I0137958

Contesting Realities

Gender, Culture, and Politics in the Middle East
miriam cooke, Simona Sharoni, and Suad Joseph, *Series Editors*

OTHER TITLES IN GENDER, CULTURE, AND POLITICS IN THE MIDDLE EAST

Arab Women's Lives Retold: Exploring Identity Through Writing
NAWAR AL-HASSAN GOLLEY, ed.

Beyond the Exotic: Women's Histories in Islamic Societies
AMIRA EL-AZHARY SONBOL, ed.

Faith and Freedom: Women's Human Rights in the Muslim World
MAHNAZ AFKHAMI, ed.

Gendering the Middle East: Emerging Perspectives
DENIZ KANDIYOTI, ed.

Intersections: Gender, Nation, and Community in Arab Women's Novels
LISA SUHAIR MAJAJ, PAULA W. SUNDERMAN,
and THERESE SALIBA, eds.

Intimate Selving in Arab Families: Gender, Self, and Identity
SUAD JOSEPH, ed.

Masculine Identity in the Fiction of the Arab East since 1967
SAMIRA AGHACY

Muslim Women and the Politics of Participation
MAHNAZ AFKHAMI and ERIKA FRIEDL, eds.

Pioneers or Pawns? Women Health Workers and the Politics of Development in Yemen
MARINA DE REGT

Representing the Unpresentable: Historical Images of National Reform from the Qajars to the Islamic Republic of Iran
NEGAR MOTTAHEDEH

Contesting Realities

The Public Sphere and Morality in Southern Yemen

Susanne Dahlgren

Syracuse University Press

First Edition 2010

10 11 12 13 14 15 6 5 4 3 2 1

For a listing of books published and distributed by Syracuse University Press, visit https://press.syr.edu.

ISBN: 978-0-8156-3246-7 (hardcover)

Library of Congress Cataloging-in-Publication Data

Dahlgren, Susanne.
Contesting realities : the public sphere and morality in southern Yemen / Susanne Dahlgren. — 1st ed. p. cm. — (Gender, culture, and politics in the Middle East)
Includes bibliographical references.
ISBN 978-0-8156-3246-7 (alk. paper)
1. Ethics—Yemen. 2. Yemen—Social conditions. I. Title.
BJ149.Y4D34 2010
953.3505'3—dc22 2010032730

The authorized representative in the EU for product safety and compliance is Mare Nostrum Group B.V.
Mauritskade 21D, 1091 GC Amsterdam, The Netherlands
gpsr@mare-nostrum.co.uk

It requires a great deal of fortitude to try to set up one's abode in these distant regions where everything seems at first to be so awkward and difficult, all the more so if one wants to try to take someone there. Besides, one is never sure of really being there. . . . [T]he fact is that the way to these regions is clearly marked, and that to attain the true goal is now merely a matter of the travellers' ability to endure.

—**André Breton,** *Manifestoes of Surrealism*

Susanne Dahlgren is an Academy Research Fellow of the Academy of Finland at the Helsinki Collegium for Advanced Studies. She has studied anthropology and Islamic studies at the University of Edinburgh and the London School of Economics and Political Science, and she received her Ph.D. from the University of Helsinki in 2004. Dahlgren has published on legal history in southern Yemen and on everyday notions of morality, sexuality, and urban space.

Contents

Illustrations

Maps

Photographs

Tables

Acknowledgments

DURING THE COURSE of writing this book, I have received assistance from a number of people and institutions. To start with, I am indebted and grateful to all Adeni people, who allowed me to enter their lives to make my inquiries. In my initial stay in Aden in 1988–89, the General Union of Yemeni Women and in particular the legendary Radhia Shamshir kindly assisted me in starting my fieldwork and provided me with a letter of recommendation that I needed to enter workplaces, government offices, factories, and institutions. I also received a substantial amount of support from the union's Aden Branch and its several clubs around town. I am particularly grateful to Khawla Sharaf, a longtime activist and leader of women's activities in Aden. I greatly admire both Radhia and Khawla and dedicate this study to their courageous fight.

After Yemeni unification in 1990, when the national capital moved to Sana'a, I needed to obtain a research permit to carry out my studies in Aden. I am thankful to the Yemeni Centre for Studies and Research in Sana'a, especially its director, Dr. Nasir 'Uthman, and its deputy director, Muhammad al-Maitami, who kindly issued me with all the permits I needed, including travel permits to Aden. I am grateful to Dr. François Burgat and Dr. Jean Lambert, directors of the Centre Français d'Archéologie et de Sciences Sociales de Sana'a for facilitating my travel to Yemen and opening the center for me. While in Sana'a, I was taken good care of in Bayt al-Ajami and given the chance to participate in all the center's activities, including using its excellent library. I am also grateful to Dr. Marta Colburn, director of the American Institute for Yemeni Studies, for assisting me and allowing me to use the institute's equally excellent library in Sana'a.

While I was in Aden, so many people helped me that I cannot possibly mention them all here. Dr. Murshid Shamsan Ahmad, director of the Yemeni Studies

Centre in Aden, welcomed me to the center, including its seminars, and gave me all possible help. My cooperation with Dr. Rokhsana Isma'il, director of Women's Research and Training Center at Aden University, has been extremely useful and allowed me to participate in all the center's activities. Throughout the years from 1988 to 2001, I was allowed to attend court sessions in the Aden Divisional Court and am grateful to everybody who made that possible.

During my time in Aden, many people always supported me, even at the stage when they did not yet know me well. I was lucky to have enjoyed an extensive amount of cordiality, hospitality, and friendship, for which I am humbly grateful. In order to stretch my sincere thanks to all of them, I dedicate this book to them all. In particular, I spent the best moments with my friends Munira, Faruq, Muhammad F., Faiza, Ma'isa, Muhammad S., Nadhira, Muna, and Su'ad. Several people also assisted me in doing interviews and visiting places, and I thank in particular Nahla, Ahmad, Huda, Muna N., Samira, Ma'isa, Muna, and Gamila. Several Adeni scholars generously helped me, among them Dr. Ja'far al-Zafari and Dr. Asmahan 'Aklan al-'Alas, to whom I remain eternally grateful.

I started my postgraduate studies in 1994 with an Erasmus Grant in the Department of Anthropology at the University of Edinburgh. I am grateful to Dr. Iris Jean-Klein for supervising me while I was outlining my dissertation. I learned a great deal of anthropology in the inspiring atmosphere of this distinguished department as I attended courses and participated in postgraduate seminars convened by Professor Anthony P. Cohen and Dr. Jonathan Spencer.

After returning to Helsinki and staying at home for two years following the birth of my son, Chang, I resumed my studies in the Department of Cultural Anthropology at the University of Helsinki. I am particularly grateful to Professor Sondra Hale of the University of California and Professor Jukka Siikala of the University of Helsinki for their mindful and critical comments on my dissertation, on which this book is based.

During the course of my studies, I have had the chance to participate in two important Finnish research projects. I could not have started my Ph.D. studies without the encouragement and mentorship of Professor Ulla Vuorela, first supervisor for my Ph.D. dissertation. Her research project "Gender and Society in the Middle East" provided an excellent scholarly atmosphere for all of us who participated in it. Ulla's next project, "The Rich, the Poor, and the Resourceful," under the women's studies academy professorship, brought me into contact with the Minna Project.

After managing to engage Dr. Martha Mundy from the London School of Economics and Political Science (LSE) as my cosupervisor, I had the chance to pursue my studies in the inspiring atmosphere of the LSE's anthropology department. My cordial thanks go to Martha for her commitment, intellect, and expertise in mentoring me. My sincere thanks go also to all my other teachers and colleagues, both in the Department of Anthropology and in the London Law Seminar—in particular Professor Maurice Bloch, who convened the postgraduate seminar I attended. While in London, I had the chance to stay in Bayt Shelagh, the meeting place for Yemeni scholars around the globe. My sincere thanks go to Shelagh Weir for her friendship and support. I am indebted also to Professor Fred Halliday of the LSE and Dr. Maxine Molyneux of the School of Oriental and African Studies for their encouragement and support during the long period I have been engaged in Yemeni studies.

Several people commented on my work and provided me with insightful new ideas: Sherry Ortner, Inger Marie Okkenhaug, Petri Hautaniemi, Ziba Mir-Hosseini, Salwa Ismail, Saba Mahmood, Samuli Schielke, Annelies Moors, Saija Katila, Amira El-Azhary Sonbol, Annika Rabo, Marko Juntunen, Val Moghadam, Anna Würth, Lucien Taminian, Marina de Regt, Soraya al-Torki, and my colleagues at the Helsinki Collegium for Advanced Studies.

Writing this book has been made possible with grants from the Academy of Finland, the E. J. Sariola Foundation, the National Graduate School for Anthropological and Ethnological Sciences, and the Finnish Institute in the Middle East as well as with a postdoctoral fellowship at the Helsinki Collegium for Advanced Studies. The Association for Middle Eastern Women's Studies granted me its Junior Scholar Prize in 2001.

Several people have assisted me in reading handwritten and printed Arabic texts: Munira Ba-ʻUmar, Zaynab Maʻsum, Nafisa Bintayah, Muhammad Matuq, Salim Banafa, and ʻAli Khairy. I cordially thank them all. Gareth Griffiths, Kirsi Reyes, and Mette Ranta have done an excellent job of proofreading my English, and my sincere gratitude goes to all of them.

Last but not least, I thank my family, Niranjan and Chang, for their endurance during the long period it took to produce this book and for their love and support.

A Word on Transliteration

I have used three systems of transliteration in this study. Words and place-names common in English usage, such as "Qur'an," "Sana'a" and "Aden," are written in the way they appear commonly in English texts. In writing standard Arabic words and sentences, I have used only the ayn and hamza for diacritical marks, except in the glossary, per Syracuse University Press style. In transliterating spoken and colloquial language, I have tried to respect the individuals' pronunciation. All translations are mine unless otherwise indicated in the text or citations in notes.

Helsinki, January 14, 2009

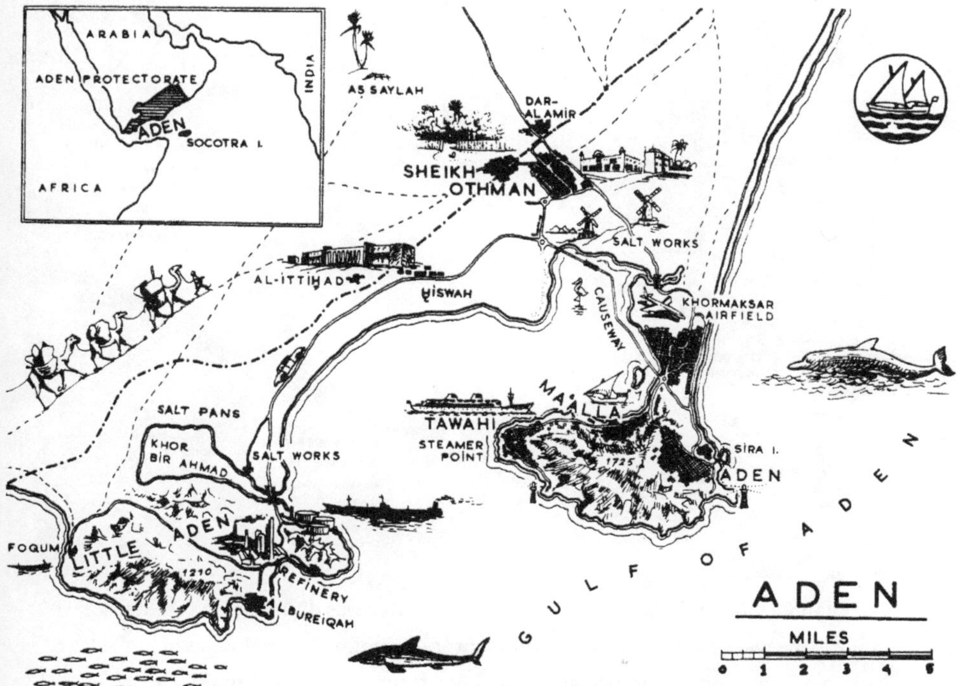

1. Aden in the late colonial era, including *(to the right)* the peninsula of Aden and the districts of Crater, Tawahi, and Ma'alla; *(to the left)* Little Aden peninsula and the district of Little Aden. First printed in *Welcome to Aden: A Comprehensive Guidebook*. 2d ed. 1963. Guides and Handbooks of Africa. Nairobi: East African Printers Kenya.

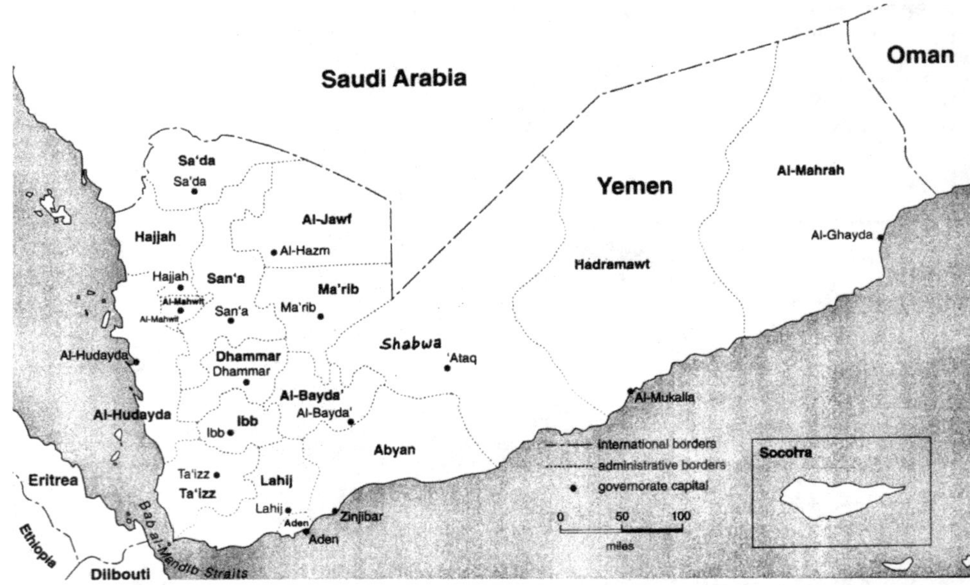

2. The Republic of Yemen in the 1990s when the country was divided into seventeen governorates. The place names may follow different transcription styles than used in the text. Map drawn by author with information compiled from many online sources.

Contesting Realities

1 Introduction

> Since the Zandes' interests are primarily practical rather than theoretical, the logic of their beliefs can only be made apparent in the context of their application; "they only appear inconsistent when ranged like lifeless museum objects."
>
> —EDWARD EVANS-PRITCHARD, *Witchcraft, Oracles, and Magic among the Azande*

THIS BOOK is based on my ethnographic interest in Aden, Yemen, during the period spanning the years from 1988 to 2001.[1] This era in Adeni history witnessed the final years of what was the People's Democratic Republic of Yemen (PDRY), the only Marxist regime in the Middle East ever to be followed by unification, in this case of the two Yemens in 1990. The difficult period of the Republic of Yemen's early years that culminated in a civil war in 1994 was followed by years of rebuilding after the war. No particular event occurred in Adeni history in 2001, but that year represents a personal point in time in which I wrapped up my experiences in Aden.

My interest in Yemen started a little earlier than 1988. In the summer of 1982, as a young student, I headed to Aden to participate in an international student camp in the countryside of Abyan, some thirteen miles northeast of Aden. The camp was organized by the Yemeni youth organization ASHEED in the spirit of "international solidarity" after the devastating floods earlier that spring that had affected the countryside outside Aden. Upon my arrival, I became aware that the camp was an all-male affair and that the "youth organization" was little more than a boys' organization. This period, however, was one in which the South Yemeni government was making a sincere attempt to introduce to the remotest

1. I spent in Aden some two years altogether, October 1988–November 1989, June–December 1991, March–June 1992, October–December 1998, and January–February 2001.

countryside a policy called *tahrir al-mar'a,* women's emancipation. The organizers were happy to see me arriving, the only girl in the twenty or so foreign participants and about a hundred Yemeni boys. My presence provided them with an excuse to invite local young women to the camp, an impossibility had the camp been all male.

This area was untouched either by the modernizing politics of British colonialism or by the government that had taken over with independence some fifteen years earlier, in 1967. In gatherings organized locally and in Aden to celebrate the international camp, I was asked to make speeches on "women's role in society." One of these gatherings was organized in an open-air cinema in Zingibar, the center of the Abyan governorate. After a Yemeni bagpipe orchestra played popular march melodies, I had the most peculiar experience as a woman speaking to an audience of some five hundred people, all of whom, as I could see when I looked down from the stage, were men.

My experiences in South Yemen in 1982 inspired me to return to this country that I found so fascinating yet so little studied. In the autumn of 1988, I arrived in Aden with the intention of carrying out anthropological fieldwork. I was given the chance to do so in the capacity of coordinator for a small Finnish health project carried out in the al-Mahra governorate, some six hundred miles east of Aden. I was on my own in Aden and had to take care of everything that the project required. My work consisted mainly of hanging around in government offices, waiting for people to arrive to work and trying to persuade them to work for me. I had a flat in a block of flats in Khormaksar, an area built by the British for the cantonment in the middle of the twentieth century. My neighbors were people with government jobs, both Yemeni and non-Western expatriates. From my balcony, I could see both comfortable British-built villas and huts butting up against them, erected by people without any proper place to live. Many of the families who lived in these huts were newcomers from the countryside, in particular from Abyan. My neighborhood provided me with some of the first contacts to Yemeni homes, whereas my work allowed me to meet men and women who held different positions in the administration.

For my anthropological work, I decided that I wanted to obtain the cooperation of the General Union of Yemeni Women. It was the official women's association that at the end of 1980s was struggling to promote women's liberation in a declining atmosphere for anything of that kind. Activists in the central office and in the neighborhood women's clubs were helpful but bothered very little about the content of my study, allowing me to carry out investigations on my own. Because I did not have a formal research permit, the Women's Union issued me a letter so that I could visit workplaces without interference by the security forces. In entering homes, I did not need a permit or official letter; people were simply interested in letting me in and talking to me. Very few people ever refused to talk to me.

My interests in the present study are morality and propriety and how they affect social dynamics in this town. I focus in particular on how the principal relations of society, gender and family relations, have historically been regulated and how they are constituted in everyday practice and discourse.

Aden is situated at the southernmost tip of the Arabian Peninsula, alongside the waters by the Horn of Africa that separate Africa and Asia. It was once a British colony (1839–1967), then became the capital of the PDRY (1967–90), and now acts as the "economic capital" and "winter capital" of the Republic of Yemen (established in May 1990). I was led to my inquiry on morality and propriety after spending some time in Aden and noticing how people nurtured virtues and positive personal capacities in their everyday life. When observing everyday life, I noticed how positive morality stood at the center of all action, deeds were evaluated from the point of view of propriety, and, in speech, distinct formulas of propriety informed statements on practice. This practice was quite contrary to what I had read in Middle Eastern studies literature, which was saturated at that time with the honor/shame approach. My interest in morality as a target of "making" was sparked also by the scarcity of anthropological literature on morality. Without a doubt, positive morality was fascinating for a student coming from a cynical Western background where even the term *moral* had suffered bankruptcy and was considered something old-fashioned and a hindrance to personal freedom.

In chapter 2, I outline a social history of Aden, from the late colonial period to the early twenty-first century. I suggest a continuity rather than a disruption between the different regimes. By applying an intersectional approach,[2] I attempt to draw a line on how different social groups, divided by ethnic and religious

2. We must bear in mind that unequally empowered social groups tend to develop unequally valued cultural styles, as Nancy Fraser (1992, 120) reminds us.

background, social origin, race, and gender have accessed modernization and the public sphere. In chapters 3 and 4, I scrutinize how gender relations have been regulated in law as part of state politics and how the legal discourse has participated in the construction of public argument during the three regimes named earlier. In chapter 4, the topic is also the historical formation of a civil society and public media in the form of newspapers, associations, and clubs. At issue is the emergence of women into public space. This analysis of the structural prerequisites of the society forms the background to the examination of how various normative representations come up in everyday discussions and how they are discursively linked to institutionalized forms. I then focus on how people in their everyday agency observe contesting normative ideas and how they move from one set of norms to another, paying attention to available resources and limitations. In chapter 7, I discuss the theoretical problems that have come up in preceding chapters, such as different notions of "traditional" and "modern," as well as the questions of the public sphere and varying notions of Islam. I further contrast notions of propriety to ideas regarding a "pariah" type of social category, the *akhdam* (literally "servants"). All these studies lead me to approach the public sphere both in its historical formation (the coming of newspapers and civil societies and the emergence of women to public space) and from a pragmatic viewpoint—that is, as lived and commented reality.[3]

Although it has been suggested that most Muslims share inherited conceptions of ideas of the common good (Salvatore and Eickelman 2006a, xix), in this book I argue that Adeni social reality[4] and the notion of the common good are constituted in a tension between contesting representations of propriety and morality. The parallel prevalence of competing normative representations does not, as I attempt to show, manifest as chaos or as an anomaly, but instead in social dynamics where people have to consider the contextual nature of public propriety. In short, what is proper in one context might be improper in another. This complexity challenges agency; it is not a matter of "manipulating" situations and stakes within them, but of learning to manage in diverse situations. This learn-

3. See Salvatore 2001; Salvatore and Eickelman 2006a, xvi–xvii.

4. I acknowledge that the term *social reality* is vague. Nevertheless, I find it more useful than talking about "the Adeni culture" or other similar (holistic) categories that tend to describe the totality in a vocabulary common to "Othering" and leaving the scholar outside the field observed.

1. Tawahi hills: a view from the hills overlooking Tawahi with rare trees in otherwise almost barren rock. Photograph by the author, 1988.

ing process results in both habitual comportment and conscious application of available resources and limitations. It is a matter of making proper comportment *(adab)* an art in everyday life.

In this book, I outline three main normative representations that in local terms are called: "our customs and traditions" *(adat wa taqalid haqqana),* "our religion" *(din haqqana),* and "our revolution" *(thawra haqqana).* The people of Aden discuss such basic elements of culture as social order, the family, gender roles, and religion in different ways in all three representations. That Islam receives diverse interpretations is to my mind a reflection of the plurality of local religious manifestations and points to the complex relationship between Islam and society. In the analysis, I call these normative representations "moral frameworks" by introducing concepts from Charles Taylor's moral philosophy in applicable measure.

Studies on Moral Ambiguities

In *Recognizing Islam,* Michael Gilsenan (1982) tells about a young man he met while working as a teacher for the British Voluntary Service Overseas in Hadhramaut, which was at that time part of the Eastern Aden Protectorate. It was the late 1950s, and the struggle against the British had started in Aden, with occasional outbreaks in the Eastern and Western Aden protectorates as well.[5] The young man of the story, Gilsenan's student, surprised him with his ambivalent behavior. While walking in the street, the student acted with deference before two members of a local sharif[6] family by kissing their hands submissively and thus acknowledging the social hierarchy. But then this same student engaged in severe criticism of the despotic rule that the high family represented. "We kiss their hands now, but just wait till tomorrow," the young man said to Gilsenan. In his analysis of the ambivalent situation that had struck him, Gilsenan elaborates: "The hand-kissing was a show, but a show with diametrically opposed meanings for the actors. It secreted hidden interpretations, reversals, and denials" (1982, 10). For him, two different interpretations of religion had met in the encounter in the street.

In the image Gilsenan draws, the two young sharifs, who in the street acted out the hierarchical position inscribed to them by birth and who behind closed shutters listened to Western pop music and spoke of their boredom, represented the old, autocratic, and hierarchical Islam. The student, Gilsenan explains, for his part stood for the new, unautocratic Islam, free of any human mediations and part of a global struggle.[7] In a later passage, Gilsenan calls the act of kissing the sharifs' hands "feigned" (1982, 264), thus indicating that it was all theater and belonged perhaps to the sphere of everyday interaction that in another context he calls *kizb*, "lying."[8] For Gilsenan, changes in ideologies and their representations

5. The British formed the Eastern Aden Protectorate and the Western Aden Protectorate out of emirates and sultanates that surrounded Aden colony.

6. A social category of noble people.

7. "For the student, the men whose hands he kissed were not only obstacles to independence but had nothing to do with true Islam, which had no need of sheriffs, no need of reverence for wealthy merchants and landowners in green turbans or of deference to a religious hierarchy. The real Islam was free of such mediations with God and was embodied in the Quran and the traditions. It was an egalitarian force for the unity of all members of the community and part of a global struggle, an Islam that went hand in hand with a fight against local sources of corruption and alien power" (Gilsenan 1982, 10–11).

8. Gilsenan elaborates: "*Kizb* is a vital theme in ideology and the code of honour, in social practice and social structure, and in the worldview and belief system. The last sphere in which it is

of Islam are linked to social transformations. People are the carriers of those ideologies and adjust their religious views accordingly.

Even if my starting point is similar to Gilsenan's problem, the question of what lies behind the seeming ambivalence in social interaction, I follow a different path. Instead of linking Islam with "old" or "new" worldviews, I focus on how social processes that manifest a diversity of social norms are constituted in the dialectical relationship between structures and agency. Ideologies certainly inform people's actions, but the way they do it is another matter and deserves a more concrete study. What Gilsenan means by "lying" I discuss as techniques in operating in the contesting reality. Based on the idea that social interaction is contextual and spatially bound, I focus on elements that contribute to constituting these contextually informed dynamics. These elements can be called "orientations," "habitual patterns," and "schematic understandings" that agents carry, as William Hanks explains (1996, 230). How these elements interact with structures is critical to understanding how social dynamics operate.

Ambiguity in terms of morality and propriety has been pointed out in many anthropological studies. Janice Boddy explains that in the northern Sudanese village Hofriyat that she studied, a "partial contradiction" prevails: "villagers' system of meanings both provides for ambiguity and seeks to contain it" (1989, 90). She draws an image of the "Hofriyati system" and describes how it contains a discourse of belittling women (109–13).[9] In a typical "empowerment studies" manner, she thus describes the ways women confront this ambiguity. Such an analysis, however, is not useful for my purposes. My focus is on the process—what happens "during"; as such, the outcome, the "restoration of order," is not my concern here.

Another study that discusses moral ambiguity is Dale Eickelman's *Moroccan Islam* (1976).[10] In line with Boddy's, this study gives a one-sex perspective

---

also thematic is that of dramaturgy, situational interaction, and the creating/performing of a self" (1993, 167).

9. In her study, Boddy speaks in terms of "Hofriyati thought" and "villagers' system of meaning" as if there prevails a unanimity in people's understandings and reactions to a surrounding world divided by social and other categorizations, least of which is gender.

10. This study is located in a middle Moroccan town, Boujad, but Dale Eickelman speaks in terms of a "Moroccan worldview," asserting that the same applies even beyond national borders.

on the "Moroccan worldview," this time the male one. Eickelman discusses key concepts through which Moroccans comprehend social experience: God's will, reason *('qal)*, propriety *(theshshem; hshumiya)*, obligation *(haqq)*, and compulsion *('ar)*. This analysis is clearly more refined than the honor/shame dichotomy that characterized Middle Eastern anthropology at the time Eickelman's book came out. To elaborate the system of propriety, Eickelman introduces the concept of *qa'ida*, "the right way" or "the code of conduct." He explains: "Reason concerns the 'inner' state of a man only in so far as he has the ability to exercise control over his impulses. Proper conduct is linked principally to efficacious performance in the social order, not to one's inner state or to abstract moral or ethical principles" (1976, 134). Eickelman does not elaborate on why he presumes such a separation of "inner" and "outer" and why moral principles should be "abstract."

He explains further on that a majority of Boujadis assume that *qa'ida* is based on, if not identical to, Islamic law. These two together provide "recipe" prescriptions for acceptable social action. As such, there is nothing surprising about the explanation that local custom is "based on" sharia. Nevertheless, Eickelman points out that because most Boujadis are illiterate, "there are no effective criteria by which the claim to immutability can be demonstrated" (1976, 131–32). Even though the latter claim is disputable, Eickelman's idea of a shared "code of conduct" based on propriety is interesting from the point of view of my argument. The problem here arises not only in Eickelman's separation of knowledge from a person's "inner state," whatever that means, but also from his tendency—in line with the honor/shame approach—to view propriety merely from the angle of negative considerations and as acts of avoidance or a lack of something.[11] In Eickelman's book, propriety is a question of how to avoid losing one's face, losing self-control, or breaking another man's reason. The limits of his analysis become manifest when he explains that "principal elements" of propriety in a woman are modesty, obedience to her husband, and the avoidance of any behavior that would publicly imply that she is not subordinate to him (1976, 139).

Anita Fábos's work (1999), in yet another study linked to Sudan, is more useful for my purposes here than the previously mentioned ones. In her

11. Eickelman explains that propriety in the Moroccan context is synonymous with deference, respect, circumspection, and embarrassment (1976, 138).

examination of the exiled northern Sudanese community in Cairo, Egypt, she elaborates on how *adab,* "proper comportment," acts as a positive tool in creating identity. According to Fábos, by emphasizing propriety *(adab)* as a boundary marker over linguistic, phenotypical, or other markers of difference, the northern Sudanese in Cairo are able in certain contexts to minimize or negate a unique ethnicity in favor of other identities shared with Egyptians (1999, 3). In the case of the exiled Sudanese community, a distinction is made by applying the notion of moral superiority as manifested in the refinements of *adab,* which the Egyptians are said to lack. Fábos's approach is solid in that she describes identity making from a positive perspective, not simply in terms of fear of negative consequences. She treats *adab* as an embodied knowledge (even though she does not give very many ethnographic examples of how it works in practice)—thus avoiding the Cartesian dualism—as a tool in causing things to happen, and as something that can be talked about, which I refer to in this book with the Hanksian term *ideology.*[12]

Honor, Respect, and Manners

As I came to understand while I was in Aden, a variety of ideals and norms coexist alongside each other, informing people how they should act in front of others. Proper comportment or good manners *(adab)* in Aden constitute nothing as shallow as etiquette; rather, they are a set of building blocks for being a respected person in front of others. As I pointed out earlier, the conventional approach to studying morality in the Middle East is the honor/shame scheme, but I find *adab* a more fruitful concept for studying the principal notions that inform people's moral evaluations and acts. If we take, for instance, an everyday situation in a mixed-gender workplace where nonrelated men and women meet on a daily basis, people do not use honor as a reference in their comportment. It is, after all, socially acceptable to work with strangers belonging to the other sex. What matters, rather, is the person's reputation *(karama),* manifested in how the

12. "When we say 'ideology' in this context, we denote something rather unlike classical ideologies, understood as ideas. Given the concept habitus, value orientations are embodied both in corporeal practices and in mental presentations, being distributed over what the Cartesian perspective takes to be the different domains of mind and body" (Hanks 1996, 234).

person takes care of his or her tasks, how he or she behaves toward colleagues, and what is known about the person outside the workplace. Notions of honor (*sharaf, 'ardh, karama,* etc.) and shame (*'ayb*) come up, but people do not consider their lives in negative terms as a series of acts to avoid negative consequences. *Adab* is not a fixed entity but instead has a variety of manifestations. It is not tied simply to Islam or to any other single system of meaning, and it varies according to a person's social position in the community. *Adab* also forms a social dividing line between people who have a claim to respect and those who do not have it, such as the lowest social category, the *akhdam*. *Adab* is not something outside a person's capacity to influence and cause agency.

Adab has been studied very little in the present-day Middle East so far.[13] When I asked an Adeni intellectual and university professor how he would advise me to study *adab* in everyday life, he told me to focus on greetings, celebrations, and rituals. These occasions are certainly instances in which proper comportment is required, but *adab* is practiced in more than the performed forms of culture. In everyday conversation when people talk about other people, they often use moral commentary on that person's acts and behavior. Nevertheless, *adab* is not expressed in a performed manner only, as in greetings, where the greeted person's respect is manifested, or in celebrations, where corporate dignity is celebrated; it is expressed in embodied ways, too—in postures, gazes, the way a person presents himself or herself in front of the others, and how he or she walks and talks. This embodied expression can be compared to what Charles Taylor calls "modes of deference and presentation." These modes include different styles of bodily comportment people conform to in learning on how to defer to others, how to hold themselves, and how to be a presence for others. According to Taylor, the modes of deference and presentation encode even the subtlest nuances of social position, the sources of prestige, and all that is valuable and ideal for that particular person in the eyes of others (1993, 58). When veiling reemerged in Aden in the early 1990s, some women who were not motivated by claims that the *hijab* is a religious obligation, explained their shift to the use of

13. Fábos 1999, Farag 2001, and Meneley 1996 are some of the exceptions. Islamic *adab* has been studied in South Asia; see Metcalf 1984b. Interestingly, the expression *bayt al-adab* (house of *adab*) refers to a water closet in classical Arabic.

the head scarf with the idea that people would not think them a good person or a good mother if they did not acquire the new costume.

Parallel with the focus on propriety, another methodological point that informs my work is legal pluralism. This notion, as I take it, does not have so much to do with law and legality—and there are many problematic issues related to it (see Dupret 2005)—but instead with norms and ideas of right and wrong. Legal pluralism has not been widely applied in Middle Eastern ethnography, even though the idea that Islam is not the only value structure in these societies has been discussed theoretically (Dupret 1999). Salwa Ismail takes up the important point that all projects of (Islamic) self-cultivation take place within a social context and are enmeshed with power relations (2007, 1). Normative pluralism allows me to avoid the problematic secular/religious divide, which in actual terms only produces arguments over what is "real Islam" and what is not—in other words, political statements.[14] In Aden, people link norms and regulations not just to state regulation or Islamic institutions. A third, equally powerful domain is what is locally called *'adat wa taqalid,* which can be translated as "our customs and traditions." It is worth noting that Adeni *'adat wa taqalid* has very little to do with Indonesian *adat,* where the state is involved in promoting "customs." On the contrary, after independence was gained in 1967, the state revolutionary discourse rose from a critique of what is understood as *takhalluf,* traditions as a source of backwardness and "feudal" *(iqta')* attitudes.

These three main normative frameworks—customs, revolution, and religion—have to do with gender relations in the sense that they promote ideals, norms, and rules for how gender relations should be ideally organized. Even though norms do not dictate behavior and rules do not predict what happens, people do have to take into consideration these normative structures in their daily life. I argue that Adeni social dynamics are constituted in an ever-changing tension between parallel and competing normative frameworks. The point is not to show how people make a particular normative framework into a project of self-fashioning, although that happens, too, but to discuss how the simultaneous existence of contesting norms is manifested in daily practice.

14. For other problems stemming from this divide, see Abu-Rabi' 2004, 115. For the background of secularism debates in the Middle East, see pages 93–113 in that work.

2. Street scene in Crater before commercial billboards arrived. Photograph by the author, 1989.

Adab—the Embodiment of Virtue

The Arabic word *adab* has two interrelated sides, a literary and a socioethical.[15] The socioethical side is the primary one and involves agency, where "*adab* designates a wide range of social and ethical virtues, like good manners, tact, grace, indulgence towards friends, refined taste, courage, erudition and literary skill" (Bonebakker 1990, quoted in Rooke 2000, 198). As Brinkley Messick (1993) explains, this side of *adab* refers to a complex of valued intellectual dispositions and appropriate behaviors.[16]

15. Iman Farag suggests that *adab* also can be seen as education (2001, 95).

16. A verb from the same root *(a-d-b), aduba,* means "to be well mannered, cultured, and urbane and to have refined taste"; another verb form, *addaba,* means "to educate," "to discipline," and "to punish." The noun *adab* refers to literature and to manners (*Hans Wehr Dictionary* 1976, 9–10; Messick 1993, 77).

References to manners have meanings linked both to Islamic tradition and to other traditions. In Islamic tradition, the concept of proper manners bears qualifications valued highly in Islamic education and upbringing. In Qur'anic schools, not only are holy Scriptures memorized, but proper Islamic comportment is learned as well.[17] In the Islamic concept of *adab* lies the conviction that Islam alone defines what humans ought to be; only those who fulfill Islamic values are fully human (Metcalf 1984a, 2). The Islamic textual heritage includes a rich collection of *adab* manuals that discuss different aspects of proper Islamic conduct. Even though *adab* as social ethics links classically to Islamic tradition, the present-day uses of this concept go beyond the Islamic discourse. A person who is *adabiyy* or *adabiyya,* expressed in the Adeni colloquial *'alehu/'aleha akhlaq* (he or she has good manners), is respected for his or her knowledge, integrity, and generosity.

All of these good qualities might be embodied in physical appearance and comportment. All in all, *adab* is about being a *mu'addab,* a well-mannered, civic, and urbane person, in contrast to being a *badu* (uncivilized hick), a *dahbash* (northerner), or an *akhdam* (person lacking respectable origin). *Adab* is also a gendered concept, manifested in different expectations for men and women. When linked to sexual segregation, *adab* informs about patterns of gender avoidance, too. It can be ascertained, as Fábos does in reference to the northern Sudanese in Cairo (1999, 127), that gender norms and gender relations are fundamental expressions of the cultural concept of propriety. More than that, however, I focus on how the gendering of *adab* constructs differences between men and women, thus producing what is locally understood as "*gandar*" (gender). The *adab* of a child—that is, bringing him or her up with good manners and cultivating intellectual and gendered dispositions in him or her—is in principle the parents' responsibility. After all, expectations of boys and expectations of girls differ from the time they are a rather young age.

Proper comportment is central to a person's expectations in the eyes of others. Therefore, *adab* does not refer to such shallow qualities of behavior as observing an etiquette, but to properties that a person is supposed to embody in his or her

17. On the acquisition of knowledge in traditional Qur'anic schools in the northern Yemeni town of Ibb, see Messick 1993.

social interaction.[18] Proper comportment is manifested in the way a person presents herself or himself in front of others—in addressing others (greetings, etc.), in using certain body postures (in walking and carrying the body and the outfit), in showing deference to people with *karama* (honor, respect), and in speaking eloquently, among other things. *Adab* discourse is also about making a distinction from less-valued cultural practices, such as using a normal voice when in the company of others rather than shouting. All in all, "good manners" are part of a person's education and socialization—in other words, a part of growing up and becoming a respected person. In addition to that, *adabiyy* is contrasted not only to being unmannered and uncultivated, but also to lacking reason *('aql)*, a lack that is linked not only to children and youth, but also in some contexts to women.

Each person has his or her own expectations regarding *adab* (provided the person is considered to have any in the first place) that are linked to the basic divisions of the society—that is, gender, age group, social status, and so on. Personal expectations thus vary for "modes of deference and presentation," as Taylor calls the different styles of bodily comportment. *Adab* is about learning how to defer to others, how to hold oneself, and how to be a presence for others. According to Taylor, these modes encode the finest nuances of social position, the sources of prestige and everything that is valuable and ideal (1993, 58). They are the embodiment of gendered social position, yet they are also something more than that.

In the anthropological literature on Yemen, very little is said about the concept of *adab*. Besides what Messick (1993) has written, few scholars discuss this aspect of social relations. Paul Dresch (1989) mentions it in one sentence only, as being opposite to *'ayb* (disgrace).[19] An exception is Anne Meneley's *Tournaments of Value* (1996), a study of *adab* among the elite Zabidi women. She explores the concept in three separate social practices: in the exchange of visits, in the practice of piety, and in social expressions of emotions. According to Meneley, Zabidi

18. Nicolas Haddad, a Christian Syrian Lebanese scholar, suggested in his book *The Paths of Life: Perseverance, Work, Economy* (1903) that human survival is associated with the ideals of life expectancy *(al-ajal al-madid)* and "good luck" or quality of life *(al-hazz al-sa'id)*, which come together in the concept of *mustaqbal*, "future" (cited in Farag 2001, 107).

19. He mentions *adab* in connection to a comment on whether honor *(sharaf, 'ardh)* is the opposite of "shame" *('ayb)*. Paying little attention to the concept, Dresch states that *adab* is a "central value in all Middle Eastern societies and the one ethnographers tend to leave out" (1989, 40).

women's *adab* is marked by such qualities as hospitality, personal hygiene and cleanliness, the welcoming and greeting of others in a proper way, generosity in giving and deference in receiving, and adornment of the body. The etiquette of visiting is central in constituting moral personhood (1996, 99–117).[20] However, Meneley does not take her analysis to a convincing conclusion. In the end, she turns the whole issue into the conventional argument of how the upper-strata women participate in keeping up the family honor and thus contribute to reproducing the social hierarchy.

Adab is an ancient term in the Arabic cultural lexicon. In pre-Islamic Arabic usage, as Ira Lapidus points out, it referred to norms of correct behavior inherited from one's ancestors. In the Islamic context, it refers to ethical and practical norms that regulate the life of a good Muslim (1984, 38). To examine the concept in the Adeni context of the present day, I study in the following chapters what *adab* means, but not only in terms of Islam or in reference to "grandfathers'" knowledge. I also focus on cultural categories linked to "proper comportment" that emerged with the revolution. The "revolution" is the local name not only for the politics carried out during the PDRY era, but also for ideas personified and institutionalized outside the politics. Of particular relevance to this politics is the idea of "women's emancipation" *(tahrir al-mar'a)*[21] that emerged with what is understood as the revolution. "Revolution" is a particular discourse where the ideas linked to traditions and religion are reapplied and new meanings constructed in dialogue with and in critique of earlier understandings of them. Alongside the Islamic *adab* and the *adab* of the grandfathers, I discuss the rhetoric of revolution and how within it the *adab* concept has been used intentionally in order to introduce "new ideas" to the society at large. These ideas concern how

20. Zabid is a town considerably different from Aden, and some Zabidi women give negative commentaries on Adeni women, which Meneley fails to treat as a discourse of distinction. Instead, she makes the contrast of Zabidi women's manners to Adeni women's supposed lack of manners (1996, 99–100).

21. This emancipation is also called *al-mar'a al-gadida*, "the new Yemeni woman" (in colloquial Adeni, the *g* is pronounced as in *good*). These expressions are the same as the famous book titles of the pioneering Egyptian modernist and advocate of women's rights Qasim Amin, who lived at the turn of the twentieth century. These idioms were accordingly applied also in the Egyptian women's movement. See al-Ali 2000, 56, and Badran 1993.

a person embodies the revolution's idealized qualities and how these qualities are socially displayed.

The following chapters show not only how *adab* is argued in what I later call "repertoires of knowledge," but also how the coexistence of these repertoires causes tensions in everyday life and how people cope in such conflicting situations. I also explore how *adab* in each repertoire constructs idealized gender qualities. Idealized notions of family and kinship, the way they inform law and legal practice, and how they are manifested in institutions are also central. By focusing on how *adab* is argued differently in relation to men and women and how men and women apply it differently, I want to emphasize that studying one sex only—it does not matter which one of the two—gives a peculiar idea of society in the first place. According to one of the slogans of the revolution, "women are half the society" *(al-mar'a nusf al-mugtama').* This slogan can be put in another way: that men are (only) half the society. I argue that *adab* is a site where contesting gender ideals are manifested and where they become embodied in human agency. As both an inclusive and exclusive type of talk and agency, *adab* is a marker of arguing social divisions and hierarchies and thus is critical to the social dynamics at large.

Context and Approach

Starting from the Habermasian notion of the public sphere,[22] scholars writing in the framework of critical theory and Middle Eastern studies have taken that notion in new directions.[23] The focus in Middle Eastern studies tends to be on "public Islam" as personalized in religious scholars and activists of all kinds and on the idea that Islamic parameters increasingly define the public good (Salvatore and Eickelman 2006a, xii, xx). In this book, I aim to approach the public sphere as made up of historically formed moral spaces encompassing the emerging sphere of the social in the modern era (Habermas [1989] 2003, 103). Although the public/private divide, the notion of private individuals joining together, and

22. For Habermas ([1989] 2003), the public sphere is a locus, form, and activity of communication, convincing enough without the external support of the speaker's authority.

23. These scholars include Nancy Fraser and other contributors to the collected volumes Calhoun 1992; Salvatore 2001; Salvatore and Eickelman 2006b; and Salvatore and LeVine 2005b.

the absence of religion in Jürgen Habermas's early work are problematic, equally questionable here would be to presume a hegemonic role for Islam. During the course of the fifty years that this book discusses (1950 to 2001), Islamic parameters have never alone defined the public good.[24] Islam has been intertwined with other ideological representations that also constitute locally characteristic forms of religious reasoning. Although these representations have changed over time, they have formed the stuff where reciprocity and mutual obligations have attached bases for shared mechanisms of anticipation (Eickelman and Salvatore 2006, 17).

As I started to write this study, I found useful William Hanks's (1996) "baseline of practice approach."[25] In particular, it was applicable in examining how *adab* (proper comportment) is embodied. In Aden, women in particular use bodily metaphors in describing existential positions. A typical such metaphorical rendering is, "Where do you sit?" meaning "Where do you live?" Such statements can be treated as actors' ideological evaluations in the sense that they embody broader values, beliefs, and self-legitimating attitudes. Following Hanks, we can say that such evaluations are metalinguistic or metadiscursive to the extent that they bear directly on language or discourse, serving to fix its meaning (Hanks 1996, 230). I suggest that residual Cartesianism can be avoided by approaching the existential question from an action point of view. As Brenda Farnell (1999) asserts, human beings everywhere engage in complex structured systems of bodily action that are laden with social and cultural significance. Such dynamically embodied signifying acts generate varieties of forms of embodied knowledge involving cultural convention and creative performativity. Such *techniques du corps*—the "ways in which from society to society [people] know how to use their bodies" (Mauss 1979, 97)—are everywhere constitutive of human subjectivity and intersubjective domains (Farnell 1999, 343).

As I was analyzing things that go beyond practice, I started to look for theoretical tools from Charles Taylor's moral philosophy. Because I understood that

24. During the course of the 2000s in Aden, Islam has increasingly taken the leading role in defining all social communication; see Dahlgren 2006b.

25. Focusing on communicative practice, Hanks divides practice into three elements: (semi) formal structures (language), semistructured processes (communicative activities), and the actor's evaluations of the two (ideology) (1996, 230).

theories written as part of Western history of philosophy cannot be universalized to non-Western contexts, I had to apply Taylor's ideas in limited measure while combining them with other theoretical considerations, such as Suad Joseph's (1999, 2003) theorizing on psychosocial dynamics inside the family. Juxtaposing these elements to what has been written about the notion of *adab* (proper comportment)[26] and contrasting *adab* with Pierre Bourdieu's (1977) concept of *habitus* finally brought about the kind of theoretical tools I needed (see chapter 7 for a full discussion of *habitus*).

This book is ostensibly about the ambiguous nature of social interaction in the public sphere. I found this apparent vagueness not only in human intercourse, but also in talk about it. Basic notions of culture appear to receive diverse representations, applicable in particular contexts. A plurality of norms prevails; in one situation something is acceptable, whereas in another it is not. Different moralities are modeled side by side. I found that people in Aden can flexibly change from one morality code to another when changing social contexts, without making an issue of it. Aden, a port town, has historically embraced communities of various origins. Nevertheless, these communities with different roots and histories have found a common ground in Aden, and conflicts have seldom arisen. The apparent ambiguity lies not in the communal diversity, but in how people operate in a social world with a flexible attitude, accommodating encounters according to social contexts. What informs this context-based awareness and how it is constituted (i.e., the procedural side of the public sphere) are the questions this book addresses.

I attend to these questions from the perspective of everyday practice, and thus I participate in developing a "praxiological" concept of the public sphere, as Armando Salvatore and Mark LeVine (2005a, 2) put it. Yet before this practice can be outlined, it is necessary to focus on the prevailing structures, such as social organization, language, and thought as well as the institutionalized forms of knowledge. After all, something that is processural in character can best be scrutinized in practice. But first it is necessary to define what I mean by "structures." According to Claude Lévi-Strauss, a structure consists of a model that meets with several requirements: that the model exhibits characteristics of

26. In particular, Lapidus 1984 and Metcalf 1984b.

a system; that the model allows transformations resulting in a group of models of the same type; that these properties make it possible to predict how the model will react if one or more elements are submitted to modifications; and, last, that the model needs to be constituted so as to make immediately intelligible all the observed facts (1977, 279–80). This definition seems to presume the outcome of events on the basis of structural prerequisites, and thus it is not useful for an analysis that aims to focus on process rather than outcome.

From a different angle, Marshall Sahlins argues that structure is the symbolic relations of cultural order and thus a historical object (1985, vii). He suggests that cultural order exists and interacts in two forms: as constituted in the society and as lived by the people. He calls these two forms "structure in convention" and "structure in action"—that is, virtual and actual. People submit these cultural categories to empirical risks as they engage in practical projects and social arrangements; they are informed by the received meanings of persons and things (1985, ix).[27] This definition sounds more suitable for my purposes here. If I follow Sahlins's ideas here, I can suggest that structures in convention are the normative representations, which I discuss in chapter 5, whereas structures in action are communicative activities, which I focus on in chapter 6.

Following Michel de Certeau, I aim to exhibit something that a purely normative (or structuralist) study would leave out—namely, coincidental incidences and irregular occurrences that do not manifest quantifiable behaviors, stereotypes of the staging of social intercourse, ritual structures, or other descriptive schemas.[28] But I do not mean to argue in favor of fluidity in social interaction or a creolization of culture as suggested in relation to disconnected and diasporic social groups (Eickelman and Anderson 2003b, 10). My aim is to show structural continuity with irregular examples.

27. Sahlins (1985) concludes that to the extent that the symbolic is pragmatic, the system is a synthesis in time of reproduction and variation.

28. Certeau explains that in scientific analysis, the full natural context where a proverb is uttered or a joke made—that is, the right space and timing—tends to be left out. Thus, of the practices themselves science will retain only movable elements or descriptive schemas, "leaving out aspects of a society that cannot be so uprooted and transferred to another space: ways of using things or words according to circumstances" (1984, 20).

In recent anthropological literature, the relationship between structures and human agency has been seen not as a contrasting dichotomy that involves only the notions of dominance and resistance, or, if viewed from another perspective, tacit consent and resisting creativity (i.e., Abu-Lughod 1986; Hale 2005; Mahmood 2005). As Andre Gingrich has argued, focusing on specific, narrow aspects of social hierarchies and doctrines or putting too much emphasis on resistance and creativity distorts both structure and agency and hides a wide range of intermediate situations that might be more significant to the way the proceedings become communally significant (1997, 153). Saba Mahmood has suggested that we should think of agency not as a synonym for resistance to relations of domination, but as a capacity for action that historically specific relations (of subordination) enable and create (2001, 203). In the spirit of subaltern studies, my aim is to bring out discourses and structural conditions that have historically contributed to the constitution of particular circumstances of inequalities, discriminations, and silences.[29] This task is vital for Aden, whose history has so far been told to the Western audience only from the point of view of ruling powers. Nevertheless, the aim here is not to produce another history to complement the previous ones, but to accept that histories change over time, a matter I learned while residing in Aden.[30]

Islam, Knowledge, and the Public Sphere

Scholars of the anthropology of Islam have asserted that Islam is knowledge rather than a belief (e.g., Asad 1996; Lambek 1993). It is a particular kind of knowledge that people apply when practicing their religion and making meaning in their lives. This knowledge is not directly linked to the Islamic holy texts; rather, it is humanly mediated. In the present study, I focus on the Adeni case, where there is not just one "knowledge" of Islam, but several. Knowledge of Islam is embedded in other knowledges, contributing to a variety of local religious and ideological

29. For instance, Chakrabarty 1997. On the scarcity of studies inspired by subaltern studies in the field of Middle Eastern studies, see Webber 1997.

30. The Western notion of "history" is problematic anyway in the Adeni context. Based on the idea of a division between past and present, "history" fails to address traditions that move among past, present, and future. See Certeau 1988, 2.

manifestations. In Aden, people draw on three different culturally embedded knowledges of Islam. This does not mean that there are several "Islams," as Abdul Hamid el-Zein (1977) argues. Instead, the basic notions of culture are argued in a multiple way, and these knowledges are manifested in the public sphere in a variety of ways. I discuss how this happens in chapters 5 and 6 and the theoretical problems that arise in chapter 7.

In the Middle Eastern cultural context, it is difficult to draw definite and stable lines between public and private. Mohsen Kadivar's (2003) definition of what is private from an Islamic point of view—as forbiddance of unwarranted inquiry, on the one hand, and as recognition of the right to freedom in action, on the other—does not require fixed, permanent entities. Fadwa El Guindi has ascertained that the public and the private do not form categorical dichotomies (1999, 77–78). Instead, the private is a flexible concept that is temporally and spatially determined. Thus, any place can act as a private place for a particular purpose and for a given time in the same way that homes can be both public and private. There is no principle that would make homes permanently domestic or private.

During the course of this book, I take the reader to both private places such as homes and public places such as government offices, factory floors, educational institutes, health clinics, women's neighborhood clubs, public meetings, courtrooms, taxis, newspaper offices, farming fields, construction sites, streets, bars, cars, and nightclubs. But the dividing line between private and public does not always tally with the division between the home and the public place. Even homes can act as public spaces; visits, feasts, and *makhdaras*[31] of all kinds make homes places where public spaces are built and public conversations are held. Workplaces and clubs can likewise be temporally made into private places. Even the street can become temporally and partially private; in performing the *salat* prayer, a person can temporally occupy any clean place for that purpose and thus render it sacred and private.

Even though I focus on many public places in this study, I do not consider these spaces alone as constitutive of the public sphere. In Muslim communities, studies on the public sphere have focused on emerging Islamic voices such as

31. The *makhdara* is a tentlike shelter erected outside the entrance of a house to accommodate more people than the house itself can and sometimes also to observe the segregation of the sexes or other groups.

"public Islam" and the new media (J. W. Anderson 2003; Eickelman and Anderson 2003a; LeVine and Salvatore 2005; Salvatore and Eickelman 2006b). In this study, I approach the notion of the public sphere from a different angle. At issue is the way ordinary people engage with metadiscourses of the public sphere. By understanding that the public sphere is *metatopical,* as Taylor suggests (1995, 271), we can consider that public places are not the only places relevant to its constitution and that they often manifest only dominant social formations. In a society with lively oral communication, everybody's business is everybody else's business, owing to *kalam nas* (people's talk), despite the segregation of the sexes and patterns of avoidance of a variety of degrees. In the Aden of any of the three periods of time this study covers, the public sphere is a sphere where various voices and representations of the modern and traditional are contested. In this study, I am particularly interested in seeing how gender, the family, and the social order are voiced in different forums. As Nilüfer Göle reminds us, women's issues and gender questions are pivotal in the shaping of political debate and the public sphere in any Middle Eastern society (1997, 62).

Segregation and Anthropological Inquiry

In the past few decades, some the most popular topics in Middle Eastern anthropology have been gender, the family, and society. Ever since Middle Eastern gender studies successfully moved out of the harem, as Lila Abu-Lughod (1989) puts it, and the "woman as victim" phase was more or less passed,[32] a more varied approach has gained space. Nevertheless, the idea of Islam as the all-encompassing frame of explanations still informs many studies. The new approaches include studying women in the labor market and as economic agents (Hoodfar 1997; Mundy 1995); as part of nationalist projects (various articles in Joseph 2000 and Joseph and Slyomovics 2001; Najmabadi 1998; Shakry 1998); as targets of and subjects in popular movements, Islamic or other (Abu-Lughod 1998; Al-Ali 2000; Badran 1993; Hale 1993); before the law of various kinds (Hirsch 1998; Mir-Hosseini 2000; Moors 1995, 1999); as bodily and sexual subjects (*Rewriting the History of Sexuality*

32. Elizabeth Fernea has asserted that in earlier years of Middle Eastern gender studies, research carried out about *hijab* and intersex avoidance could be classified into two categories: "dignity studies" and "oppression studies." See Moghadam 2002, 597.

2006); in history that was earlier forgotten (Keddie 2002; Lutfi 1991; Meriwether and Tucker 1999; Nashat and Tucker 1999; Tucker 1993); and as agents in their own right in a variety of fields of life. In spite of these new approaches challenging the earlier public/domestic dichotomy, the focus has remained on women's lives as separate from men's. It is as if women had more or less forcefully penetrated fields previously occupied by men only and would now encounter men simply in hostile terms, as part of an "accommodated protest."[33]

Rather than viewing men's and women's lives in opposing terms, I look at them as part of the same culture divided only partly by gender—a gender that is embedded in other significant distinctions. This intersectional approach, common from postcolonial feminist studies, has influenced me throughout my work and particularly in the way I discuss gender and social categorizations in this book.[34] I especially want to emphasize that the women and men I discuss here do not form any uniform categories such as "Adeni women," "Adeni men," "Adeni people," or, as the British colonizers used to put it, "*the* Adenese."[35] To avoid any such false coherence, I have given indicators of the person's social and other distinctive background when discussing particular people. It is more than evident to me that the young, poor, illiterate woman who took care of her blind parents at home and whom I met in the Women's Union literacy class had very little in common in terms of life options with the young woman I met in her first job at the university, full of enthusiasm regarding her new prospects and with her parents' full support in all her aspirations.

Because the division between sex and gender[36] has become the target of criticism in both feminist and anthropological studies (H. Moore 1999, 151–52), it is appropriate here to explain what I mean with these two categories. Throughout my work, I have found it problematic to define sex and gender when looking at the question from the point of view of my ethnographic material. While in Aden, I did not encounter problems in discussing gender, but this does not mean that

33. Arlene MacLeod (1991) introduced this expression.

34. On postcolonial feminisms, see Vuorela 1999.

35. The point of false coherence is discussed in Mohanty 1991a, 7. Mohanty also stresses the fact that Western women such as I should not expect some sort of "bonding" when meeting women in other cultural frameworks (1991b, 53).

36. Initially suggested by the American anthropologist Gayle Rubin (1975).

my understanding of this category would tally with that of the people I was in communication with. The fact that standard Arabic has only one word for the whole issue, *jins* (sex and [grammatical] gender),[37] which divides people into two categories, *dhakar* (male) and *untha* (female), complicates the issue further.

In Yemeni academia, efforts have been made to introduce the word *gandar* (the term *gender* pronounced in "an Arabic way") into the local vocabulary (see Badran 2000). As Margot Badran notes, gender appeared in the vocabulary of Arab countries, Yemen included, in the 1990s as part of the "gender and development" scheme and as a result of foreign funding devoted to improve women's living circumstances. Women's studies programs, with a development focus, appeared at about the same time in Arab universities (Badran 2000, part 2). Although it is clear that "gender" as a concept has come from the West, women's studies *(al-dirasat al-niswiyyat)* now have roots in Yemeni academia, where the term *gandar* is developed on the basis of local considerations, as Ra'ufah Hassan al-Sharqi of Sana'a University asserts (1998, 7). These local considerations link the notions of "male" and "female" to social and cultural aspects specific in time and place (al-Sharqi 1998). Nevertheless, it is evident that in Yemen, as elsewhere, gender tends to refer to women only, as if men do not have any gender at all. Although much of the ethnography on gender discussed in this book actually is about women, thus reflecting the particular Adeni gender question as a women's question, it does not mean that the material presented here would originate from women only or that discussions on women would not take place in reference to both genders.

Among Yemeni social scientists and other members of academia, *gandar* is understood, first, to stand for the distinguished roles of man and woman in the society generated by civilizational, cultural, and social components of that society and, second, to describe relations between man and woman in that society at a specific place and time. The latter notion views gender relations in light of the distribution of social roles for each sex in obtaining resources that enable them to meet the needs required for performing those roles, as Manal al-Kanadi (2000) explains. Viewing gender from the perspective of health, Husnia al-Qadri, a medical doctor and lecturer at Sana'a University, explains that the term *sex*

37. The word *jins* means also, among other things, "race," "class," and "nation," and the word *jinsiya* means "citizenship."

stands for biological differences between men and women, whereas *gender* refers to particular social and cultural aspects. She suggests that a gender approach (to health) would mean considering the critical role that social and cultural factors and power relations play between the sexes. These inequalities create, maintain, and exacerbate exposure to risk factors that vary according to sex. They also affect access to and control over resources such as decision making and education. Because these hierarchical inequalities usually disfavor women, gender analysis must address women's problems in particular, Dr. al-Qadri (1998) asserts.

In these two considerations on the difference between sex and gender, the idea that sex is linked to biology but gender is linked to society and culture becomes explicit.[38] Considering the importance of gender and sex to such social categories as "woman," "man," and "family" that this book addresses in different historical, social, and particular contexts, it is sufficient to say that I approach these notions in their particular historical and social constitutions. As Henrietta Moore has put it, anthropological studies should work back toward these categories rather than take them as a set of starting points (1994, 27).[39] For me as a scholar, it has been important to listen to and learn how people talk about these notions.

In Middle Eastern anthropological studies, sexual segregation has often been taken as a barrier that has consequences not only for men and women who live in the particular society, but also for the anthropologist who studies the society. According to this understanding, men and women's lives seldom crosscut and indeed form two separate fields—fields that consequently require separate studies.[40] In Aden, the level and intensity of cross-sex contacts vary according to generation, social class, the general and particular context or place, and the temporarily prevailing ideals that organize intersex communication. For me as a

38. This definition, of course, takes biology as constituted outside discursive practices that are part of knowledge and power systems. For critical perspectives on the sex/gender divide, see H. Moore 1994, 8–27, and 1999.

39. In a later text, Moore suggests that scholars should not try to define absolutely the boundary between sex and gender but should instead benefit from the different ideas that the sex/gender debate brings up (1999, 168).

40. Wikan 1982/Barth 1983 and Dorsky 1986/Stevenson 1985 are two examples of such studies carried out by an anthropologist couple, where the woman anthropologist studies "women," but the male scholar, even though focusing only on men, describes "society."

3. An extended household on the slopes of Mount Shamsan in Crater. Photograph by the author, 1992.

scholar, it was not difficult to spend time and have conversations with both men and women, a fact I am extremely grateful for.

The Ethnographic Field

I collected material for this book during several ethnographic field trips. In addition to these trips, I studied British colonial files stored in the India Office

Records in the British Library in London. I went through, in particular, files that were kept on individual persons or that dealt with religious matters, prostitution, social matters, civil societies, and newspapers. It was in these files that I expected to find "real" people.

At the very beginning of this study in 1988, I did interviews and collected structured information in people's homes, women's union clubs, and various workplaces, including government offices, schools, colleges, the Aden Divisional Court, factories, cooperatives, state farms (in the neighboring governorate of Lahig), health centers, hospitals, newspaper offices, and the television station. The structured part of my fieldwork consists of some 311 families and provides data on socioeconomic background, family and household size, work history, attitudes toward women's extradomestic work, education, and problems women face in working outside the home. I also asked about attitudes to social and political changes that had taken place after independence and then after Yemeni unification as well as about aspirations for the future. Because there are so very few anthropological studies on Aden, I felt that I needed to collect this kind of "sociological" data simply to know what kind of community it was. I did not want to limit myself to one sociological category, so I made efforts to include people from all social categories, from both sexes, with various backgrounds, and from all parts of the town.

In carrying out the interviews in workplaces, I always asked someone from the administration, often a supervisor or foreman (man or woman) to do the structured interviews. This approach allowed me to concentrate on listening to what people said and to formulate additional questions when something interesting came up. I found that group interviews were more fruitful than individual meetings: first, because they promoted discussion among the participants and, second, because people would offer comments to me afterward regarding what some other person had said, thus providing me with more background to what had been said. I did not find that the presence of a male foreman hindered women from expressing themselves because everybody's affairs, family problems included, were known by everybody else in the workplace anyway. The foreman's presence also did not seem to limit expression of opinions on critical issues, either, however political in nature these opinions might have been. In one of the factories, I found out in a group interview about internal tensions, and people often complained about broader political issues. These visits did not provide my only material about working life in Aden, however. I was living there, after all, in the capacity of a health project coordinator, hanging around in government offices and other places to do my job every day.

I never carried out secret observations while undertaking my work; I always told my work colleagues and the people I met that I was also a university researcher. People usually felt very positive about my interest and helped me. In visiting various workplaces, I made new contacts and sometimes visited the homes of people I had met this way. I soon made friends, too—both men and women—and started to spend extra time with them, visiting their homes, sitting with them at my own place, and going out with them. I also started chewing *qat*,[41] which involved me in numerous social gatherings with interesting discussions and new people to meet. Hanging around and socializing with people provided me perhaps with the best source of knowledge on what was going on and what it was like to live in Aden. My Arabic improved steadily as I took courses in standard and colloquial Arabic, but still today I cannot claim fluency.

In the beginning of my fieldwork, I had the intention of studying the impact of the 1974 Family Law on women's lives. After spending some time in Aden, I realized that this topic would not be that interesting to investigate. Instead, what I found fascinating to follow was the interaction between men and women, and thus I decided to concentrate on looking at gender relations in various fields of life and how these relations had changed in the course of the revolution. I carried out the first part of my fieldwork from October 1988 to November 1989, the period before unification. This part of my fieldwork consisted of material on life during the PDRY era. Soon after I returned to Finland, the unification of the two Yemens was announced in late 1989, and in less than six months Aden was no longer the capital of the PDRY. At that moment, I decided that I had to return and study the changes that unification was bringing about, especially because I now had material for a comparison.

I returned to Aden in June 1991, one year after unification, and started a new investigation in a changed atmosphere. I stayed until December of that year and went back yet again in March 1992 for three months. From October to December

41. *Qat* is a mild narcotic leaf chewed in societal gatherings. According to local Islamic interpretations, *qat* does not belong to the category of narcotics prohibited in the Qur'an. On social aspects of *qat* chewing in North Yemen, see Weir 1985a and 1985b.

1998, I carried out further investigations, this time in the very depressing atmosphere and declining economy that followed the devastating civil war in 1994. Between 1992 and 1998, I made three short visits to Aden, which gave me a chance to follow what was happening and to keep in contact with my old friends. In January and February 2001, I did the final part of my fieldwork for this book, so what I describe here does not expand beyond that date.

While in Aden, I used to take long walks and kept my camera with me. In this way, I wanted to get to know every corner of the city that fascinates me so much and to record the disappearing colonial town scenery. It was also a good way to meet new people and visit homes. Many people asked me to take a photo of them. I also took photos at weddings and other celebrations, even though by the end of the 1990s not so many women volunteered to be photographed, and some families destroyed their wedding videos. I still have a video from one wedding, though, made by a private photo studio that specialized in shooting wedding videos.

In the capacity of my work as a health project coordinator, I learned about matters of health, where gender constitutes a big difference. I visited health units, hospitals, and health administration offices throughout the country and in the al-Mahra governorate in particular. These visits gave me an insight into life in the countryside, from where many Adenis have only recently come.

To learn about the Family Law and how it was practiced in court, I visited the Aden Divisional Court, where I met barristers and both female and male judges and sat in court sessions where family disputes were litigated. These sessions were interesting not only from the point of view of how much detail they gave about the litigants' lives and how they articulated social normativity, but also in regard to how social hierarchies are played out in a court session.

At Aden University, I asked, with the help of a teacher, two classes of English-language students (a total of thirty-four female and male students) to write an essay on the "ideal marriage" or on a "Yemeni marriage." Most of the students were not (yet) married, and what they had to say about marriage focused very much on the dreams, fears, and expectations they have of the opposite sex. Even though arranged marriages, where the couple meet for the first time at their wedding, no longer take place in Aden, starting an intimate life and a family continues to be a source of anxiety. Some of the students had chosen their future spouses on their own, without any parental involvement, but marriage still seemed to be a matter of excitement and concern. It was interesting how both topics produced similar ideal discourses on gender, family, morality, values, and local customs.

In 1998, I focused in particular on notions of normativity in family life and on observing how the revolutionary discourse survived in the postunification atmosphere and how the religious discourse was strengthening. To contextualize the students' views on marriage, I discussed with people of the elder generation about contracting marriages, gender roles in the family, patterns of closeness in kinship relations, and issues of supernatural forces.

Finally, in 2001, I devoted time again to observing litigation in family disputes in the Aden Divisional Court and finding out about practices related to marriage payments. I also studied marriage and divorce records from the 1950s to the year 2001 archived in the Ministry of Justice and Waqf (Religious Endowments). Outside the normal hanging around, I visited people and places I had come to know since 1988.

As I stated earlier, people I concentrate on in this book are seldom adherents of a particular normative representation. In order to avoid giving the idea that such representations are tied to people and that their proponents "bring" them to the public sphere, I have deliberately kept such activists in side roles. Instead, I focus on encounters with people, men and women, for whom the diversity of normative rules is a matter of coping in a social reality that happens to be constituted that way.

Rapid economic, political, and social changes are sweeping over the Middle East. Within the past fifteen years, Yemen has stepped into a multiparty parliamentary democracy.[42] It has received hundreds of thousands of returnees and refugees from abroad, and its economy has collapsed, impoverishing even what might be called the middle classes. In Aden, the former PDRY capital, these changes have meant marginalization, the polarization of society, and the loss of many rights that women had gained during the earlier rule. To understand what has happened in Aden, though, it is not enough to refer to such political and economic changes. I have written this book in an attempt to provide a tool for understanding the social dynamics and how ideological conjunctures play an

42. With increasing popular unrest in the southern provinces and a war in the northern province of Sa'ada at the time of writing in November 2009, it was not certain which way the country would go and whether it would survive at all.

important role in what happens. By writing this book on morality and propriety, I want to focus on the positive driving forces behind people's actions.

The book's argument can be summarized in the following way: social interaction takes place in a tension between mutually contrasting normative frameworks that do not determine practice as such, but encode a certain cultural understanding. People act in reference to these normative frameworks, but practice is never imposed by rules. Focusing simply on norms would give an inadequate view of social practice because events do not follow a rule, and particular ideals seldom become targets of self-discipline.[43] Even though the three normative frameworks—customs, religion, and revolution—are hegemonic in the sense that they dominate talk, few people are proponents or opponents of any, a fact that speaks for more complex situations rather than for one that can be reduced simply to a question of dominance and resistance. More accurately, the book is about what lies in between submission and defiance. It is a preliminary study, and many themes have had to be left without proper discussion. This book is in no way intended to stand as *the* ethnography of Aden. What is said here naturally involves Aden only and should not be generalized to cover other parts of Yemen.

43. Because I want to present common, "ordinary" social interactions in this study, I do not focus on activists and people for whom a particular normative (and political) program is a target of disseminating public morality or the cultivation of a self.

2 From Colonialism to a Neocolonial State

Aden, Mukalla, Mascate sont au nombre de ces "enfers" que mentionnent les dictons des marins. [Aden, Mukalla, and Muscat are among the "hells" mentioned in sailors' tales.]

—ELISÉE RECLUS, *The Earth and Its Inhabitants*[1]

THE ARGUMENTS presented in this book need a contextualization of the society as a morphology of all kinds of interests, be they political, ethnic, economic, or ideational in nature, so in this chapter I give a short historical introduction to Aden as a concentration of movement of things, ideas, and people. By "social morphology," I mean the structure of a town made up of interconnected or interdependent parts joined together in an urban community. This chapter discusses what these parts are.

Throughout its history, Aden has seldom left a visitor indifferent. Such is the spell of this arid place, hot and humid most of the year. Descriptions of the harsh life of the people living here, with few natural resources, have filled literature on this Arabian port.[2] A peninsula filled with rocky hills and flat sands, the place is said to shine satanic light in the full moon (Little 1968, 120). There is no arable land in Aden, which means that its food supply depends on the surrounding areas and on trade with foreign lands.[3] Its appeal rarely comes with the first impression: at first glance, the dull colonial architecture makes the place seem somewhat unattractive to the eye of the visitor who is exhausted

1. Quoted and translated in Nizan 1987, 92.

2. Brian Doe, referring to the traveler and historian Ibn Al-Mujawir (1986), mentions that in ancient times there were 180 sweet wells in Aden (1965, 10–14). See also Hunter [1877] 1968, 10, and Shukry 1986, 329–42.

3. Ibn Battuta described Aden in the fourteenth century as a large city without seed, water, or trees (Doe 1965, 12; Hunter [1877] 1968, 7).

by the heat and ready to reboard the ship or plane to leave again right away. But once she learns the ways of Aden, she will find it difficult to leave. Aden is a place thick with contradictions, which, perhaps, is the very reason for its being so fascinating. Contradictions and how they organize everyday life are what this book is about.

Two physical factors, climate and physical morphology, structure Aden as a town. They influence how daily life is organized, how houses are built, and how subcommunities are imagined. The position of the sun dictates where the open-air market is erected and where food is served in street restaurants. Aden requires different rules of orientation in the daytime and evening. In actuality, it is not one place, but rather consists of several towns, making it a polynucleotide city, with mountains and the surrounding sea dividing it into separate and detached subtowns. The name "Aden" refers locally only to the oldest part of Aden, an area surrounded by extinct volcanic slopes and connected to other districts only through narrow openings in the cliffs. The British introduced the name "Crater" to this part of Aden during the time when the town extended to other areas in the congested peninsula, but even today the Arabic form of the new name (Kritr) has not replaced the old name "'Adn."

From March to October each year, during the season that is understood as summer, Aden is very hot and humid, with suffocating winds called *shimal,* blowing, as the name says, from the north. The extreme heat has been a source of several stories throughout the years, and the one presented by the Indian Adeni historian Abdulla Yaqub Khan, who wrote in the late 1930s, is perhaps the most illuminating. In a humorous manner, he describes the heat as "just enough for Shams-e-Tabrez to roast his meat" (1938–39, 616). In November, the moist climate finally gives way to a milder temperature and moderate humidity. During the summer months, activities outside of ventilated and cooled indoor premises are reduced to a minimum. The pace of life slows down, and people adapt to the requirements of living in a harsh place, where every activity has to be measured by the given heat. The desolate hills made the British repeatedly talk of "the barren rocks of Aden."[4] Captain F. M. Hunter, in his famous

4. The "barren rocks" seemed to act as a metaphor to the British. It is the most common expression used to describe Aden in memorial literature on colonial British; see, for example, Trevaskis 1968, Paget 1970, and Lunt 1966, which is titled *The Barren Rocks of Aden.* A traditional

Account of the British Settlement of Aden in Arabia from 1877, described the climate as being "so bad that it turns wine into vinegar in the space of ten days" ([1877] 1968, 191).

It is evidently not necessary to own a watch in a place where daily routines create the pulse of the day. Such routines are repeated every day with a tempo dictated by the sun, except on Fridays (and, later on, Thursdays, too, when it was made into a weekly holiday). When the sun shows its first rays behind Sira Island at five o'clock each morning, people begin to appear in the streets, many called by their vocation. The quiet morning hours belong to the fishermen, bakers, taxi drivers, and tea hawkers. People who have spent the night sleeping in the rough on the beach or in the open street wake up and proceed to their daily activities, whatever they are. Yet even before this movement outside, there is already full activity going on inside many homes. In numerous families, women start their mornings with the sunrise prayer, bake bread, and prepare breakfast for the rest of the family. Later on, they wake the children and clothe and feed them while their husbands and other male folk continue to sleep.

Between 6:00 and 7:00 A.M., the city starts slowly to gather in outdoor activities. Onto the streets come the factory workers, first the women, who start their work day at 7:00 A.M., as they catch the bus provided by the workplace. The next groups of people to enter the streets are the workingwomen who are taking their little children to relatives and who are the dutiful office employees—the secretaries, messengers, and others in the lower ranks of the office hierarchy. With the pulse ever increasing, more and more cars fill the streets as men in senior positions drive to the office, the last ones to come out. Shops and markets are open for a few hours before noon and close again after the midday call to prayer. By that time, those who reached the workplace last are the first ones to leave, and many make their way to the *qat* market. Children come home from morning classes and then return to school a few hours later for the evening session. The last people to arrive home are those—mostly women—who work according to the clock card or are dependent on transportation provided by the employer. By that time, many people have already finished lunch and taken their rest.

---

military song, a Scottish two-four bagpipe march, is also entitled "The Barren Rocks of Aden"; for the tune, visit http://www.nigelgatherer.com/tunes/tab/tab1/ aden.html (visited on June 9, 2007).

In the afternoon, the streets become hot and quiet. Everybody seeks the coolness of the shadows and the few occasional gusts of wind. Those who are in the habit of chewing *qat* withdraw to their favorite chewing place, whether it is home, a friend's house, a public chewing club, or just a spot outdoors where the heat is minimized. When the *mu'adhdhin* calls for the afternoon prayer, movement in the city remains slow. Life resumes in the streets only around four o'clock, when most of the heat has passed away. This is the moment for shopkeepers, street hawkers, and others who sell items that are not intended to be consumed the same day. Meat and fish markets are closed; the hectic bargaining is over in half-empty *qat* markets, and the few late buyers have to settle for what remains.

Late afternoon, before the blue moment approaches, is the best moment of the day. The sun is gentle, making colors full. Women, if free from their household chores, visit relatives, neighbors, and friends. Men gather in teahouses and coffee shops to kill the time they have to spend outside the home. By sunset, mosques fill with praying men, the most popular moment to gather for joint prayer. Now the market starts to become fully alive, women and men with children filling the streets in the main market, which is organized in clusters according to the merchandise sold. In makeshift hut areas, where there is no electricity, the sunset provides a natural moment to retire for a new day to come.

After the last prayer call, the activities start to slow down, and men can return home for their dinner. Families gather round the television to follow the news and the daily Arabic soap opera. Those who do not have a home to return to look for a quiet place to lie down for the night. Families who get daily food by begging in their particular sector of the town feed the children, but many are already asleep.

This is the hour that nightlife in Aden begins. Before unification and on a reduced scale afterward, the city was full of bars, restaurants, and nightclubs, where music, alcohol, and dancing attracted those who desired it. In the late 1980s, the town districts of Tawahi and Khormaksar had an active nightlife, whereas Crater, Shaykh 'Uthman, and other districts in the mainland, where no entertainment was to be found, became quiet after the market closed. In the late hours of the night, one could meet people not encountered during daylight. Old drunkards, hookers, and people who sailed the seven seas filled the bars. This is still the port town of Aden, with exciting people, a fascinatingly decadent atmosphere, and a large share of tolerance for different lifestyles.

The town finally becomes quiet in the early hours of the morning, with only occasional soldiers patrolling the streets, checking that everything is alright. Now it is the time for stray dogs, cats, and rats to fight and look for food and for disoriented roosters to announce the dawn when it is still time to sleep.

Social Stratification and Communal Diversity in the Colonial Era

During the colonial era, from 1839 to 1967, Aden was divided into separate "ethnic" and religious communities. The division was due in part to the British policy of exaggerating communal differences among the colonized subjects (divide and rule) and in part to the local tradition of emphasizing a person's descent *(nasab)*. Each community had its own symbols and practices, which strengthened communal unity and distinguished it from the others. The European community consisted of the British service personnel, both military and civil, and British businessmen who relied largely on supplying the increasing demand of the military base. Other Europeans, who came mainly from Italy, France, and Greece, ran commercial firms and a few industries. Their number was small, but their share in the total economy was considerable. The role of Europeans in running the town's economy increased in the 1960s when Aden became one of the busiest ports in the world. The most prominent businessman during the entire colonial era was undoubtedly Antonin Besse, the French tycoon who gave his own color to the town's colonial charm with his taste for the music of Wagner, which he used to listen to with his friends on the roof terrace of his 'Aydarus Road residence (see Footman 1986).[5]

Early-twentieth-century Aden was a society of contractors and brokers who contracted everything from daily foodstuffs to luxury goods and labor. The foreign brokers moved from one market to another in search of business deals. Their only concern and interest in community affairs was where to make money fastest. Because the land was not good for cultivation, all food was imported during colonial times, either from the two Aden protectorates[6] or from Africa or Europe.

5. On French colonial interests in Aden before and after independence, see Taminian 1998.

6. The Aden Protectorate was divided into the Eastern Aden Protectorate and the Western Aden Protectorate. Together they are sometimes referred to as "the protectorate." See Naval Intelligence Division 1946, 342–54, for the administration of those areas.

An increasing number of service personnel and their accompanying families made a market for European styles of consumption. Transit passengers in the port brought a demand for tax-free items. Peculiar to the time, there were a few local industries, including a gin factory, a cigarette manufacturer, and a Coca-Cola company.[7] The city was full of needs that could not be satisfied by a local supply. According to Kennedy Trevaskis, the high commissioner of Aden from 1963 to 1965,[8] "With the exception of a minority of local Arabs and a few others, whose only home was Aden, this whole polyglot mass of people was parasitic. They were mere visitors who had come to Aden to make money and remit it to their distant homes" (1968, 4).

The main part of the labor force came from outside Aden and involved a powerful group of headmen (*maqadima*, sing. *muqaddam*) whose dealings entailed recruiting labor from the two Aden protectorates and the Kingdom of Yemen and organizing everything from board to lodging for these migrant workers. In the early years of the British settlement, the first *maqadima* came from Mocha, in the southern part of the Kingdom of Yemen. The British allowed this system to flourish in Aden (Gavin 1975, 59). Another "class" of people characteristic to the Adeni labor market was the *surung*, persons who supplied labor on a daily basis wherever manpower was needed. They tended to come from the same villages or tribes as the laborers and formed pockets of men who worked, resided, and socialized together. In 1955, a total of 35 percent of the entire population of Aden came from the Yemen, 13.7 percent from the protectorates, and 11.4 percent from India. Local Adenis with resident rights accounted for only 26.7 percent of the population living and working in the town. The influential Europeans and Jews comprised 3 percent and 0.6 percent, respectively, of the town's population in that period (Aden Colony 1955a, 12).

7. Aside from these and some other minor manufacturing, in the late colonial period Aden's industries consisted mainly of the saltworks, ship repair, and the huge Aden oil refinery, which in 1969 employed 60 percent of the whole industrial labor force (Shukry 1986, 256). According to Abd al-Hafiz Mahmassani (1962), the only important local product was salt, which was made from seawater.

8. The highest representative of the London-based Colonial Office in Aden was called "governor" during the years 1937 to 1963 and after that was referred to as "high commissioner."

The ethnic diversity and the number of temporary residents left their mark in the geography of the town. Homeless people and those living in temporary huts and makeshift shelters on the slopes of Ma'alla and Tawahi and in the district of Shaykh 'Uthman were often temporary workers, either from the Yemen (called *jebelis,* "people of the mountains") or from the protectorates. *Akhdam* people (literally "servants"), the native social category treated as pariah, had their separate shanty areas in Crater, Ma'alla, Tawahi, and the mainland districts. The Somali population was concentrated from the early times of colonial rule in some quarters of Ma'alla, which were called "Somalipura" in the local Arabic-Indian dialect. Jews had their own streets in Crater near the Esplanade. Close to the Jewish quarters, on the other side of the main market area along the Jinnah and Gandhi Roads, lived Hindus, the so-called *banian* traders and merchants and white-collar government employees. Small congregations of Bohoras and Khojas, two Shi'ite sects active in trade who had moved to Aden from India, a small Zoroastrian community with Parsi traders, and an Indian Muslim trade community (after 1948 called "Pakistanis") also resided in these quarters.

Tawahi was the European sector alongside the new cantonment town of Khormaksar, with comfortable villas and an air of colonial splendor. Banks, luxury shops, hotels, clubs, and bars gathered round a crescent, where a statue of Queen Victoria was placed, and formed the European center of the town. Paul Nizan, a young French author who lived for a short period in Aden during the 1920s, describes with disillusion the European Aden he knew: "Aden was a highly concentrated image of our mother Europe, it was Europe compressed. A few hundred Europeans huddled together in a space as cramped as a prison ship five miles long by three miles wide. . . . The Orient reproduced the Occident and is a commentary on it" (1987, 110).

The colonial era consequently provided a town scene of separate communities, rarely interacting yet most of the time living in harmony alongside each other. Public holidays celebrated in colonial Aden reflect this communal diversity. Their observation was legislated in the Public Holidays Ordinance, enacted in 1941 (Aden Colony 1941, no. 14). Christian celebrations included New Year's Day, Good Friday, Easter Monday, Christmas Day, and Boxing Day. Alongside these holidays were the colonial celebrations of Empire Day and the king's (later the queen's) birthday. Id al Fitr (two days), Id al Haj (two days), Muharram 10,[9] Rajab 27 (Leilat al-Ma'araj),[10] and Rabi al-Awal 12 (Maulid an Nebi)[11] were among the Muslim holidays observed.[12] The Muslim holiday Aidarus Day (Rabi' al-Thani 13) was also observed; on it, observers make a pilgrimage *(ziara)* around the mosque and tomb of the patron saint of Aden, the *wali* Abu Bakr bin Abdullah al-'Aydarus, a Hadhrami sayyid who had lived in Aden during the fifteenth century (see Luqman n.d., 177–79). His *ziara* has been held annually since 1469.[13] From the Hindu calendar came the Divali holiday, called in the ordinance the "Hindu New Year Day." The most peculiar celebration was Jamshedi Navroz,[14] the New Year festivity according to the Persian solar calendar and celebrated after the spring equinox on March 21. It was added to the public holidays' calendar for the small Parsi community. The anniversary of the Fire Temple was also marked in Aden.

Old people still recall how the different groups in town used to celebrate each other's holidays. As in other British colonies, the weekly rest day was Sunday, in contrast to the surrounding "hinterland," as the British used to call the sheikhdoms, emirates, and sultanates that formed the Western and Eastern Aden protectorates.[15] There was, however, as elderly people still remember, some flexibility with working hours in order to allow everybody to perform religious duties.

Each religious community had its places of worship, celebration, and mourning. The Christians had churches, schools, and missionary stations for, among

9. That is, *ashura*. This holiday was celebrated by Shi'ites as a day of passion for the martyrdom of Husayn, but Sunnis celebrated it as a day of blessing conforming to similar holidays in the Jewish calendar. On that day, a *ziara*, pilgrimage, was organized in a mosque in Crater (see Bawazir 1997, 47–48).

10. That is, *leilat al-mi'raj*, the night journey.

11. That is, *rabi' al-awwal*, the Prophet's birthday *(mawlid al-nabi)*.

12. The different spellings of these holidays given here and later in this chapter are as given in the Public Holidays Ordinance.

13. The mosque itself was built in 1470, after the pilgrimage had already started (Bawazir 1997, 65).

14. "Navroz" refers to *naw roz*, "new light" (Persian). In the Public Holidays Ordinance, it is called the "Parsee New Year Day."

15. The weekly rest day was changed to Friday on April 19, 1963, by the government and commercial houses' agreement (*Welcome to Aden* 1963, 121).

others, Catholics (including Europeans and Goans), the Church of England, the Danish Lutheran mission, the Baptists, the Methodists, and the Presbyterians. The couple hundred Parsi Zoroastrians, ancient Persian settlers from Bombay, had the Fire Temple, known as "Adenwala Agiary." It was opened in 1883 with an eternal fire brought from Bombay. The Tower of Silence farther up the hill was the place where the deceased were left to be picked clean by the vultures (*Three Hours in Aden* 1891, 10, 34). During colonial times, the lively Parsi community was in the habit of holding parties for the cream of the town in the gardens of the Fire Temple, whether a sacred place or not (J. Knox-Mawer 1961, 93–94). Today lying abandoned, both the temple and the tower can be seen halfway up Mount Shamsan overlooking the Crater vegetable market.[16]

The Daudi Bohora community, Musta'ili Isma'ilis, originating from India,[17] comprised merchants and shopkeepers, among other professionals. Their mosque is situated in a closed compound in the market area of Crater, and it has room for other functions, too, such as communal feasts, sports activities, and a school. The community's spiritual leader, *dai,* has his seat in India. The Indian-style mosque is open for women, too, with their own separate section for praying in the main hall of the mosque behind a *sitara* (curtain) and upstairs.

Bohora women can be distinguished from other women by their costume, sewn from colorful thick cotton, with separate upper and lower parts and a hood for the head. The Khoja community was divided into Nizari Isma'ilis (Eastern Isma'ilis[18] and followers of Aga Khan) and Twelve-Imam Shi'ites, called Ithn'asharis. The

16. The Holy Fire, Atash, was taken back to India in 1976, when most of the Parsi community left Aden. It was taken to Adenwala Agiary in Lonawala, Maharastra. Its transport in a special air flight was organized by the Adeni-Parsi businessman and banker Cowasjee Dinshaw. See Daruwala 2002.

17. "Bohora" comes from the Gujarati word *vohorvn,* "to trade." It refers originally to a Hindu caste who converted to Islam during the early period of Isma'ili proselytizing in India before the eleventh century. The Musta'ili (Western) Isma'ilis are a branch that split with the Nizari (Eastern) Isma'ilis in 1094 and does not recognize the *aga khan* as its spiritual leader. The Adeni Bohoras have a sister community in Jabal Haraz in northern Yemen (Kour 1981, 26). Both are independent of the central authority in Egypt, from whom they split in 1130. The seat of the Dawah was moved from Yemen to India four centuries ago.

18. The Khojas originate mainly from Cutch or Kathiawar in India, representing the same group of immigrants as those who settled in Zanzibar and on the mainland of East Africa early in the nineteenth century (J. N. D. Anderson 1964, 21).

4. A British-style clock tower in a roundabout in Crater. The clock was removed after unification and replaced with roundabout decorating art from South Korea in the manner of the new Yemen capital city, Sana'a. Photograph by the author, 1988.

latter group, also called Ja'fariyya or Imamiyya, comprises a community that at the end of the twentieth century had some eight hundred members and a mosque in Crater. Their spiritual leader is presently in Iraq. In this Shi'a community, too, the mosque hosts various communal services, but other people are allowed to go and make a vow *(nadhr)* there. Women pray in a separated area, and weddings and other communal celebrations are held in the mosque compound.

Some Isma'ili families became very influential in the political scene of the colonial era. The Luqman family was one such family, who originated from the northern Yemeni area of Hamdan, but who had had to flee from Zaidi oppression to India in the eighteenth century. The patron of the family, Ibrahim Luqman, settled in Aden in the late nineteenth century and established successful businesses with British backing. His grandson, Muhammed Ali Luqman, an advocate and writer, published the first Yemeni novel in 1939, *Sa'id*.[19] A few

19. Originally published in 1939, reprinted in al-Hamdani 2005, 395–454.

years earlier his book *Bimadha taqaddum al-gharbiyyun?* (Why Has the West Advanced? 1933),[20] a critique of the "backwardness" of the East and a call for Western modernity, was reprinted and debated in the newspapers. He started the first local Arabic language newspaper, *Fatat al-Jazira*, in 1940. He also played an eminent role in the political scene of the 1950s and 1960s, first in the Arab Reform Club, a loose association of Adeni intellectuals, and later in the Aden Association, which embarked on promoting the independence of Aden under the British Commonwealth, in the same style as Singapore, as a state separate from the protectorates (Douglas 1987, 72–73; El Habashi 1966, 76–77; Muheirez 1985, 207; Tahir 1981, 25).

Land of Hope and Glory

Out of all the different nationalities and ethnic or religious communities,[21] Hindus were the group of people closest to the British apart from the Jews.[22] Owing to their position in between the ruling British and the ruled ones, they developed a distinction from the local people and culture. Perhaps Aden was the place where the humiliating experience of colonialism in India could be compensated for as large numbers of Indians joined the British-Indian government overseas recruitment program. In Aden, they were no longer colonial subjects but were offered white-collar positions. British high commissioner Trevaskis wrote about the Indian community's affinity to its colonial masters: "With India so recently independent I was surprised to find them so openly attached to the colonial regime.

20. Available in reprint in al-Hamdani 2005, 59–138.

21. This section's title refers to the British composer Edward Elgar's (1857–1934) March no. 1 of his famous piece *Pomp and Circumstance*. With A. C. Benson's lyrics, "Land of Hope and Glory" became a popular patriotic song: "Land of Hope and Glory / Mother of the Free / How shall we extol thee / Who are born of thee? / Wider still and wider / Shall thy bounds be set / God, who made thee mighty / Make thee mightier yet /God, who made thee mighty /Make thee mightier yet."

22. Aden was part of British India during 1839–1932 and was ruled from the Bombay Presidency. As a result, a number of Indians seeking a career in the colonial administration arrived in Aden. In 1937, Aden became a Crown colony directly under the Colonial Office in London. After the independence of India in 1948, the role of Indians in Aden continued as before. High Commissioner Trevaskis called Aden an Anglo-Indian colony where "largely British and Indian hands . . . made the wheels go round" (1968, 4).

For all their tea parties to celebrate Indian Independence Day, they tended to behave as their grandfathers had when educated Indians, such as Gandhi himself, had felt no shame in admiring the British Raj. They would ask you politely about current affairs in Britain and one evening in the Orient Club, which many favoured, an old man spoke to me of the 'King Emperor'" (1968, 4).

Only a few Indians who came to Aden with colonial rule stayed on after independence. Those who stayed were either remnants of the former trading community or men who had married locally. The Indian Hindu community—with newcomers brought by foreign firms, international organizations, and the government—continued to be distinct from other communities after independence, too. The Gandhi house in Crater is the place where Indian National Day and other celebrations are organized with family gatherings, badminton games, music performances, and food prepared by the community women. Out of the seven Hindu and Jain temples in Crater and Tawahi, only the Jain temple and two Hindu temples located in Crater have stayed intact. After the devastating civil war of 1994, the temple that was built under a cliff has lain unused, with a lock on its gate and a homeless Muslim family occupying it.

The number of Jews in Aden decreased from 7,290 in 1946 to 800 after the 1947 anti-Jewish riots and massacre in Aden, when thousands of Jews took aliya and immigrated to Palestine. A large number of them, however, moved to London.[23] Aden was once an important Jewish town, though. Magen Avraham, the principal synagogue in Aden, was one of the most magnificent in the world and could accommodate a thousand people (Burman 1991, 15).[24] Jews lived in the old quarters of Crater in a section of five streets where they had seven synagogues *(mi'lama)* and separate schools for girls and boys. These streets had their own Jewish names, such as "Chaplat al-Hamra" (Red Street, but renamed Solomon Street by the British), "Chaplat Banin" (named after the community president Banin Messa), "Chaplat al-Chobz" (Bread Street because of its several bakeries), and "Chaplat al-Mullah" (named after the Persian mullahs living there). Before

23. Ahroni explains that a total of 6,500 Adeni Jews and 2,500 Yemeni Jews, the latter refugees in miserable conditions in both Aden and nearby refugee camps, left Aden after the 1947 riots (1994, 244). The famous Operation Magic Carpet in 1948, the airlift from Aden to Israel, involved refugee Yemeni Jews, not Adeni Jews.

24. The image of this huge synagogue is reprinted in Tobi 1994b, 58.

the 1940s, a fifth street, Chaplat Zafaran, was also inhabited by Jews (Burman 1991, 8; Tobi 1994b, 59). In addition, smaller communities of Adeni and Yemeni Jews had synagogues in other areas of Crater, Tawahi, and Shaykh 'Uthman (Government of Aden 1939, 102).[25]

Well-off male Jews socialized in separate clubs for men only, such as the Hatikvah Club and the Judean Club. It was customary that women did not go out, not even to the market because the husband or servant took care of the shopping. Jewish women had barely any social activities outside the home, a situation motivated by their "traditional role": "Seeing that the family was properly clothed and fed were the main female occupations. This was no small job, particularly when the number of children was often between six and 13, and ready-made food and clothing were not available," as a booklet on Adeni Jews published by the Jewish Museum in London puts it (Burman 1991, 14). This remained the case until the Halus ha-Sa'ir organization was introduced in Aden with mixed-gender activities. Its functions resulted in a major social change in the community, which had earlier been strictly sexually segregated. Uncontrolled male-female interaction and girls in Halus uniforms in the streets of Aden appalled the community Jewish elders, who fought for the "traditional" values of seclusion for women and who resented the Zionist call directed at both sexes to join the mission in Palestine.

Jewish girls were also recruited in the Aden branch of the Ha-Berit Ha-'Ivrit Ha-'Olamit, a social organization with a strong Zionist and nationalist orientation. Boys and girls spent time together in cultural activities with ideological inclinations in the Young Pioneers' movement. Segregation of the sexes continued, however, in the Jewish community both in the educational system and in the many social activities up to the end of the Jewish era in Aden in 1967, with the exception of the Halus movement, which enabled girls to take advantage of educational and cultural activities to which their mothers had had no access (Ahroni 1994, 192–94).

As I stated earlier, of all the local communities in Aden during the colonial period, the Jewish community was closest to the British and assumed elements

25. The Jews had ten synagogues altogether in Aden (Burman 1991, 15). The ancient Jewish cemetery, overlooking the port in Ma'alla, has the oldest gravestones in the town, some of them seven to eight hundred years old (Goitein 1964, 46).

of the British way of life. Enjoying full rights as British subjects, Jews could travel freely to Europe and elsewhere with their British passports. In the course of the twentieth century, Jewish women changed their usual attire from trousers and a "coarse dress" over them to the modern European dress. Links to European and American Jewish communities, tied to the Adeni Europeans in the Scout movement and other joint communal activities and the emergence of Westernized education, contributed to the gradual Westernization of the Adeni Jewish community. This trend distinguished it from other Jewish communities in the Aden protectorates and Yemen, which the Adeni Jews considered backward (Ahroni 1994, 143–44). By the time of independence in the late 1960s, all Jewish families had moved from Aden, many of them to London, where the Adeni Jewish community has kept its traditions.[26]

Despite the particular customs and habits of each religious and "ethnic" community in Aden during the colonial period, they all shared some local customs not practiced by fellow believers in other lands, such as chewing the leaves of the plant *qat (Catha edulis)* in societal gatherings and smoking *mada'a* or *shisha* (two different types of water pipe).[27] Likewise, the language of Adeni Jews during the colonial period was Arabic mixed with Hebrew, Hindi, and Gujarati, just as other Adeni linguistic groups were blended with all these languages and English.[28]

The "ethnic" divisions were reflected in the labor market as well. The colonial administration was composed of the British, who managed the senior executive posts, and Indians brought to Aden by the British-Indian rule, who manned the junior executive and clerical positions. The latter were a cause of bitter feelings among the local population, who believed that the Indians had seized the opportunities that colonial rule had offered. By the 1850s, Indians had replaced all Arabs and Jews in the settlement's clerical positions (Gavin 1975, 60). Only during the course of the twentieth century were lower administrative posts manned by other "ethnic" groups alongside the Indians, but the Indians nevertheless filled

26. In contrast to the London Adeni Jews, those who went to Israel have, according to Ahroni, become alienated from their traditions (1994, 245–48).

27. For *qat* chewing as a custom, see Luqman 1960, 208–9, and for *qat* chewing among the Jewish population, see Ahroni 1994, 125.

28. On the language of Jews in Aden, see Ahroni 1994, 173–83 and 278–99; and on Adeni Arabic, see Muheirez 1985, 204–5.

the majority of these positions. As Doreen Ingrams explains, "The influence of the Government of India lay heavy upon Aden with its ugly, unimaginative government offices and official houses, and the innumerable Indian clerks, traders, police officers and schoolmasters who, through no fault of theirs, as it was the Government of India that gave them their jobs, delayed the opportunities for the native born Adeni to take their place" (1970, 3).[29]

A few local elite families could enter administrative posts that were closed to the rest of the population by limited access to education. At that time, education, from a qualification perspective, involved learning English, which remained the official language until 1959. In the 1955 *Census Report,* literacy was classified as "literate in English" and "literate in Arabic." In the category "Adeni Arabs," as the British called the local population, 2 percent of women were literate in English and 15.3 in Arabic,[30] and the rates for men were 24.4 and 58.5 percent, respectively (Aden Colony 1955a, 30).

The Jewish community in Aden was headed by a president *(nassi* or *nagid),*[31] the patron of the rich and influential merchant Messa family, often called "the Rothschilds of the East." On average, Jews were well-off people, and many were engaged in trading and commerce. Some were owners of proper shops and stores, and others worked as employees therein. The shops were located along the main road bordering the Jewish quarter, in the main bazaar area, where the Indian and Parsi traders also had their areas, and in Steamer Point (Tawahi), where they provided transit passengers with luxury items (Burman 1991, 13). Some Jewish young men worked as *karranis*, clerks, in the colonial administration. The Jewish craftsmen were famous for silver and gold, and others worked as tailors, bookbinders,

29. Doreen Ingrams was the wife of the British resident adviser to the Eastern Aden Protectorate; she published a study on life in the protectorate (D. Ingrams 1949).

30. It is worth comparing these figures to those of other ethnic category women. Among the British women, 96.4 percent were literate in English and 1.5 percent in Arabic, whereas only 61.4 percent of other European women were literate in English and 6.0 in Arabic. Indian women were not in a much better position: only 16.0 percent could read English and 13.0 percent Arabic. Of all the "ethnic" groups, the least literate (according to the British definition) were Somali women, of whom 1.5 percent knew English and 2.3 percent Arabic (Aden Colony 1955a, 30).

31. Burman calls the head of the Jewish community the *nassi* (1991, 9), whereas Ahroni calls this person the *nagid* (1994, 47).

and moneylenders. The Greek-owned cigarette factory employed Jewish laborers. There was a Jewish monopoly in the fez *(tarbush)* industry and in the ostrich feather trade. According to Reuben Ahroni, most Jewish families in Aden were not very wealthy (1994, 111), and their image as prosperous among the Adeni people was perhaps based on the wealth of their leader, the head of the Messa family. However, Adeni Jews were well off if compared to protectorate and Yemeni Jews, who occasionally sought refuge in Aden, where they lived on the streets. The division of labor inside the Jewish family was strict: the man was the breadwinner, and the woman the housekeeper (Ahroni 1994, 111; *Three Hours in Aden* 1891, 12).

In the Indian community, there were prosperous merchants, junior officials in the colonial administration, and semiskilled laborers. The community itself was divided by religion: Hindus; Muslims, who were subdivided into "Pakistanis" (Hanafis), Bohoras, and Khojas (Ithn'asharis); Parsis (Zoroastrians); and Goans (Catholics) (Bujra 1970, 195). Each commercial community had its own trade specialization and its own quarters in the bazaar area, with the exception of the Goans, who worked almost entirely in clerical positions. Hindus and Hanafis formed the main group of government employees, brought over by the overseas recruitment program. A very small number of Indians worked as manual or semiskilled laborers (Bujra 1970, 195). The group closest to the local Arab Muslim population was the Hanafis, who converged in the mid–twentieth century into a communal organization called the Jinnah Volunteer Corps, which later became a more Arab-oriented society with the name "Muslim Association." It was more common among Indian women than Arab women to work outside the home. It was mainly the Hindu, Catholic, Bohora, and Khoja women, among whom no strict purdah was observed, who worked in hospitals, schools, industries, and others' homes. Parsi women enjoyed a freedom of movement outside the home similar to European women's and likewise seldom worked outside the home (*Three Hours in Aden* 1891, 10). Both Parsi and European women were, however, active in various charities that flourished in the town during the late colonial period.[32]

The Adeni Somali population were Shafi'is, like other African people, who visited and lived temporarily in Aden. In earlier history, Somalis were occupied in small-scale trade, peddling goods and cattle between Aden and the Somali coast.

32. I describe women's charity work in Dahlgren 2007b.

They were basically seasonal immigrants who came from the Berbera fair on the Somali coast (Gavin 1975, 52–53). The permanent Somali male community was involved in casual work in the port, whereas Somali women worked in domestic employment and were called *ayahs*. An *ayah* helped with the children and did the washing and other housework. Some *ayahs* lived with the family and had to be available all the time. Few flats and houses had servants' quarters, though. The working hours included mornings, 7:00 A.M. to 2:00 P.M., and evenings. Most of the Somali women employed as *ayahs* were just teenagers, with the minimum legal working age, twelve years old, providing a cheap labor reserve for well-off Adenis and Europeans (*Welcome to Aden* 1963, 108–9). A few Somali women also worked as prostitutes, alongside women from all other groups except the Europeans.[33]

Semiskilled and unskilled laborers, called "coolies," came mainly from the protectorates and Yemen. Labor contractors *(surung)* offered work on a daily basis and on longer assignments in the port, in the saltworks and a few other industries,[34] and on construction sites. Some immigrants were engaged in petty trading, street hawking, or *qat* trading. These men usually brought families with them only after having a permanent position in the labor market and a decent flat for family life. After settling in Aden, the women in these families seldom took jobs outside the house. In their home village, they had been accustomed to heavy work in the fields, tending cattle and carrying water and firewood. The difference in their workload after they moved to town was often notable. Also, their freedom of movement became limited to inside the residential compound and its neighborhoods. These women even had to adopt to different purdah rules (sexual segregation)[35] and observe the city's dress and comportment patterns. After mov-

33. According to lists provided by the Aden police, there were no European prostitutes in Aden. See the following documents from the India Office Records (IOR), British Library, London: R/20/A/1284, Lists of Prostitutes; R/20/A/1285, Venereal Disease; R/20/A/1375, Prostitutes; R/20/A/2212, Prostitutes; R/20/A/2213, Prostitutes; R/20/B/990, Prostitutes; and R/20/B/991, Prostitutes. See also Fayein 1957, 25; Hunter [1877] 1968, 146–47; and Khalifa 1951, 18–20.

34. In the 1930s, the main industries were the saltworks, the *dhow* building, manufacturing, dyeing, and cigarette making (Government of Aden 1939, 128). In the late 1950s, construction works and the Aden Refinery became the biggest labor opportunities.

35. The word *purdah* came from British India, where it was commonly used to describe gender segregation. In Aden, it was pronounced *burda*.

ing to Aden, many protectorate-born women put on the veil for the first time. These women often stopped going out altogether and instead received relatives and neighbors at home. In visiting distant relatives, women became dependent on the men in the family, who organized transportation.

Young boys from the countryside and Yemen often came to Aden for work with elder brothers and relatives and acted as housekeepers and servants in well-off families (Aden Colony 1955a, 10). A few boys were engaged in prostitution, too, providing services to adult men. However, not everybody from the protectorates came to Aden to seek any available work just to survive. Prosperous people from the protectorates, too, were drawn to Aden by the market and its business opportunities. A number of Hadhrami merchants and traders formed the affluent upper strata of the town. There were many notable sayyid families from Hadhramaut,[36] among them the al-'Aydarus family (Bujra 1970, 193–94; Government of Aden 1939, 128, 130; W. Ingrams 1937, 166).

The "ethnic" composition of the Aden police force in 1948 offers an interesting window into colonial labor politics. The force was divided into the Armed Police and Civil Police units. In the Armed Police, out of a total of 270 men, only one man was a "colony-born Arab," as the British called Adenis, and most of the men came from the protectorates (206). Indians were classified into two groups: "Indians" (8) and "local Indians" (11). A considerable number of Somali men worked in the military police (42), but only two Yemenis were qualified. For most of the 1950s, no man born in the colony was allowed to join the Armed Police, and the one who in 1948 succeeded in joining had his contract terminated by the early 1950s. The "ethnic" composition of the Civil Police was quite different. Out of the 353 manned Civil Police force engaged in traffic control and other tasks not involving armed policing, 118 were "colony-born Arabs," and 132 originated from the Aden Protectorate (Aden Colony Police 1948, n.d.).[37] For a locally born young man, it was easier to enter the civil constabulary than the military one.[38]

36. A historical area some six hundred kilometers east of Aden and, after independence, one of the governorates.

37. In 1960, some fifteen Aden-born officers worked in the Armed Police (Aden Colony Police 1961).

38. For a study on colonial police activities in Aden, see Willis 1997.

The Adenization Committee, set up in 1959, was to ensure enhanced access of local people to the civil service and to obtain skills needed to become a civil servant. Women were grouped according to the male guardian's civil position and did not have the right to vote or stand for elections. Because women in general did not enjoy full citizenship rights, no man without access to "Adenese" categorization could obtain it by marrying an Adeni woman. According to the British, the absence of any political rights for women was said to be owing to "local customs," which allegedly made it impossible to introduce any changes.[39]

To make things more complicated, franchise for the Legislative Council elections of 1959 was defined in a different way. The right to vote was limited to people enjoying full residential and political rights: male members of the population who were born in Aden or were British subjects or British-protected subjects provided they had lived in the colony for seven out of the previous ten years. In the end, only 21,500 people, all men, out of a population of 183,000 had the right to vote in the 1959 elections. Turnout in the elections was further minimized by the nationalists' boycott.[40]

Uneven Opportunities

In 1955, one out of every ten women age twenty-one years or older worked outside the home in Aden, and nine out of ten men had paid work. This was the period when the labor market expanded rapidly; the port, a few industries, and construction works provided employment for men, and schools, hospitals, industries, housework for well-off families and cleaning work gave livelihood to women (Aden Colony 1955a, 14). It seems that Aden attracted female labor as well, which came mainly from Somalia, Eritrea, and the protectorates. Among them were also street hawkers. Aden was an attractive market for prostitution, too, if that is considered a work option. Mohsin Khalifa explains that for the Aden Protectorate and Yemeni women, Aden was a foreign country where no relatives were around, so there was no fear or shame before one's own tribe or clan (1951, 19).

39. See chapter 3 about this attitude.

40. Only 27 percent of the eligible electorate took part (Bujra 1970, 200, 203; Halliday 1975, 172–73).

Interest in developing education during the British period shifted from social welfare measures to a need for trained labor for the expanding job market. This education involved preparing clerks for the administration and training craftsmen—both job options for the permanently settled male population with qualifications in English.[41] Because the local qualified male population was far from abundant, and loyal persons were needed to run the administration, the British contracted managerial and middle-level officers from India and other parts of the commonwealth. After primary- and intermediate-level schooling,[42] boys could acquire academic secondary education at Aden College, a prestigious government school built on the mainland, and at the Technical Institute at Maʿalla, where instruction took place in English—both schools established in the early 1950s. The Girls' College in Khormaksar had intermediate and secondary classes, which led to the Cambridge School Certificate Examination. Government schools were restricted to citizens of Aden Colony, whereas the so-called aided and unaided schools, which were run by religious communities, welfare organizations, and private families, were open to all. In 1958, only 231 females attended secondary education, in contrast to 1,083 males together with 65 male teacher trainees (Aden 1961, 43).

Only wealthy families could send their children abroad for further studies. As a consequence, wealth and education divided the local population in their contact with foreign rule and the overseas possibilities it opened. This distinction turned out to be a form of gender division, too, because the few families who

41. According to Saeed Al-Noban, this tendency becomes clear in the Adenization scheme (1984, 108). Gavin, in contrast, argues that the British developed educational possibilities before World War II only as a part of social welfare measures (1974, 324). The need for skilled labor in junior positions started after the economic expansion of the 1950s, when both the commercial circles and the colonial administration started to recruit clerks and skilled men to fill the posts in offices and workshops.

42. During the colonial period, school enrollment included four years of primary school, three years of intermediate school, and four years of secondary school. Primary and intermediate education could be attained in English, Arabic, Urdu, Hebrew, or Gujarati, depending on the community one belonged to, but secondary education in English only (Aden 1961, 41). After independence, unity schools of eight-year enrollment were substituted for the previous primary and intermediate schools, and secondary education remained at four years. Schools were in principle separate for boys and girls in the British era, but there were no restrictions on admitting a boy to a girls' school and vice versa.

could afford schooling for their children tended to favor their sons over their daughters. Even though in the 1950s and 1960s there were already education possibilities for girls, "traditional" values in families prevented many girls from pursuing their education beyond primary school.[43] Even the labor market did not encourage girls to obtain an education because there were few possibilities for women to act in a respectable profession and to work in a place where cross-sex mixing and blending with lower classes could be avoided, both of which were considered harmful for the reputation and marriage prospects of girls from better-off families.

The few women who worked outside the home in the mid–twentieth century were employed in offices, schools, and Aden Radio (D. Ingrams 1970, 148). A small number of women worked in manufacturing, cleaning coffee, incense, gum, and oyster shells. Women who worked as domestic servants were basically of Somali origin, but, as mentioned earlier, domestic work was mainly a job opportunity for young boys from the protectorates and Yemen. A few women worked in the government health service (Aden 1961, 9). Labor statistics from 1958 reveal that 818 women were employed outside the home. The statistics were classified accordingly: port (41), building and construction (0), industrial undertakings (540), retail and wholesale trade (0), government and other services (237), and miscellaneous (0). The entire manpower of the colony consisted of 35,191 persons. It is noteworthy that in the previous year (1957), no women had worked in the port, and 30 women had worked in the retail and wholesale category (Aden 1961, appendix I, 139). However, women's role in the extradomestic labor market was not limited to those few women who had paid work: some women acted as volunteers in various clinics and social welfare institutions and thus contributed to government services.

Sex and Gender in Aden

The presence of a European power for more than a hundred years (1839–1967) and an unbalanced sex ratio among the population evidently had an impact on

43. In September 1958, there were seventy-one students from Aden and the protectorates pursuing higher studies abroad at public expense. Only four of them were women, three medical students and one nursing student in Britain (Aden 1961, 44).

gender relations. Throughout the colonial period, gender disparity was uneven. In the 1955 census, the number of males exceeded that of females by more than 52,000, and out of a total population of 138,230 only 31 percent were women. This figure was only slightly higher than during the three years after the British capture of Aden. The disparity was undoubtedly a result of making Aden a garrison and, in the early years, a coaling station for ocean steamers.[44] As a contrast, in 1839, the year the East India Company arrived and captured Aden, women had formed the majority in a town population numbering a thousand or so (Gavin 1975, 59 and 109ff.).

In the mid-twentieth century, among northern Yemenis the sex ratio was even more unbalanced, with 5,944 men for every 1,000 women. This asymmetry was a result of, on the one hand, the nature of immigration, where women were left behind, and, on the other, a lack of housing. In 1955, 9 percent of the Adeni population were classified as homeless. The number of people living in temporary dwellings erected in the slopes of Ma'alla and Tawahi and in big areas in Shaykh 'Uthman was as high as 12 percent of the population (Aden Colony 1955a, 31; see also Khalifa 1951, 7–9). With regard to geography, the most poignant disparity in the male-female ratio was in Little Aden, the district built in the late 1950s around the oil refinery, where for every 1,000 women there were 6,124 men. In contrast, the most balanced areas were Shaykh 'Uthman and Crater, with only two men for every woman (Aden Colony 1955a, 10). As a result of this disparity, Aden had a huge male population that lived without the care and services normally provided by a family, which resulted in a vast market for teahouse owners and restaurant keepers, errand boys and prostitutes.

These immigrant workers normally could enjoy home life only when they visited their home village approximately every two years. Some workingmen who slept in the streets owned their bed, often a simple date tree mat that they left with a friend or a familiar shopkeeper during the daytime. They kept personal belongings in a small box that was likewise stored with a shop owner from the same village or tribe. Those laborers who did not possess a bed used the open-air "flop-

44. Already in 1842 the male/female ratio was 2,670 men per 1,000 women. Some communities—such as "banyans" (Indian traders), Bohoras, Parsis, and some Europeans and Africans ("Sidis")—did not at that time have any women at all (Kour 1981, 26).

houses," where in the early 1950s one could rent a bed for one anna[45] per night. The municipality provided public baths and latrines in those areas where immigrant workers were concentrated, but a washing place in a mosque also served the same purpose. Because these men had no place to stay outside the working hours, many favored working every day of the week without taking a rest day. They attempted to earn as much money as quickly as possible in order to be able to return home or to marry and establish a family in the town (Khalifa 1951, 8–9).

Women and men had different contact with the modernization that came along with the British. Even though the British were careful not to irritate the local people in matters considered to belong to "custom and religion," the presence of a European power with different lifestyles from the local ones paved the way for alternative models of sex/gender relations. The British influence was seldom direct. British colonial rule was basically military in nature and brought to Aden single servicemen. Wives of service personnel started to arrive in Aden in large numbers only after the 1950s, when the British presence was expanded, and the new oil refinery enlarged British interests. Big housing projects in Maʿalla, Khormaksar, and the mainland districts of Shaykh ʿUthman, al-Mansura, and Little Aden, in particular, involved erecting family housing for the British service personnel.

The British wives lived a secluded life in their own community and seldom encountered local women (D. Ingrams 1970, 125).[46] One such wife, June Knox-Mawer, gives a derisive account of colonial contact:

> Being a good Colonial wife of course entailed the duty of being-nice-to-the-locals. It was the white woman's share of the burden. But it need not involve anything more strenuous than an inter-racial cocktail party once a year, an occasional lunch to which one invited one or two of the jollier Arab notables and a squire's-wife type of appearance at the odd tea party which after all often provided hilarious material for bridge-table anecdotes the following morning. ("—and the food, my dear, you couldn't tell the flies from the currants!"). For

45. The currency was until 1951 the Indian rupee.

46. June Knox-Mawer (1961), journalist and wife of the British chief justice of Aden in the late 1950s, recalls that only exceptional women among the British community "mixed" with local women.

> many of the commercial and service wives life was even more restricted—an Arab was simply that irritating creature in the kitchen who always forgot to put the salt in with the potatoes or someone who took two whole days to mend a simple leak in the bathroom drainpipe. (1961, 108)

The arrogant attitude toward the local people was known locally as *kibr inglizi,* "the English pride." Another author of a colonial times memoir, Doreen Ingrams, who, like Knox-Mawer, did "mix" with the local people, confirms this attitude: "It always seemed strange to me that so many British women could live for years in Aden without even speaking to an Arab other than their servants or the shopkeepers. They had no interest in 'natives,' did not attempt to speak a word of Arabic, and were astonished if a compatriot did not conform to their way of life—bridge, tea parties, the exclusive British Club" (1970, 125).

Europeans tended to minimize contact with local people and maintained separate and isolated social networks for whites only. Indians had their own exclusive clubs where they could socialize in the colonial manner. As long as the local men had positions in the town's business and administration, they had the chance to learn the colonizers' systems of management and to be in touch with their way of life. Such men also had the opportunity to learn English, the official language of the colony until 1959 and the only way to make direct contact with the Europeans. Because local women lacked these opportunities and had fewer chances to go to school, fewer direct links were formed between the local women and Europeans than between Europeans and local men. Europeans tended to have no interest in learning Arabic because Aden was not seen as a permanent station post, but instead as a crossroads where different interests sometimes met.[47]

Two groups among the Europeans were an exception to this inconsiderate attitude. The first group was the Christian missionaries, who were eager to visit

47. Tom Hickinbotham, governor of Aden from 1951 to 1956, describes this temporality well: "The European community on the whole look upon Aden as a place of exile from their own land, a place of temporary abode in which to earn a living and leave for a better land as soon as possible. They are not interested in the local people as human beings, but only as potential or actual customers for their merchandise, or as passengers in their ships, or as servants in their houses. They only mix with them socially when it is unavoidable" (1958, 201).

local homes if allowed to enter. Older local women still remember European ladies who were not particularly welcomed in any home. Watching the missionaries' activities in the locals' compounds through the window opening of their adjacent homes was long-term entertainment for them during their childhood, as one woman recalled to me. Another exception was the women's societies, where European women cooperated with local elite ladies in welfare and charity work. These societies also enlightened local women on the tenets of modern housekeeping and gave instruction on child care, running the household, and all in all how to promote the modern values of health and hygiene in the local home.[48]

After the nationalist struggle started in Aden in the late 1950s, some of the local ladies active in these women's societies challenged the Europeans' hegemony in leadership and made the societies into independence platforms.[49] In promoting modernity in homes, the women's associations had on their side intellectual and commercial elite men, who promoted good housekeeping, domestic technologies, and consumer culture in the local newspapers. These papers had special pages devoted to women, where "superior Western" lifestyles were contrasted to "Eastern" ones.[50]

If the memoir literature of colonial times gives the impression of very little contact between European and local women, the local elder women I have talked to have confirmed this position. Instead of direct contact between the colonizers and the uneducated colonized, there was the local elite, who had an instrumental role in promoting European gender and family ideals. Some elite women even acted as trailblazers in giving up the purdah.[51]

48. The names of the voluntary services that attracted women of "all races" are telling: Ladies Child Welfare Committee, King Edward VII Charitable Dispensary, Aden Central Poor Relief Committee, Aden Women's Voluntary Service, Sheikh Othman Children's Milk Scheme, and Hospital Visiting Committee, among others (Khalifa 1951, appendix; Aden 1961, 52).

49. In particular, the Aden Women's Club, later renamed the Arab Women's Club, under the leadership of Radhia Ihsanullah and others, (see IOR R/20/B/2813, Arab Women's Club; J. Knox-Mawer 1961, 121; and the interview of Ihsanullah after her return from a long exile in the newspaper *14 Uktubr*, Apr. 20, 22, and 26, 1992).

50. More on these issues in chapter 4.

51. Doreen Ingrams mentions among such women those with "Persian origin" and in particular the Hassanali and Jaffer families (1970, 126).

5. Men's open-air hotel in Crater. Owing to labor migration from outside Aden and shortage of housing, this guesthouse was still in place in the late 1980s. Photograph by the author, 1989.

In His Majesty's Service

Typical for a port town and a foreign military base, prostitution became a widespread phenomenon in Aden during the British period. The unbalanced gender ratio also contributed to the demand for prostitutes. On the offering side, scarce labor possibilities and poverty made prostitution an option for women who did not have anyone to support them or their children, if they had any. These women were often divorcées whose natal families had rejected them. For administration purposes, the British divided prostitutes into "public women" and "private women." The former were women who carried out their profession either in a public house or in the open air. Private prostitutes were more difficult to control because they practiced their vice either in the confines of a home, in a car, or in other private places on the basis of a personal network—that is, without a procuress or a pimp. When reading the colonial files on prostitution, I got the impression that some of the "private women" were simply women with a lover.

The British records—carefully organized according to district and marking the name, age, and "ethnic" origin of the workingwoman—excluded, however, young boys with adult men as clients.

According to police reports from the first part of the twentieth century, each district of the town had its own prostitutes, recorded by the local police inspector four times a year.[52] All these women came from native and immigrant communities. Licensed prostitution was legal until 1945,[53] and Shaykh ʿUthman and Maʿalla in particular had streets lined with several public brothels. Even after 1945, suppressing prostitution was not on the agenda of the colonial power, and the authorities tended to become involved only if the matter threatened public order. Such interference happened, for instance, when venereal diseases started to spread among the British troops or when prostitutes were smuggled inside a military area. A public petition would sometime force measures against prostitution. In 1940, the director of a brothel in Maʿalla sent a petition to the commander of the Royal Air Force (RAF). She complained that her house had been excluded from those public brothels that, according to her, the RAF paid the rent of and had reserved for its soldiers "for the purpose of sexual intercourse." In her petition, she described how women in her brothel had always served His Majesty.[54] The usual method of curbing prostitution that disturbed public order was deportation.

52. IOR R/20/A/1284, Lists of Prostitutes; R/20/A/1285, Venereal Disease; R/20/A/1375, Prostitutes; R/20/A/2212, Prostitutes; R/20/A/2213, Prostitutes; R/20/B/990, Prostitutes; R/20/B/991, Prostitutes—all covering the years from 1900 to 1941. The police issued licenses even to beggars (see Khalifa 1951, 14–15).

53. The Morality Offences Ordinance (also called the Suppression of Brothels Ordinance) was enacted on January 18, 1945. The same year another ordinance that had to do with prostitution came to force, too, the Venereal Disease Ordinance. See *Laws of Aden* 1955, 2:chap. 99 and 3:chap. 162. Even a third ordinance from the same year was instituted in connection to prostitution, the Vagrants and Undesirables Ordinance, which allowed the deportation of homeless people, beggars, and young boys who were engaged in prostitution.

54. IOR R/20/B/991, letter dated September 9, 1940, by Fatima bint Ali Bosti on behalf of eighteen Arab, Somali, and other prostitutes to the Senior Medical Officer, RAF Hospital, Steamer Point and Officer Commanding Royal Air Forces, Headquarters in Aden. The addressees investigated the matter, and it was found that the RAF did not keep up or pay the rent of a brothel.

Marriage in Colonial Aden

It seems that immigration generally did not change marriage patterns among those who had roots in Aden or among those who had moved there for employment. But intergroup marriages did take place, such as between an Indian Muslim man and an Adeni-born Arab woman. A few British women married Adeni men and converted to Islam. In the mid–twentieth century, marriages between Adeni Muslim men and Adeni Jewish women were not uncommon. In the Somali community, marriages also took place between immigrating men and Arab women. Male migrants from the Kingdom of Yemen sometimes took a local *akhdam* woman as a wife.

Traditional patterns of marriage familiar in the surrounding countryside and in the Kingdom of Yemen survived even longer stays in the city, which attracted labor but did not provide a means for family life. Marriages were contracted among the kin, tribe, or village.[55] Arranging a marriage involved family cooperation and required that the groom-to-be traveled home to discuss the matter. This happened only after he had been successful enough to obtain means in Aden to provide for a family and, most important, gathered the wealth for what was usually a very high dower *(mahr)*.[56] The custom of organizing a *makhdara*

55. Although the customs vary locally, the overall principle in contracting a marriage is through negotiations between two families (whether related on kinship, tribal, or residential terms) where matters of marital residence, bridal (and possible other) payments, purchases, and wedding expenses are settled. On contracting a marriage in some locations outside Aden, see Bujra 1971, 47 and 93–97; Chelhod et al. 1985, 63–97; Meneley 1996, 76–78; Mundy 1995, 126–38; and Naumkin 1993, 239–44. On incidences of provocation against the conventional marriage arrangements, see Bujra 1967, 361.

56. It seems evident that the economic upswing and increased possibilities for immigration contributed to an increase in the *mahr* sums demanded. In marriage records for the Sira District (comprising Crater, Khormaksar, and Shaykh 'Uthman), usual sums paid in 1951 ranged from five to eight hundred rupees. A *thayyiba* (a woman who was no longer a virgin) expected lower amounts than a *bikr* (virgin) (see Dahlgren 2005). In a 1951 social welfare report, Khalifa writes of a working family originally from the Aden Protectorate whose son, when marrying in the late 1940s, paid three hundred rupees as *mahr* although he had only a sixty-five-rupee monthly salary (1951, 4–6). June Knox-Mawer mentions three thousand East African shillings as the usual amount

for the groom, a party where men were invited to chew *qat* and contribute to the wedding expenses, eased the financial burden of the groom and his family to meet the high demands for the *mahr* and an expensive wedding party.

The criteria for selecting the group among whom a spouse could be found varied from place to place and among social categories. For those who could afford to choose and had the moral capital that allowed choice, the three most important qualifications were social compatibility *(kafa'a)*,[57] descent *(nasab)*, and promising political or business alliances. For lower social categories, anyone from the same village would suffice.

A professional "bride searcher" *(khatiba)* was sometimes contracted to find suitable candidates. Her work took time as she went from house to house in a village or a residential area in Aden inspecting bride candidates and reporting her findings in detail so that the man could make initial contact with the girl's family. That the prospective groom's and bride's fathers belonged to the same occupational category served as an indicator of how big of a dower could be negotiated from the suitor. No legitimate marriage was possible unless the two parties agreed on the terms.

Marriages were initiated among clusters of men from the same village or tribe working and residing together in Aden. Residential areas where families from the protectorates were concentrated were another place to look for a bride for an immigrant man. One such area was the Armed Police Lines, a residential area erected by the British for the protectorate-born recruits of the colonial army.[58] In the old times, the three main personal criteria for a bride

---

paid in the late 1950s among the middle-income groups (1961, 96). The currency was changed from the Indian rupee to the East African shilling in October 1951. In 1953, the rate was approximately one hundred shillings to sixty-six rupees. See *Colonial Reports Aden 1953 & 1954* 1956, 20–21, and Reilly 1960, 8.

57. *Kafa'a* refers to the "equality" principle, among other things, in choosing a spouse. There are many interpretations of *kafa'a* in marriage, but in general the rule means that a man may marry one social category lower than his, but a woman may never do so. Among the *sada* (sing. *sayyid*, descendants of the Prophet's family), women could marry only among their own group. *Kafa'a* predates Islam, which incorporated it. See Serjeant 1981, 227n1, on the origin of *kafa'a*, and Bujra 1971, 94, on one interpretation of it in a Hadhrami town.

58. Just as with the police force, army units were recruited from the protectorates, and local-born people were not admitted.

(once her social background was accepted) were beauty, the right background (*nisba,* "kinship"), and a good temper—as a man who migrated to Aden in the early 1950s from the Aden Protectorate explained to me. When the *qadi* (judge) performed the marriage contract ceremony, it was his duty to ensure that the requirements were met.

Marriages contracted between people from the countryside had to consider matters of descent; this was not always the case among Aden-born people. Because the roots and origin of Aden-born Muslims varied, ranging from Iranian to Egyptian to Indian to Somali and other African-born ancestors, the small communities tended to regulate marriages inside the group if the family possessed large properties or had specialized skills in the town's division of labor. In this way, matters of financial or symbolic capital and inheritance were controlled. Among the lower social categories, however, such concerns were not an issue, and marriage expenses and social propriety directed the choice in marriage. Wealthier people also socialized in a group's own communal association or club, a place where adult men gathered to exchange news on home-community affairs.

My field survey indicates what social compatibility meant for people who contracted marriage during colonial times. A slight difference emerged between people who were born outside the colony and those who were born in Aden. Among colony-born people, a man tended to marry from an equal or one-step-lower social category. In a marriage contracted in 1966, a guard gave his daughter to a driver, an occupation that had slightly better pay and higher social respect. Similarly, in a wedding that took place in 1967, a messenger (someone who prepares and serves the tea in a government office) was able to marry off his daughter to a car mechanic. In 1955, a marriage was negotiated by a seaman and a man who had a steady white-collar position in the Aden municipality. In 1962, a customs' inspector received a municipal sanitary inspector as his son-in-law.

Among protectorate-, African-, and northern Yemeni–born families in my field survey, there are cases where the father gave his daughter to a man who did not have as high a social position as himself. A white-collar government employee gave his daughter to a driver in a marriage that took place in 1958. Both families came from the town of Mudia, in the Western Aden Protectorate. Similarly, a shopkeeper *(mudakkan)* who had come to Aden from Sana'a, accepted a lorry driver as his son-in-law in 1962. However, socially equivocal marriages were contracted among this group, too. Another shopkeeper from the Kingdom of Yemen married off his daughter in 1964 to a man involved in "free trade"—that is, a private entrepreneur. A businessman from Asmara on his part negotiated a marriage to his daughter with a man who worked as a petty clerk.

According to my field survey, during the time prior to independence Aden-born people tended to honor the principle of social compatibility in the choice of marriage, whereas people originating from the protectorates, the Kingdom of Yemen, and countries outside South Arabia considered belonging to the same lineage, residential unit, tribal confederation, or ethnic group more important. But it is not possible to draw any definite conclusions on the basis of these limited data.[59]

The End of Bangala Shaytan

At the time of independence in the late 1960s,[60] the social composition of Aden changed dramatically.[61] Withdrawal of the colonial administration and the military base resulted in the expulsion not only of the British administrative and military personnel, but of large numbers of businesspeople who had been drawn to Aden by opportunities provided by the foreign rule and its access to the world market. The economy was in ruins, suffering from the evacuation of the foreign base and all the economic activities it attracted and from the exodus of foreign companies. A big blow to the town's economy came with the Suez crisis in 1967 as the number of ships arriving to Aden port dropped from 6,246 in 1966 to 1,568 in 1969 (Ismael and Ismael 1986, 104). An imminent crisis in the new nation's economy came after Britain suddenly withdrew both its direct and its indirect

59. This part of the field data consists of 311 families, collected in 1988–89 and 1991 around the town on a random basis.

60. In November 1967, the People's Republic of South Yemen was established, comprising the two earlier protectorates, with Aden as the capital. In 1970, the name of the country was changed to the People's Democratic Republic of Yemen.

61. The Bangala Shaytan referred to in the section subhead was the Masonic Hall of the Lodge Felix (Arabia Felix), established in 1850. Its members included not only European Christians, but also local and Indian Muslims, Zoroastrians, and Jews. Children feared this secret building that was situated at the start of Madram Road in Ma'alla. See Tahir 2001.

support of the local economy, which it had promised to continue after independence.[62] With the British left groups that had cooperated with colonial rule, such as the rest of the Jews, European businessmen, and a large part of the Indian community that had occupied junior posts in administration, education, and health care. As the labor market collapsed, labor migrants from the surrounding countryside and North Yemen returned to their villages, fixing their gaze on the booming oil economies in other areas of the peninsula. The departure of the administrative personnel and of the manual and skilled laborers created a lack of some eighty thousand qualified people in a period that was crucial to the establishment of the national economy (Ismael and Ismael 1986, 80). This lack resulted in a call for women to join the labor market.

The social hierarchy of the town was also shaken. Some of the new rulers belonged to the lower social strata, which previously had not been allowed entry into the administration. The new government directed measures against hierarchies of all types, be they based on descent, religion, country of origin, or sex. Most of the elite *sada* families left Aden after the government's politics were radicalized following the Corrective Move of June 22, 1969,[63] and after the nationalization of banking, insurance companies and some other businesses took place. Members of the former upper strata felt threatened as their traditional respected role in society was questioned[64] and some were persecuted.

62. The British naval installations in Aden accounted for as much as one-quarter of local gross national product, and the closing down of the base caused the loss of some fourteen thousand to twenty-five thousand jobs. See Ismael and Ismael 1986, 79–80.

63. The June 22, 1969, Corrective Move was the radicalization of the NLF and its allies' policies after the NLF's left wing took power from the moderate forces. This radicalization also brought "women's emancipation" *(tahrir al-mar'a)* onto the national agenda. On these events, see Halliday 1975, 237–44, 249–253; Lackner 1985, 60–69; and Wenner 1984, 130–31.

64. The *sada* were originally immigrants who came to South Arabia in the second and third century A.H. from Iraq. There have been conflicts between local groups and the *sada* throughout history. In Hadhramaut, the conflict between Alawis (descendants of the Prophet Muhammad through his daughter Fatima, who came to Hadhramaut in A.D. 952) and Irshadis (members of Jam'iyyat al-Irshad, the Reform and Guidance Association, established in 1914 in Indonesia) is one of the longest conflicts. See Bujra 1967, 355–73.

With the advent of independence, many communal groups left Aden, and the communal variety diminished.[65] Religious establishments were left to decline. By the end of the 1980s, not a single Jewish synagogue was open, and the number of Hindu temples was reduced to two. The few Europeans and Asian immigrant workers made arrangements so that some of the churches had at least a weekly church service. The two Shi'a mosques continued their activities. A few Pakistani and Parsi traders still occupied particular trading niches and streets in the main bazaar. Indians ceased to form a community in the old sense, and new residents with varying origins moved into the streets formerly occupied by Jews.

The new rule's housing policy disfavored residential areas with particular social classes or "ethnic" communities, except for some areas restricted to new rulers, which were distinguished by tighter security. In sharp contrast to the colonial force and its divide-and-rule politics, the new administration promoted nationalism with the aim of one united Yemen (see al-Saqqaf 1999, 152–53). An expression of the new rule's radicalism was the giving of equal possibilities to everybody irrespective of origin, "ethnic" or racial belonging, religion, or sex. The new system of social recognition was proclaimed to rest on competence in work and participation in building up the new nation.

In the same way that public holidays celebrated during the British era reflected the nature of its politics of religious and "ethnic" diversity, public holidays enacted after independence marked the symbols hailed by the new regime. Holidays such as Muharram 1 (Hijra New Year), Rabi'a Awwal 12 (Prophet Muhammad's birthday), Rajab 27 (Leilat al-Mi'raj, the anniversary of the Prophet's ascension), *'id al-fitr* (Shawwal 1–2), and *'id al-adha* (Dhul Hijja 9–11) symbolize the Islamic nature of the nation, whereas New Year's Day, May Day, and Women's Day (March 8) indicate adherence to a "modern" nation-state with "secular" inclinations.[66] Special holidays for the trade union and the women's movement reflected the new govern-

65. Nevertheless, many people had roots in other countries. In a booklet published around 1973, a table listed Adeni citizens as having been born in nineteen countries outside the PDRY, listed from most to least: North Yemen, India, Somalia, Ethiopia, Tanzania, Pakistan, Kenya, Indonesia, Egypt, Sudan, Saudi Arabia, Burma, Soviet Union, Kuwait, Bulgaria, Bangladesh, Palestine, Lebanon, and Nigeria (UNICEF and Ministry of Local Government 1973, 359, table 238).

66. In *Aspects of Economic & Social Development in Democratic Yemen,* Women's Day is not marked as a public holiday (1981, 8–10), but in actual terms March 8 was a public holiday until Yemeni

ment's political priorities. The third category of holidays symbolized the nationalist scheme: June 22 (the day of the Corrective Move, the political radicalization that took place in 1969), National Independence Day (November 30), and October 14 and September 26, the revolution days of the South and the North. Celebrating North Yemen's 1962 revolution symbolized the unity of the two parts of Yemen. The new regime created symbols linked to Islamic, national, and "modern" discourses in its building up of a new nation and eradicated "priestly, feudal, bourgeoisie and colonial ideologies," as the documents of the first General Congress of the Women's Union put it (General Union of Yemeni Women 1977, 10).[67]

In dramatic contrast to the colonial times, most of those who earlier had a high position in society by wealth or social rank were forced either to conform to the new rules of social recognition or to leave the country. But building up a nation-state cannot be described simply as a break with the former colonial rule. First, the British had already attempted to unite Aden with the two protectorates and to form a federation with a central rule, but with no success. Second, the modernizing project that the new rulers carried out after independence was to a large extent a continuation of the one the British had started. However, modernization was given a new content and color. Schoolchildren continued to wear school uniforms as earlier, but the color of the costume was altered. After independence, the red British post pillars continued to stand in street corners but were now repainted yellow. The English administrative system was maintained. The British had relied on the principle of not touching "custom and religion," which they considered stagnant but outside the scope of colonial administration. This policy echoed the one practiced in British India.

Drawing a contrast to the earlier hegemonic Islamic discourses as personified in two prominent Islamic scholars, Shaykh 'Ali Muhammad Bahamish and Shaykh Muhammad bin Salim Bayhani,[68] the new regime declared a break with

---

unification, when its official celebration was terminated. Here spelling of these holiday names is again as given in the Public Holidays Ordinance.

67. In political rhetoric, the social and economic system that prevailed during colonial times in the countryside areas of Lahig and Abyan outside Aden is called "feudal" *(iqta')*. See also Ghanem 1981, 10.

68. Bahamish was a longtime *qadi* of Aden and famous for his tolerance of various forms of religious practice and women's concerns, whereas Bayhani was a scholar and mosque imam with Wahhabi inclinations. I discuss these two prominent personalities further in chapter 4.

"priestly ideology" and promoted new, "progressive" interpretations of Islam in conformity with the aims of the revolution. Nevertheless, quite contrary to this aim, the dropping of certain Islamic holidays from the calendar of public holidays must have pleased the most orthodox circles of the town. These holidays included not only days celebrated by the different Shiʿa communities, but also Aidarus Day, considered by the intolerants as "Sufi" or "un-Islamic." An annual *ziara* for ʿAydarus (visitation to the saint's tomb) continued after independence but no longer as a day off from work.

Independence and the subsequent economic crash brought changes to the town's sex ratio. After the departure of immigrant laborers, by 1973 the male-female divide was almost balanced, with 1,260 men to every 1,000 women. By 1988, the gender disproportion had pretty much been eliminated, with 1,020 men to every 1,000 women.[69] This balance naturally improved bachelors' marriage possibilities.

No Rich, No Starving, No Americans

Aden of the 1980s was a peculiar society with neither extremely wealthy nor devastatingly needy people. The absence of these two extremes created an unrealistic but comfortable atmosphere. Rich merchants and high-estate families now carried out their businesses and other activities in more favorable surroundings in North Yemen, Saudi Arabia, or England. Poverty and the scarcity of resources were part of the daily life in Aden, but rather than pushing anybody to the brink of survival, they were shared by a large number of people. When I asked people about their family's social standing, most replied "middle class" *(mutawassit)*. This big "middle class" turned out to be a very flexible concept, indeed, comprising families where the main supporter was anything from the head of a governmental office to a factory worker. The homes of these "middle-class" people ranged from former colonial villas in Khormaksar and Tawahi to makeshift huts erected from whatever wood or corrugated metal plates could be found in the shanty towns al-Qahira or al-Hashish.[70]

69. See *Aspects of Economic & Social Development in Democratic Yemen* 1981, 40, for the 1973 figure and PDRY 1990, 56, for 1988.

70. Al-Qahira, "Cairo," is a small residential area next to Shaykh ʿUthman on the mainland. Al-Hashish is the area behind the Crater vegetable market where a civil hospital was earlier located.

The idea that everybody should be given a chance "to improve himself or herself" gained momentum and gave possibilities in particular to women and members of the lower strata of society (see also al-Saqqaf 1999, 153). This happy "middle-class" town was to survive only until autumn 1991, when Saudi Arabia deported Yemeni business owners (and workers) and sent them, among other places, back to Aden as a result of the Yemeni president's siding with Saddam Husayn in the 1991 Gulf War. Despair spread in the streets when beggars and other homeless people started to pour into Aden from the northern towns during the same period.

How did independence affect Aden? Owing to the political change, the town's social composition became more unitary. As Ziad Mahmoud Abu-Amr claims in regard to all of the PDRY, the transformation of society was well under way when the leftist National Liberation Front (NLF) took power following the expulsion of the British. Among other factors, a well-organized trade union movement, a variety of newspapers, political militancy as reflected in the independence struggle, intellectual activities in societies and clubs, women's organizations, and Arab nationalist calls from other parts of the Middle East paved the way for changes. According to Abu-Amr, the British presence had raised social and economic expectations. Although the empire had no intention of meeting these expectations, the British left behind a functioning infrastructure run earlier mainly by British and Indian hands, which included the oil refinery, bunkering facilities, a road network, the airport and seaport, the administrative system, and housing establishments—all of which facilitated later transformations (1986, 169–70).

Characteristic to Aden as a former colony, even years after the British left, the infrastructure and everyday systems of management resembled the way things were run on a daily basis in Britain. In those parts of Aden where little construction took place after the British left—Crater, Maʿalla, and Tawahi—the town scene in the late 1980s still spoke the language of the early 1960s, with the same old advertising signs, shops, restaurants, and cars, some not functional and others just rusted with time. For those Adenis who left after independence, this stagnated town view meant that no development took place during the years of socialist rule. But the changes in the socialist period were not manifested in road building or construction of fancy villas, as in North Yemen. Instead, in Aden development meant educational, political, health care, and job opportunities for women and previously disfavored social groups.

The New Society

In 1988, when I arrived in Aden with the intention to carry out anthropological fieldwork, I faced the problem of a scarcity of studies on Adeni society from the 1970s to the present day.[71] This scarcity led me to carry out a small survey on what kind of people lived there during the years of the socialist rule. This survey should in no way be taken as a comprehensive social survey on Aden. The number of families involved was only 311, and even though I collected the data in various parts of the town on a random basis, the survey can be taken only as background material to the ethnography I present here. Because information was collected on the basis of the household, and because most of those interviewed for this purpose were female household members,[72] the survey is biased toward women. A proper sample of the town's social structure would naturally require a bigger sampling and adequate statistical methods.[73] Therefore, the statistics I present here should be considered relevant only from the point of view of providing implications regarding the field material I have collected. A comparison to

71. Books that deal with the PDRY, mostly in English, German, and Russian, have little if no information on Aden. Arabic-language books deal mainly with the (political or military) history of Aden, but not with the current society.

72. The mere fact that women know about the household business better than men motivated me to talk to them instead of to men for the purposes of the survey. My own observations confirmed what Hilma Granqvist (1931) argued concerning her study of the Palestinian village of Artas. Men's role is more balanced in other parts of my field material, in particular in open interviews and discussions.

73. I collected information for this small survey while doing interviews and observing male-female interaction mainly in various workplaces. This approach resulted in a bias toward working-women. Furthermore, because it was my interest to meet people in various life situations and in as many different work positions as possible, I did not collect my data with the idea of presenting the most typical and statistically "average" people. As a consequence, the data include the rare woman in a profession such as judge, television announcer, and artist alongside women in the typical housewife or factory positions. A sample that has been collected from a woman's point of view is a quite unorthodox representation of the household, which locally is always viewed from the male head of household's point of view, provided there is a man to head the household. This male point of view is reflected in what households are called: Bayt Ahmad Salim (Ahmad Salim's house), Manzil al-'Aydarus (al-'Aydarus family dwelling), and so on.

the available official statistics would point out the possible exceptional character of the data.

The women involved in my survey ranged from fifteen to fifty-seven years of age, and men ranged from eighteen to seventy-five. The largest number of women belonged to the age group twenty-five to forty, whereas most of the men were between thirty and forty-five years of age. The rule that the husband should ideally be a couple of years older than the wife is clearly evident in the sample (see the tables in appendix A). Because the existence of social hierarchies during the PDRY era did not fit in with the official slogan "equal opportunities to all," there are no official statistics on the town's social composition in this period.[74] However, according to my understanding, a new hierarchy surfaced during the PDRY era based on social recognition and respect *(karama)*, gained by participating in building up the society instead of by depending on earlier roots *(asl)*, religious piety, or wealth. Now a person's descent was said not to set any limit to his or her advancing in society, a modern element distinct from the old social markers. In contrast to the past, a woman could gain a social position and reputation separate from her male guardian on the merit of her personal professional career or political activity.[75]

As a consequence of the possibilities given to women, some of them reached higher positions in working life than their husbands. When I asked these women if they had any difficulties at home or if they faced a lack of cooperation while acting in a senior position in their working life, most replied that there were no problems. According to them, men respected women at work. The only occupational

74. Neither were the British too keen to publish such statistics. Colonial-era statistics categorized people according to "ethnic" or religious background, age, gender, and place of birth, whereas during the PDRY era the relevant categories included education and employment as well as gender and age.

75. One of the most well-known cases of a woman paving her own way is that of Aida Sa'id. During the 1980s, she was chairperson of the Women's Union and a leading politician, and her husband was a highly placed Socialist Party official. The couple fell into political disagreement and separated following the events of January 1986, when an internal struggle in the party leadership led to a bloody two weeks of fighting and left the town devastated and the people disillusioned for years to come. Aida's choice to divorce her husband rather than to change her political position raised feelings of admiration. Her decision was seen as a sign of integrity of character. In another political situation, her choice to "leave her family" would have easily been condemned. *Aden's Bloody Monday* (1986), a booklet issued afterward by the party, is a dramatic account of the events of that devastating January in 1986.

field where most women in senior positions had experienced problems in daily interaction with male subjects was engineering. In particular, female civil engineers complained of men's lack of respect. The female engineers that I met on a big construction site voiced their concern that men should "learn new attitudes." Even though some women occupied high positions in the PDRY government, not a single woman ever became a cabinet or Socialist Party politburo member.[76] Many women and men I met thought that there should be more women in the country's leadership, on the one hand to give women a positive role model and on the other to change the view of those men and women who still believed in women's mental deficiency.

As I mentioned earlier, after independence the new government propagated social reckoning on the basis of merit in building up the society. This new system in part replaced the old hierarchy based on descent and in part substituted it by allowing members of the old elite positions in the new system. These elite individuals after all had educational skills and experience from the old administration. Position in the labor market and professional or political career were not the only means to achieve high esteem socially. The authorities did try to introduce new values, but it was not easy to curb the old value basis in which a person, man or woman, was evaluated in his or her surroundings as a "total personality" and his or her morality and virtue were monitored. In this study, I refer to such an embodied state with the concept *adab,* as I explained in the introduction. An ability to cultivate social assets allocated to each and everyone in different shares contributes to this system of reckoning. In contrast to the old social hierarchy, the new one stressed individual achievement at the expense of the reputation of the collective family and their honorific paternal roots. As I pointed out earlier, some of the *sada* (sayyids, those who claim their descent from the Prophet Muhammad) left Aden during the years of the PDRY, but the other traditional elite group, the *mashayikh,*[77] in part maintained their positions and became engaged with the new principles of rank and prestige.

76. The highest position a woman ever held in the PDRY was deputy minister of culture and information, and that was during the 1980s.

77. Descendants of Qahtan, the mythical forefather of South Arabians, and residents in the area older than the *sada,* who came after Islam was introduced in the southern part of the peninsula. Islamic scholars and jurists traditionally came from this elite category. See Serjeant 1980.

Even though many people who earlier belonged to groups lower in the hierarchy could now improve their position, it is hardly surprising that those who already had an education and social capacities could more easily benefit from the new government's reforms, attaining a professional career, accessing higher education, and gaining positions in the administration and politics. However, some *mashayikh* families became impoverished and lost their earlier higher status. One such family I met had its roots in a small town in Abyan, northeast of Aden. While living in the village, the patron of the family was a *qadi*, charged with questions of justice and religious endowments *(qadhi fil-'adal wal-'auqaf)*. His income was not enough to support the family. His wife, illiterate and without any previous work experience, had to take a job in the local school as a cook. In the early 1960s, the daughter of the family married a local man who worked in Aden as a driver in the British Petroleum (BP) Company. His income was not very high, but the family with six children could survive until he died in 1982, when the wife had to take a job. Like her mother, she had no qualifications, nor could she read and write. At that time, anyone who wanted to take factory work had to have a basic education,[78] a measure taken to increase literacy among the adult population. Because this woman did not qualify for factory work, she could only take a job as a messenger in a college. Her tasks included preparing and serving tea for those who worked in her section and running small errands inside the workplace. The family's work history links to service work, which traditionally is considered degrading to upper-strata people.

Residential patterns and family type seem to have had an impact on social position genderwise, in particular during the PDRY era, when a woman's social reputation was no longer necessarily determined by her male guardian's position and when many women became the main breadwinners in the family. The patrilocal residential rule, which is often presented as the ideal rule, comes from the representation of the family as a male lineage where male roots and lines are counted at the expense of female roots and lines. However, when talking with young men who were recently or soon to be married, I found that patrilocal residence was not the preference. Instead, many wanted to become the head of an independent

78. Basic education meant that the person could read and write. Attending a Qur'an school was not considered proof of literacy. In the late 1980s, this qualification was dropped, and anyone could qualify for factory work.

household and step out of their fathers' shadow. Becoming the head of the household was possible either by obtaining a separate flat from the paternal family, which was difficult considering the shortage of housing in Aden, or by moving into the wife's household if its senior male had already died. As a consequence, it is no surprise that the most popular residential pattern in my field survey was uxorilocal, where the newly wed couple moved to the bride's parental home to live with her old mother. From the young women's point of view, too, this was preferable because she could then remain with her natal family. But the most popular choice among young people, men and women alike, was to move into a neolocal residence separate from parental households. Both of these patterns, the most favored one and the most common one, are to this day affected by the chronic shortage of housing, which has deteriorated the more Aden's population has increased over the years.

Neolocal residence is not the best option from the point of view of child care and shared household chores. For a working couple with children, living with an (elder) female family member provides needed assistance in both running the household and taking care of the children during working hours. In my survey, one-third of the families consisted of nuclear families with children.[79] Regarding whether any help was received in performing the household chores, 79 percent of women in extended families did get help, whereas only half of those in nuclear families were assisted. In light of this information, it is interesting that young women still prefer neolocal residence. Many young women anticipated bad relations with the mother-in-law. A recent trend among young women, irrespective of educational level, to quit their job and stay at home after giving birth to the first child contributed to the preference for independent housing. Many highly educated young women I met who were approaching their thirties and desperate to get married were vocal in announcing their willingness to stay at home if the husband so preferred. In most cases, a workingwoman received help at home from her mother or from her eldest daughter once she was old enough. In rare cases, the husband participated in household chores. According to my data, these cases involved mostly factory workingwomen whose husband, too, worked odd hours.

In cases where the new couple moved in with the woman's mother, not only young women could expect trouble from the senior woman of the house. A

79. The number of married women in the data is 211.

fifty-two-year-old woman complained about her own widowed mother, who even in her senior years continued to make trouble for the daughter's husband. The woman jokingly hoped that her mother would pass away so that she could finally have harmony at home.

Because houses in Aden as a rule are small in size, an average of approximately 1.2 families (pl. *usar*, sing. *usra*) lived in a dwelling (pl. *masakin*, sing. *maskin*) at the time of my survey. The average number of people living in a dwelling was 7.1, slightly higher than what the official statistics state (6.8) (PDRY 1990, 62). The usual way to accommodate a newly wedded couple in an extended household was to erect an extra room on the roof. However, because most of the houses in Aden were built either during the colonial period for the needs of the colonial service personnel or after independence as a part of foreign aid and according to foreign architectural thinking, many Adenis lived in blocks of flats where no extra space could be reclaimed. As a consequence, some married couples lived separately, as if the marriage had never taken place. One woman I met, with a good position in a government office, told me desperately that after two years of marriage, she and her engineer husband had still not yet found a place to live together. Both remained living in their natal homes.

The housing shortage not only created difficult conditions for newly wedded couples but obliged some families to live in spaces that were originally not meant for residential use. In Crater, I visited a home that was made by reclaiming the space under the stairs. An old woman's home was so small that her sofa/bed occupied most of the space of the single room plus kitchenette. In Khormaksar, near the block of flats where I lived, I visited huts erected on the side of a house, its wall serving as the support for the scavenged building materials piled up as makeshift walls and shanties attached to an electric transformer cabin. Large areas in Crater, Ma'alla, and Tawahi and in the mainland in Shaykh 'Uthman, al-Mansura, and areas surrounding them have big shanty towns where all kinds of building materials have been used in erecting homes for extended families. The oldest and most permanent areas among them have electricity and some kind of piping for running water and drainage, but the latest areas, which started to fill with people arriving in the early 1990s, either as refugees or as returnees sent back from the gulf states, are entirely without such necessities. Not all shanties are miserable places, though—far from it. In Crater, I visited a police inspector's home, which from the outside looked like a temporary hut but from the inside was a decent place, furnished like any home. It had the typical huge double bed, fitted carpets, television set and VCR, table fan, and refrigerator. The only apparatus that was missing was a butagas stove. Like in many homes, the kitchen was situated in the open air, surrounded by a makeshift fence to prevent the smoke from entering the rooms and to provide fresh air for women preparing the food.

Out of all the extended-family households in my survey, the biggest was that of a couple in their midforties. Their roots lay in the countryside, northeast of Aden, and they now shared a flat in a block of flats along the Madram road in Ma'alla with eleven children, some of them already with a family of their own. Twenty-four people altogether lived in this three-room flat, originally designed during the early 1960s by a French architect for the British service personnel families with servants. Only one of the couple's daughters had moved out.

Piety, Purity, and Prestige

The new system of hierarchy characteristic of the postindependence period requires further elaboration. As I pointed out, the new system bears the "modern" element of personal accomplishment in contrast to inherited qualities and virtues that are linked to membership in a larger community and that hold particular cultural and social meanings. The question of whether the new system is a class, prestige, or status system is relevant, too, from the perspective of what kind of daily manifestations the new hierarchy has and what kind of implications it has regarding family and gender. In particular, I argue that this hierarchy acts with regard to status considerations in social interaction and social production, but not so much in manifested forms of distribution of social capital.

In the official propaganda of the early postindependence period, presented as a part of the revolution's goals, people irrespective of descent were encouraged to benefit from education and to join the working life. However, status considerations did not disappear from people's minds; rather, status behavior adapted new forms. As authorities discouraged the use of names that refer to status, such as calling the *akhdam* by that derogatory name, people started to avoid talking directly about status matters. A plethora of commonsense rationalizations arose for not socializing with particular people in place of comments on their status. Arguments that had to do with hygiene and purity, convenience, decency, and personal qualities were common. When social stratification formed an acknowledged part of social interaction, such rationalizations had previously been used to motivate the hierarchy, but now they were applied to explain patterns of social interaction, which is in fact the very same thing.

By suggesting that the new hierarchy emerged on the basis of merit in building up the new society and that it maintained aspects of the old social prestige system, I remain critical of Abu-Amr's definition of a "new social class structure" that supposedly emerged after independence in the PDRY. According to Abu-Amr, "the old ruling class of tribal leaders, Sada, big landlords and members of the bourgeoisie ceased to exist and were replaced by the petty bourgeoisie, the workers and the peasants" (1986, 197). The fourth social class in Abu-Amr's "new social class structure" is "bedouins." If this characterization were applied to Aden, however, where no farming takes place and where nobody functions as a bedouin, the only applicable social classes would be petty bourgeoisie and workers. This categorization instead seems to refer to economic activity, not to the relationship with the means of production, as classical political economy has it. In Abu-Amr's scheme, the "petty bourgeoisie" category includes both those who own the means of production and those who rent their labor. He divides this petty bourgeoisie into four subgroups: first, "emigrants who reside and work abroad"; second, the "segment with private ownership" (consisting of two subgroups, those who employ wage labor and those who are involved in contracting); third, employees; and fourth, the intelligentsia. If this scheme were applied to Aden, such influential groups as party functionaries, politicians, newspaper people, writers, and legal professionals would be in the same category as clerical workers, nurses, and messengers.

However, Aden has never been a full-fledged capitalist society where social standing is based on a relationship to the means of production. During the colonial period, when Aden was connected to the capitalist world market, the control of productive forces as such was not a quality by which one could claim high social standing among locals. The old social hierarchy was based on an inclusive and exclusive system where a person's origin preset the limits in the social hierarchy. In addition to descent, such personal or family-related capacities as generosity, piety, and learning mattered, too. They formed the basis of an excellent communal reputation. As a consequence, a pious but poor *qadi* enjoyed a higher social standing than a rich businessman without merits.

In colonial Aden, each community had its own social hierarchy, and in the majority of the Muslim Arab population's eyes a wealthy Jewish merchant did not enjoy the same high position as he had in his own community or among the British. For Jews, wealth and position in the town's business life mattered much more than the community's actual size. For example, the Jewish community had always been a minority in the town's entire populace, but it lost its favored position after it no longer played a leading role in commercial life.[80] Owing to this communal variety, it is difficult to draw a comprehensive social hierarchy for colonial Aden. The position each person had always depended on the point of view of the one who made the categorization. Women did not have a role of their own in any of these hierarchies but were counted according to the male guardian's position.

In a way similar to Abu-Amr's study, sociologist Abdalla S. Bujra, who wrote about Aden of the early 1960s, analyzes social hierarchies in terms of economic position. However, Bujra rightly divides the Adeni population into different communal groups using his own categorizations. Nevertheless, I find his characterization of the Aden-born community lacking some important groups of people. According to Bujra, the "Adenese" of the 1960s were an urban group that was "internally stratified on a basis of differential achievement. It has had a long time to develop its own élite composed entirely of the leading rich families. Below the rich élite are the large merchant class and white-collar workers who form a big middle category. Below this category is a small number of artisans, petty clerks and semi-skilled labourers. Within this hierarchy there is a constant mobility both up and down, as some people move up through the administration, or by becoming wealthy, and others move downwards for failing to maintain or raise their economic status" (1970, 192).

In his portrayal of the elite, Bujra (1970) forgets two traditional religious elite groups typical to southern Arabian towns, which he in another framework (1971)

80. "The standing of the Jewish community in the commercial life of the Colony has also suffered severely and the members of the Community no longer play a leading part in commerce," Governor Tom Hickinbotham wrote in a letter to London dated November 25, 1955 (IOR R/20/B/2681, Jewish Community), explaining the changed British attitude toward the Jewish community in regard to their appeals for converting into grants the unpaid loans made by the British after the 1947 riots. However, in his memoirs Hickinbotham refers only to the diminished number of Jews in Aden as a reason for their having "ceased to be a factor in the affairs of the Colony" (1958, 87).

describes in fine detail: the *sada* and the *mashayikh* and consequently all men of religious learning, who seldom could boast of owning large properties. Another social category he forgets for some reason is the *akhdam*,[81] which he likewise discusses in detail in his study of the Huraydah town in Hadhramaut. Artisans and semiskilled laborers cannot be squeezed into one category because the nature of the work performed divides these occupations into "respectable" and "despicable" according to local characterization. Artisan and manual jobs where one had to be in contact with "wet" and "unclean" material or human excrement and service tasks in general were (and still usually are) reserved for particular categories of low-status people, the *akhdam* included. A carpenter *(naggar)* enjoyed a considerable higher position than a barber *(hallaq)*, a messenger *(murasil)*, or a porter (whom the British called a "coolie," *hammal*). Tribal men from the countryside and the Kingdom of Yemen who claimed *sharaf* (honor)[82] tried to avoid menial jobs or having to serve another person if they possibly could, which in actual terms they were not always able to do. But Adenis of the 1960s were strict about not carrying out duties judged improper to a person's social rank.

In a slightly different vein from both Abu-Amr and Bujra, Tareq Ismael and Jacqueline Ismael attempt to combine an economic approach with a status approach in their political analysis of the PDRY. According to them, social hierarchy during the colonial era was a "socio-economic class system" where "social divisions did overlap with wealth and occupational divisions" (1986, 8, based on Bujra 1971; Omar 1970, 1–41; and Stookey 1982, 4–9). In practical terms, this configuration meant that the *sada* tended to own more of the means of production than did those at the bottom end of the scale. In towns, certain occupations were carried out by members of a given social group, a system further reinforced by the existence of occupational guilds. In Aden, however, the "caste-like status system" based on genealogical stratification was replaced in the colonial era by an "ethnic" one, "with European administrators heading a hierarchy comprised

81. The reason that Bujra excluded both the traditional elite and the *akhdam* might be that his article deals with the question of political participation in the colony. Strangely enough, though, the exclusion thus suggests that the *akhdam* did not participate in the liberation struggle, which they certainly did.

82. Groups with claims to *sharaf* include, with local variations, the *sada*, *mashayikh*, and *qaba'il* (tribal men).

(in descending order) of East Indian merchants and civil servants, Arab artisans and workers, and unskilled Somali labourers" (Ismael and Ismael 1986, 8). Again, the *akhdam* are missing, and the overall attempt to draw one system of hierarchy for an entire town with distinct communities remains problematic. As I pointed out earlier, not all members of the traditional elite, the *sada* and the *mashayikh*, managed large properties. If the social system from the colonial period is viewed from the point of view of social interaction and social reproduction, as I tend to do in this work, Ismael and Ismael's analysis appears to be the most relevant.

My small survey includes families whose second generation was able to break the chain of unfavorable origin and its social implications. They improved their position either through marriage or by gaining an education and making a professional career. In one such family, the father was a barber who married his daughter to a man who had a stable white-collar job in a ministry and who eventually was promoted to chief of section. However, when the son-in-law died, the daughter, who did not have any education, had to take a menial job as a messenger. In another family, a man who worked as a "coolie" *(hammal)* in the port and whose wife worked as a school sweeper had an accountant *(muhasib)* as a son-in-law. Both these marriages were contracted in the 1970s by parents who originally came to Aden from Hadhramaut and Tihama,[83] respectively. The daughter in both cases was only fourteen years old, and the groom one or two years older. In yet another case, the daughter of a factory worker (father) and a carpenter (mother) gained a university degree and advanced to the position of chief of section in a ministry. Her husband, whom she originally met in the university, was an architect working likewise for a ministry.

Patterns of Women's Labor History

Obtaining a job outside the home tends to be the desired option among the younger generation, at least until a married woman has her first child. It is not surprising that the number of "housewives" among the women from whom I gathered the survey data is lower than the number among their mothers. Because the women in my data vary between fifteen and fifty-seven years of age, however,

83. The coastal area along the Red Sea that belonged to North Yemen.

their mothers came from very different generational backgrounds. Full-fledged job opportunities became available to women only after independence, so the older generations did not really have the option of taking a job in their youth. In addition, the number of unemployed women in my survey does not reflect the actual number of women seeking jobs, described in official statistics for the late 1980s as being high as 17.1 percent of the total female labor force. The same figure for men was only 8.8 percent (PDRY 1990, 57).[84]

If we divide my field survey data into three generations, depending on which period of recent history the person reached adulthood, we can gather information about women's changing job opportunities and choices.[85] Those who came of age during the late colonial period, the oldest generation in the data, performed menial work in offices, factories, and schools, if working at all. They were illiterate women in their fifties who were forced to take a job after the breadwinner of the family, the husband, died or divorced her. Typical occupations for these women's husbands were driver, mechanic, police inspector, accountant, and different menial jobs such as porter. The father of such women often worked as a farmer, guard, shopkeeper or street hawk, private in the army, or sweeper in the municipality. For this generation of women, possibilities for women's education were limited, and many stayed at home when the call to join the labor force came after independence. Most women with whom I spoke seemed to think that women should stay at home unless they have some education or job qualifications. Only then, they argued, is it right for them to work outside the home.

84. According to the same source, 14.5 percent of the female population in Aden around 1990 worked or was unemployed (PDRY 1990, 57). The remaining 84.5 percent did not consist of housewives only, but also included retired people, children, students, and others. However, in another table of the statistics for 1988 the percentage of unemployed women in the total female labor force is given at 60.2 percent (PDRY 1990, 126)! It is evident that the number given of employed females in the workforce is not accurate in that, according to the same table, only 331 women worked in production. The female labor force is given as 35.9 percent of the total labor force in Aden (PDRY 1990, 124–25). The labor force of the total population in Aden was only 31.8 percent at the time (PDRY 1990, 62). More than half of the unemployed women were seeking a job in clerical and related fields (PDRY 1990, 124, 126).

85. I have suggested elsewhere a "generational approach" (Dahlgren 1998–99). According to this tool, I have divided Adeni women into three generational groups. The point is not to construct neat generation categories, but to allow a focus on common social and political circumstances that individual women share when coming to age, contracting a marriage, and so on.

The older women I met often led a life "inside four walls," as the local expression has it. Some of them never went out even to the street. This did not mean that they had no social life and never met people, however. Neighbors and family members came to visit, and a women's sphere was created in the confines of a big block of flats, and men killed time outside the home on street corners and in teashops and *qat* chewing places. Accustomed to moving long distances in the countryside, women who had migrated from the countryside to Aden often had problems in adapting to the congested and restricted city life. During the colonial period, many flats were built for the needs of the Europeans and thus lacked an inner yard, the only place for many women to breath fresh air.

The daughters of these elder women can be called the "women of the revolution" generation because it is this group that in large numbers seized the opportunities in education, the labor market, and politics offered to them by the revolutionary government in the name of *tahrir al-mar'a* (women's emancipation). This change was described to me by many women as "the woman joining her brother to build up the society." Some women wanted to emphasize that "the woman no longer lived inside four walls." Even though not every woman of this generation went to work, had a career, or pursued education, the changes were viewed positively. The mere idea that there was a choice was valued. Women who in the 1990s reached their late thirties or early forties were both highly qualified professionals in top administrative posts and machine operators in big factories. Some of these women were active in the Women's Union in the early years after independence but dropped out once they had children.

The youngest generation included in the survey spent their early adulthood in insecure times at the turn of the 1990s, patterned by economic and moral uncertainties that culminated in the anomalous transitional period following unification in May 1990. This period included the coming to Aden of the new veiling phenomenon, which was common a little earlier in other Middle Eastern towns (see El Guindi 1999; MacLeod 1991; Shirazi 2001), and the reintroduction of sexual segregation. In particular, young women, some with more and others with less enthusiasm, adopted these two phenomena that had often been resisted by their mothers. Both higher education and the labor market were open to these women, but they often preferred to stay at home once they married and had children, another phenomenon their "revolutionary" mothers could not always comprehend. Getting married was the first priority to this third generation of women, a social convention reinforced by religion as well as by customs and traditions that only female medical students were said to resist.[86]

In the late 1980s, Aden was a tolerant place. When struggling with the economic hardships that came after the unification and other misfortunes that occurred in the early 1990s, people tended to look back at that time with nostalgia. No militant movement was imposing its way of life, and by that time even the rulers were tired of imposing anything.[87] According to a World Bank report, by the late 1970s the PDRY was among the world's most egalitarian countries in distribution of domestically earned income. Men and women enjoyed equal pay, and it was accepted that a woman could be the main breadwinner in the family, especially considering the meager economic situation. The gap between the highest-paid government employee and the lowest paid was only a ratio of 3.5 to 1.0, whereas before independence the highest salaries were eleven times the lowest ones (World Bank 1979, page unavailable; see also Stookey 1982, 88).

In the evenings in the 1980s, one could choose whether to go see an anti-Communist film in the nearby cinema or listen to a Socialist Party lecture. Men could choose between going to the mosque to pray and drinking beer in the street outside a bar. Patronizing discourses were absent in the public sphere, and in general women's movements outside the home were not limited. When going out, women did not face problems in mingling with men, and they could attend public activities the way men did. Again, later on, however, when women's freedom of movement was curtailed, many people looked back with nostalgia to these years when women could go to the cinema or enjoy New Year celebrations in a restaurant with the family. Some women complained about the lack of public activities in the late 1990s: there was nothing else to do except chew *qat* in somebody's home, it was explained to me.

86. It is believed that women who choose medicine as a career consider this choice against the background of remaining unmarried because the odd working hours make it difficult to manage family life.

87. Abou Bakr Al-Saqqaf, a northern intellectual, describes the PDRY period in similar terms: "personal liberty in the South [Yemen] was kept intact and enjoyed greater freedom in absence of the destructive hand of the preacher and the watching eye of the security forces" (1999, 154).

6. The old and new meet in the streets of Aden—a colonial-era car and women chatting in the street. Photograph by the author, 1989.

The New Atmosphere

Aden changed rapidly at the turn of the 1990s. As a prelude to unification, the border between North Yemen and South Yemen, previously heavily guarded on both sides and also a site of inter-Yemeni warfare, was opened in May 1988 for all Yemenis carrying identity cards.[88] In Aden, this new policy resulted in a caravan of Toyota Land Cruisers pouring into the town on Thursday afternoons. Each car carried northern men eager to enjoy the liberties of this port town: alcohol, belly dancing, and inexpensive prostitutes. The northern driving style and these visitors' occasional bad behavior produced feelings of resentment toward anything that came from the North. It was also believed that when these same visitors returned home, they spread stories of low morality among Adenis.

88. The border had split many families. To visit relatives on the other side, one needed to obtain a permit and to have a passport. People who had contacts with people on the other side of the border were harassed and persecuted by the security apparatuses in both North and South Yemen.

In 1990, people without a place to stay and a means of income started to flow into Aden in large numbers. They included both refugees from the horn of Africa and Yemenis returning from Saudi Arabia and other gulf countries following the Gulf War. Despair spread around the town as congested refugee camps with no electricity or running water were erected with makeshift huts. In Crater, the old open-air swimming pool, lying empty since the mid-1980s,[89] was converted into a miserable refugee camp with hundreds of needy people who had been forced to leave Somalia because of the civil war there.

The next group of people to arrive were beggars and people from the North who provided small services in traffic-light areas. Some of these people cleaned windshields; others sold newspapers or items drivers were expected to need. For all these people, Aden offered a completely new market.[90] These beggars were not welcomed, and some residents simply told them to go back to North. "The messengers of Ali Abdullah Salih,"[91] as they were called, were believed to be *akhdam* originating from Tihama on the coast of the Red Sea.

Wealthy families who had fled Aden after the radicalization of the government (the Corrective Move of 1969) to continue their businesses abroad were the last "new" group to arrive in the 1990s. When the postunification government started to give back nationalized housing and property, the best hotels filled with these people. Some claimed noble descent and came to see if they could restore their lifestyle and position of respect *(karama).* As both the rich and the starving returned and with them came a rise in consumer prices, social origin started to matter again.

Also among the newcomers were northern civil servants sent by the central government in Sana'a to serve in leading administrative posts in Aden, a measure

89. The Holkat Bay swimming pool was opened in 1955 and had one afternoon set as a "purdah" day for women only (Foster 1969, 22). This practice continued after independence. Many people recall that during the women's days, the nearby hills were filled with men eager to get a glimpse of a woman.

90. It was not the first time that beggars came to Aden from outside the town. In the colonial period, a group of professional beggars called the Ga'di tribe used to walk the streets and visit homes to ask for food, which they put in a *masab,* a goatskin wallet (Khalifa 1951, 14).

91. Ali Abdullah Salih, the president of North Yemen, became the chairman of the five-man presidential council of the new Republic of Yemen and later its president.

not exactly welcomed in Adeni government offices. With the returnees and the newcomers also came people engaged in dishonest or criminal activities. Looting, house breaking and robbery had been basically unknown during the previous years, but now the talk of the town was crime. Aden obviously changed in a short period of time.

By this time, segregation of the sexes started to structure the town. Particular areas became restricted to one sex only. In restaurants, a separate "family area" was reserved to allow women to have ice cream or a meal undisturbed. In its most modest form, the family area was simply a windowless and suffocating back room isolated from the main restaurant by a plastic curtain. Women disappeared from cinema halls entirely. To see a film, formerly "women's most popular entertainment,"[92] women rented a cassette from a video store and watched it at home. Women appeared on beaches draped in black cloaks and refrained from going into the water. Public transportation remained unsegregated, though. In contrast to many other public areas, taxis and buses became places where men made efforts to allow women to remain alone. This exception naturally challenged the widespread belief common at that time that because men cannot control themselves, women have to disappear from sight.

Women's covering clothing contributed to new behavioral patterns alongside avoidance. Even though some women took to the *hijab,* religious headgear, with great enthusiasm, many young people in particular considered it just a new exciting fashion and instead called it a *mandil,* head scarf. Some women thought negatively about the new dress code, saying that it interfered in women's own affairs. Force was not so much the issue in women's adopting this new outfit. More important was the coming to the forefront of ideologies that favored traditional family-related role models for women and the curbing of women's "unnecessary" movement outside the home. The new atmosphere made many women who were less convinced about the necessity of the new costume confront questions such as "Am I a good person if I do not cover my hair?" "What will people think of me as a mother?" and "Am I showing a good example to my children?" Those who resisted and refrained from using the outdoor covering costume were harassed in the streets as adolescent boys took the chance to pinch and grope them.

92. As Farouk Luqman describes in *The Aden Guide* (1960, 207).

Women's sports activities also ran into difficulties. The Women's Union, which earlier had organized volleyball, table tennis, and other sports for women in town clubs, had to drop sports after the atmosphere became unfavorable and some families complained. Successful sportswomen had to abandon their careers because of the lack of support. The Ministry of Youth and Sports became the Ministry of Male Youth and Men's Sports. For some activist women, this concession was one of the saddest made owing to the "pressure from the North," as the new atmosphere was called.

Segregation spread in many homes, too, where it had not been the custom earlier. Most houses in Aden are small, with the entrance directly connecting the street and the living room. Now, if a man wanted to enter a house, he had to announce his sex by utterance from outside the door. Once he was given permission to enter, he was expected to lower his gaze in case "forbidden" women were present and to cross the room rapidly without acknowledging or greeting anybody. Segregation in schools followed after the 1994 civil war, when conservatives were given the chance to sweep "heretic" elements in Aden. Workplaces and public transportation were left outside these measures of forced segregation, however.

All these types of phenomena indicated the coming of a new era in gender regulation in comparison to the previous period, when a woman's role was declared to be alongside her "brother" in building up the society and when men were expected to respect every woman as his "sister." In the new era, such "unregulated" male-female interaction was targeted, but not without resistance. A lively debate flourished in newspapers and other forums on the desired role models for women in both society and the family. Avoidance structured the town in a new way. The changes discussed here cannot, however, be considered a return to the preindependence situation.[93] Before independence, the town had embraced various lifestyles alongside each other. Although the British brought modernization to Aden, it was made obtainable to nonelite women in the same way as for men only after independence. The British stabilized gender relations in their attempt to avoid communal unrest. Segregation and gender avoidance were commonplace during the British period, but no alternative patterns of intersex communication were attainable in the public sphere, as they are in the unsegregated labor

93. I compare sexual limits in these three periods in Dahlgren 2006a.

market of today. Women disappeared again from public places, but their role in the public sphere did not vanish.

Throughout the twentieth century, the idea of what Islam is and what stands outside it has become polarized into two positions represented by two prominent figures, Shaykh Muhammad bin Salim al-Bayhani and 'Ali Muhammad Bahamish. During the PDRY period, the kind of Islam personified in al-Bayhani was left little if no room to function, and the blind shaykh himself was forced to leave Aden some years after independence was achieved. During that era, the rulers favored a tolerant Islam without political ambitions, a line that had its roots in the colonial period and that was personified in Bahamish. After unification, when the state control of religion lapsed, Wahhabism and other earlier suppressed forms of Islam could flourish again.[94] A mosque carrying the name of Shaykh al-Bayhani was thus erected in Khormaksar with foreign money (Bawazir 1997, 146–50).

By the beginning of the twenty-first century, life had become hard again in this town with a cosmopolitan past. People felt that the new rulers, representatives of the Yemeni president's party, the People's General Congress (locally known as *mut'amar,* did not respect Aden the way it should. Although Adeni families have seldom had properties outside the residence they occupy, the new elite busily engaged in distributing land and properties to anyone loyal to the northern rule. After the 1994 civil war, Adenis came to feel that the town had come under northern occupation *(ihtilal shimali),* as though they were living again in a colonial state, but now run by less capable hands than during the period of British-Indian colonialism.

In the following chapters, I deepen my analysis of Adeni society and look in particular at the state's role in regulating the family, where social attachments are concentrated, and the key notion in most social deliberations.

94. During the colonial period, Aden had only two *qadi*s, one in Aden proper and another in Shaykh 'Uthman; after independence, a third *qadi* was nominated in Tawahi following popular demand. Since unification, some thirty to thirty-five *qadi*s have functioned locally, causing confusion for authorities who try to keep registration in order. The Bohora and Ithn'asharis sects have had their unofficial *qadi*s during the whole of this period.

3 Law and Court

The Making of Familial Ideologies During the Colonial Era

Like Melrose Abbey, Aden should be seen by moonlight.

—*Three Hours in Aden*

THIS CHAPTER focuses on the practice of law as a specific field of gender regulation. As I suggested in the introduction, it is vital to understand structural factors and which of them provide the limitations and resources for people to constitute practice. We are dealing with a field where moral frameworks are acted out and where they get their meaning. In looking at the legal field and state regulation in it, I am particularly interested to see what kinds of gender ideas the court practices have produced and what the origins and bases of such ideologies are. The present chapter discusses the legal field in colonial Aden, and chapter 4 discusses the legal issues during the PDRY era and the period that emerged in unification.

I start by looking at family legislation as a construction that has practical consequences to the community in the form of court rulings mediated by legal experts, Muslim scholars, and court judges. Family legislation is a form of state intervention in family matters, and it both informs and is informed by the prevailing sex/gender systems. I examine how the British colonial court system presented family relations and interpreted Islamic law and discuss the local responses to the British intervention in familial relations, a field that both the British and the local people considered the core of local culture. In chapter 4, I take a look at how the PDRY era provided another form of accommodating family relations and Islam to state rule. By focusing on how Islam was transformed after independence to serve new purposes and not just set aside, I want to avoid the dubious contrast of the secular and the Islamic. In such a false approach, the colonial rule and the Marxist government are presented as "secular" institutions with assumedly distinct religious domains in contrast to ritual practices and the Muslim scholarly tradition. As Nikki Keddie suggests in her study on postcolonial Muslim societies, state control over religion would be a more accurate designation than an established secularism (1988, 11). In both the colonial and the PDRY eras, it was basically a question of weakening the social stratum most identified with Islam, the ulema (religious scholars).

The legal field has perpetually been a site of contesting normative representations, and the question of religion has not been simple at any time. The postunification family legislation is in no way a "return" to the preindependence or precolonial state of affairs. Scholars of postcolonial legal systems have emphasized this point, too (Keddie 1988, 9). Therefore, this historical review gives a perspective not only on the changes in family legislation that took place after the unification, but also on the changes that were made after independence. As Sally Falk Moore has suggested, small-scale legal "events" bear the imprint of the complex, large-scale transformations. Legal disputes have an immediate internal logic, but they also have an external logic that is linked to conditions on a larger scale over long periods of time (1986, 11). In a colonial setting, local and outside influences are linked together and form new meanings.

Legal discourse is a specific field of gender negotiations. It is where the public and private meet, if the former is understood as state intervention into family regulation and the latter as family affairs that the people involved want to settle on their own. Strictly speaking, the practice of law involves only families whose marital relations have come to the point that they look for an outside settlement. In a more general way, however, court rulings act as preventive or encouraging examples to all people, not only to those who consider their possibilities in court. As Carol Smart has suggested, the practice of law always contains power relations because the ideal of law implies a claim to "truth" and sets itself above other knowledge, such as common sense (1989, 10–11). In a court setting, where a couple's private matters are discussed in a public forum, gender relations are negotiated in a manner different from the way they are negotiated in the family sphere because the legal discourse provides a framework to the discussions. It is a question of state intervention in the family, where the attitudes of court judges toward women also need to be taken into consideration, as I later show. The way women are treated in front of the law tells not only about the prevailing communal attitudes toward women and normative expectations directed at them, but in a colonial setting also about the interpretations of those attitudes and expectations by the colonial agents, who are presumed to stand for *the* local custom.

In legal discourse, everyday cultural understandings provide material for argumentation, so the discourse on familial relations communicates between law and culture. In the legal process, the argumentation negotiates cultural meanings (Mann and Roberts 1991, 24). Finally, legal discourse constructs women and men as gendered subjects, presenting them as wives, husbands, mothers, fathers, sons, and daughters, thus applying dominant familial ideologies or assumptions over them. By "familial ideology," I refer to a set of norms, values, and assumptions about the way in which the family life is expected to be organized in a normative way. Familial ideology represents a set of ideas that are naturalized and universalized to such an extent that such ideas have come to stand for commonsense thinking about the family (Kapur and Cossman 1996, 13).

Law is also a domain where prevailing gender roles have been challenged, as Ratha Kapur and Brenda Cossman suggest (1996, 12). The nationwide debate on the Draft Law of Personal Status (1971), conducted in the PDRY in the early 1970s (Ghanem 1976, 191; *The Middle East,* Feb. 1983, 47; Molyneux 1989, 205), is a case of an active period of battle between contesting gender concepts in the framework of law. It was followed in 1991 by quite a different process, when the postunification rulers in Sana'a, the new capital, issued a new family law during the fasting month of Ramadhan to avoid public challenge. Even though there eventually came some debate both against and in favor of the draft law, the process of enacting the law in the legislature did not consider this debate relevant because the debaters were not considered to retain an authority on Islamic law similar to that held by those who drafted it. The flourishing discussion on family, women, and education that was going on at the same time in the media and various other forums constituted a separate but parallel discourse to the process of enacting a new family law for the unified Yemeni Republic.

Linking the practice of law to people's actual circumstances allows us to move beyond a dichotomized understanding of law as simply an instrument of either oppression or liberation. As Smart points out, law constitutes, rather than just a tool, an institutionalized and formalized site of power struggles that can provide resources for people in varied ways (1989, 138). According to Adeni legal professionals and women's rights advocates, knowledge of law and legal rights and duties is low among people, especially the nonliterate part of society. For this reason, one of the Women's Union's main tasks, ever since it was founded in 1968, has been to inform women about their legal rights. This focus also guided the activists of the "re-Islamization" process *(al-sahwa al-islamiyya)* that started in the late 1980s and gained momentum after the 1994 civil war,[1] though toned down by 1998. That Islam guarantees women all the rights they need was the essence of a critique of the 1974 Family Law and the allegedly secular rule.

The question of women's and men's rights, if "rights" are understood as resources available to each sex in varying degrees, cannot be approached merely by studying rights as they are established in law texts.[2] In a hierarchical society, alleged equality before the law presents a case of its own when varying divisive factors are brought in. Equality should not be equated with sameness, but, as Kapur and Cossman outline in what they call a substantive approach, attention should be directed to the prevailing historical and systemic disadvantages (1996, 16). Just as knowledge of law varies among people of different strata, so does awareness of legal means available to work for a positive court ruling.

In anthropological studies of Middle Eastern societies, legal systems and state order are also discussed as fields where competing and conflicting ideas struggle over the meanings of various symbols (see, for instance, Geertz 1993, 193–233). As Michael Meeker (1976) puts it, law can be seen in terms of structuring that derives from a cultural system of meaning.[3] The relationship between legislation and legal practice should always be viewed in a historical and concrete framework. In the Middle East, common factors include widespread illiteracy, the centrality of oral tradition, locally emerging forms of Islamic practice, prevalence of customary laws, legal pluralism, and the coexistence of various religious communities with family legislation of their own, to mention only a few. In analyzing the ways Islam is present in any cultural setting, one should be careful not to take sharia merely in a normative way, from text to practice, and use Qur'anic verses to explain local practices. In the Yemeni framework, sharia should not be seen in the conventional meaning as "Islamic law" but can be better character-

1. On the rise and fall of Islah Party in Aden, see Monet 1995.

2. For a critique of a textual reading of legal practice, the usual case prior to the 1970s in studies conducted by orientalists, see Moors 1999, 142.

3. Without hesitation, Meeker adds, "This system of meaning is directly related to the concept of honor in the Near East" (1976, 244).

ized as a "total" discourse, wherein "all kinds of institutions find simultaneous expression: religious, legal, moral and economic," as Brinkley Messick asserts following Mauss.[4] This totality, however, should not be understood as presenting a single discourse, but rather a variety of conflicting discourses on what is "real Islam." The judicial domain should likewise not be regarded as manifesting coherent cultural assumptions, but instead conflicting ideas on "the right interpretation" (see S. F. Moore 1986, 10). This multiplicity was further emphasized during the colonial times by the presence of a dual apparatus in interpreting the Islamic law, as I later show.

In Aden, colonial institutions transformed Islamic law into a specific legal discourse that both contributed to the endurance of the "traditional" roles ascribed to men and women and brought along a religious-legal practice that was cultivated in other parts of the British colonial empire, in particular India.[5] As Richard Roberts and Kristin Mann suggest, the practice of (Islamic) law provides an excellent window to the colonial period because of its centrality to colonialism and the political domination it helped to maintain (1991, 4). In the colonial legal system in Aden, local Islamic scholars *(fuqaha')* were left outside the court system with an unofficial "advisory" status. In family dispute cases litigated in the Supreme Court that are reprinted in the Aden law reports, the British judges never relied on such out-of-court legal advice (see also J. N. D. Anderson 1954, 38–39).

During the PDRY era, Islam was also transformed to serve the purposes of the government. On the one hand, Islam was interpreted in ways that did not conflict with the ideas of the revolution, and on the other hand it was allocated a central role as the official religion.[6] This approach can be contrasted to the system of accentuated religious diversity that the colonial rule favored in the manner of divide and rule. During the PDRY, the influence of religious scholars in public affairs was minimized, and mosques came under state control with per-

4. Marcel Mauss, *The Gift* (1967, 1), cited in Messick 1993, 3.

5. On this legal practice and its connections to other parts of the British Empire, see J. N. D. Anderson 1954, 33–39; M. Anderson 1990; and Schacht 1964, 94–97.

6. The 1970 PDRY Constitution enacts that "the state shall preserve the Arabic and Islamic [*heritage*]" (part 1, chap. 3, art. 31) and proclaims Islam as the state religion (part 2, chap. 3, art. 46). In the same article, the freedom of belief is guaranteed to other religions as well.

sonnel appointed by the Ministry of Justice and Waqf (Religious Endowments). This process can be described as both emphasizing the role of Islam in society and simultaneously minimizing its influence in areas considered political. With regard to proselytization, religion became a private matter, in line with the policy of creating new meanings to such central cultural concepts as religious faith, tradition, state, society, and the family.

Whenever anthropologists have looked at women's legal rights in the Middle East, they have focused exclusively on personal status and family law and left other forms of law unexamined, as Safia K. Mohsen suggests. This preoccupation has its background in the notion that family law, with roots in sharia, is a repository of traditional values and reflects the most "authentic" aspects of Middle Eastern culture (Mohsen 1990, 15).[7] A variant of this thinking is manifest in how the 1974 Family Law was locally understood as the "women's law" *(qanun al-mar'a).* The assertion that family law represents the legislation that involves women in particular is, however, problematic. This issue came up in the criticism that Women's Union activists and others directed at the 1992 Personal Status Law. What they opposed, among other things, was the idea of reducing women to persons "situated" inside the family under male guardianship. Thus, the legal discourse constituted only men as citizens or objects of legislation at large. During the colonial era, when the British policy was to leave family laws of each religious community outside direct colonial intervention, criminal law was the platform for changes in personal status law in general. For example, the Criminal Procedure Ordinance was developed to regulate the terms for maintenance orders (i.e., spousal and child support) issued in the Aden Divisional Court.[8]

The Anglo-Muhammadan Legal Practice

Throughout the colonial era, a variety of sources of law were applied in Aden. Colonial law prevailed primarily in relation to public and administrative law, whereas other areas of legislation, such as family relations, were considered to

7. For the fallacy of such thinking, see also Mir-Hosseini 2003.

8. Criminal Procedure Ordinance on the Maintenance of Wives and Children, cap. 38, *Laws of Aden* 1955, vol. 1. See also Ghanem 1972, 89–90. J. N. D. Anderson discusses the problems the courts faced with the issue of the maintenance of wives and children (1954, 36, 38).

belong to the sphere of "religion and custom", which the British were not eager to touch in their attempt to avoid communal unrest (Bujra 1971, 125; Amin 1987, 31).[9] This policy was drafted in Bombay Regulation 4 of 1827, section 26, which stated that in the absence of specific enactments, the court should apply the "usage of the country" and the "law of the defendant" (J. N. D. Anderson 1954, 2).[10] Various religious communities were allowed the means to settle family disputes in their own way.[11] Such disputes were distinguished from issues considered to have a political character, which subsequently belonged to the colonial administration.

Because Aden was under the government of Bombay, legal development and practice followed Bombay and the decisions taken in its High Court (J. N. D. Anderson 1954, 33, 37). In 1932, the control was transferred to the "governor-general of India in council" until 1937, when Aden became a Crown colony ruled directly from the Colonial Office in London (Naval Intelligence Division 1946, 309). Between 1944 and 1963, Aden had a legislative council, nominated by the British governor up to 1955, when some of the council members were elected by an electorate of male British subjects. During 1963–67, the British ruled under a state of emergency and suspended the legislative council (Amin 1987, 25).

9. In British India, from where Aden was ruled during the period 1839–1937, the East India Company and later British Crown administrators followed the practice of awakening least resistance by relying on local intermediaries and on the military and police force to ensure control. Part of this policy was to adapt to the precolonial political systems, including law (M. Anderson 1996, 4–5). In South Arabia, the latter meant indirect rule by incorporating sultans, emirs, and shaykhs ruling the countryside into the colonial system with a carrot-and-stick policy, allowing autonomous rule in exchange for loyalty to the British interests in the area. The result of the British policy was that during the colonial era the countryside was kept unchanged (Halliday 1975, 164, 172).

10. The Bombay Regulation was later applied in the Interpretation and General Clauses Ordinance of 1937, which gave the British judiciary authority to apply sharia law in Colony Courts (J. N. D. Anderson 1954, 33).

11. During the nineteenth century, "their own way" meant by a *qadi, rabbi,* or the *punchayet* council for Hindus (Kour 1981, 87–88). The various Indian-, Persian- and Yemeni-origin Muslim minorities resident in Aden—namely, Ithn'asharis, Isma'ilis, Musta'li Bohoras, and Zaidis—tended to solve their family disputes within their own communities in respective Community Councils and not to bring cases to court, as J. N. D. Anderson reports based on his conversations with Indian lawyers of the Aden bar (1954, 37).

The colonial period contributed to founding a Western statutory system of law and public administration in Aden, both of which were kept and maintained throughout the PDRY period.

The British viewed Aden as "ethnically" and religiously divided in terms similar to India and thus introduced the British-Indian legal system to Aden. In India, the system was drafted in the Hastings Plan of 1772, where civil and criminal courts were charged with the tasks of applying indigenous legal norms in matters regarding inheritance, marriage, caste, and other religious institutions. "Indigenous norms" included "the laws of the Koran with respect to Muhammadans" and "the laws of the Brahmanic Shasters with respect to Hindus" (M. Anderson 1996, 5). In Aden, this application meant the establishment of a judicial system wherein local Islamic scholars were excluded from the colonial court system, which applied a specific type of Islamic law that in other parts of the empire was called "Anglo-Muhammadan law." These courts appointed British judges and Indian barristers, so it would be misleading to call this system "an organised hierarchy of shari'a courts," as al-Hubaishi does (al-Hubaishi 1988, 183).

The British courts set up in Aden relied on a legal scholarship that included English translations of Arabic and Persian law manuals, a variety of legal commentaries, and the precedent court cases as recorded in the courts of Aden, British India, and even Great Britain (M. Anderson 1996, 4).[12] The colonial policy was not to make any fundamental changes in what they considered the sharia, and the ordinances issued throughout the colonial period had the intention of reproducing legislation in Aden parallel to that in India and British East Africa (J. N. D. Anderson 1954, 34; Ghanem 1972, 87). As Norman Anderson, a British

12. British judges in Aden consulted the famous Shafi'i manual *Minhaj al-Talibin* by Muhyi al-Din al-Nawawi, translated into English by E. C. Howard from an earlier French rendering and published in 1914 (al-Hubaishi 1988, 54; R. Knox-Mawer 1956, 511). Because no English translation of *Al-Tuhfa* by Ibn Hajar was available, this manual, which local Shafi'i jurists considered equally authoritative, was not used in Aden courts (R. Knox-Mawer 1956, 511). Ghanem claims that the local nineteenth-century manual published in English and Arabic, *A Treatise on the Muhammedan law, Entitled "The Overflowing River of the Science of Inheritance and Patrimony," Together with an Exposition of "The Rights of Women, and the Laws of Matrimony,"* by Shaykh Abdul Kadir bin Muhammed al-Mekkawi, originally published in 1886 and reprinted in 1899 (in Syria) and in 1959 (in Cairo), was also used in Aden courts (Ghanem 1972, 139). However, the British judges did not treat this book as equally authoritative to some Indian law manuals.

jurist whose book *Islamic Law in Africa* (1954) was used as an authoritative reference book in Adeni courts, describes the intentions of the British: "Sharia law appears in South Arabia largely as the tool of the centralized government" (1954, 11). According to him, sharia was easier to control administratively than the customary law *('urf)*, and it besides gave the colonial rule the chance to pose as a champion of Islam, a manner imitated from Saudi Arabia and the Kingdom of Yemen (J. N. D. Anderson 1954, 12n; see also Messick 1993, 6–66). This approach obviously made it easier to motivate the state of affairs in courts where the judiciary consisted of British judges and Indian barristers.

The British legislated on the duties of the *qadi* in the Qadi Ordinance from 1943 to include only the right to register Muslim marriages and divorces.[13] To avoid competition, they carefully selected among the *qadi* candidates only those loyal to the colonial rule.[14] Because marriage and divorce registration was the only legal function the *qadi*s had outside the unofficial role of advising the colonial rulers, and considering the fact that all Islamic scholars were excluded from court practice, it is understandable that the local people did not consider these courts to be sharia courts, so that demands that such courts be established were raised. These demands took the forms of petitions signed by local notables and political speeches delivered in different social occasions, most notably by Shaykh Muhammad bin Salim al-Bayhani. In the early 1960s, the British finally considered allowing the *qadi* of Aden, Shaykh 'Ali Muhammad Bahamish, to act as a divisional magistrate in the Magistrate Court. However, the experiment was soon terminated because it turned out that Bahamish had difficulties in combining trial procedures with the provisions of the Islamic law and consequently resigned.[15]

The British "sharia courts" differed from the earlier practice that prevailed before the time of the British occupation. At that time, Aden was under the rule of the sultan of Lahig, the powerful Abdali Sultanate north of Aden. His local

13. *Laws of Aden* 1955, chap. 133, Qadi Ordinance. See also J. N. D. Anderson 1954, 35, and Gavin 1975, 60. In the Jewish community, the rabbinical court (Bet Din) had a similar role (Ahroni 1994, 145).

14. India Office Records (IOR) R/20/A/2210, Qadi, and R/20/B/2833, Religious (Sharia) Courts. The British authorities in Aden also participated in finding and nominating a *qadi* for British Somaliland (see IOR R/20/B/1000, Qadhi).

15. See IOR R/20/D/327, Religious Courts.

Table 1. Crime and punishment in Aden prior to the colonial era

Crime	*Punishment*
Theft	The loss of a hand, a flogging, or a fine
Homicide	Death; if the victim was shot while committing robbery, no charge
Not saying prayers	Reprimand and sometimes a fine
Breach of promise of marriage	Obligation to marry or to refund all money received
Infidelity	Flogging of both culprits, wife and children discarded
Sale of spirituous liquors	Flogging and a fine

Source: Kour 1981, 86–87.

representative was the *qadi* to whom all disputes were usually referred. The executive powers were in the hands of the *dawlah* (state power). Whenever the sultan or any other Abdali chief was present in the town, they superseded both the *qadi* and the *dawlah*. The law applied in passing judgments was a combination of the sharia and local customs *('urf)* as Zaki Kour (1981) explains, relying on British Settlement Papers.[16] The list of punishments applicable in that period gives further evidence of the judicial system and the prevailing ideas of what was considered illegitimate (see table 1).

Kour mentions some of the principles applied in Aden both before and some time after the conquest in contracting and dissolving marriages and in dividing inheritance.[17] A father could marry off his daughter at any age, but a girl who did not have parents had to be fourteen before she could be given away. Upon separation of spouses, the mother lost her children because the custody of both female and male children was allotted to the father. No limit was set to marriage payments or the dower, and the dower was to be decided by the parties in the case where the woman was without male guardian. Orphan children were set under the protection of a chief or *qadi*—girls until the time they married, and boys until they reached manhood (Kour 1981, 86–87). Inheritance rules followed classical sharia, but local custom seems to have influenced the marriage practice. The situ-

16. Minutes by Governor, Sept. 6, 1854, BSP 291, in Kour 1981, 86.

17. Al-Mekkawi ([1886] 1959) gives another idea of how sharia was interpreted in that period.

ation was, of course, made more complicated at that period by the existence of slavery in that some people who were considered the property of another person thus became a party in any legal deal.

Under the governorship of Captain S. B. Haines from 1839 to 1854, the first British political agent, the legal practice just described was maintained, with the exception of mutilation for theft. From then on, the British seized the right to nominate the *qadi* and other public officials (Kour 1981, 88). Characteristic of British policies, the *qadi* remained the only official position occupied by a local Arab, whereas all other public offices were already by 1850s manned by Indians, who started to arrive in large numbers from British India (Gavin 1975, 60).

In the British courts, the court language was English, which further alienated the local people from the judicial system. The Anglo-Muhammadan law as practiced in Aden differed from the local Islamic law in referring to Shafi'i *fiqh* (Islamic jurisprudence) in an eclectic manner devoid of the particular local history of that school in South Arabia. As Abdulla Maktari has asserted, the Shafi'i school of jurisprudence developed in various parts of the Muslim world under the influences of different local traditions and under the practice of provision of legal views by the spirit of reasoning *(ijtihad)* practiced by the local *fuqaha'*. In South Arabia, in particular, where the Shafi'i *madhhab* (school of law) was introduced at the end of the fourth century A.H., the school had to confront and integrate a well-established system of customary law *('urf)* (1971, 4–5).

Other differences between the Anglo-Muhammadan law and local Islamic *fiqh* have to do with the court practice and process of litigation. In his study on the Indian colonial legal system, Robert Kidder (1978, as cited in Mann and Roberts 1991, 37) asserts that although the colonial legal system was designed to preserve "religion and custom," the working of the colonial courts nevertheless altered processes of litigation, expressions of conflict, and litigants' strategies. The process of litigation turned marital conflicts into separate "cases" void of larger social aspects where the clear-cut right and wrong was to be distinguished and duly ruled.[18] Furthermore, the colonial legal system favored single, exhaus-

18. Sally Falk Moore describes a similar situation in Kilimanjaro: "When parties come to a Primary Court on Kilimanjaro, from the point of view of the Court, the most important thing is that their situation becomes a case, in other words, that its disposition should fit into one of the general categories from which prescribed consequences flow. A highly personal and idiosyncratic situation

tive definitions of the local custom and a careful recording of precedent cases. Rules of evidence restricted the content of evidence that was considered relevant. All this—accompanied by the colonial power's implicit arrogance toward the "primitive" local law, occasionally voiced aloud by British judges, and an assumption of the inferior status that this local law was presumed to allocate to women—contributed to layered biases in court rulings, as I show later in this chapter.

Because the primary tenets of the British legal system maintained that all persons should be treated equally before the law and that justice should be blind, local status differences and hierarchies were in principle set aside from the process of litigation. These provisions for equality did not, however, apply to the assumed gender hierarchy, as the sample law cases I give here show. In India as well as in Aden, the principle of equality before the law violated the prevailing status system, in India embedded in the caste system and in Aden based on the hierarchy of descent *(nasab)*. As Kidder (1978) also suggests, the notion of isolated law cases in which distinct rights and duties were argued simplified the complexities of local relations and violated the customary conflict settlement systems (as cited in Mann and Roberts 1991, 37). In scrutinizing Aden from the point of view of how colonial legal practice transformed prevailing gender relations, Kidder's argument is useful; however, it should be kept in mind that the court system was not the sole field where contested relations were argued.

In India, as the colonial rule gained a firmer base, large portions of Anglo-Muhammadan law were replaced by laws of British origin. Practices that the British deemed "barbarian," such as *sati* (suttee) and child marriage, were also targeted as part of campaigns for social reform and in attempts to improve women's position (M. Anderson 1996, 7–8; Kapur and Cossman 1996, 45). In India, campaigns to reform social practices through law were met with some sympathy, but the general attitude was steadfast resistance, and outcries of "religion in danger" were common (Kapur and Cossman 1996, 47). As a result of these confrontations, the mere existence and legitimacy of colonial rule became threatened, which obviously made the British careful not to attempt similar moves in Aden.

---

from the point of view of parties is easiest to deal with if it can be classified as an instance of a general category" (1977, 182–83).

The fragile coexistence of, on the one hand, the foreign military presence in Aden and, on the other, the fragmented sultanates and sheikhdoms of the surrounding countryside, organized with treaties into what was called the Aden Protectorate, was perhaps the immediate reason for not attempting to improve women's position outside Aden either.

The British therefore developed a cautious approach during the twentieth century, in particular in relation to Muslims. At the end of nineteenth century, the British Law of Inheritance (Act of Succession) caused trouble among the Jewish community of Aden.[19] The law established equal rights of succession to all children of the deceased, regardless of gender. In response, the bewildered leaders of the Jewish community organized a delegation to India to appeal for the exemption of Jews from the act, which was later granted (Ahroni 1994, 148–49). Another law that caused major protests was the Marriage (Christian) Ordinance (1940). Even though the ordinance was meant to apply only to people who professed to be Christians, a stipulation on the validity of marriage between a Muslim woman and a Christian man induced accusations that the ordinance was a "danger to religion" and "antisharia" because Muslims do not allow a Muslim woman to marry a non-Muslim man (Ghanem 1972, 84).

However, not all laws issued by the British caused public outcry. For example, the Child Marriage Restraint Ordinance, issued in 1939, ordained that the marital age for boys should be eighteen and for girls fourteen. Linked to this ordinance, the Aden Penal Code ordered that sexual intercourse by a man with a woman younger than fourteen years was considered rape, regardless of whether she was his legal wife.[20] This ordinance was not considered to be antisharia and turned out to be acceptable to the Muslim community, possibly because the marrying age for Muslim boys and girls had risen anyway. Nevertheless, the practice of marrying girls younger than fourteen persisted, especially in the countryside, but the marriage was usually consummated only after the girl's first menstruation. In such cases, the girl's age was simply declared to be fourteen in the marriage contract, if such a contract was drawn up in the first place.

19. This law was applied to Jews alongside other non-Muslim people, whereas inheritance among Muslims was litigated according to what the British judges interpreted as sharia. See also Tobi 1994a.

20. See *Laws of Aden* 1955, chap. 22, and J. N. D. Anderson 1954, 35.

7. A wedding in the open-air Alf Layla wa Layla (Thousand and One Nights) wedding club in Shaykh 'Uthman. Photograph by the author, 1989.

Hanafi Doctrine Gains Space

During the colonial period, an eclectic choice *(talfiq)* from the four schools of Sunni jurisprudence, with an emphasis on the Hanafi doctrine, became the court custom owing to the practice of judge-made law (Ghanem 1972, 115). Out of the four major schools of Sunni doctrine, the British relied in particular on the Hanafi school, which the majority of Indian Sunni Muslims who came to Aden followed. Some of the texts that British judges consulted were Egyptian, which was also Hanafi. Norman Anderson suggests that this amalgam was compiled as a measure to favor women (J. N. D. Anderson 1954, 35–36, and 1959, 22, 26, as cited in Lateef 1990, 57).[21] However, not every woman could demand the application of the Hanafi interpretation because only those "brought up as a member of the Hanafi school" were entitled to do that (see Ghanem 1972, 79–173, especially 121–22). Religious adherence was considered to follow the mother's religion because the mother was responsible for her children's religious upbringing. However, the practice of consulting other Sunni Islamic doctrines alongside Shafi'i, the main school of law among Muslims in Aden, also came from elsewhere other than Anglo-Muhammadan law (Ghanem 1972, 106–11, 128–29). The local scholar of Islamic law Shaykh Abdul Kadir bin Muhammed al-Mekkawi's manual from 1886 interprets the law with reference to both Hanafi and Shafi'i schools.

In reality, the eclectic legal choice practiced during the colonial period resulted in a legal practice that was more alien than familiar to various Muslim communities and in a way that was similar to what happened India.[22] Another problem was the mere concept of "Muslim" itself. In Aden, the Muslim population was far from a united community. It had two Sunni schools (the majority being Shafi'is and most of the Indian Muslims professing the Hanafi school) and four different Shi'a schools: Zaidis following the Hadawi school, who came to Aden from the northern part of the Kingdom of Yemen; Nizari Isma'ilis, or Khojas;[23] Twelvers, whom the British called Dodekites (Ithn'asharis, another

21. I am grateful to Dr. Salah Haddash for pointing out this question to me. Hanafi law might be favorable to a woman with respect to marriage arrangements where her own consent is needed and that of her guardian is not required if she is *baligh (at the age of maturity) and her husband is kufu'* (equal); but according to Hanafi law, it is very difficult for a woman to arrange for a divorce without her husband's consent (Coulson 1963, 185; El Alami and Hinchcliffe 1996, 29).

22. M. H. Awbali claims in his book *Ihtiyal Britaniya li-'Adan wa al-Janub al-'Arabi* (1971, 67) that in the Qu'ayti Sultanate in the East Aden Protectorate, this eclectic judicial system was more appropriate from an Islamic point of view than was the case in Aden (cited in Ghanem 1972, 99n). On India, see M. Anderson 1996, 8, and Parashar 1992, 150.

23. In India, Nizari Isma'ilis followed customarily personal laws of Hindu inspiration; see M. Anderson 1996, 21.

section of the Khojas); and Musta'ili Isma'ilis, or Daudi Bohoras. These religious schools differed little in scholarly terms, but there were marked differences in their customs and religious practices. Khojas, for example, had legislated away women's inheritance rights and opposed any application of sharia that would allow women their rights of succession because that would force families to divide their financial holdings.[24]

As I mentioned earlier, one aspect of British administrative technique was to attract loyalty from various communal or religious groups other than Muslims by allowing separate family legislation alongside sharia (e.g., see *Laws of Aden* 1955, vol. 1). This approach, however, contributed to conservatism regarding women's legal position in the case of both Muslims and groups other than Muslims. A Hindu widow gained inheritance rights over her deceased husband's property only in 1937, when the Hindu Woman's Right to Property Act was passed in India and applied to the Adeni Hindu population.[25] Unilateral repudiation by the husband and the possibility to take a *sarah*, cowife, remained as legal rights of men in Jewish legal practice, even though the latter was discouraged by the Bet Din rabbinical courts and was more widespread in the Kingdom of Yemen. In Aden in particular, widowed Jewish women were not allowed to remarry, which led to expressions such as "the living-dead women in the city of Aden" and "an Adeni Jewish woman dies with her husband" (Ahroni 1994, 147). As Reuben Ahroni describes the life of Jewish women during the mid-1900s, "despite the many advantages the British rule in Aden brought to the Jewish woman, she continued to be the victim of some deep rooted customs. . . . Following her marriage, the bride began to assume the subordinate role traditionally assigned to her in a society, which like the other communities in the region, was generally patriarchal and hierarchical, stratified on the basis of sex and age" (1994, 142).

Adherence to precolonial systems of law contributed to stagnation in the regulation of family matters in general, but judge-made law and the practice of referring to the Hanafi doctrine brought some judgments that favored women more often than other schools of jurisprudence would have. A case where the judge-made law eventually acted in favor of the female litigant is Civil Suit no. 828 of

24. The Cutchi Memon Act of 1920 (Lateef 1990, 70).

25. On the process of introducing this law in India, see Parashar 1992, 79, and Sharma 1994, 36.

1957,[26] in which an Adeni Hanafi woman who had lived for nine months with her newly wed Indian Hanafi husband in India and supported him while there in vain requested maintenance or support *(nafaqa)* from the husband, who stayed in India after the woman moved back to Aden. The principal legal issue the judge was concerned with had to do with the litigants' domicile. Because the husband had never actually resided in Aden, the judge had to decide whether the case could be dealt with in Aden or if the wife had to travel to India to obtain her divorce. In his ruling, the British judge decided to rely on "the principles of natural justice"—to the woman's benefit—because he could not find any reference in available *fiqh* manuals to the problematic question of the litigants' domicile. The judge thus ruled that the woman was entitled to have a divorce in his court because the husband had not replied to her request and thus proved not to fulfill his marital obligations toward her. In a normal case, no dissolution of the marriage would have been granted until evidence of the husband's destitute status was produced in the court and after official channels had been used to forward letters to the husband, a procedure typical of the colonial administration (J. N. D. Anderson 1954, 36–37). Because the case met these requirements, the judge granted the wife her divorce.

Can a Woman Contract a Marriage on Her Own?

A field of litigation where the practice of consulting the Hanafi doctrine brought rulings more favorable to women than would the Shafi'i school involved the issue of *jabr* (compulsion, compulsory marriage) and a guardian's consent to a woman's marriage. However, it must be remembered that the Hanafi doctrine was consulted only in those cases where one or both parties concerned were professing that school and in the case of *jabr* only if the husband was a *kufu'* (equal), a matter that is a further condition in Hanafi law for a legitimate marriage where the wife's guardian's consent is not manifest. A case of interest is Civil Suit no. 577 of 1958 (3 Aden L.R., 71–72),[27] where a father wanted his daughter's mar-

26. The lawsuit is reprinted in Aden Colony, *Law Reports,* vol. 3 (1962), covering cases from 1956 to 1958 and subsequently referred to in the text as 3 Aden L.R., 43–44, and discussed in Ghanem 1972, 94–96.

27. Ghanem discusses the case in his master's thesis, "Social Aspects of the Legal Systems in South-West Arabia" (1972, 117–18).

riage to be dissolved by a court order because it was contracted without his consent. Both the father and the daughter were Hanafis. The judge, Chief Justice Campbell, ruled that the marriage was valid, in regards to both the question of the guardian's consent and the question of whether the husband was *kufu'* (in this case equal to his wife's social status). The daughter was seventeen when she contracted the marriage. For his verdict, the judge relied on Hanafi manuals he had at hand, which were *Mohammedan Law* by Amir Ali[28] and *Hedaya*[29] published by the New Book Company in Lahore, but he also consulted a precedent case from the Bombay judiciary (Case B.H.C. 236 [R.4.Bom. L.R. (Bombay Law Reports)], 611), wherein a husband brought a suit against his father-in-law for the unlawful detention of his wife. In the verdict of the Bombay case, the judge stated: "According to the doctrines of the Hanafi Moslems a female after arriving at the age of puberty without having been married by her father or guardian can select a husband without reference to the wishes of the father or guardian though according to the doctrines of Shafei a virgin whether before or after puberty cannot give herself in marriage without the consent of her father" (3 Aden L.R., 72). It is noteworthy that the practice of consulting precedent cases in considering a verdict comes from the British legal practice, not from the Islamic legal tradition.

This lawsuit bears the legal and moral problem of whether a woman herself can choose her husband. As the judge in Bombay noted, according to the Shafi'is, a virgin cannot give herself in marriage before or after her puberty without her guardian's consent. But according to the Adeni scholar Shaykh al-Mekkawi, it is recommended that she be consulted by sending to her some "trustworthy women" to sound her opinion (al-Mekkawi [1886] 1959, 253–54, also quoted in 4 Aden L.R., 65,[30] and Ghanem 1972, 120). He adds that the guardian should not organize a marriage in case there is any enmity between him and the woman to be married or between her and the husband-to-be. In Civil Suit no. 577 of

28. A modern Hanafi law manual written by an Indian scholar who, contrary to the principles of Islamic law, consulted precedent cases in his discussion of various aspects of Islamic law (see 3 Aden L.R., 44).

29. That is, *Al-idayah fi sharh bidayat al-mubtadiyy*, a famous Hanafi manual that was also applied in Indian courts.

30. 4 Aden L.R. is the reference for State of Aden 1964 (*Law Reports*, vol. 4: *1959–1960*).

1958, the judge noted that the father of the woman whose marriage he wanted to dissolve had lived in Ethiopia for the past eight years, during which time he had neither kept any contact with his family nor provided maintenance for them. He even claimed to have divorced his wife, the mother of the daughter, but the wife denied it. To prove his claim, he had invited his sister to the court to give testimony regarding his divorce, but he himself failed to appear in the court (he was represented by an advocate), a fact the judge noted with disapproval.

In another similar case, Civil Suit no. 154 of 1959 (4 Aden L.R., 64–69), a nineteen-year-old daughter of a well-known family in Aden sought a declaration that the marriage her father contracted for her be made null and void. The case is slightly more complicated than the previous one because the daughter, the plaintiff in the suit, wanted to marry another man. She had earlier asked her uncle, her father's brother, for help. The latter had taken his father, the woman's grandfather, and went to see the *qadi* of Aden, Muhammad Bahamish, to ask him to perform a marriage between his niece and the man she had chosen. The *qadi* had refused because he saw that the proper guardian of the woman, her father, was not with the uncle. Then the woman's father had gone to see the *qadi* and asked him instead to perform a marriage between his daughter and the man he had chosen for her. The *qadi,* who saw that the woman was not agreeing to this marriage, had tried to delay the marriage and had suggested to the father that the families should endeavor to settle the matter among themselves. The father had then gone to another *qadi,* Shaykh Abdul Fatah al-Hitari, an unofficial *qadi,* who acted in Tawahi and whom the British considered a troublemaker. This *qadi* had subsequently performed the marriage between the daughter and the man the father had chosen. This marriage had been performed at midnight in the absence of the bride and her mother and without the consent of either. The court was now to decide whether to accept the suit brought forward by the daughter.

In the court session, acting Chief Justice Wickham indulged in a lengthy discussion on Islamic law regarding whether a father can arrange a marriage for a daughter who is a virgin *(bikr)* but at the age of maturity. In order to show the complicated nature of the case, the judge characterized the plaintiff in the following way: "For some time the plaintiff's father had intended to marry her to the second defendant [the candidate chosen by the father]. When the suggestion was first made to the plaintiff I do not think she raised any objection. She is however a girl of some education who has been to school and is able to speak English. She came to know an Indian whose name is M. and decided he would make a more suitable husband than the second defendant."

By this assertion, the judge indicated that the case involved a modern educated woman at the age of maturity who should thus be allowed to choose her husband. He further declared: "It may well be abhorrent to many people that in modern times a woman can be married to a man whom she does not like without her consent. It is not however my task to consider whether the law is good or bad, but simply to decide what it is and apply it accordingly." Having stated his attitude, the judge then proceeded to consult English-language source books he had at hand on both the Shafi'i law (the plaintiff and defendants were Shafi'is) and the Hanafi law. These books included *Minhaj al-Talibin*, *Hedaya*, Syed Ameer Ali's *Mohammedan Law*, Neal B. E. Baillie's *Digest of Moohummudan Law*, Roland Knyvet Wilson's *Anglo-Muhammadan Law*, Faiz Badruddin Tyabji's *Muhammadan Law*, and the Adeni jurist Shaykh al-Mekkawi's book. He noted that there was no agreement among these authorities regading the question of whether a father can marry his virgin daughter without her consent.

The judge then contrasted the present case with a precedent from an Indian court,[31] in which the judge, after consulting most of the same authorities, had reached the conclusion that such a marriage is null and void. The British judge in Aden concluded that the Indian court ruling was made without regard to what the authorities maintain and decided on his own behalf to dismiss the suit with cost. At the end of his lengthy judgment, he declared, "I arrive at my conclusion with reluctance; but I have no doubt what the law is, and it is my duty to apply it." However, he could have reached a similar ruling to the Indian one by relying on Shaykh al-Mekkawi's book, which asserts that "it is recommended that her [a virgin whether a minor or past puberty] permission should be asked for, that is, he should send to her some trustworthy women to see what is in her soul (i.e. to sound her), and the mother is more fitted for this" ([1886] 1959, 253–54, and as quoted in 4 Aden L.R., 65). Despite quoting this statement in his verdict, the British judge considered his own reading of sharia to be more trustworthy than the local Islamic scholar's elaboration.

31. Case number AIR Madras 1285 from the year 1928.

Virgins and Nonvirgins

In the case where the woman is no longer a virgin, but a *thayyiba*—that is, a woman who has lost her virginity and is thus socially considered a person who already has been married—the Shafi'is, too, maintain that her consent is required in choosing a spouse for her. Civil Suit no. 190 of 1960 provides an interesting detail in a lawsuit concerning the validity of a marriage that was contracted against the woman's will. Here, like in some other lawsuits, what mattered to the British judge was the daughter's religious adherence, not her father's, because the two were not adherents of the same school. The case is interesting from the point of view, too, that the judge reached a quite contrary decision to the one in the previous case, even though he consulted the same books as the judge in the previous case and irrespective of the fact that the situation now involved a *thayyiba*. In general, British judges' eclectic method in consulting Islamic law manuals reflects poorly on the British principles of equity and justice.[32]

The plaintiff, age fifteen when the suit was presented in court and considered a minor, was represented in court by her mother, who was her legal guardian. The plaintiff contested the marriage her father had contracted for her on three grounds: first, because she was brought up as a Hanafi Muslim, she could not be married without her consent, even though her father was a Shafi'i; second, she was too young to be married; and third, her father had married her to the defendant (the husband) from motives of enmity. In his ruling, Acting Chief Justice Gillett, although consulting the same Islamic law manuals as the judge in the previous case, reached the conclusion that the marriage would have been void even if the plaintiff was a Shafi'i. He elaborated: "I note that even the Shafi'i doctrine lays down that it is 'commendable' that a father or guardian as to marriage of a Shafi'i girl should consult her wishes before marriage, although it is not compulsory." He based his decision on his reading of *Minhaj al-Talibin*, the well-known Shafi'i manual, regarding the question of the need to obtain a virgin's consent in marriage (*Minhaj al-Talibin*, 284, as reprinted in the lawsuit, 4 Aden L.R., 45). However, the judge dismissed the plaintiff's claim regarding

32. As J. N. D. Anderson put it, "the views of two or more jurists have often been so combined in a single matter as to produce a result which is, in effect, wholly new" (in *The Muslim World 40*, no. 4, 244, as quoted in R. Knox-Mawer 1956, 516).

her young age in marriage even though she brought a medical report confirming her physical immaturity. The report stated that the girl, age 14⅞ when the marriage took place, was physically not yet fully mature and that she had been menstruating for only five months. The doctor thus recommended the marriage be postponed for a couple of years. The judge ignored the report and ruled that the claim was invalid.

The judge took more seriously the plaintiff's two other claims. He stated that the girl, when reaching puberty, was fully entitled to change her school of religion, but because that has not happened, he had to decide whose school should be considered, the daughter's or the father's. For his argument, he sought support from a precedent case from India. It is an interesting case wherein a daughter, one month after attaining puberty, went to a *qadi* in Bombay with a written note signed by herself denouncing her school of religion (Shafi'i) in order to become an adherent of the Hanafi school. As for her motivation, she stated in court that she had noted her father's "great aversion and unkindness toward her from her birth, and her consequent desire [was] to renounce his doctrine."[33] The Adeni judge, however, considered the present case different from the precedent, and because the plaintiff had been living with her Shafi'i father and had not renounced that doctrine, he ruled that she should be regarded "by the Shariah law" as a Shafi'i, too. But because the plaintiff also put forward evidence that she was brought up as a Hanafi by her mother, the judge came to the conclusion that her announcement of being a Hanafi could not be disregarded and that no renunciation of the Shafi'i school was needed. It is noteworthy that the father had divorced the plaintiff's mother some ten years earlier and that he had unsuccessfully applied to the Supreme Court for guardianship of his daughter, who was now in the mother's guardianship and custody. As a result of the divorce, the court had ordered him to pay maintenance for the daughter. The father had, however, obtained an order from the Magistrate Court only a fortnight after the daughter's marriage to excuse him from paying further maintenance for the plaintiff because she was now married. The daughter used this fact as proof that there was enmity between her and

33. A lawsuit treated in Bombay (R. 4 Bom. L.R. 611), published also in *All India Digest 1811–1911*, 6:s500.

the father. This fact made the judge consult Shaykh al-Mekkawi's book, which considers a marriage contracted without the daughter's consent to be invalid in the case where such enmity exists. As a consequence, the judge announced the marriage to be void on the basis of two of the claims put forward by the plaintiff, a result that might have been different had the judge interpreted the consulted law manuals in a different way.

It is interesting to note that the judge in this case decided to interpret the case according to the school of law followed by the plaintiff, a fifteen-year-old girl. This choice was, however, not so unusual. In cases of conflict where the litigants represented different schools of law, the custom in the Adeni courts at that time was to follow the law of the defendant's school.[34] In this case, however, the defendant was the husband, who was not a party in the dispute over the woman's consent to her marriage. According to J. N. D. Anderson, by that time, 1960, the court in Aden, when dealing with the legal issue of an adult woman's consent in her marriage, had started to follow the Hanafi view, even when all the parties were Shafi'is. This change had occurred, he explains, owing to a tendency among British judges to be influenced by British ideas of equity and justice. As legal means to announce a marriage contracted against an adult virgin's consent void, the judges sought to see possible enmity between the woman and her father—that is, relying on Shaykh al-Mekkawi's reading of Islamic law. In a case where no such evidence was available, the judges relied on "modern" Muslim jurists such as the Indian scholar Ameer Ali, who states in his book *Mohammedan Law* (1929) that any compulsion in contracting a daughter's marriage is foreign to Islam. But as Anderson notes, such a reading does not reflect a proper knowledge of historical texts (1954, 36). Isam Ghanem suggests that the practice to follow Hanafi rather than Shafi'i law was a result, first, of most barristers' being Indian and trained in Hanafi law and, second, of the dearth of English-language reference books available for British judges in Aden courts, in particular on Shafi'i law (1972, 128–29).

34. As stated by J. N. D. Anderson after consulting "the British Judge, a leading Indian Muslim lawyer, the Qadi, and two or three of the most learned local jurists" in the early 1950s (1954, 36).

8. Family and friends greet the arriving wedding couple with ululations in the Alf Layla wa Layla wedding club in Shaykh 'Uthman. Photograph by the author, 1991.

The Regulated Divorce

In colonial legal practice, divorce between Muslims was regulated according to *talaq* and *khul'*. Such a divorce became legal after the husband had reported it to the *ma'dhun*, a *qadi* whom the British had appointed as a marriage notary (*Laws of Aden* 1955, vol. 3, chap. 133, Qadhi Ordinance of 1943). *Khul'* divorce, as initiated by the wife, required the husband's consent and the wife's payment of compensation to him. In contrast to *talaq*, the husband's unilateral right to repudiation, a woman whose husband did not agree on divorce (or who was absent) had to go to court to seek for a judicial dissolution of the marriage, litigated in the Supreme Court. If the court found in favor of the woman, the husband had to pay the remaining share of her *mahr* (deferred dower or what had not been paid of the prompt dower) and maintenance during her *'iddat.*[35]

In divorce cases that came to court, British judges did not necessarily advocate similar voluntarism in protecting suffering women as might have been the case concerning compulsory marriage. A case in point is Civil Suit no. 10 of 1938 (1 Aden L.R., 6–8),[36] litigated before Chief Justice Lawrence. It is a divorce case where the legal problems the judge specified included what constitutes a divorce in writing; a false allegation by a husband of his wife's immorality before marriage; and whether the court should grant the wife a divorce. Both the plaintiff (the wife) and the defendant (the husband) were Hanafi Muslims. The dispute focused on the husband's allegation that the wife was not a virgin (called *virgo intacta* in the court proceedings) when the marriage was consummated. The husband then approached his wife's father, demanding him "to pay all back or make good monies spent on the marriage," as his counsel formulated it in a letter to the father. The plaintiff on her part brought a claim to court demanding a declaration that the defendant had divorced her. According to her, the words "she is of no use to me" (as stated in the husband's counsel's second letter to the plaintiff's father) and the husband's refusal to admit liability to maintain her, together with the demands for damages for the marriage, implied in writing a divorce, according to the Hanafi doctrine. The defendant on his part declined having implied divorce and instead demanded compensation from the wife's guardian. The judge, however, ruled that the allegation of immodesty, even when declared false in the court, concerned a time prior to marriage and could therefore not be considered a basis for the wife to be granted a divorce.

The judge could have taken another approach to the matter and treated the husband's false allegation, which is a serious accusation both from customary and Islamic legal points of view, as cruelty toward the wife and on that basis declared that the wife was entitled to a divorce. However, as Ronald Knox-Mawer pointed out in 1956, in Aden courts mental mistreatment of a wife was no basis for divorce. In his brief essay on Adeni legislation during the 1950s, Knox-Mawer, who by that time acted as chief justice of Aden, compared Adeni law practice

35. The *'iddat* is the waiting period, normally three menstrual cycles, that the woman has to observe before being able to remarry. I discuss divorce practice in colonial Aden in Dahlgren 2004.

36. 1 Aden L.R. is the reference for Aden Colony 1955b (*Law Reports*, vol. 1: *1937–1953*).

with that of India, to the benefit of the latter. In India, the colonial authorities issued in 1939 a law—prepared in cooperation with some local members of the ulema, most notably Mawlana Ashraf Ali Sahib—to counteract the "unspeakable misery [the suffering caused to a divorced woman by the absence of provisions in Hanafi law that should protect her] to innumerable Muslim women in British India" (1956, 517). Knox-Mawer consequently demanded similar legislation in Aden to protect a woman from a husband because "so frail is the marriage tie which binds him to his wife that even though he pronounces the words of repudiation unintentionally, or by way of jest, when he is drunk, or in his deathbed, the divorce is nevertheless legally effective" (517).

What the judge considered the principal legal problem in the case previously described was the validity of an immorality accusation that referred to a time prior to the marriage. As the judge deliberated, "It appears that, according to Hanafi doctrine, allegations of adultery made by a husband against his wife during coverture would entitle her to a divorce. The only authority produced in support of the proposition that allegations of immorality before marriage made by a husband against his wife would entitle her to a divorce, is a decision of some Kazi in Algiers and I do not feel called upon to follow this decision. The suit is dismissed" (1 Aden L.R., 8).

To my understanding, however, the question in this case concerned a husband's seeking compensation for getting into marriage with a *thayyiba* (non-virgin) instead of with a *bikr* (virgin). As is the custom in Aden, *mahr* paid to a *thayyiba* is considerably lower than the one paid to a virgin. Also, the wedding ceremony tends to be more modest than in the case of a virgin marriage, if one is held at all. From the wife's point of view, the legal issue was to get a divorce as compensation for falsely being accused of immodesty. As noted earlier, the court held that the accusation was false. Instead of leaning on this latter legal fact and ordering the parties to seek arbitration to the marital dispute, the judge followed a line of reasoning that proved entirely negative to the woman concerned. It is interesting to note that, according to Robert Bertram Serjeant, the *qadi* of Aden were in the custom of issuing a certificate to a father of a child born without a hymen as proof of her virginity, which was then handed in due course to the daughter's bridegroom. Such a child was called *bint al-nathra* (J. N. D. Anderson 1954, 38n).

Judicial dissolution of marriage is usually followed by litigation concerning custody of children and maintenance of the wife during her *'iddat,* the waiting period before she is able to remarry. Regarding the issue of custody, the judges of the colonial period tended to consider the children's benefit in their decisions (R. Knox-Mawer 1956, 511–12). The woman was usually considered the best custodian for young children, and the man for older offspring.

A more complicated issue is the question of maintenance of the wife during her *'iddat* because different schools of jurisprudence do not agree on the qualified terms. The Shafi'i school maintains that an irrevocably divorced woman *(mubana)* is entitled to maintenance during her *'iddat,* but only in the case where she is pregnant, and in that particular circumstance the maintenance is actually granted to the fetus, not to the woman. However, she is entitled to lodgings. This was the opinion of Shaykh al-Mekkawi, too ([1886] 1959, 177–78). The Hanafi school, by contrast, maintains that the wife should be granted maintenance during her *'iddat* even in cases of irrevocable divorce (El Alami and Hinchcliffe 1996, 23; Ghanem 1972, 129–30).

To make the law practice regarding maintenance more straightforward, the British issued a Criminal Procedure Ordinance entitled *The Maintenance of Wives and Children.*[37] This ordinance is a good example of how a particular familial ideology informed the basic presumptions of the law text. The mere title of the ordinance defines the ones being provided for and the one who is accountable for the legal consequences. The law text provides a ready-made gendering of the parties of litigation. The law is based on what the drafters of the law, the colonial authorities, presumed was the customary sexual division in the family, which is prevalent in Islamic law, too. The way the law is written rules out cases such as Civil Suit no. 828 of 1957 discussed earlier, where it was the woman who had provided for the husband. The only compensation the law could give her was to grant her a divorce.

However, not all wives were entitled to maintenance. Section 327.4 of the ordinance rules that "no wife shall be entitled to receive an allowance from her

37. Criminal Procedure Ordinance, cap. 38, the Maintenance of Wives and Children, *Laws of Aden* 1955, 1:chap. 30. The entire text is reproduced in Ghanem 1972, 89–90.

husband . . . if she is living in adultery, or if, without any sufficient reason, she refuses to live with her husband, or if they are living separately by mutual consent." Only when the dutiful wife fulfills her marital duties to her husband does the law see fit for her to receive maintenance from him.

Divorce cases where the wife brings the suit to court were extremely rare in preindependence Aden, as Ronald Knox-Mawer (1956) asserted. Nevertheless, it is reported that in the 1950s, *talaq,* divorce by repudiation, was rather common. According to the official *Reports for the Years 1957 and 1958,* marriage and divorce registers show seven to eight dissolutions of marital relations for every ten marriages (Aden 1961, 58; see also J. Knox-Mawer 1961, 92–93, and R. Knox-Mawer 1956, 512). However, I have some reason to doubt the accuracy of these high figures. I went through the Marriage and Divorce Register from the Sira District[38] on *zawj* (marriages) and *talaq* (divorces) stored in the Ministry of Justice and Waqf in Tawahi and calculated marriages and divorces for an average month in the early 1950s (October 1951).[39] My calculation showed that 110 marriages and 23 divorces were registered. Even though these figures include records only for Crater and Khormaksar, they show the tendency that prevailed in the 1950s. It is likely that divorce numbers were higher in the Shaykh ʿUthman District, where immigrants from the surrounding countryside and from Yemen tended to reside. Marriages as a rule were contracted in the immigrants' place of origin, whereas when any of them wanted a divorce, it was likely that they reported it to the nearest *qadi* in their present residence, which was Aden. It is also possible that not every marriage was registered, but that people were more eager to register the divorce. However, Ronald Knox-Mawer explained that one reason for the high divorce rate was the custom for the husband to divorce the first wife when he wanted to take a second wife (1956, 514). This consecutive polygyny would then be explainable by the lack of such housing that would accommodate two wives in an acceptable way and by other financial matters. Because men initiated most divorces, it can be said that women did not prefer divorce however difficult their situation was in the marital home. In 1955, the number of divorce petitions

38. The Sira District comprises Crater and Khormaksar. In Aden Peninsula, the other two areas, Maʿalla and Tawahi, form the Mina District.

39. During the hot summer months, fewer marriages are contracted. Likewise, Adenis tend not to contract marriages in between the two *ʿids*—that is, *ʿid al-fitr* and *ʿid al-adha.*

presented before the Supreme Court that were initiated by the wife was only eighteen (R. Knox-Mawer 1956, 513).

As pointed out earlier, in those divorce cases where the wife was the one who took the initiative, the possibility that she would receive maintenance for herself from her previous husband was considered nonexistent based on the different schools of Islamic jurisprudence. Her only option was to return to her father's house or to take a job. Considering the slender labor options for women in pre-independence Aden and the few or nonexistent qualifications most women had at that time outside the normal household chores, she most likely would not be able to find decent work. Based on that fact, Knox-Mawer claimed that about 70 percent of the prostitutes in the mid-1950s were divorced women (1956, 513). If a divorced woman wanted to keep her children, she should at least not marry a "stranger" after her divorce—that is, a man unrelated to her children—because she then risked losing them.

Following the practice in Aden courts of consulting different schools of Islamic jurisprudence, the question of the legal basis for judicial separation *(tafriq)* on the wife's instigation remained a perplexing one. The Hanafi doctrine does not recognize the dissolution of marriage on a juridical decree, but annulment *(faskh)*[40] can be ordered on the basis of nonconsummation of the union or the husband's prolonged absence. Other Sunni schools, however, recognize judicial separation or the dissolution of a marriage contract instigated by the wife on the grounds of the husband's failure to fulfill his marital duties.[41] Although *talaq* was easy for any man to take, he did not escape the communal disapproval in the case where leaving his marriage was considered unjust and caused great distress to the rejected woman and her children.

Because the court under British rule never considered the husband to have a similar duty in marriage as the wife—namely, to make himself available whenever his wife wants sexual intercourse—this was no grounds for divorce. Even

40. *Faskh* refers to the judicial dissolution of the contract of marriage, and it can be initiated even by a third party or the court. *Faskh* is mandatory in the case where the marriage contract is irregular or void (Welchman 1999, 170).

41. Grounds for a wife to ask for judicial dissolution include the exercise of her right of rescission on coming of age, the husband's impotence, and, according to some jurists, his lunacy or certain grave chronic diseases (Schacht 1964, 164).

though in actual life women's sexual satisfaction is considered a requirement for a successful marriage, in colonial-era courts the wife's dissatisfaction provided no legal grounds for liberating her from an unhappy union. Only after independence, when the legal system was entirely reformed, did the courts start to consider it a legitimate reason for divorce. The Shafi'i, Maliki, and Hanbali schools are favorable to court termination of the marriage in the case where the husband fails to provide maintenance for the wife, and the Maliki and Hanbali law schools recognize also the husband's prolonged absence as a legitimate ground for the wife to obtain judicial dissolution. Only the Maliki school considers *dharar* (prejudice, "cruelty") as grounds for a court divorce (El Alami and Hinchcliffe 1996, 30–31). How *dharar* was considered in the Adeni courts varied from case to case, if it was considered at all. As I show later, severe physical abuse was not necessarily considered cruelty with legal consequences.[42]

What Is a Marriage?

The question "What is a marriage?" had legal consequences for maintenance, custody, and succession. It drew up both the husband's and the wife's duties and rights and fixed the conditions for a legitimate child. A court case from 1955 (Miscellaneous Application no. 180 of 1955; 3 Aden L.R., 6–9; discussed in Ghanem 1972, 144) shows the rationalizations that the British judge used on the question of the prerequisites for a marriage to exist in the first place. The case involves an application for an heirship certificate that a widow had filed to claim inheritance rights for her daughter, who was born six months before the marriage took place. The husband had first denied paternity of the child, but after the marriage he acknowledged her as his daughter by accompanying his wife to visit the registrar of births, who issued a birth certificate with both the mother's and father's names on it. The girl was consequently given the father's name. The child had been born out of a relationship similar to the one after marriage but that lacked the legitimacy of a proper marriage and was thus considered *fasid*,

42. As J. N. D. Anderson explains, "[cruelty] is never held to entitle the wife to a judicial dissolution of marriage, but is regarded as an adequate defence to a petition for 'restoration of conjugal rights'; and this, coupled with the wife's continued right to maintenance in such circumstances, would normally induce her husband to divorce her" (1954, 36).

"irregular."[43] The legitimacy of a child requires a relationship either between a man and his wife or a man and his slave, according to the reading of the Islamic law by the British judge. In the court, the child was considered to be an offspring of *zina*, an illicit sexual relationship and thus without the legitimate rights of an offspring in the male lineage. In the court decision, the judge ruled that the girl was not a legitimate child and hence not an heir, and the heirship certificate was issued without her name.

This ruling stood, however, against what Shaykh al-Mekkawi in his book describes as the conditions for a marriage. According to him, the existence of a marriage between a man and a woman who cohabitate and possibly have children is "one of the twenty-six questions which are established by notoriety or hearsay evidence." Thus, it is enough if a reliable witness, such as the couple's neighbor, bears evidence of a marriage. In this situation, it is immaterial to know who performed the ceremony of the marriage contract (al-Mekkawi [1886] 1959, 217–18). In the case just described, the husband had considered the cohabitation as a marriage, which the parties had been unable to perform earlier because of resistance from the respective mothers. For the British judge, the legal question had to do with the moment of marriage taking place, even though the father had later acknowledged the daughter as his legitimate offspring.

An essential condition for a marriage to be valid is that it has been consummated—that is, sexual intercourse *(dukhul)* has taken place. There is, however, no unambiguous view among the schools of Islamic jurisprudence on what the requirements for *dukhul* are. The various interpretations that judges in colonial Aden courts made in cases dealing with the problem of the consummation of marriage can be read also as statements of what they considered sexual intercourse. Following the practice of eclectic choice *(talfiq),* all the main schools of Islamic law were consulted in order to make a court ruling. It was established that the Maliki school is rather vague in its description of *dukhul,* maintaining that it is the staying together of a man and a woman in a place without intrusion for a relatively long time. This interpretation takes it for granted that sexual contact will take place once a man and a woman are left together in a place without

43. An irregular marriage is legally not the same as a marriage declared as void—that is, legally not valid.

outside disturbance: no proof otherwise is needed. The Hanafis differ from this understanding only in respect of the time spent together, indicating that this time does not have to be long.[44] The Hanbali view is more precise on the matter of what should take place between a man and a woman. A legitimate consummation is, according to this *madhhab,* one in which a lustful coveting takes place between the two after the marriage contract. This interpretation naturally raises the question of evidence, as in the Shafi'i view. The Shafi'i idea of *dukhul* requires that "normal and complete sexual intercourse" take place. The evidence problem was resolved in colonial Aden courts, as it was explained, by relying on the view of most Islamic jurists—that the woman's witness should be considered more credible than the man's in such matters after she has taken the oath (Ghanem 1972, 155).

The question of the consummation of marriage was irrelevant in what was called a "regular marriage." It involved a contract signed in the presence of a *qadi* and a public and loud wedding ceremony. Particular importance is appointed to consummation in the marriage ceremony, where *lailat al-dukhla,* "the night of penetration," is the name of the night where the ceremony culminates. In earlier times, the bride's virginity—thus, a penetration—was to be proved by a specialized wedding assistant *(muqaddiyya),* a woman who went from wedding to wedding and who showed a blood-stained bride's underskirt *(futa)* to the groom's and bride's closest female relatives. This practice has been rejected as shameful, and it is considered enough if the groom is satisfied with his bride's virginal quality. Such issues were nevertheless seldom discussed in the colonial courts.

The Disobedient Wife

Interesting data on prevalent gender ideas can be traced in lawsuits that had to do with questions of appropriate accommodation the husband was expected to provide to the wife (*bayt shar'i,* or sharia quarters) and of a disobedient wife *(nashiza).* These trials raised legal definitions on both the husband's and the wife's marital duties. Civil Suit no. 73 of 1951 (1 Aden L.R., 32–34) involved the

44. Note that here it is not a question of cohabitation, but simply of a man and a woman "staying together" in a closed room.

rather common problem of whether a wife was entitled to leave her marital home on the basis that her husband had failed to provide her with sharia quarters. The husband was the plaintiff, demanding restoration of his conjugal rights. In the Supreme Court session, the circumstances of the marriage were described in both the wife's and the husband's testimonies. The British judge drew a conclusion on the basis of these two testimonies but felt the need to raise the question of the woman's trustworthiness: "There may be circumstances in which such a plea [for sharia quarters] would provide a defence [against restoration of conjugal rights], but each case has to be decided on its merits. In this case the wife lived with the husband only for ten or twelve days. There is no evidence at all that during this period she demanded sharia quarters. In fact it is clear that she did not raise the point until she had failed to get her own way over the cupboard. She then demanded her sharia quarters and almost immediately left her husband."

Judge Nunn established that the wife's dissatisfaction was of earlier origin and had to do with the husband's inability to provide her material needs. It was agreed before the marriage that the husband would buy her a cupboard on the occasion of the *subhia,* the tea party given by his mother after the wedding to female relatives and friends to introduce the new daughter-in-law.[45] However, the husband failed to provide the *subhia* gift. On this basis, the judge felt it proper to raise the issue of her being disobedient *(nushuz)* and ruled in favor of the husband.

The details of this judgment indicate that the housing arrangement was very congested. The husband had taken his wife to live in his father's house, a typical Aden house with one room, a kitchen, a courtyard, and a veranda.[46] The husband's father was the head tenant in the house and lived with his wife (the husband's stepmother), his married daughter, and unmarried daughter. The married daughter's husband was a seaman who resided in the house only occasionally. In the court, the husband asserted that the family had given the only room to the

45. *Subhia* gifts form a part of the wedding expenses that the husband has to stand for and that are agreed upon between the families when a wedding is negotiated. See my article on *mahr* and other marriage expenses (Dahlgren 2005).

46. The British used the term *veranda* for an open-air courtyard that separates the gate to the alley from the door to the living room. It is often a congested space whose only purpose is to limit the view from the street into the house.

new wife, but it became evident that while the husband was out at work during the night, other family members used the room. On this basis, the judge ruled that the housing arrangement did not meet the legal qualifications for sharia quarters. From the point of view of the legal issue at stake, he nevertheless considered this fact irrelevant. Instead, he pointed out that the wife's attempt to stay in her new home was not serious. The length of her stay and the fact that she had caused trouble to her husband when she did not get her way in a quarrel over a cupboard indicated her character to the judge. On that basis, the judge ruled that she had not made enough effort to fulfill her marital duties and thus decided the case in the husband's favor.

In making his decision, the judge consulted Shaykh al-Mekkawi's book, too, where this nineteenth-century Adeni legal expert discusses the problem of housing a newly wed couple in the light of the practical circumstances that this arrangement raises. According to al-Mekkawi, if the wife is not willing to live with her husband's people, he is bound to lodge her in a separate house ([1886] 1959, 188). This requirement, however, the British judge considered to be too much to demand against the background of the bad housing situation. Instead, he preferred the interpretation of a British expert on Anglo-Indian law, Sir Roland Wilson in his book *Anglo-Muhammadan Law*. The judge considered this manual, popular in British India, as "authoritative" in comparison to al-Mekkawi's book, which he described as "a useful little treatise." Wilson interprets sharia quarters as premises that "allow her the use of an apartment from which she may exclude all persons except her husband himself."[47]

However, as Ghanem points out, the British judge had used only part of what the Adeni expert on marital customs maintained. Shaykh al-Mekkawi deals in detail with the question of whether the husband is bound to lodge his wife in a house without his relatives. He asserts: "Yes, if she is not willing to live with his people; or if he has a plurality of wives, each of them can dun him for a separate house, which should have a kitchen and privy. If he vacates for her a tenement of the same house, provided with bolts and locks, it would suffice for her. The house varies (in description and dimensions) with the condition of different people"

47. Sir Roland Wilson, *Anglo-Muhammadan Law*, 6th ed., 132, as reproduced in the judgment (1 Aden L.R., 33).

([1886] 1959, 187–88). The learned shaykh deals here with the actual problem in the Adeni virilocal system—that is, that the wife has to get along with her husband's relatives. This fact the British judge put aside even though he maintained that the demand for sharia quarters was a consequence of a quarrel between the wife and her in-laws about the use of her room. According to al-Mekkawi, a new wife should have her own kitchen and toilet, which would liberate her from submission under the hierarchy of the in-laws' house. However, al-Mekkawi's interpretation of sharia quarters did not become established in the colonial courts. One of the reasons for that might have been the continually deteriorating housing situation in Aden in the middle of the twentieth century.

The lawsuit involved a legal problem, which at that time often came up in the magistrate courts. This particular case, however, was litigated in the Supreme Court. This fact led the judge to allow himself to comment on the question of proper accommodation in a broader light, taking into consideration the prevailing social circumstances: "I desire to add certain observations by way of *obiter dicta.* It is common knowledge that in Aden it is extremely difficult for the less wealthy classes to obtain houses or even separate rooms in houses. It is customary for brides either to continue living with their parents after marriage or to go to live with their husbands' parents, and it is not unusual when a domestic quarrel takes place for the wife to withdraw from the husband and then, but not till then, put forward a claim to sharia quarters, which she knows very well the husband cannot satisfy because of the housing shortage" (Ag. Judge Nunn in 1 Aden L.R., 34). In this statement, the judge revealed his attitude toward the defendant, the wife. He saw her as one more example in a row of incidences where women used questionable means to solve domestic problems. The statement indicates his distrust of local women and tells of prejudices regarding women's alleged manipulative behavior.

This attitude comes up also in another decision the same judge made in a similar lawsuit. In Criminal Appeal no. 39 of 1951 (1 Aden L.R., 118), the respondent-wife had lived for some months with the husband (the appellant) in his parents' house. When domestic quarrels arose between her and his family, she made the claim for sharia quarters. The appellant was unable to provide separate quarters for her, so she left him. After that, the appellant refused to maintain the wife, and she obtained an order against him in the court of the chief magistrate for the payment of a monthly maintenance allowance. The husband appealed for a revision of the court order on the allowance payment. The judge dismissed the appeal. The judge stated in his decision: "It has been held by this court that if a Muslim husband does not provide his wife with the separate quarters to which she is entitled under the Sharia law, she is justified in leaving him and claiming maintenance. The fact that it is customary in Aden for wives to waive this right cannot prevent them from claiming the right if they wish: nor can a wife contract out of the right: nor is the great difficulty in obtaining houses a defense to the husband when she does claim the right." In order to highlight the "injustice" of the case, the judge added at the end: "The husband has his remedy since he may divorce the wife at will." On the one hand, the judge's attitude toward "wives who waive this right" tells of his sincere attempt to judge and take into consideration the prevalent social circumstances where the law is implemented, but on the other hand it neglects the social conditions that made women use this legal option and the fact that in divorce cases women had very few legal assets on their side, a matter of fact that the judge indirectly acknowledged by stating that the husband could have his compensation anyway.

These law cases show how the colonial court system established a system of "facts" relevant to the hearing of a case. As David Cohen reminds us, in the British court system there was a remarkable distinction between what the courts saw as appropriate, relevant, and correct facts and arguments and what the litigants on their part saw as relevant, appropriate, and correct. This situation created two discordant discourses in the courts: one consisting of what the court wanted to hear and the other of what the litigants and their advocates presented (1991, 241, 252).

These divorce cases are just two examples of many that bear evidence against the assumption that a European colonial power would improve women's position before the law. It should be kept in mind that the legal status of women in Britain at that time was not the same as it is today and that even there a male bias informed the British law and legal practice.[48] For example, the British never brought female judges to work in Aden courts. Thus, in regard to what remained the only legal step the British took to improve women's position before the law, the Child Marriage Restraint Ordinance (1939), it would be inadequate to argue,

48. As William Cornish and G. de N. Clark assert, the Victorian vision of marital relations proved resilient and continued to inform the law during the twentieth century (1989, 382). I discuss the legal question of the disobedient wife in Dahlgren 2003.

9. A mother dances with her bride daughter in the Alf Layla wa Layla club after the club was extended and covered with a roof. Photograph by the author, 2001.

as Sayed Hassan Amin does, that "in the area of family law, the British had taken several steps to remove customary laws which discriminated against women" (1987, 36).[49] After all, as pointed out earlier, the British were reluctant to change matters of "religion and custom" in concerns that did not stand as an obstacle to the colonial rule. This fact can be read in Criminal Appeal no. 39, where the judge unburdened his frustration regarding the "inadequate demands of wives": "Since by the Law of Aden the domestic relationship of husband and wife is governed by their domestic law, the courts are obliged to recognise Sharia law in cases such as these" (Ag. Judge Nunn in 1 Aden L.R., 118).

The British Family Compared

From Civil Suit no. 839 of 1956 (3 Aden L.R., 24–26), we can get an idea of the kind of attitudes that prevailed in British courts in regard to gender division in

49. In another context, Amin, otherwise sympathetic to the British, admits that the British colonists' impact on the legal system in Aden "is by far less than what it has been the case of other former British colonies such as India and Pakistan" (1987, 35).

the British family. This case involved a deserted wife whose husband had ceased to pay the rent of the house where the wife and their children lived, resulting in an attempt by the head tenant to evict the family. The wife had tried to pay the rent on her own, but the head tenant refused to receive it. In his judgment, the judge saw fit to compare the wife's position to that of a deserted wife in Britain. In order to do that, he referred to three preceding cases in British courts. In one of the cases, it was held that "[t]he reason is because a wife, so long as she behaves herself properly, has a special position in the matrimonial home. She is not the sub-tenant or licensee of her husband. It is his duty to provide a roof over her head" (1 K.B., 0. 311 [1950], as cited in 3 Aden L.R., 17). As this statement makes clear, a wife's obedience was an issue with legal consequences in British courts as well at the time. However, in the Adeni case the husband-defendant stated that the law concerning the deserted wife in Britain was not applicable to deserted wives in Aden. The judge responded: "It is true that the rights of a wife here are very much less than in England. She can be divorced at will and she can claim no right to maintenance after divorce. Nevertheless I think that her position in all essentials is the same and that she has this 'very special position in the home' referred to." In this particular case, the judge's positive ruling in favor of the woman lay in his basing his decision on the fact that the wife was not divorced. According to the "domestic law," a husband was liable to continue maintaining a wife he had not divorced.

In the two cases on sharia quarters, the court took as a vantage point the question of whether the legal requirements for a marriage were present or not. These requirements were measured, on the one hand, by the extent the parties fulfilled their duties and, on the other, by how well they could obtain their marital rights. In these judgments, it can be read that the husband's duty was to provide his wife with acceptable accommodation, and if the latter was provided, the wife's duty was to be present there. In another court case from 1958, Chief Justice Campbell referred to the husband's conjugal rights: "to have his house run by his wife, to have marital relations and to have his children looked after by her in his house."[50] Classical schools of *fiqh* are not unanimous about the duties

50. Chief Justice Campbell in Civil Suit no. 951 of 1957, as quoted in a judgment delivered on October 25, 1958, 3 Aden L.R., 69–70, discussed also in Ghanem 1972, 162.

of a husband and wife in marriage. Judge Campbell's opinion tells more about his own attitude toward the matter than about his careful study of the various judicial opinions.

The lawsuits concerning a disobedient wife *(nashiza)* provide more information about the husband's and wife's duties as constituted in the court practice. In each of these cases, the husband brought the suit in order to get a legal order against his wife requiring her to return to the marital home and resume performing her marital duties toward him. If the wife disobeyed, she could be declared in court a *nashiza*—that is, a disobedient person and a runaway, who would then no longer enjoy the rights, including maintenance and moral respect, attested to a dutiful wife. Islamic law does not recognize a disobedient male, and a husband who fails to fulfill his marital duties does not risk a similar legally sanctioned moral stigma. In Civil Suit no. 951 of 1957, the chief justice considered the wife's claim of legitimate departure from her marital home to be based simply on a "trifling quarrel" and thus declared her a runaway (3 Aden L.R., 69–70).

Another case of interest where the woman was declared a *nashiza* is Original Civil Suit no. 575 of 1958 (3 Aden L.R., 67–68). This lawsuit concerned restoration of the husband's conjugal rights, which the wife contested on the basis of cruelty and absence of sharia quarters. The house where the married couple and their child lived together with the husband's mother and stepdaughter consisted of a room, a courtyard (where the cooking and most of the household work was performed), and a cabin. The husband made the wife's departure from this home dramatic by assaulting her and accusing her of stealing money. He filed an allegation of theft that same evening in the local police station. He found the money afterward, however, and withdrew the charge. In the judgment, the judge explained: "This is a suit for the restitution of conjugal rights. It is resisted by the wife upon the usual grounds of cruelty and absence of Shariah accommodation."

By taking the attitude of "the usual grounds," the judge revealed his bias. He expressed little sympathy toward a woman who came to court because of domestic hardship. The judge also ruled against the defendant's claim that the dwelling did not fill the requirements of a sharia accommodation based on the claim that the only adult stranger to the wife was her mother-in-law. In the cruelty issue, the judge's decision informs us of what he thought was to be considered cruelty. It was established in the decision that the evening the defendant left her husband, he had beaten her, and there was blood on her face. But according to the judge,

"I cannot find, however, that this is evidence of persistent cruelty which would make it dangerous to her health for the defendant to return and live with her husband." Instead, what the judge did consider cruelty was the husband's charge of theft and his reporting the matter to the police station: "I think that this was the most horrible thing for a husband to do and it showed that he must be completely devoid of any affection for his wife and shows that he can have no decent feelings whatever."

The judge was obviously conscious of the moral problems in his considering an accusation of theft made to the authorities as cruelty, yet he did not feel the same about a woman's being beaten in the face so that she bleeds, and he tried to rationalize this behavior by claiming that it was in accordance with the local customs and values. He clarified: "this court must regretfully accept that the marriage contract of these persons is a business arrangement only, and the matter of mental cruelty can, I feel, not be allowed to have very much weight in Aden." The wife was thus given ten days to return to the husband's house and restore his conjugal rights. In failing to do so, she would risk being declared a *nashiza*.[51]

Another lawsuit offers further evidence of this British judge's attitude regarding domestic cruelty. In Original Civil Suit no. 686 of 1958 (3 Aden L.R., 75), the husband had twice locked his wife inside the marital home before going to his office. As a result, the wife left him. The suit involved the husband's demand for restoration of conjugal rights and the wife's resistance on the grounds of mental cruelty. The judge ruled in favor of the husband on the grounds that, according to his understanding, under the sharia law a Muslim wife must not leave the marital home without her husband's permission. Likewise, because it was impossible to hold that locking up the wife inside the home against her will was actual cruelty, there was no basis for her leaving him. The judge elaborated: "The husband says he did this for her protection and she could have got out as she had a key, which she could have given to neighbours who would have unlocked the padlock. I am satisfied he is telling lies as he had to admit that there is an inside lock which

51. Ghanem is not happy with the label "business arrangement" and explains: "[the rulings] regarding mental cruelty [show] how some Colonial Judges were prejudiced in their outlook upon Muslim society, and it is submitted that a Muslim marriage is far from being a business arrangement." This label, according to him, reflected "a poor attitude towards the Aden community by the Chief Justice at the time" (1972, 165).

would have protected her equally well." Having said this, however, the judge anyhow ruled in favor of the husband and ordered the wife to return to him within ten days. No conditions were attached to the court order to ensure that the husband would not repeat this action.

Conclusions

These examples of legal interpretation and practice in the colonial Aden court draw a picture of a particular familial ideology. This ideology has both moral and economic aspects. On the moral side, the familial ideology outlines the duties and rights of both husband and wife, which differ in function but complement each other. Obeying her husband and carrying out her duties are the requirements for a woman, entitling her to the rights that a wife's position brings about. Her moral value is constructed in her fulfilling her marital duties, and thus it is only as a dutiful wife that she safeguards her moral dignity and legal rights. The family is seen as a unit, which has clear division of duties so that all members contribute to the unit's well-being. As a consequence, the family is constructed as a moral necessity, a social unit that both determines its members and allows them to fulfill the moral obligations these family roles require. Outside the security of the family, a person lacks both the moral legitimacy that the unit effects and the chances that it allows to fulfill the moral obligations reserved for both sexes. This moral aspect of the familial ideology naturalizes gender roles because the family is presented as the only site where the morality of the sexes can be properly created and nurtured. However, the family's economic aspect can be viewed as being equally important to the naturalization of the gender roles because it complements the moral dependency the spouses enjoy in the familial ideology. By acting disobediently, the wife loses her means of subsistence, as manifested in the practice of law.

Even though the colonial period family legislation was not based on codified law, legal practice was constructed on the economic dependency between the man and the woman. However, men and women's contributions to the single unit were not viewed in similar terms. Once the family dissolved, the legal practice considered all the property accumulated during the marriage as belonging to the husband, unless the wife could prove in court that particular property belonged to her, such as her *mahr* (dower). But even the latter was not automatically allotted to the wife. In Civil Suit no. 12 of 1938 (1 Aden L.R., 11–13), the judge ruled in favor of the husband in a dispute concerning property the wife had brought to the marital home. A Somali couple permanently residing in Aden had contracted a marriage in Aden and divorced there at the husband's initiative. Even though it is customary in Aden for the bride's family to provide furniture to the marital home at the wedding, the judge dealt with the issue as a Somali custom called *dibad* in its particular application in the British Somaliland. After listening to several witnesses' interpretations of this Somali custom, most of them laypeople without legal authority and all of them men, the judge ruled that the property belonged to the husband-defendant. With a different legal approach, the ruling might have been favorable to the woman.

In divorce, the wife kept her solemn right to her *mahr,* including any delayed part of the dower *(daf'a mu'ajjal),* provided she did not instigate the divorce. She did not have the obligation to maintain the family from her own property. In a divorce case, the wife was entitled—provided she did not spoil her chances with "improper behavior"—to maintenance (food, clothing, and lodging) under particular circumstances during her *'iddat,* the waiting period before she could remarry. In cases where the wife also participated in a subsistence economy outside the home, her own income did not have the same legal status as the husband's.

The wife's duties were further demonstrated in the legal term *nushuz,* "disobedience." Even though *nushuz* is a legal concept in Islamic law, the way it is applied, if at all, varies from one country to another. By obeying and fulfilling her duties toward her husband, the wife was established as having secured the moral and economic well-being she would receive as a dutiful member in the marital home. By failing to conduct herself properly, she risked not only losing that security, but also being proclaimed an outcast in a public court. This way, the legal discourse contributed to making her comply with the familial ideology. In contrast, the legal claim of the restoration of marital rights is in Islamic law reserved for men only; women could attain a divorce only in cases where the husband did not fulfill his duty to maintain her.

However, the familial ideology cannot be described as patriarchal as such. As the court practice indicates, women had few legal assets on their side in comparison to men. In addition, concrete circumstances made it often more difficult for women to pursue their legal interests because it was considered shameful for women to appear in the court in the first place (Bujra 1971, 159). However, the legal practice manifested aspects that can be viewed as "mother's right," too. The mother's contribution to the education and upbringing of the children was considered more enduring than the father's. As pointed out earlier, children's religious adherence, for example, was considered to follow the mother's in cases where the spouses adhered to a different school of Islamic jurisprudence. Likewise, in disputed cases regarding whether a marriage had been consummated or not, the woman's testimony in court was considered more reliable than the man's. Besides, the familial ideology did not represent a devaluing discourse on women's duties in the family—that is, raising children and running the household; on the contrary, these duties were seen as being equally important to the family's well-being.

The European colonial power transformed Islamic law to serve its rule by accommodating a certain colonial form of Islam, known as "Anglo-Muhammadan law" in other parts of the empire. In principle, the legal practice was not meant to change the local custom in family matters, but in actual terms it did form a particular practice unique to the background of Adeni history, both before and after the British rule. In particular cases, the colonial reading of Islamic law stood against the interpretation of the local *fuqaha'*, Islamic scholars. In part, this transformation stemmed from British judges' preferences for different authoritative reference books than those used by the local ulema. The colonial legal practice reformed gender relations only in details, and the biggest contribution to women's legal rights had to do with the application to the Hanafi doctrine—which in some aspects was more favorable to women, such as in cases of consent for the marriage of postpubertal virgin women. Nevertheless, this "contribution" was no novelty in Adeni legal practice, as al-Mekkawi's treatise demonstrates.

The Child Marriage Restraint Ordinance, enacted in 1939, remains the most important law reform of the colonial period. However, in contrast to Africa, where during the early years of colonial rule the European officials sometimes looked with sympathy on women who testified that they had been forced into marriage against their will, as Roberts and Mann assert (1991, 41), in Aden the British practitioners of law often evidenced an unsympathetic attitude toward female litigants based on their reading of Islamic law as being unfavorable to the woman in the first place. The way British judges interpreted Islamic law and treated female litigants in court contributed to the endurance of traditionalist attitudes and practices toward women and thus to the permanence of gender relations unfavorable to women.

The legal discourse referred to in this chapter in the form of law texts, commentaries on Islamic law, and court judgments offers examples of official interpretations of family and gender relations. As the cases discussed show, the authoritative discourse represents solely male voices because no women were involved in this discourse in the colonial period, as either Muslim scholars or court judges or authors of commentaries on Islamic law. This absence of women was not owing to some limitations on women to act as judges, as was the case in North Yemen during the time of the Arab Republic (Ghanem 1981, 12). Nor did the British bring female judges to Aden, and they thus contributed to the male dominance in legal practice. Indian and local barristers and solicitors were men, too. The conflict between the colonial judges and the local Islamic scholars, as manifested in the struggle to control the sharia practice in Aden courts, did not involve gender relations because the British adjusted to what they presumed a stability in the local sex/gender system. Instead, the British attitude mirrored a colonial hierarchical relationship, where the ruling power accommodated its allegedly secular legal practice and systematic hierarchy of courts to a field they understood as religious, as Islamic jurisprudence and hierarchy of the learned were treated.

However, it is questionable to consider the British colonial practice as being devoid of Christian and Enlightenment values: on the contrary, these values contributed to the understanding of Islamic law as "religion" and the colonial legal practice as "secular" and thus based on rationality in contrast to faith. The British judge's reluctance to rule in favor of a woman respondent in a divorce case, because "it is customary in Aden for wives to make excessive demands for sharia quarters," was rationalized with the statement that Islamic law was the "domestic law" in Aden and thus governed marital relations, whether fair or not. The British idea of not touching "religion and custom" can be thus seen to represent a colonial outlook where the law was viewed from a rule-oriented approach and where the inferior local custom was contrasted to the empire's rational practice in the name of establishing and maintaining a superior political order and domination.[52] Let us then see how independence transformed the state legal scene.

52. See Roberts and Mann 1991 on the role of the rule of law in maintaining political dominance in colonial Africa.

4 The Making of the New Yemeni Woman

> The family ties, in all [their] forms, were not subject to a unified system except the feudal relations which made of the noblest human ties a business house and made the fate of the Yemeni women in the hand of the highest bidder.
>
> —Preamble, Law no. 1 of 1974 in Connection to the Family (PDRY Ministry of Information translation)

IN THIS CHAPTER, I discuss the emerging familial ideology that patterned the PDRY era (1967–90) and what happened to it after Yemeni unification. In an attempt to show how this new ideology did not simply emerge from nothing and that it did not represent a radical break with the previous period, I describe its roots within the background of the local history. I also discuss in detail the first codified law on the family: the Family Law of 1974 (Law no. 1 of 1974 in Connection to the Family; see appendix B) and compare its provisions to the demands for reform that were made earlier. I then describe the process that brought about the unified code for the family of the new Yemen Republic in 1992. I discuss these legal changes against the background of court practice and the opening of the legal profession to women.

After independence, Islamic law of the Shafi'i school and the local custom (*'urf*) became the main sources of law (Amin 1987, 28). However, the Hanafi school remained a reference, too, even though most Indian Hanafis had left the country with the withdrawal of British rule beginning in 1967. In the early years of independence, no big changes were made to the legal system, and colonial laws remained in force as long they did not contravene the new regime (Molyneux 1985, 150). Members of the judiciary affiliated with the colonial rule were dismissed in the early years of independence, and before local judges could be trained abroad (Ghanem 1972, 167), Sudanese law specialists came to replace the colonial judges with interpretations that better suited the new regime's aspirations. The court language was changed from English to Arabic as part of the measure to Arabicize the administration. The training of indigenous legal personnel, including women for the first time alongside men, started in 1972 when the Institute for Legal Studies was opened, and the training of judges began one year later. The Law Faculty of Aden University was established in 1978 (Ismael and Ismael 1986, 50). In the late 1980s, the number of female law students climbed to 125 in comparison to 283 male students (PDRY 1990, 92).[1]

One of the big tasks set for the revolution was to transform the family and free women from "the oppression and subjugation of colonialism and feudalism [and from] subjugation to the fathers, brothers and husbands," as it was described in the documents of the first congress of the General Union of Yemeni Women, held in Sayun in 1974 (General Union of Yemeni Women 1977, 10–11).[2] It was maintained that both society at large and the family were responsible for the oppression of women. The primary condition for a woman's emancipation was set in her economic independence from a man. As I suggested in the previous chapter, the normative family ideal in the colonial era established a provider/dependent relationship between the man and the woman in marriage. The revolutionary discourse applied the idioms of "women's emancipation" *(tahrir al-mar'a)* and "the new Yemeni woman" *(al-mar'a al-gadida)*[3] so that this relationship was held as a starting point for the criticism of the earlier state of affairs.[4] Educational and job opportunities were accordingly established for women as safeguards of their economic independence. As Maxine Molyneux has suggested, this discourse linked the politics of women's emancipation to the gender equality ideology characteristic of the "socialist modernization" politics of countries such as the German Democratic Republic, the USSR, and Cuba (1991, 267). However, as I argue here, the new politics should not be viewed only against this socialist

1. During that period, university faculties of medicine and education had more female students than male.

2. The draft analysis, discussed in the women's congress, was written by Salem Bukair, at that time lecturer and later rector at Aden University and member of the politburo of the ruling Yemeni Socialist Party.

3. I am following here the colloquial pronunciation where *g* is pronounced as in the English word *good*.

4. As I pointed out in the introduction, these idioms have their root in the Egyptian reform movement at the turn of the twentieth century. See al-Ali 2000, 56, and Badran 1993.

background: after all, the foundation for the changes had already been laid during the time of colonialism, when there were no links to these socialist regimes. According to Ziad Abu-Amr, the new politics were based on the need to begin political, social, and economic transformations to undermine the old "social class" composition of society (1986, 197–98)[5] so that the traditional elites (the *sada* and the *mashayikh*) and the new elites of the local bourgeoisie and members of the previous administration (as well as tribal leaders and large landlords in the countryside) would be stripped of their privileges and material bases.

After independence, the British military base and its service community left Aden and with them a number of European entrepreneurs and other businesspeople. One of the most urgent needs felt by the new rulers was to establish national production to replace the foreign industries and to train local people to take positions earlier occupied by foreigners. In the early years, it was obvious that women were needed in the workforce simply because of a labor shortage, but later this was no longer the case. Economic necessity does not explain the call for women's emancipation in the context of the revolution. First, although the founding of a national industry was an urgent need of the newly established state, the roots of women's emancipation lay in the times preceding independence, when changes were demanded from various directions both in family relations and in women's position at large, as I later show. Second, the official[6] women's liberation policies were not limited to the call for women to join the labor market.

In political speeches and pamphlets, earlier customs and ideologies linked to the family were severely criticized. Salim Rubaya 'Ali, the country's second president, declared the family as the site of women's oppression, where the father, brother, or husband practiced absolute authority over the daughter, sister, or wife and stripped her of her basic human rights, such as choosing her husband, leaving the home whenever she preferred, and practicing control over the joint property

5. See chapter 2 for critical remarks on Abu-Amr's concept of "social class."

6. By "official" during the PDRY period, I refer to the state policies of the ruling government and the parties that formed it. These parties included the NLF, its ally parties, and the later coalitions, most notably the Yemeni Socialist Party. Formed in 1978, the party is a coalition of the NLF, the Ba'ath Party (pro-Syrian Ba'athist), and the small Communist Party People's Democratic Union (earlier called al-Salafi Youth). On these parties' politics, see Halliday 1975, 214–22, and 1979, 10; PDRY 1974, 64.

created during the marriage.[7] Thus, her economic liberation was not enough. In the analysis of women's position before independence, early marriage was pointed to as a result of paternal domestic authority, who considered only his own personal interests in signing a marriage contract on her behalf.[8] The family was presented as a unit where a woman's work was not given any value and where she was treated as economically dependent, no matter how hard she worked in the household or outside in doing wage labor or in cultivating the land and tending cattle.[9]

The official discourse presented woman's subordination to be manifested also in the form of popular proverbs *(amthal)*. Proverbs such as "The minds of women are in their knees" and "Whoever listens to women is of them" were given in Women's Union documents as evidence of a culture of men's domination over women. Furthermore, the mere word *woman* was explained to be such an evil metaphor that after uttering it, one needed to purify oneself by adding the expression "May Allah honor you."[10] Saying it was similar to encountering the evil eye *(al-'ayn)*, which required purifying measures to get rid of the harm and misfortune it was believed to bring to one.

The Women's Union documents further maintained that the earlier system and its abuse of Islam, which they termed "priestly feudalism," imposed the veil on women. The most outrageous custom of that era, the documents explained, was that in some areas of the country the wife was obliged to veil in front of her brother-in-law even if they all lived in the same house. This exceptional practice was considered despicable because it limited a woman's movement inside her own home. At that time, the popular proverb "The chaste woman does not frequently leave her husband's house" was further given as evidence of a woman's inferior status (General Union of Yemeni Women 1977, 13). Her life was confined "inside four walls," as another popular expression described it.

The critique of the state of affairs in the family before independence established the principles for the new Yemeni woman. This discourse became the

7. Speech by Salim Rubaya 'Ali at the first congress of the Women's Union (General Union of Yemeni Women 1977, 4).

8. Study on conditions of Yemeni women (General Union of Yemeni Women 1977, 13).

9. Speech by Salim Rubaya 'Ali (General Union of Yemeni Women 1977, 4).

10. Study on condition of Yemeni women (General Union of Yemeni Women 1977, 12–13). See also al-Zafari 1997.

official rhetoric on woman, man, and the family after independence, but it was toned down at the end of the 1980s. In official texts, such as speeches by leading politicians, governmental five-year plans and programs, and party documents, the policy was referred to in a general manner,[11] but it was elaborated more fully in the Women's Union documents and speeches by leading male politicians before women's gatherings.[12] It was held that the woman should be liberated from the yoke of the patriarchal family and that her moral value should be rehabilitated. Eradicating illiteracy and securing women's educational opportunities up to a university level were seen as important steps in this work.

The Producer and the Mother

In the new state constitution, the woman was presented as a "producer" and a "mother" and in these two capacities given equal rights to men. She was now called "half the society" *(al-mar'a nusf al-mugtama'),* as it was commonly expressed in Adeni colloquial speech. In this basic law, work was presented as a duty for every able-bodied citizen. Women's emancipation was also an important aspect of the larger social transformation that the new regime was aiming to accomplish. The new policies were far more radical in the countryside than in Aden because the former had been left untouched by the colonial rule and largely isolated from the outside world. As I later show, the demand for women's emancipation in Aden was not something new brought out by the revolutionaries, but was common already during the colonial era within varying circles eager to modernize the society and eradicate "backward" customs and traditions.

An essential role in social change was allotted to the new family, which was to bring up new citizens who would acquire "new ideas." Such ideas were based on economic, social, and educational equality irrespective of race, ethnic origin, religious adherence, language, level of education, social status, or gender, as inscribed

11. See, for example, the 1974 interview with Abdul Fattah Isma'il in PDRY 1974, 58–59; 'Ali 1977 (unpublished document), 8, 10–11, 19–20, 44; PDRY 1977, 32, and 1979, 130; and Yemeni Socialist Party 1979, 77, 181.

12. For example, General Union of Yemeni Women 1977; the extraordinary congress held in 1981 (*Watha'iq al-mu'tamar al-istithna'iyy 1981* 1983); and the fourth congress (*Watha'iq al-mu'tamar al-'am al-rabi'* 1986).

in the 1970 Constitution of the People's Democratic Republic of Yemen (chap. I, art. 34, 19). In this project, women were given a central role as mothers, who bear the main responsibility for the upbringing of children in the "new family."

The new familial ideology constructed the woman in a dual role of producer in the national economy and mother of the future enlightened generation. Her role as principal educator of children was in continuity with the earlier ideology that limited the woman's role to the kinship domain. The marked difference from the earlier situation was that the woman was now allowed the role of mother as an educated person, rational *('aqliyya)* enough to make her own decisions and capable of judging what is right and wrong. The new familial ideology liberated the woman from the irrational capacity linked to her earlier position, but not from the burden of tending children. In this way, the new ideology relieved men of the important and respected role of bringing up the children.

Even though these aims seem radical, they were continuous with the modernization that the British had brought along in Aden but left incomplete. Thus, the socialists in actual fact only expanded the field of the modern and incorporated new groups, most notably women, to the field of modern society as they literally changed the color of the British modernity. The new familial ideology was described as being based on gender equality, but in actual terms it was based on the notion of complementarity in gender roles. Complementarity has roots both in Islam and in local custom. In both, the complementary roles of man and woman are explained as contributing to the founding of a "happy family." In everyday life, this happy family provides a strong ground for individual self-presentation, which is gendered in line with the complementary roles the family assigns to each sex.

The complementarity of family roles links to relationality, where the person sees himself or herself in relational terms to others. As Suad Joseph has asserted, relational self-images have fluid boundaries between one's own and the other's needs. This feeling of connectivity, if linked to patriarchy, creates hierarchical family formations. Patriarchy, according to Joseph, means the privileging of males and seniors and the mobilization of kinship structures, morality, and idioms to legitimate and institutionalize domination by gender and age (1999, 12).[13]

13. In terms of everyday life, patriarchy entails cultural constructs and structural relations that privilege the male and senior initiative in directing the lives of those counted to stand under their "protection." Connectivity adds to all this the need of those under protection to invite the

In the socialists' rhetoric, families were to be reformed and eradicated of patriarchy to allow women to participate "alongside the man in building up the new society." Still inside the family, woman-the-mother was expected to contribute to the family's well-being and carry the responsibility for child upbringing.

This "higher goal," the family's welfare, can be compared to other ideologies present in the larger Yemen. Self-presentation among the tribesmen of the northern Yemen highlands is linked to a similar "higher goal": the purity of descent and the idiom of shared honor *(sharaf)*. Knowledge of ties based on patrilineage is central to an individual tribesman's *(qabila)* self-presentation. Descent is the basis for group identity, too, as members of the same group claim descent from the same root *(asl)* and share the honor of their ancestors. There is subsequently a complementary relationship between the group identity and the individual identity (Dostal 1989, 2–3; Dresch 1989, 43–44; on tribal identity, see also Miller 2002). In Aden, the idea of complementarity can also be seen in the old social stratification, where each stratum and profession played its characteristic role in the whole, or, as Louis Dumont (1980) describes this kind of hierarchy, it was a holistic system where every stratum had its own function in the whole, with mutual reciprocities and obligations (see also Ortner 1989, 360).

The postindependence familial discourse constructed the man as a producer, but no longer as the only provider of the family. In the 1974 Family Law, perhaps the most radical change to the earlier law was the stipulation on maintenance: "Both husband and wife share their joint life expenses after marriage, but where either of them is unable to do so the other spouse shall be liable for maintenance and for shouldering the burdens of the married life" (*Family Law* 1976, chap. IV, art. 20, 12).

In other words, the wife could become the major provider of the family in the case where the husband was unemployed or for some other reason was unable to acquire an income. This stipulation is a clear deviation from sharia, which constructs the man as the sole provider of the family, in a law that otherwise is merely a restatement of sharia interpretations (see also Mueller 1985, 227).

---

male's and the senior's involvement in shaping the self. In this way, patriarchy and connectivity work toward the same aim from the two poles of a patriarchal relationship and form what Joseph calls patriarchal connectivity.

Following the policies wherein women were invited to take part in building a new society, women were also encouraged to leave home and take positions in the public fields that were previously occupied by men only. These policies acted also to downplay sexual segregation, which was considered incompatible with the new gender ideals in which the woman's place was said to be "alongside the man" and in which she was presented as the "sister" of every man. The latter formulation utilized the speech code common in Aden whereby family terms are used metaphorically to describe relations to people outside the kin group. Accordingly, every man should respect any woman irrespective of whether there was a legitimate (i.e., kinship or marital) relationship between them. However, this guideline was directed at disciplining such men who had not yet acquired the new thinking and who still considered women to be respectable only if they were visibly under the protection of a particular man and that women who moved outside the home on their own need not be honored.

A Family Code Emerges: "Vitamins to Old Ideas"

The new Family Law, drafted in the early 1970s, represents a modernizing interpretation of the sharia. The process of drafting the new law involved, alongside some prominent *qadi*s (Molyneux 1982, 9), people who earlier had never been consulted on matters of sharia and legal reasoning and who were not previously in a position to be allowed to give an interpretation on these matters.[14] The draft and its provisions were discussed by the ruling party, mass organizations such as the Women's Union, the press, and people with legal qualifications but not necessarily with knowledge of the Islamic *fiqh* (jurisprudence) (Ghanem 1976, 191).[15] The draft was also discussed in public meetings organized by the government with local authorities over a period of four months in the main cities, in the towns, and throughout the countryside. One of the matters debated in these meetings

14. Accusations of *ijtihad* were raised, the deduction of the rule of law from the recognized sources of sharia, a right that can be claimed only by a *mujtahid* (person with right to practice *ijtihad*) (Ghanem 1976, 191).

15. In the early 1970s, the ruling party meant the National Front, successor to the NLF, a leftist coalition that ruled in alliance with two smaller parties, the Popular Vanguard Party and the Communist People's Democratic Union.

was the legal question of how long a woman has to wait to divorce a husband who has migrated and left her on her own. The process of amending the draft lasted three years. Some of the notaries in the drafting committee later recalled that during the public discussion women were more in favor of radical reform measures than men (Molyneux 1982, 9n14). It has been reported that during these meetings members of the drafting committee were at pains to defend the new law within the Islamic context because it was a new, different interpretation of the sharia. As one member of the committee later recalled, "We researched the old books of hadith [tradition] to show that we had not created anything; everything is in Islam. We only gave vitamins to old ideas, to have them triumph" (quoted in *The Middle East,* Feb. 1983, 47).

According to Maxine Molyneux, South Yemen's jurists instanced the Tunisian Law of Personal Status from 1957 as the main influence for the new legislation (1985, 158). The process itself, she maintains, was influenced by the "gender equality" ideology typical to socialist countries, the German Democratic Republic in particular (1989, 195, and 1995, 422). According to Molyneux, the way the Constitution pledged to advance women's emancipation reflects the postindependence rulers' political goal to further that cause by legal reform consistent with the policy of the socialist states (1989, 193, 195).[16] Her macrosociological analysis is based not on local legal developments, but rather on theories of state intervention, modernization, and the development of socialist states. Her approach can be contrasted to that of Leila Ahmed, who analyzes the development of women's rights in some Middle Eastern countries against the background of larger historical developments. Ahmed claims that the policy of women's emancipation in South Yemen was a result of a living tradition in the Arabian Peninsula of strong independent women and a history of women's agency. During the independence struggle in Aden, she argues, women participated in the political fight and were able to transform their own aims as part of that fight; it was not a case in which the fight tapped women to achieve its nationalist goals, as in Algeria. Women's aims reflected a convention of strong women, which Ahmed calls an indigenous tradition of "feminism" particular to the Arabian Peninsula (1983, 169–70).

16. East German jurists were consulted when the Constitution was drafted.

In postunification Yemen, the 1974 Family Law was attacked, among other issues, from the point of view that it is an alien element in Yemeni culture. However, Abu Bakr al-Saqqaf, a northern Yemeni intellectual and prominent figure in the postunification opposition, refuted such allegations in a newspaper article he wrote to debate the 1991 Draft for Personal Status Law. According to him, the critics of the 1974 Family Law were wrong in their attempts to claim that this law is alien to the local culture. Unlike many other laws introduced by the Socialist Party regime, the Family Law was rooted in the political, educational, and trade unionist struggle that Adeni men and women waged against the colonizers. In fact, it was where the aspirations of different political movements met. Not only was this struggle directed against the foreign rule, but its aim was also to fight local tendencies that opposed any social progress that would include women. The demand for women's emancipation was raised long before the leftist government took power from the British, al-Saqqaf maintains (al-Saqqaf in *Al-Ayyam*, Mar. 25, 1992, 12).

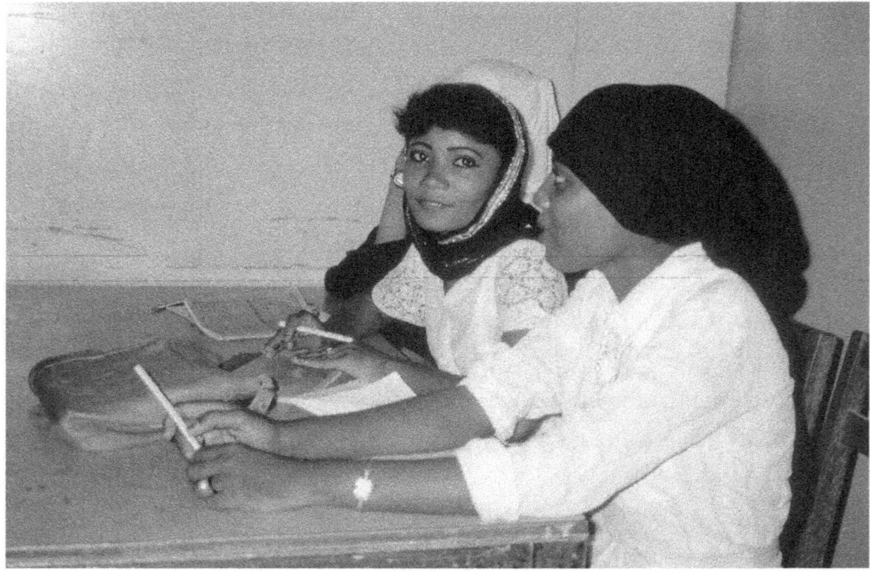

10. Two students in a literacy class run by the General Union of Yemeni Women branch in Ma'alla. Photograph by the author, 1989.

The Ignorant Woman and the Reform Movements

Owing to many influences, mid-twentieth-century Aden was a cosmopolitan town. There was the European colonial power and a lively business community of European, Asian, and African origins. The port allowed a link to international markets, and the status of Aden as a free port with tax-free shopping attracted large numbers of tourists.[17] Even more remarkably, Aden was a center of rising political, cultural, and ideological appraisals in reaction to the colonial rule and the imamic power in the Kingdom of Yemen, reflecting nationalist aspirations in the Arab world at large. New ideas were introduced to Aden by both visiting Arab intellectuals and prominent local personalities who had spent time abroad. By the middle of the century, radio broadcasts from abroad brought new ideas; the most popular of these broadcasts came from Sawt al-ʻArab radio in Cairo and the BBC Arab Service in London.

In the 1930s, cultural and political debate centered around the Arab Reform Club, a loose discussion group established in 1929 in Tawahi by a number of male intellectuals from prominent Adeni merchant families with contacts to centers of political debate in other parts of the Middle East as well as Europe. Even though the Arab Reform Club was small, its activities gathered occasionally big crowds. In 1958, its celebration of the Islamic holy day *mawlid al-nabi* turned into an anticolonial rally with two thousand participants.[18] In 1930, the Islamic Arab Reformatory Club[19] was started in Crater and Shaykh ʻUthman. It, too, was a loose club where male intellectuals gathered and shared thoughts. It influenced intellectual discussion up to the 1950s and gathered newspapermen and writers who had access to wider audiences in newspapers and journals that started to appear in Aden after World War II. Discussion clubs, newspapers, and journals presented a wide interest in cultural, political, social, and religious affairs. In

17. Even in 1968, after the closure of the Suez Canal and the withdrawal of the British military base, more than ten thousand tourists visited Aden (H. Luqman n.d., 13). The number was many times greater during the early 1960s.

18. See India Office Records (IOR) R/20/B/2810, Arab Reform Club.

19. See IOR R/20/A/3452, Reformatory Club.

these circles, demands for women's education, legal rights, and the "freedom to discard the *hijab*" *(tahrir al-mar'a min al-hijab)* were also raised (Tahir 1981, 26).

The first Arabic-language newspaper was started in 1940. It was the popular *Fatat al-Jazira,* launched by a member of an influential merchant family, Muhammad Ali Luqman, the prominent intellectual, lawyer, and author of the first Yemeni novel *Sa'id* (1939, republished in al-Hamdani 2005, 395–455). The newspaper was initially financed by the British in order to distribute allies' war propaganda in Aden, at that time bombarded by Italian troops (Douglas 1987, 72–73; Stark [1945] 1986, 13). After the war, the paper went its own way and disengaged from British interests. Luqman was a leading figure in the political scene with his organization Aden Association, which promoted the slogan "Aden for Adenis" and a separation from the "backward" *(takhalluf)* hinterland with its "reactionary" customs, as reflected in, among other things, women's inferiority *(inhitat al-mar'a).* In 1956, when the British started efforts to form a federation between Aden and the two Aden protectorates, the association announced that the town should remain on its own, in the style of Singapore, as part of the British Commonwealth. In this respect, Luqman was a typical member of the Adeni elite, whose nationalist thoughts differed from the mainstream of Arab nationalism, in particular the Movement of Arab Nationalists, which had possessed a branch in Aden since 1959. The movement promoted Arab unity, freedom from colonialism, and unification of the whole Yemeni homeland (see Halliday 1975, 191, and 1990, 19, 57; Lackner 1985, 37).[20]

In contrast, for Luqman and his associates Aden represented a civilized oasis in a desert of backwardness and reaction. Thus, its development relied on contact with the "advanced" West, as he called it. He was also an advocate of modernity, which in his mind meant education for the population at large.[21] The Aden Association demanded general suffrage, equal rights for women, and the appointment of qualified Adenis to senior administrative posts from which they had been excluded by the colonial policies. In his book *Bimadha taqaddum al-gharbiyyun?*

20. There were other views within the Aden Association, too. Some of its members did not oppose unity with the protectorates as such but objected to tribal law that would replace Aden's constitutional safeguards. The two tendencies split in 1958 (Nagi 1984, 248).

21. Government schools were limited to Adeni citizens only, and even the private schools stayed beyond the reach of many families at the time.

(Why Has the West Advanced? 1933),[22] he pointed out three main reasons for the East's "backwardness": insufficient opportunities for education, including the absence of a university; the "shameful position of women as objects of pleasure for men only"; and the aimlessness of youths without future prospects. The book gained a wide audience, especially in various newspapers where it was quoted and discussed (A. A. Tahir 1981, 25).

Luqman's newspaper *Fatat al-Jazira* became the number one newspaper in Aden until it was closed down in 1967 and reflected his ideas of modernity and advancement. In every issue, the paper introduced ideas and improvements from the "advanced West." A regular column during the 1950s and 1960s, entitled "Our Beautiful Half!" ("Nisfna al-halwa!"), was devoted to female readers. In this column, together with small pieces of news on the same page, women were informed on, among other things, the benefits of a refrigerator or electric cooker, the wonders of plastic surgery, the U.S. First Lady's cooking recipes, and useful tips from German housewives on matters of housekeeping (from headlines in *Fatat al-Jazira,* 1961 issues). In 1961, as part of its advocacy to bring about "advancement" in Aden, the newspaper published a special issue devoted to the needs of a "modern home." The advertisement section of the issue displayed how trading houses and importers of foreign goods could provide for kitchenware, furniture, and technical solutions that would make the Adeni home step into the twentieth century. The mission was felt to be so urgent that the newspaper offered free translation and editing help for foreign firms that wanted to advertise their products.

The women's column also had articles on women working outside the home, on problems in a marriage between an uneducated "ignorant" woman *(al-ummiyya al-gahila)* and an educated man, and on the activities of the Adeni Women's Association. The latter was a charity and welfare organization that devoted its energies to educating and helping women in need. In the beginning in 1958, it was chaired by British and other European women, but later it was run by wives of Adeni politicians and the elite, such as the wife of *Fatat al-Jazira*'s chief editor, Luqman himself.

22. *Bimadha taqaddum al-gharbiyyun? Bahuth akhlaqiyy wa durus ijtama'iyy* (1933), reprinted in al-Hamdani 2005, 59–138.

In post–world war Aden, women's inferior position *(inhitat al-mar'a)* and marriage problems were discussed in various literary circles, the most important of which in the 1950s was the Abu al-Tayyib Camp, which held its meetings at the *Fatat al-Jazira* offices (Muheirez 1985, 207). But not only intellectuals and men of letters initiated the discussion. In February 1961, in its page devoted to female readers *Fatat al-Jazira* reported on a public meeting organized by the Youth Section of the Aden Tennis Club. In this open meeting, the obstacles young men encountered in getting married were discussed. The article described how the debate was organized to reflect the problems young men faced in the customary marriage, especially the fact that the groom was expected to amass a large sum of money before he could even consider marrying. The problem lay in the economic boom of the early 1960s at the world's third-busiest port. When the economy grew better, the wedding expenses and the dowers requested also grew. Despite the economic upswing, young men found it difficult to meet the ever-rising demands. Another serious problem these young men faced was the appalling housing situation. At the height of the colonial rule, the city attracted thousands of immigrants from neighboring areas, all in need of accommodation. To make things worse, the young bride-to-be often pressed her fiancé to provide her with a home separate from his parents'.

Given the urgency of the problem, it is no wonder that the meeting attracted sixty young men to discuss these matters. The meeting began with a young man's introducing the theme of the evening. In the discussion, wedding expenses and the increased amounts of dower were pointed out as the main problems. Among the participants was Muhammad bin Salim al-Bayhani, the famous religious figure and graduate of al-Azhar University in Egypt. He acted as the imam of al-Asqalani mosque in Crater and sat on the board of the Tennis Club Youth Section, even though the blind shaykh was no longer in his youth and hardly played tennis. Al-Bayhani promoted his ideas not only from the pulpit of his mosque or in public events, but also in books he authored. Among those ideas was a call for a religious reform that would purify Islam of practices of idolatry *(wathaniyya)* and adoration of forces other than God *(shirk)*. The British called him a troublemaker, and his opponents called him a Wahhabi.[23] His presence in such a club indicates

23. IOR R/20/B/2904, Sheikh Mohammed Salim El Beihani.

the active political climate in Aden, the city that at that time was a haven for clubs and societies of all kinds.

In addressing the meeting, Bayhani suggested that the gathering should establish a committee to start troubleshooting the problems. He demanded that the *daf'a,* the amount paid by the groom to the bride upon *khutba* (engagement) should be limited to 3,000 shillings (150 dinars) and that the *mahr* (dower) written in the marriage contract should be limited to 1,000 shillings (50 dinars).[24] He also suggested that in case the wife initiates a divorce without a legal (sharia) cause, she should pay back half of the *daf'a.*[25] He attacked in particular the heavy spending that was customary in Adeni weddings. According to him, such licentious behavior turned weddings into feasts of excessive squander. He demanded that *qat makhdara*s (*qat* parties for men in connection to weddings) should be banned, and he discouraged people from collecting money with such methods.

Regarding the housing problem, the learned shaykh suggested that the state should take measures to ease the shortage. The latter proposal did not satisfy all the participants, and it was suggested that an endowment should be started to find solutions to the blatant lack of housing. The fund could also assist young men in solving their financial problems and thus facilitate marriage. Finally, the shaykh proposed that a limit should be put on how much a person who earns less than 500 shillings (25 dinars) a month should be expected to spend on a wedding and that at least he should not be required to organize a *qat makhdara.* In conclusion, the meeting participants decided to start the Committee to Facilitate Marriage Arrangements and for Help of the Family (Lajna Tashil al-Zawaj wa Is'ad al-'Usar), with members from the Tennis Club board. The committee was supposed to start negotiations with the authorities, religious scholars *(rigal al-din),* and the press to facilitate cooperation (see *Fatat al-Jazira,* Feb. 1961).

24. During this period, the dower payments registered in marriage records varied for a virgin bride between fifteen and fifty dinars among workers and lower-middle-strata people but were much higher among more wealthy groups. It is possible that the young men gathered in the public meeting were from modest backgrounds; otherwise, Bayhani's suggestions would hardly have impressed them. See my study on *mahr* practices in Dahlgren 2005.

25. He is obviously referring to *khul'* divorce, which I discussed in the previous chapter. Because Islamic law has no set limits to the compensation a wife should pay for her *khul'* divorce except for a general notion of "moderation," the shaykh's proposal can be seen as beneficial to women.

This example shows how the prevailing marriage customs were debated in the early 1960s. These same demands continued later and are raised even today. Throughout the 1990s, the Islah Party, the leading "Islamic" party in the unified Yemen, organized group weddings with occasionally tens of couples participating, in order to cut the expenses and provide a "real" Islamic occasion for a wedding. In those celebrations, no music was played, and no wealth or fancy clothes were on display; instead, participants in strictly segregated separate parties for men and women engaged in singing religious songs and in reading the Holy Book. Unlike other weddings, these occasions were not photographed or videotaped.[26]

The Tennis Club meeting tells of the sentiments of young men who from a very practical point of view saw marriage as a cost they could not easily meet. But it was also a platform for Shaykh al-Bayhani, one of the most outspoken men of religion at that time, to preach against what he considered the "bad customs" that people in Aden were engaged in. The talk of greed was directed not only at families—that is, fathers and mothers who negotiated the marriage deal for the daughter—but also at young women. It was clear that neither al-Bayhani nor the young men present at the meeting had an understanding of the security that the *mahr* provides for a woman. In the early 1960s, few women worked outside the home, and because girls seldom went to school or learned a profession, marriage was the only future for them. If the marriage failed, and the woman became alienated from her natal family (or if all earning members of her family died), she had few options to support herself and her children. She could either remarry, in which case she lost her children, or she could take up prostitution, a vocation that had a good market in a city full of guest workers and a colonial army—in other words, men without their families.

From two different frameworks of interest, the thoughts presented in the Tennis Club Youth Section meeting reflected the urgency felt in Aden, even before independence, for reform in the way marriage was arranged. This is important to remember when we look at the process of drafting a family code in the period after independence was gained. Presented in the framework of Islam, Bayhani's

26. In fear of religious purifiers, some families have stopped videotaping their weddings. In those weddings that are still taped, the local video shops are hiring female photographers to replace the earlier male ones.

suggestion to cut the dower to a nominal sum tallied with the leftist government's measures to add such a limitation in the new law. In the 1974 Family Law, the *mahr* was limited to a symbolic amount of 100 Yemeni dinars (2,000 shillings), either paid promptly *(mahr mu'ajjal* [with an ayn] or *mahr muqaddam)* or deferred (*mahr mu'ajjal* [with a hamza]) or paid in two parts. According to Adeni marriage records, during the 1970s this amount (100 dinars) was the sum that men with a good salary and with a profession such as physician, teacher, or state employee could easily afford to pay to a virgin bride. The various amounts paid to a *thayyiba* (nonvirgin) were considerable lower, such as 7 dinars 50 fils, which was the prompt dower a fifty-five-year-old mechanic paid to a widowed woman age forty-five in September 1970.

Al-Bayhani was an active debater and dominated the religious and social scenes in Aden in the 1950s, together with 'Ali Muhammad Bahamish, another graduate of al-Azhar University and for the British the trusted *qadi* of Aden in the late 1950s. Bayhani's book *Ustadh al-mar'ah* (The Teacher of the Woman, 1950) drew both positive and negative reactions. The book discussed, among other themes, religious obligations, life-cycle rituals, practices related to women's health and child bearing, superstitions and idolatry, the "problem" of lesbianism among Adeni women, and female circumcision *(khitan)*, which the shaykh recommended and claimed even to be obligatory for Shafi'is (al-Bayhani 1950).[27] Some Adeni women were reported to have reacted to his teachings by asking, "What has that old blind man got to do with telling us how to behave?" (Serjeant 1962, 194n).

Bayhani was a student of Ahmad al-Abbadi, a prominent figure of religious learning in Shaykh 'Uthman. The latter was a devout opponent of the practice of venerating local saints (*awliy'*, sing. *wali*) and visiting their tombs (see Knysh 1993; Messick 1993, 49n, 37–40; Serjeant [1957] 1981). According to Captain Frederick Mercer Hunter, there were fourteen such tombs in Aden alone in the mid–nineteenth century ([1877] 1968, 175),[28] and later veneration centered round two notable Adeni saints, Abu Bakr al-'Aydarus, who lived in the fifteenth century and whose tomb and mosque are in Crater, and Hashim al-Bahr, whose

27. On *khitan*, see al-Bayhani 1950, 80. Muheirez (1985, 209) and Serjeant (1962) discuss al-Bayhani's book.

28. Most of those tombs are still there, but no visiting takes place.

ziara (pilgrimage) in Shaykh 'Uthman became more important than visiting the tomb of Shaykh 'Uthman, after whom the area was named (Bawazir 1997, 63–70, 118; Nagi 1976, 57). Saint veneration involved an annual pilgrimage that gathered thousands of people and was respected as a national holiday, at least in the case of al-'Aydarus.

Al-Bayhani called for religious reform that would purify Islam from practices he considered idolatry *(wathaniyya)* and adoration of forces other than God *(shirk)*. Women in particular were involved in practices such as *zar* (spirit possession) and other healing techniques that he considered idolatrous, which is perhaps why he devoted his book to educating women. As part of his religious mission, Bayhani was an advocate of women's education, but only in moderate terms, and he debated the issue publicly against Bahamish, who together with some mosque imams disputed his ideas. The subjects discussed by these two religious camps included the questions of whether women should give up purdah; whether dancing, singing, and the watching of films should be allowed; how much education women should acquire; and whether saint veneration should be practiced (Muheirez 1985, 209). During 1948–50, Bahamish published the religious and social newspaper *al-Dhikri,* which presented the views of some Islamic scholars centered around the Islamic Welfare Society. Bayhani and his teacher al-Abbadi represented in this debate the "reforming" Islam, whereas Bahamish and many of the mosque imams stood for an Islam that was tolerant of local customs and practices. These two main views characterize religious debate in Aden still today.

The Rise of Women's Societies

In preindependence Aden, women's issues, marriage, and the family were also debated in various clubs and organizations for women. As I mentioned earlier, during the colonial era Aden was the ideal place for clubs of all kinds based on a variety of principles, such as communal, tribal, or religious attachment; literary, political, religious, or ideological sympathies; sports activities or hobbies; occupational affinities or welfare purposes. Clubs and societies devoted to women had in common the understanding that because of purdah women were confined to homes where they supposedly lacked educational opportunities and intellectual stimuli and that they should be drawn out of the home in order to participate in activities for their own good and for the benefit of the needy elements of society. Activities organized for women in these clubs and societies centered around teaching useful skills in home management, in providing chances to get a job outside the home within the fields reserved for women (clerical, nursing, and manufacturing), and around participating in welfare activities. In contrast to men's clubs, these societies tended to have an "all race" membership, as the British put it, but in practice they attracted women from communities where observing the purdah was unheard of or less strict, such as the European, Jewish, Parsi, Hindu, Khoja, and Bohora communities and, socially, the wealthier strata.

The names of these clubs and societies during the 1950s and 1960s are illustrative of the nature of their activities: Aden Women's Voluntary Services (established in 1950 by the governor's wife, Lady Champion), Aden Ladies' Child Welfare Committee, the League of Good Fellowship (started in the early 1960s by Sister Francesca of Crater Catholic Convent), Women's Corona Society (which organized social gatherings for the wives of civil servants), Aden Girl Guides Association, Government Guards' Family Association, Aden Protectorate Wives' Club, Hospital Visiting Committee, and Boys' Clubs (with branches in Shaykh 'Uthman, Tawahi, Crater, and Ma'alla) (Aden 1961, 52; Aden Colony 1954, 28; *Welcome to Aden* 1963, 114–15). Most of these women's societies and clubs gathered in the Besse Women's Education Center, started by Antonin Besse, the leading businessman in Aden during the British era who contributed to the promotion of education in Aden, but who at the end of his life donated his property to establish St. Anthony's College in Oxford University (on Besse's life, see Footman 1986). Later on, the Besse Center was run by the government Education Department (Aden Colony 1954, 25; Parfitt 1996, 168; *Welcome to Aden* 1963, 115).

Women's activities in the late colonial period were not limited to these clubs, but also included, with the gradual increase in educational opportunities for women and their expanded participation in the labor market, political and trade union activities. In March 1962, it was reported that students at Aden College went on strike to promote a demand for equal opportunities for women to complete their exams. The strike resulted in the closure of the college until October the same year (*Welcome to Aden* 1963, 223, 227). This college was the site of many uprisings against the colonial power, and it was the school of many later prominent figures in Yemeni politics and women's organizations.

After closing the British Council in 1951, the British opened a club for women called Aden Women's Club. The club was led in the beginning by Mrs. W. A. C. Goode, the wife of the colonial chief secretary. Its activities included instruction in Arabic and English, dressmaking, embroidery, "simple home nursing," child welfare, and cookery (Aden Colony 1954, 29). As Doreen Ingrams describes the intentions of the British, "The British Council opened a club for women in Aden, in hope of bringing them into more active participation in the community, but it was uphill work as few men would allow their womanfolk such emancipation as joining a club, and it was largely patronised by Indians, Somalis, a few Europeans, and by Hasanali-Jaffer[29] families. The strictly purdah bandage-making parties, however, were successful in attracting a number of more secluded women especially as they were thought to be working in a good cause" (1970, 126).

By the end of the 1950s, radicalization spread to the Women's Club, and the activists changed the British leadership into a local one. A new name was introduced, the Arab Women's Club, to reflect its reformed aims. In its fight for women's education, the club occasionally collided with the colonial authorities, and the government kept a keen eye on its activities. In 1962, the *Aden Recorder,* an English-language newspaper, reported how "Aden's suffragette demands rights." In the article, Mahiya Nagib, Aden's first female editor of a women's monthly magazine, *Fatat Shamsan* (The Maiden of Mount Shamsan), was reported to have "criticised the pace of progress in the field of women's education in Aden, and demanded, as a matter of urgency, the immediate attention of the Government to this aspect. She said that had the Adeni woman been given appropriate attention earlier in the field of education she would have been by now a very useful component of society" (*Aden Recorder,* Jan. 7, 1962).

On another occasion, when the director of education wanted to prohibit a lecture by a male speaker due to be held in the Besse Center, one of the society's leaders, Radhia Ihsanullah, declared: "The community in which man lives

29. The Hasanalis and Jaffers were families of Persian origin whose women were, according to Ingrams, the "most emancipated" in Aden and went out of doors without a veil, wearing only the *shaidor,* an outdoor garment (1970, 126).

separately from the woman. A community equal to the bird which attempts to fly with one wing! Take out the turban, oh Education Department! We know what benefits us from traditions!"[30]

The problem was not that a man was being allowed to enter a clubhouse designed for women only, but more likely that the speaker represented the anticolonial front. In 1960, when the Arab Women's Club considered joining the International Alliance of Women, the Aden government contacted London to get instructions on how to deal with such a membership application. The alliance's slogan, "Equal rights—equal responsibilities," included demands for civil and political rights, equal property rights, and, among other issues, equal moral standards for men and women. London replied that joining should be encouraged. However, this affirmative attitude from London did not stop the club's problems with the local government. A few years later the club had a meeting in the Muhammedan Combined Club in Crater, at which Girls' College students' problems with the English headmistress were discussed. In the anticolonial frenzy, one of the participants was reported to have announced: "All this is the fault of this Queen Elizabeth, this British bitch, who sends people abroad to colonise others. She is finished."[31] By 1960, the Arab Women's Club and its rival, the Aden Women's Association, had three hundred members each.[32]

All these activities to engage women during the late colonial period had in common the idea that women should be drawn out of doors to "participate in the community" (the British), to gain education in "moderate terms" (Bayhani and other religious purifiers), and to participate in the "political struggle" (the liberation movement). All attempts were directed against segregation, considered by all to contribute to women's ignorance and the prevalence of "bad customs" *('adat sayyi'at).* During the colonial period, pressure for reform came from many directions, but legal measures came only after independence because the colonial power refrained from legal changes that would touch "custom and religion," as I explained in the previous chapter. The sketches given here from the preindependence times clearly indicate how demands for changes in women's situation were

30. British translation from *al-'Amal,* June 7, 1959, in IOR R/20/B/2813, secret file, Arab Women's Club.

31. Aden Colony Police, report, Feb. 8, 1962, in IOR R/20/B/2813.

32. Government of Aden, memorandum, May 20, 1960, in IOR R/20/B/2813.

11. A judge at her bench in the Aden Divisional Court. Photograph by the author, 1989.

made from different platforms and from different perspectives before the leftist government took over.

The Women's Law

The specific demands made in the meeting organized by the Youth Section of the Adeni Tennis Club and the specifics of other calls for a change are similar in content to the first ever marriage code promulgated in South Yemen, the Internal Circular or a Marriage Law, issued in Zingibar, a town northeast of Aden in 1971. It was drafted by the governor, local *qadi*s (judges and magistrates), and some other local people.[33] The circular was issued by the time the drafting of a family law was announced in Aden, but it then became apparent that the enactment of

33. The issuing of such a circular as a law text is one example of the popular eagerness for reforms that occurred in various parts of the countryside after independence because the new regime had not yet issued new legislation. However, the practice of issuing circulars was common in Hadhramaut before independence and in Sudan as well. See Ghanem 1972, 102, 111–12.

the law would take several years. Even though the circular was not valid in Aden, it is interesting to see what it contained and how it was received. The introduction proclaimed: "The popular revolution is determined to change society, which is backward as a result of all its rotten relations, into a new progressive society." Further, it declared that women were considered as chattels sold and bought by high dowers and that this meant that many of the young people were unable to get married simply because of a lack of money. Polygamy was characterized in the circular as "tragic" (quoted in Ghanem 1972, 100, and 1976, 192). Among the circular's provisions were:

- The dower is to be limited to four thousand shillings (two hundred Yemeni dinars);
- The consent of the bride is required; a court clerk has to listen to her and take her signature of approval;
- A girl may not marry before the age of maturity *(sin' al-rushd),* specified at fifteen years;
- *Talaq* (divorce by announcement) may not take place under any circumstances outside the shari'a courts, and a good cause must be shown to be acceptable to the shari'a;
- Marriage is restricted to one wife at a time except in the following cases: the wife's chronic illness, infertility, or infidelity;
- If the husband deserts the matrimonial home for a period exceeding two years, the court must first warn him, and if he does not comply, it dissolves the marriage. (*al-'Arabi* 162 [May 1972], 127, 130, as quoted in Ghanem 1972, 100–101)

Some of the provisions in this circular tally with the demands to improve women's position described earlier. Restrictions on polygamy were new, but not the demand to curb polygamy. These stipulations followed the Iraqi 1959 Family Law (Law no. 188 [1959]), which orders that marriage to more than one wife is not allowed except with the judge's permission, unless the man has sufficient income, and when there is a lawful benefit (El Alami and Hinchcliffe 1996, 66; Rateb 1988, 88). Provisions regarding the husband's prolonged absence are common from court practice in the Aden Supreme Court during the colonial era. In many respects, the Zingibar Circular was in fact more radical than the Draft Law of Personal Status, the code the new government issued in 1971, which after three years of discussion was enacted with the name "Family Law" (Law no. 1 for the Year 1974 in Connection to the Family).[34]

Al-'Arabi magazine reported also on popular reactions to the Zingibar Circular. The sharia *qadi* of Zingibar, Yahya 'Abdullah Qahtan, was one of the initiators of the circular and was reported to have said, "At the beginning there were always difficulties, but we found a general awareness which enabled us to apply the clauses of this Circular which need to be further established to convince the people. The Circular is not inconsistent with Islamic shari'a, and the Qur'an ordained that 'if you fear that you shall be unjust, then one [you should take one] (wife only)'" (quoted in *al-'Arabi* magazine 162 [May 1972], 127, as quoted in Ghanem 1972, 101, and 1976, 193).

For the duration of its validity (1974–92), the Family Law was called the "women's law" *(qanun al-mar'a)*. The law established man and woman as equals in rights and duties.[35] This provision can be seen as a matter of principle only because the enactments did not in reality treat men and women equally when it came to marriage payments, polygamy, divorce, or custody. Even girls and boys were not treated equally when it came to defining the age each was eligible to contract a marriage or become liberated from an adult guardianship. In this respect, the law cannot be characterized as allocating equality between the sexes, but instead as assigning to women some rights that they did not enjoy earlier. Thus, the law and its provisions were a continuation of the colonial-era debate and the ongoing discussion on women's rights rather than an attempt to introduce a principle of equality in marriage. When the law was later criticized, it was for allowing women "too many rights" rather than for bringing equality between the sexes.

Concerning the question of consent for a marriage (point two in appendix B), the law was clear in requiring the woman's consent, but it did not say anything about whether her guardian's consent was needed. Thus, the father's consent was left outside the legislation, making it a family matter. One consequence was that a father could no longer bring to court a demand for the dissolution of a marriage contracted against his will, as was allowed during the colonial era. On the

34. Official English translation issued by the Information Department of the Yemeni Ministry of Information in 1976.

35. The law's main provisions are reprinted in appendix B.

one hand, this provision allowed families to settle disputes on their own, and on the other it was meant for the protection of women. Among the young women I talked to, it was considered one of the most important rights that the law and *tahrir al-mar'a* (women's emancipation) politics brought to women. It was generally understood to establish a free-choice marriage. As one young woman who was not yet married expressed the idea to me, "In the past, the woman had no right to choose her life partner because that would bring disgrace [*'ayb*] to her family. Neither was she allowed to work alongside her husband. Now the woman has full right to choose her husband, and she can work beside him outside home."

Such a provision was, of course, no legal novelty; the classical law schools had already addressed it. For example, whereas Hanafis allow women in their legal majority to arrange marriages for themselves, the Malikites demand the guardian's consent for the woman's first marriage.[36]

Nevertheless, the law did not eradicate old customs in contracting marriages, and complicated court cases sometimes came up involving people trapped in an irregular marriage *(fasid)*. A good example is the exchange marriage *(nikah al-badal* or *nikah al-shighar)*. This practice continued after the promulgation of the law and provides an instance where a conditional use of Hanafi doctrine persisted. The exchange marriage is a marriage arrangement where A marries B's sister and B takes A's sister for marriage, and no dower *(mahr)* is paid. Exchange marriage was prohibited during the colonial era in Lahig, the sultanate north of Aden, but in Aden there was no legislation regarding it. In Lahigi law, the prohibition was based on a hadith, and such an exchange was considered harmful to the parties.[37] Shafi'i doctrine is negative toward it, but Hanafi keeps it conditional.[38] The Family Law of 1974 did not prohibit such a marriage but implicitly stated that a marriage is a contract between one man and one woman only, rendering a multiparty marriage void (*Family Law* 1976, part I, chap. I, art. 2).

36. For a comparison, see Moors 1999, 149. The Libyan 1984 Family Law (Law no. 16) stipulates that the court can allow a marriage that does not have the consent of the woman's guardian (art. 9; see also El Alami and Hinchcliffe 1996, 183, and Rateb 1988, 76, 83, 85).

37. Lahigi Laws of the Sharia Courts of 1950 with supplements in 1954 and 1957, according to Ghanem 1972, 96.

38. According to Hanafi doctrine, the contract is valid in case a proper dower is entitled, which, of course, renders it a normal marriage (Ghanem 1972, 96).

Such exchange marriages were registered during the PDRY, anyway. In 1988, I met in the Aden Divisional Court a woman whose marriage was about to be terminated because the other partners in the contract, her brother and his wife—her husband's sister—were seeking a divorce. She was desperate because she and her husband were happy in their marriage, but they did not know how to save it. This couple was, like most commoners, unaware of the stipulations of the law. According to the 1974 law, the divorce that the court gave to the (exchange) marriage was not irreversible provided it was not the third divorce, and thus the marriage could be restored officially after the ninety days compulsory *'iddat* (waiting period that the wife has to observe before she can remarry) and if the husband obtained a Return Certificate from the marriage registrar *(madhun),* provided the wife agreed, as was the case here (*Family Law* 1976, part II, art. 27 and 28). However, it is possible that additional circumstances complicated the case further.

A stipulation on legitimate age for marriage was meant to protect young girls in particular from getting married too early. Already during the colonial era, child marriages were criticized as a token of "backwardness" that should be rooted out from the society. In contrast, the limitation of marriage between people whose age difference is more than twenty years, provided the woman has not past thirty-five years of age, was an innovation that had no basis in the sharia. As such, it was against the prophetic sunna that tells about Prophet Muhammad's marriage in old age to the young bride Aisha. In practical terms, I met young women whose marriage to a considerably older man had been terminated in court on the woman's instigation.

Such matters as incompatibility of the spouses, a lack of equal prerequisites between the spouses (the pre-Islamic *kafa'a,* or social equitability principle, that Islam adopted),[39] and the husband's unsatisfactory sexual performance were considered legitimate reasons both in the court and in public opinion for the woman to seek a divorce. When I inquired about this matter among law professionals and laypeople, men and women agreed that woman's sexual pleasure is one of the paramount concerns for a marriage to be successful. In this sense, the age-difference provision can be regarded as a measure to prevent probable divorces. From a legal point of view, it was not invented by the drafters of the law but followed the

39. See Bujra 1971, 93–94, on the *kafa'a* principle in Hadhramaut.

Jordanian Law of Family Rights (1951), which requires a *qadi*'s permission to a marriage of people whose age difference is more than twenty years.[40]

The law lists the conditions by which a man is able to take more than one wife *(ta'addud al-zawjat).* These conditions do not constitute a prohibition on polygamy but limit it for the purpose of protecting the woman.[41] In this respect, it follows the old Syrian marriage law (Law no. 59, 1953) (Rateb 1988, 91). The woman's right to stay in the house of a polygamous union should be seen against the background of protecting her in case she has lost her natal family's support and has no place to go in a chronically bad housing situation. Characteristic of attempts to protect a deserted wife, the paragraph includes the provision that she keeps this right even if she initiates the divorce. The law is not explicit, but courts usually ordered a woman to stay in the same house with the husband she had just divorced. Many people criticized this practice, and accusations of morality in danger were raised. A woman who lived in such a condition risked being called a *mufisha,* a prostitute. It is possible that this practice was there already during the colonial era. In the previous chapter, I explained that during the British era the authorities thought that about 70 percent of the prostitutes were divorced women (R. Knox-Mawer 1956, 512).

Women's Law versus Women's *'Adah*

As mentioned earlier, Family Law provisions on the maintenance of the family (see point 8 in appendix B) involve both the husband and the wife. These provisions, together with the requirement that the wife carry full responsibility in the case where the husband is unable to contribute, are alien to the Qur'anic verse

40. In the Jordanian Family Law (Law no. 61 of 1976, art. 7), the age difference of twenty years concerns women who are younger than eighteen, but the court can decide otherwise if she appeals. The minimum age for women to marry in Jordan is fifteen and for men seventeen (see El Alami and Hinchcliffe 1996, 80, and Rateb 1988, 76).

41. The Zingibar Circular was in fact more radical in that it prohibited polygamy entirely. The right of a woman to divorce if her husband intends to take a cowife is guaranteed in the Egyptian Family Code (Law no. 100, 1985, art. 2:11b), in the old Moroccan Family Law (Law no. 343, 1957, art. 31), and indirectly in the Iraqi marriage law (Law no. 188, 1959, art. 40.5). See El Alami and Hinchcliffe 1996, 58, 203, 75, and Rateb 1988, 64, 72, 88–89.

regarding man's sole burden to maintain his wife and his consequent supremacy over her (Surat al-Nisa' 4, 43). This point is clearly the issue where the law deviates from sharia, and it refers to the aim to liberate a woman from economic dependency on her husband. In contrast, inheritance laws were based on the sharia.[42] At the same time, the obligation to provide for retired parents was cast on both the man and the woman (§24). Scholars of *fiqh* support inequality between the sexes in inheritance by referring to the practice that the man carries the responsibility for the upkeep of the family, his retired parents included. Molyneux reports that a female advocate explained to her that it is customary for men to bear responsibility for aged parents and feeble relatives, a duty that women are, according to her, not ready to take (1985, 163n21). But some women complained to me about the unfairness of the inheritance rules. After the enactment of the Family Law, the man was no longer the sole provider in the family, and because the law did not recognize property accumulated during marriage—for example, property that should be divided in case of dissolution of the union—the provision that made the woman responsible for supporting her family in the case where the husband is not capable of doing so in actuality became an extra duty for which she would not get the same compensation as the man. I met many women, married and single, who supported their families, elderly mothers in particular. The inheritance law follows sharia in that respect, too, though, in that it allows a woman to keep her income and property without her husband's having any right to touch it (al-Shamiriyy 1984, 79). This stipulation contradicts the requirement that the wife support the family with her own means, as some women told me.

The stipulation to limit the amount of dower *(mahr)* to one hundred dinars is perhaps the point where the law was violated most often (see Dahlgren 2005). One hundred dinars was at the end of the 1980s about twice the monthly salary of an average worker and considered a very small sum indeed. This nominal fee was often written in the contract and paid in cash in front of the *madhun,* but it was multiplied by providing the bride with expensive jewelry—including a ring, bracelets, and a necklace—and with an expensive wardrobe. Another way to get around it was to agree on a high *daf'a,* the payment made upon engagement and

42. According to sharia, the wife inherits only one-quarter of her husband's property or, if there are children, only one-eighth, whereas the husband inherits respectively one-half and one-quarter.

providing for a luxurious wedding party. A third method that two families negotiating a marriage might have taken was to make an oral agreement on a higher *mahr* than what was written in the marriage contract.

In the Family Law's preamble, *mahr* is called a "negative custom" that transformed the family ties into "a business house" and placed the "fate of the Yemeni women in the hand of the highest bidder" (*Family Law* 1976, preamble, 6). Although some women agreed that a larger dower is not important in a marriage based on partnership, others saw *mahr* as imperative and as a woman's only property. Those women sometimes criticized their male kin for excluding them from negotiations with the groom (see Dahlgren 2005). Wedding gold is a matter of display and pride for most women. It is considered not only a reserve for bad times, but a token of the husband's love and respect, particularly if added to during the marriage. In Aden, it is not customary to pay the bride's father, as is done in some other areas in Yemen (see Mundy 1995, 131–38).

In this light, the limitation on *mahr* remained a contested issue. As I explained earlier, such a limitation was demanded already during the colonial era. After independence, the actual limitation in law was supported by those women who considered women's economic safety to lie in their access to working life and education rather than in the *mahr.* But other women tended to view it differently. Those men and women who wanted to see women equal to men in all aspects of life had a negative attitude to *mahr* and the sharia-based inheritance laws in the first place. Problems related to *mahr* were debated in meetings on the law held in 1976 and 1985 organized by the Women's Union (General Union of Yemeni Women 1986, 10, 16; Molyneux 1985, 163), but these discussions did not bring about any change. This aspect made the 1974 Family Law not exclusively a "women's law" *(qanun al-mar'a),* as it was popularly called.

Women's Divorce

Provisions on divorce in the Family Law (see points 12–16 in appendix B) made divorce a real option for a woman for the first time and protected her from unilateral repudiation *(talaq).* In Adeni legal history, it was, however, not the first time the consequences of divorce were regulated in law. In the 1930s, the British issued the Criminal Procedure Ordinance "the Maintenance of Wives and Children" (*Laws of Aden* 1946, chap. 39, cap. XXX [1948, 1227]) to allow women some procedural means to obtain maintenance after a divorce. In those Middle Eastern countries that have a codified law for the family, unilateral divorce without any legal consequences is no longer a common phenomenon and has been substituted by varying decrees that either strengthen women's rights or limit men's liberties (Moors 1999, 153–54). Some sort of compensation and maintenance is required in countries such as Egypt (Law no. 100 of 1985), Morocco (Law no. 343, 1957), Lebanon (law issued in 1933), Jordan (Law no. 61, 1976), Tunisia (law issued in 1956), North Yemen (Law no. 3, 1978), Libya (Law no. 10, 1984), Iraq (Law no. 188, 1959), Syria (Law no. 59, 1953), and Algeria (Law no. 84, 1984) (Rateb 1988, 65–93).

However, after women were given rights to divorce similar to the ones men had, divorce rates did not multiply, as table 2 shows. This result is contrary to what the critics of the 1974 law claimed.

According to Adeni marriage and divorce records for the years 1973–81, before the enactment of the Family Law, 318 divorces and 1,366 marriages were registered, making the divorce rate 23.3 percent (two to three divorces for every ten marriages). In the following years (1974 and 1975), the rate went down to 21.2 and 19.8 percent, respectively. There was a jump in 1976, when every third marriage resulted in divorce, but again in the following years the rate dropped to less than 20 percent. According to these statistics, the year 1981 witnessed the most registrations for divorces, with 895 divorces for 2,192 marriages (40.8 percent) (compiled from statistics in al-Shamiri 1984, 39 and 60). In that year, the number of marriages was slightly lower than in the five previous years. But the number of

Table 2. Marriage and divorce in Aden during 1973–1981

Year	*No. of Marriages*	*No. of Divorces*	*Divorce Rate (%)*	*Divorces per 10 Marriages*
1973	1,366	318	23.3	2.3
1974	1,472	312	21.2	2.1
1975	1,569	311	19.8	2.0
1976	1,744	558	32.0	3.2
1977	2,236	398	17.8	1.8
1978	2,247	456	20.3	2.0
1979	2,334	414	17.7	1.8
1980	2,345	555	23.7	2.4
1981	2,192	895	40.8	4.1

Source: Compiled from statistics in al-Shamiriyy 1984, 39 and 60.

divorces at this time was still far less than what was reported in the early 1950s, as I explained in the previous chapter. However, the increase in 1981 seemed not to be part of a tendency during the 1980s because in 1988 divorce records give a rate of 24.7 percent (PDRY 1990, 67). These figures and my own observations speak in favor of the conclusion that the law succeeded in curbing men's "easy divorces" as the word spread among women that they could get their rights in the court. An illiterate woman in her thirties put it to me this way: "I have the law on my side."

These statistics do not tell who initiated the divorce, but based on my own observations, after the promulgation of the Family Law litigating a family dispute in court became a real option for women, which they increasingly now employed. However, credit for this change should not be given solely to the law. What contributed perhaps more to curbing the "easy divorces" was the introduction of a marriage counseling system that meant obligatory arbitration *(tahkim)* for every couple in marital discord. Arbitration, as a legal procedure, is mentioned in the Qur'an (4:35) and recommended by the main schools of Islamic *fiqh*. However, in Islamic law the role of an arbitrator *(hakam)* is given only to a person qualified to act as a *qadi* (Schacht 1964, 189).

Marriage arbitration was practiced to varying degrees in preindependence Aden, but with the 1974 Family Law it gained legal status. According to this principle, every couple was obliged to visit either the premises of the neighborhood Popular Defense Committee (Local Defense Committee) or a General Union of Yemeni Women clubhouse. In the case where the court expected reconciliation, the couple was sent to both places on several occasions. Popular Defense Committees were neighborhood organizations designed according to the Cuban model and charged with problems of public order, minor offenses, and local social problems. The chair was usually a man. In the Women's Union neighborhood clubs located in each part of the town, a female social secretary was charged with giving counseling to couples. Counseling sessions were the only occasions when men could enter the women's clubs. Because it was likely that the couple would meet a male arbitrator in the Defense Committee and a female one in the women's club, a gender bias was expected to be avoided.[43] The judge decided each case on the basis of testimonies

43. The possibility of such a bias was a matter of concern to the judiciary, as one female judge told me.

12. Factory workers in a big mixed-sector factory in Ma'alla. Photograph by the author, 1989.

presented in the court—the immediate "facts" that according to each party led to the marital dispute, character witnesses, recommendations by either or both of the official arbitrators, as well as other evidence I witnessed in the Aden Divisional Court—so it did not matter if the two arbitrators gave different recommendations to the court. Even though arbitration is an acknowledged method both in tribal custom and the sharia, with the coming of the new Personal Status Law in 1992, it became a requirement only in the case where the wife asked for dissolution of the marriage on the basis of incompatibility.[44]

The New Yemeni Woman Lives

The 1974 Family Law survived only until the summer of 1992, two years after unification, when it was replaced by the Personal Status Law (Law no. 20 of 1992), a code for the unified Yemen. As indicated in the previous discussion, the

44. Article 54 (Al-Jamhuriyya al-Yamaniyya 1992).

Family Law reflected a popular demand for changes in the family relations and in women's legal position. Even though the Family Law was no longer valid, many people continued to adhere to regulations set in it. In marriage records that I went through, most people kept to the nominal 100 dinars (2,600 rials) dower in the period right after the law change.[45] When attending some family dispute cases in the Aden Divisional Court in winter 2001, I observed that the spirit of the law prevailed in the court, too. I witnessed a male judge, trained during the PDRY era in the Aden Law Faculty, who despite the change of law applied the principle of facilitating justice to the female litigant in the case where she was the underdog (which is not always the case) (see Dahlgren 2002).

I had attended the same court when the 1974 law was still in force[46] and observed how decisive the judge's role was in marital dispute cases. Nevertheless, the judge could not disregard the recommendations of the two popular organizations engaged in reconciliation. Female judges in particular were conscious that their verdicts were monitored from the point of view of whether they favored women at the expense of men. The court sometimes needed several sessions to reach a verdict, and in the meantime the couple was intermittently sent to arbitration.

There has been much speculation about why the southern leaders abandoned the 1974 Family Law and failed to fight for the earlier accomplishments concerning women. Even before unification, however, the law seems to have divided male members of the power elite. As a leading member of the PDRY judiciary told me in November 1989, half a year before unification, "Women have too many rights, and I will personally take care that the situation will be corrected." By the late 1980s, the Women's Union was having difficulty gaining support from the Socialist Party for reforms that would improve women's situation.

One matter of dispute was whether the Socialist Party should promote the establishment of Women's Union cells in large workplaces to keep watch over women's issues in labor conflicts. This demand was opposed by the mighty Trade Union, which wanted to be the sole public organization on the shop floor and which claimed to represent women's interests, too. As a rule, each labor committee in a workplace had to have at least one female representative on its board.

45. Marriage records for the Sira District, Oct. 22 to Dec. 31, 1992. The law change came into force in August 1992.

46. This was in 1989. See Dahlgren 2002.

There was often only one woman, whose powers were limited if she failed to get male colleagues' support. During the PDRY era, women's chances to participate in meetings were secured by the law, which ordered meetings to be held during working hours. This provision was abolished in the new labor law issued after unification, however. Even though women had the right guaranteed by the labor law to participate in decisions that concern their working conditions, many women's problems were left unsolved.

One such problem was child care for working mothers: establishing nurseries in accessible locations was no longer the government's priority. By the late 1980s, there were only some ten nurseries in the whole of Aden, most of them with restricted access. If a workingwoman did not live together with adult female relatives who could take care of her children while she worked, she would have to leave them with a relative who lived elsewhere, sometimes on the other side of the town, to which she had to travel every morning and afternoon on public transportation. Considering the rush-hour traffic jams on most of the main roads in Aden, the trip could sometimes take hours. A young woman who had a small baby and worked in a ministry described her daily nightmare in a newspaper article: "I live in Crater, and I have nobody at home to look after my baby girl. I have to take her to my mother, who lives in al-Mansura. The trip between Aden and Mansura is long and has caused my baby to fall ill often. Sometimes I have to leave her with my mother for two days, and that resulted in her stopping sucking. . . . Even my sister has the same problem, but her daughter is already three years old. This is a general problem where the state should provide a solution."[47] Her demand was more nurseries with hours extended to 3:00 P.M.

At the time just before unification, women's situation was still full of unresolved problems. Women had replied to the state call to join the labor market, but their problems were no longer addressed in the state agenda; instead, the voice of those who had grown tired of "too many rights" for women seemed to have become ever louder. The unification provided a perfect framework to readjust male-female power constellations. Why this happened is a question many have tried to answer. Radhia Ihsanullah, one of the early "suffragettes" and leaders

47. "Should We Order the Working Mother to Return Home?" *14 Uktubr*, Aug. 19, 1990, my translation of the title.

of preindependence women's activism, explained the situation in a newspaper interview she gave after returning from years of voluntary exile:

> There are conservative forces who want to return Yemen to the times of the Imamate. They see a threat in the liberated, educated and self-confident woman to those women, who still live subordinated in some parts of the country. None of those women can gain anything if she does not belong to some powerful family or tribe. After unification, those conservative tendencies have felt that their reign *(dawlataha)* is disappearing. Their methods of rule, such as terrorism, threatening with violence and brain washing are no longer effective on young people. They can no longer fight back development that is about to enter to the "Bride of the Arabian Peninsula" and the "Pearl of the Red Sea."[48]

Readjusting Women's "Too Many Rights"

It is clear that the Personal Status Law that replaced the 1974 Family Law was a readjustment of male-female rights in the family to the man's benefit. To add to the catastrophe, the 1992 law was later amended (1998 and 1999),[49] which led to a further deterioration in the status of women, as I later elaborate. Compared to the 1974 law, the Personal Status Law represents a conservative reading of sharia. Nevertheless, it allows rights to women that the northern woman did not earlier enjoy (Women's National Committee 1996, 19–20).

Disparity in women's and men's duties and rights in marriage is manifest in many of the law's provisions. The legal age for marriage is fifteen (§15). In 1999, this paragraph was amended to stipulate that a guardian can contract a marriage for a minor provided she is capable of sustaining intercourse (*saliha lil-wati'a,* §15). Only the bride's guardian can sign her marriage contract, even though her consent is required. Mere silence is a sign of consent (§23). A woman's capacity to give testimony is counted as half that of a man: for instance, a marriage ceremony

48. "After 20 Years, Radhia Ihsanullah Has Woken Up and Spoken," interview by Safa' 'Ali Ibrahim, *14 Uktubr,* Apr. 20, 1992, my translation of the title and the quote.

49. These amendments—steps backward, from women's perspective—were made possible by the 1994 civil war that resulted in the northern occupation of the South, as many Adenis tend to describe the situation, and the withdrawal of the Yemeni Socialist Party from government.

(the signing of the contract in front of a *qadi*) has to be witnessed by two men or one man and two women. The law allows the man an unconditional right to repudiation *(talaq),* and the wife cannot reverse such a divorce. In the initial version of the law (1992), the wife was entitled to compensation provided she took the case to court and the court found the divorce unjust (§71). The compensation could amount to one year's maintenance after her normal *'iddat* maintenance. But this stipulation was removed in 1998.

For the wife, the only way to leave an unsatisfactory marriage is to appeal for a court dissolution of the marriage *(faskh)* in accordance with one of the clauses stipulated by the law, such as the husband's prolonged absence (§32). She can also attempt to persuade her husband to agree on a no-fault divorce *(khul'),* where she pays compensation to him (§72–73). Custody of children in a divorce is normally given to the mother until the age of nine for boys and twelve for girls, but if she exhibits "misconduct," she risks losing them at the age of five. The husband is entitled to marry up to four wives provided he treats them equally (§12). The law regulates the *mahr* (dower), obligatory in signing the marriage contract, but it sets no limits to the amount paid (§33).

Gender discrepancy in the law is most evident in spousal duties. The wife's duty is to allow the husband free sexual access whenever he wants, to obey him in all matters, and to ask for his permission whenever leaving the house (art. 40). The husband has no similar obligations. His duties include maintaining the wife/wives and their common children. He also has to honor the living standard the wife was accustomed to prior to marriage and to treat all his wives equally. These provisions repeat article 27 of the northern law (Family Law of 1978, Yemen Arab Republic, chap. 3).[50] The law constructs the man as the provider and the woman as the one being provided for—in other words, as the one who is dependent on what the man provides. The wife is constituted in the law as a person without her own will and who needs the husband's permission even when going out for a simple errand.

50. Article 27:4 continues: "However, the husband cannot forbid his wife to go out if she has a legitimate excuse or if custom dictates and if there is nothing to bring dishonour or disregard to her duties toward him especially when she goes out to care for her assets or to perform her duty. Caring for her aged parents is considered a legitimate excuse when there is no one else to serve" (as reprinted in Amin 1987, 69).

Other legislative changes complemented what the family legislation started. Nevertheless, those who fought for women's full role in society gained a few victories. Attempts to stop women from working in the military were averted. Women maintained their positions in the working life, despite calls made in newspaper articles for their return home. Women were no longer encouraged to work as judges, and female judges' jurisdiction was limited to civil and commercial law.[51] Outside the Personal Status Law, the unified country's legislation is not bad from women's perspective, but as women's organizations and human rights groups emphasized throughout the 1990s, the implementation of laws is the problem. Women's rights are violated in various fields of administration, not only because their legal status is different from that of men,[52] but also because women are not respected in the same way as men and, furthermore, because women are not aware of their rights.

Conclusions

The PDRY-era gender ideology, officially and popularly called "women's emancipation" *(tahrir al-mar'a)* and "the new Yemeni woman" *(al-mar'a al-gadida),* constructed the woman as the partner to the man in building up the society. Even though the family legislation of that era was not based on full equality between the sexes, it uplifted women's position vis-à-vis the man and liberated the woman from male guardianship and from her dependency on the man. Important provisions in this regard included making the woman a full party in contracting a marriage. In practice, people understood this allowance to mean a free-choice marriage where the woman could choose her husband. Equally important were the stipulations that made the woman a full party in supporting her family. Reforms in education, the labor market, and health care contributed to the same goal. Although many problems remained unresolved, such as the child-care provision, the foundation for an alternative gender discourse was laid during the PDRY era. This foundation did not disappear with Yemeni unification, even

51. Women's ability to enter judge training is not limited by law, but until 2008 women were not admitted in the only school that trains judges in Yemen.

52. On women's and men's different citizenship rights, see Carapico and Würth 2000.

though the discourse itself no longer had institutional support. This gender ideology echoed the demands made during the colonial period to liberate the woman from her "inferior position" *(inhitat al-mar'a).*

This gender representation is in sharp contrast to the postunification legislative and other changes. In the Personal Status Law of 1992, the woman is again constructed as the man's dependent. The law sets strict limits to her movement within marriage and makes her agency dependent on her husband's permission. From the man's perspective, contracting a marriage means taking on the economic burden for his wife and, later on, standing alone for the children's expenses, irrespective of whether his wife has a higher salary. Free-choice *mahr* subjects him again to the market, where economic swings and a woman and her family's greediness, as men tend to view it, set the limits for him to get married in the first place. Both these regulations resonate with what I explained earlier about the colonial period. One difference from the old times, however, is that women's wide participation in the labor market, bringing them independent earnings, means that although the man is obliged to spend his income on the family, his wife no longer has the same obligation. In actual life, however, both salaries are needed to survive in the deteriorating economy.

Even though in the colonial period there was no legislation on marital duties, the gender ideology that I outlined from court rulings in the previous chapter constructed the limits for women's agency, among other details, through the legal term *nashiza* (disobedient woman), a concept that was applied widely in the colonial family court. Whereas in colonial times a woman was considered both economically and morally dependent on her family, in the present era she may have her own income, but her morality is still tied to her being a dutiful member of a family. The necessity of her moral confinement is now motivated by Islam, whereas it was based earlier on the British understanding of the local gender discrepancy. Thus, the family is again presented as the only site where the morality of the sexes can properly be cultivated.

In this chapter and in the previous one, I have attempted to outline gender discourses that emerged in legal practice and in the application of law. The emphasis has been on normative constructs and their application in institutionalized forms. In the following two chapters, I study how ordinary people, men and women, confront these ideologies in their everyday life and construct moral frameworks upon them as well as what kind of agency arises in this interaction. I start by investigating how people talk about these different moral frameworks and how they cope in situations where ambiguous and contesting guidelines for proper, decent, and virtuous action prevail.

5 "This Is Our Customs and Traditions"

As for exploiting and oppressing the woman in the house, this has become an indisputable matter which cannot be argued and when you attempt to discuss it, you simply discuss the possibility of sunrise from the direction of sunset.

—PRESIDENT SALIM RUBAYA 'ALI, speech at the first congress of the General Union of Yemeni Women, *Documents of the General Union of Yemeni Women*

IN THIS CHAPTER, I explore notions of normativity, propriety, and morality the way they appear in talk among people about the opposite sex. I focus on different spheres of life where the sexes meet and make meaning of gendered divisions, such as in marriage, family life, child raising, work, and the world of imagination. I am in particular interested in seeing how people apply notions of gender in everyday talk and what meanings such renderings carry. I then contrast such popular gender ideologies to the ones I outlined in the two previous chapters and discuss whether these two levels meet. This comparison allows me to draw more general conclusions on moral frameworks as gendered notions that organize talk about everyday life.

I start by looking at how an elderly man discursively constitutes an image of himself as "strong." "Strong" and "weak" are metaphors often applied by people when discussing male and female roles in society and echo the way social groups and strata are traditionally classified, as I later explain. This is a story of an immigrant man, Salim (all names here are pseudonyms), who settled in Aden, found a job, set up a family, and attained a respectable place in the town's social networks. He came from the countryside north of Aden in the early 1960s as a young man to try his luck in the blooming labor market of the British colony. In telling his story, I focus on "traditional marriage," or marriage that honors what are called customs and traditions (*'adat wa taqalid*), and on his way of addressing the attributes that make a man strong and a woman weak.

Salim was seventeen years old when he moved to Aden. He joined a foreign company working as a manual laborer, a job he found through contacts with people from his home area. A fellow countryman introduced the *muqaddam* (labor contractor) who gave him a job. In the beginning, the work was hard, and there was not much leisure time. However, Salim preferred to work hard because there was not much else to do, and he needed money to get married. Born in 1943, he spent his childhood in a small town in the sultanate of Lahig, the agrarian Western Aden Protectorate state, where many Adeni migrant workers came from at the time. His father had a shop in the *suq,* market, in the town of al-Hauta, where he sold luxury goods imported from abroad and transported from Aden to Lahig by a *gammala,* a camel cart. Mirrors, perfumes, needles, and ladies' creams were among the items displayed in his prosperous shop. "It was like in Suq Bohora,"[1] Salim recalled. Later on, when the asphalt road came to Lahig, the father bought his own car and started a transport business, a prosperous field of enterprise during the time when everything except food came to the countryside through the international port in Aden. The father had married Salim's mother when she still was very young, ten or fifteen years his junior.[2] In due course, she bore him three boys and four girls. Another four of her children died—the first at the age of two from diarrhea, the next also of nutritional problems and a swollen skull, and twins, a boy and a girl, after developing a high fever from malaria or something else, Salim remembered his sisters having told him.

Describing his first abode in Aden, Salim became excited about how life was different in the old days. "Everything was simple in the old days, you didn't need much," he explained. Houses were modest huts with an earth floor and thatched roof. Walls were made of mud brick: "It was a cooling material in the hot season, much better than the cement and concrete of these days." The exterior of the hut was painted with whitewash, *bidha,* made locally by burning *nurah* stone. Not everybody had a wooden bed with the legs made from date tree wood and the bottom woven from natural rope *(hibal).* Salim had a date tree carpet for sleeping. The only piece of furniture in his house was a *sanduq,* a beautifully

1. Suq Bohora is a section in Crater market that used to have many shopkeepers from the Bohora community. Today it is the main market street for perfumes, ladies' wear, and imported luxuries.

2. The ideal age gap is only a couple of years.

carved wooden box where he stored his clothes and other belongings during the daytime when he worked. When visitors came, everybody sat on the floor; there were no cushions in a poor man's house. Wealthy people had manual fans attached to the ceiling and servants to move them. Hand fans made of straw were used in "*kutcha* huts," as small houses like Salim's were called, to drive away flies and to get some respite from the sultry air. A kerosene lantern *(fanus)* gave light, and a simple kerosene cooker was used to prepare food. Houses like Salim's, a bachelor without any of his family accompanying him, did not have much kitchenware. A clay pot *(gahla)* was used for cooking. "That was enough," Salim said.

Poor people did not have many clothes either: "I did not need much, only a few clothes." New clothes were purchased only on an *'id,* holiday. A belt, *futa* (loincloth wrapped round the waist and sometimes tied with a belt), *kufiyya* (skull cap), *kaut* (tailor-made jacket), and *imama* (turban, the best ones made out of silk from India and wrapped round the head) were all he had at that time: "Sometimes I went to the shoemaker to have new leather shoes made." However, leather shoes were not the work footwear; simple sandals (*mad'as,* pl. *mada'is*) were more practical. When after a couple of years Salim joined the police force, he got a uniform and was able to save his clothes for free-time use only. Salim recalled that people did not always buy clothes readymade or have them made by an artisan. Many people relied on a home supply. Women used to sew at home, preparing *kufiyyas* for men and *niqabs* (face veils), *dar'as* (sleeveless voile dresses), and *shaidors* (black overcoats) for women.

"Food was natural, everything was bought fresh and prepared the same day." Imported food and European delicacies were not for the ordinary man, even though available in the market. Fresh vegetables from the neighboring countryside, fish from the seashore, and meat on special occasions composed the menu. Meat was lamb, goat, or mutton and occasionally cow, but Salim did not get it often. Cabbage, *kabish,* offered the daily nutrition. Instead of rice or bread made from wheat flour, he ate his meals with *ghurba,* a bread made of *jowari* (sorghum). *Ruti,* the usual bread today that is bought from a local bakery, was not available in those days. *Khubz,* flat bread made from wheat, came later on. It was baked at home in a *tannur* oven or just on a pan. Salim remembered that *ruti* and rice came to Aden around 1945–50, the same time as tea did, all from India.[3] Other food items that came from outside were wheat *(burr)* and barley, imported from the interior or from the Yemen, and sugar, which came in ships from Formosa. Before that, people used to drink *bunn* (coffee made of beans grown in highland Yemen) or *qishr,* a spicy drink prepared from coffee husks and cooked with plenty of ginger. The town was full of coffee shops where men used to sit for long hours exchanging news with passers-by, Salim remembered.

With the new daily food items—*ruti,* rice, and tea—came a big change, Salim says. People now wanted to take their daily food with either *ruti* or rice. The local man started to imitate the foreigners' way of life. According to Salim, the change in nutrition was accompanied by a similar change in medicine. Earlier, all medicine was "natural, from the trees." Then factory-made medicines arrived, and everybody started to use them. First came sulfa, then penicillin. Other industrially produced medicines followed. To get medicine, people had to go to the hospital or pharmacy and spend more money than they were used to spending. Medicine was previously either prepared at home or bought at the street corner from the *riggal salih,* the ingenious medicine man who prepared the substances from local herbs. As a consequence of the change in what was available, Salim believed, people's habits changed, and they became dependent on the outside. Life was no longer uncomplicated, where "you [did] not need much, just simple things."

In the old days, Salim commented, you could marry with little money. In 1964, he married a distant relative. The wedding was celebrated in Lahig over a three-day period. After the wedding, he brought his wife to Aden. Arranging the marriage was not a problem, Salim explains. Two years earlier, while working in the Aden Civil Police force, he had obtained a flat in Khormaksar. The British built new housing compounds in this new area, allocated to those working in the colonial administration. Even though Salim did not have any formal education, he could take evening classes for government employees to learn English, which improved his career prospects considerably, and he soon was promoted. In his

3. Frederick Hunter shows that rice was being imported to Aden in large quantities from India some hundred years earlier. According to him, each social category purchased the quality of rice it could afford ([1877] 1968, 63–64).

work, he rode a motorbike and occasionally a police car, too. To be able to marry, a proper flat in Aden was considered an asset the equivalent of a big dower. With a government job and a proper flat, Salim's value in the marriage market increased considerably. His savings would not have allowed him to marry so soon, anyway. He was not wealthy, but he was financially safe, as he put it. At that time, only the British, other foreigners, and some local businesspeople had money and cars: "If you did not have a car, you walked. Goods you transported in a camel cart. But when buses came, people became lazy." By the time of his youth, the railroad from Ma'alla to Wadi al-Khudad (northwest of Aden) no longer existed. Earlier it brought water from Lahig to Aden and transported passengers and goods in return. Already in his childhood the railroad was considered something ancient. If something was very old, it was said to be as old as the railway to al-Khudad.

Salim recalled how the natural manner of life was present also in women's appearance and body. Women's hair was "natural and long, sometimes to the thighs or knees." Women were different than they are today in other respects as well: "At that time women made *tahara* [female "circumcision"; literally "purification"], in Aden, too. It is in Islam. It is for both Muslim men and women. They cut it everywhere, but with very young girls only, within seven days and two weeks."[4] Following the custom in his family, he has had all his daughters "purified."

After independence, Salim's career took a new turn when he was recruited to a ministry. There was a short supply of literate people and those with experience in administration to fill all the posts left vacant by the British and Indians, and Salim's literacy in English became a big advantage again. He soon advanced to a senior position. He eventually retired as a chief of section in a ministry in charge of some of the vital services for the entire southern part of Yemen. From a simple background, he made his way to ever new successes, and in his old age he could look back with pride. At the end of telling me his story, Salim looked pleased and pronounced, "Wasn't it a good story?" I said, "Yes, very good indeed. Perhaps I could speak with your wife, too?" Salim looked troubled and replied, "Oh no, she cannot give you a good story."

4. Female genital mutilation or circumcision, also called *khitan*, is not widely practiced in Aden, and it is questionable whether it was practiced on a large scale even in the 1960s. In the Lahig governorate, its prevalence varies depending on the area. Nowadays, in and around the town of Lahig (al-Hauta), the operation involves cutting the tips of the labia minor. See Khalil 1972.

In Salim's account, we can follow how a man constitutes his claim to respect. In his youth, he came to a strange town without his family. But he did not get by solely on his own devices. He relied on networks of people from his home area and with a similar background to find both work and a place to stay. Even today, when *muqaddams* and *surungs* (headmen and labor contractors) no longer hire people, tribal networks and kinship relations form clusters of people in workplaces who share roots and affinities. In one office, there might be many people from Meyun, Perim Island, and in another office perhaps many people from a particular Abyani tribe. These networks are the social web people use in solving problems, obtaining information, contracting marriages, purchasing properties, and promoting careers. Being part of such a network means not only having social capital, but also being in the position to have access to resources and capacities that can be used in cultivating a person's *karama* (respect). These networks helped Salim to find his place in Aden and to reach beyond what his humble start promised. But such networks are not a personal favoring system that helps anyone with the right connections, nor would it include bribery and corruption, which came to Aden only after the unification. These networks exist, but it is up to each person to use them in the best possible way. A respectful position in the eyes of others cannot be achieved without personal accomplishments. A rich man is not respected because he has accumulated wealth, but rather because he has used his wealth in a respectful way to the benefit of the community.

In Salim's account, *natural* is the synonym for *local* and *self-made* and refers to a man's innate capacity to defend his autonomy. It stands in opposition to anything imported, manufactured, and foreign, manifesting dependence on outside help—that is, indicating a person's weakness. In a nostalgic fashion, Salim's account describes this lost autonomy that in the old times made a man feel strong and independent in his own community. Even though the British were there, they did not interfere with the way Salim lived his life outside work. Yet even if the society around him changed, his home did not. In his house, there was a strict division of labor between him and his wife. He earned the money, and his wife ran the household. Both fulfilled their duties and stayed away from the other's domain. The home is the woman's sphere, from which men have to keep away and where they are expected only at lunch and dinner time and to sleep at night. In Salim's home, the wife dominated the space, and Salim had to stay away. The unwritten "contract" served everybody's needs, and it is the way Salim thought things should be. He did not care for her company, and as he said, "She cannot give you a good story."

Women's stories are not relevant in the same way as men's. As Salim said, "The Yemeni man likes everything to be ready when he comes home." Food served warm on time, a clean house, and well-dressed children form his idea of a well-kept household and a successful wife. The good wife runs the home but remains invisible when not needed, such as when the man's guests arrive. Not only that, even her story cannot be interesting. It is, after all, the man who is mobile and sees things around him, acting for the benefit of the whole family. But this does not mean that the woman's role is of lesser importance. The man would not be complete, Salim opined, without a woman. Both man's and woman's contributions are needed to establish the happy family.

Salim explained that this natural order is established in Islam. Islam also lays down the norm for sexual relations between the man and the woman. The man is the active party, and the woman simply "nurtures his seed." As Salim described sexual intercourse between man and woman, "The man enters and puts his seed in there. The woman nurtures the seed that the man has placed there. Islam gives everything to the man and the woman. Men and women have different spheres of life because they are different by nature." The Islamic right for a man to marry

13. Men of religion sitting inside al-'Aydarus mosque in Crater. Photograph by the author, 1988.

more than one woman at a time, Salim explained, is based on practical grounds: "It is reasonable that the man can take four wives because there are so many widows. If a man sees someone he likes, it is better that he marries her than that he keeps her as a lover. It is better to have legitimate relations than illegitimate ones, like you do in the West." In order to spark debate, I asked him, "What if the woman could take several husbands, too?" "That is NOT possible," Salim replied abruptly, and the discussion was over.

The Strong Man

In Salim's account, one characteristic of a man is being strong *(qawi)* in a metaphorical sense. This is how "our customs and traditions are," as he put it. Being strong has many implications. Economically it relates to being capable to provide for a family. Socially it relates to the category of people who are capable and entitled to have the means to defend themselves and provide protection for those who do not possess that capacity, the so-called weak ones (sing. *da'if*, pl. *du'afa*). In the tribal areas in the Yemeni countryside, this means in simple terms a man's right to protect himself and his possessions and, in order to do that, to be entitled to carry a weapon. Weak people—such as women, members of socially low categories, and non-Arabs or non-Muslims—do not have the right to carry a gun but instead remain under the protection of the "strong people."[5]

However, being a weak person *(da'if)* means not only being deprived of carrying arms, but also lacking the quality called "honor" *(sharaf)*. A person who is *qalil asl*, "of lesser roots"—that is, lacking a respectable origin—cannot claim prestige and respect for his forefathers. Despised social categories, such as the *akhdam*, possess unmerited ancestral roots, which stigmatize each new generation. Salim, the son of a *mudakkan* (shop owner), did not have the high ancestry

5. For how this system functions in Hadhramaut, see Bujra 1971, 35. In Aden, carrying firearms, daggers (sing. *ganbiyyah*), and other weapons has been forbidden for a long time. The ban was started by the British and the Socialists continued it. After unification, the general feeling in Aden was that no firearms or other weaponry should be allowed in the town, and thus many considered the government decision to continue the ban that followed a period of anomaly as a victory. Throughout the countryside outside Aden after unification, rifles and daggers reemerged as part of men's everyday outfit.

that the "strongest" social groups possess. This connection to ancestry can be called the social meaning of being strong.

"Being strong" politically means having autonomy and not needing outside help. Such autonomy does not mean, however, that help from kinship, a tribal unit, or a neighbor is not utilized or called for. It is a matter of being able to benefit from the social networks that belong to a person. In the northern Yemeni tribal society, autonomy and personal integrity are part of the status of being a tribal man. In Salim's account, autonomy and integrity entail self-sustainability and self-reliance. As he explained, the change in lifestyle that took place in the mid–twentieth century alienated the Adeni man from these ideals and forced him into the dependency on the outside sources of a modern society. The British policy of not interfering with "custom and religion" meant not interfering with the local man and his family. After independence, steps were taken slowly to change the woman's position—"slowly" because the authorities knew that strong resistance to this change also prevailed. For a man such as Salim, with a like-minded wife, no particular effort was needed to keep his family outside the changes. In many cases, the family has remained the man's autonomous area, where he alone exercises control, or at least this is what men usually believe. Women often have a different idea, a matter to which I turn later.

Beyond the economic, social, and political meanings of being "strong," the sexual meaning is perhaps the one most commonly referred to. According to this representation, the Adeni man is sexually strong—not only in being able to perform sexually, but also in being potent all the time. It is a source of endless bragging, story-telling, and joking. "The Yemeni man is always ready," said a government employee, a man in his late thirties, when he described to me the benefits of the *futa,* the traditional Adeni man's attire. Not only does the *futa* allow the man to be instantly available for sexual intercourse, but the man who wears it is also immediately ready to perform. Men's ideas on male sexuality focus on penetration and on the capacity to have a long-lasting erection. The notion of the sexually dominant man somewhat contradicts the belief in women's active sexuality, which in some accounts exceeds men's capacity to perform. When I was in Aden, stories were spread of the "sexually insatiable" Soqotran women and of a woman in Aden who picked up men in her car and took them to a remote place for sex, even though nobody actually met a man who had been picked up by that woman and few had ever talked to a Soqotran person. Cars, driving, and beaches often serve as the scene for stories of illicit sexual encounters. Such stories contradict the idea of man as the active party, the one who penetrates and puts his seed inside the woman, as Salim put it.

Men often talk about sex in relation to *qat* chewing. For most men I have talked to, *qat* and sex belong together. Even though it has many social purposes, too, *qat* chewing to men links to the ability to perform well sexually. In general, men's and women's accounts of *qat* chewing are markedly different. Before unification, when few women in Aden were in the habit of chewing, no woman explained the habit to me in terms of sexual pleasure. For a woman, it would be considered shameful to make such a link. One housewife whose husband was a shopkeeper and whose children had passed the age of childhood told me that she chewed in order to get extra energy for cleaning her house. Another woman in her late fifties, a widow of a bookkeeper, explained that she did not chew "really"; she only took a little. Many women I met who told me that they were in the habit of chewing in fact took very little. It was more like social chewing where the husband, son, or other male relative took care of buying *qat* for the entire family and brought a little to the woman, too, who then consumed it while spending a brief resting moment together with her family. In men's *qat* gatherings, a person who does not fully concentrate on chewing would be called a nonchewer. Before unification, women were not supposed to chew the way men do, and even after that they were not to talk about sex in relation to chewing. If a woman chewed, she had other motivations, or she did not do it properly. Reasons for chewing were presented in a framework that was considered proper for a woman. In contrast, men usually tend to draw links between *qat* chewing and sexual fantasies, expectations for sex, and actual experiences. Another government functionary, also in his thirties, explained his habits during a good Thursday night *qat* chew. He started his afternoon by allowing his wife to serve him a proper lunch that filled his stomach for the rest of the day. He then went to a friend or colleague's place where other men also gathered, and there he chewed his favorite *qat* brand, discussing politics and other important matters with the others. After he finished chewing, often late in the evening, he liked to take a beer or a small whisky to cool down a little. Then he was ready for the pleasures of lovemaking, the highlight of the evening. With *qat* in his blood, he felt strong and capable. If he happened to have a girlfriend, he would go to her, but if not, he would settle for his wife. In the customs and discourses connected to *qat* chewing, a marked gender difference is manifested. Whereas for a woman *qat* can make her feel energetic (to perform household chores, for instance), for a man it makes him physically stronger.[6]

The Weak Woman

The notion of the strong man finds its contrast in the weak woman. Man has to be strong because woman is weak and in need of protection and moral guidance. According to this representation, the woman's weakness is manifest not only in the absence of physical strength, but also in the deficient *(naqisa)* nature of her mentality. Like a small child, the woman lacks *'aql* (reason, rationality, common sense), the quality needed to judge what is right and wrong. As Salim explained, men and women are profoundly different. Where men know religion and maintain creed as the guiding force in their behavior, women, who can neither read nor understand Islamic principles, are guided by superstitions *(khurafat)* and backward thinking *(takhalluf)*. This quality makes them ignorant *(gahila)*. From a man's perspective, these ideas are part and parcel of "our customs and traditions." For example, Salim mentioned that whenever any health problem or other trouble arises, a woman turns to the *sahib al-kitab* (local magical healer)[7] and allows him to cheat and manipulate her. He will ask her to wear an amulet *(hirz)*, perform some nonsensical rituals, and refrain from going to the doctor. Lacking reason of her own, a woman therefore cannot be trusted or left to her own devices. Instead of education, it is better to offer the woman tasks that match her qualities. The woman is the "mistress of the household" *(sayyidat al-manzil)*. This is what Islam means for the man and the woman, Salim asserted. Each gets what is good for him or for her.

Even some women consider that women lack the capacities needed outside the home, such as those that men have. When I asked women who live as housewives whether women should go out to work, many replied that they should only if they have an education. If not, it is better that they stay at home. During the

6. This belief disregards the effects of *qat* chewing on health. With long-term use, *qat* causes impotency.

7. "Magical" healing differs from the kind of healing Salim mentioned in his story—that is, applying herbal medicine.

first years of the PDRY, until the early 1980s, a person had to be literate in order to be able to take factory work. Even though this policy was later abandoned, many people still think of it is a requirement.

Some men believe that women's intellectual weakness is not innate, but that there are nevertheless objective reasons for it. This argument has variations according to which period of recent history is in question. During colonial times and when the countryside was ruled by feudal *(iqta')* shaykhs and sultans, it is explained, the woman was kept in ignorance by the reactionary ideology of the colonizers and their lackeys outside Aden. The woman was confined "inside four walls," and her going to school was prevented in families guided by backward thinking and by the rulers' deliberate policy of curtailing girls' education. After independence, when schools were opened to females on a large scale, not every woman wanted to "improve herself" and "acquire knowledge" *(tatwir min ma'arif)*. Therefore, nowadays a woman's mental deficiency might be owing to her "voluntary confinement" inside four walls and her lack of interest in developing herself by acquiring even the most basic skills of reading and writing.

The government employee who described his *qat* pleasures preferred another woman's company to that of his own wife, not only for sex, but also for intellectual stimulation. According to him, his wife had no interest in things around her. He had several times tried to push her to join a literacy class, but she always refused. The way he saw it, as a couple they were not intellectually matched. Another man, a driver in his thirties, talked in a bitter voice about the mismatched intellectual interests between him and his wife. He was disappointed in his marriage because he did not have any thoughts to share with his wife. According to him, they shared only the home, children, and a routine, unemotional sex life. When I asked him if there was anything else they had in common, he replied bluntly, "Mafish!" (Nothing!). From the wife's point of view, it might be that she felt that her husband did not value what is important to her.

In many homes, though, I observed that women deliberately kept men outside women's affairs. The practice of keeping men away from the home outside of eating and sleeping hours naturally contributes to this separation. Women might consider that the segregation of sexes and avoidance should be manifest in a clear separation of men's and women's fields of life. In more segregated parts of Yemen, the sexual aspect in male-female relations is often overemphasized, as the popular saying "out of sight, out of mind" puts it.

Men sometimes like to comment on women in terms of what they allegedly cannot do. "Women just cannot do the same things as men can," explained an army cook in his fifties: "For instance, women cannot shoot. They are not capable of that." That this man was a professional cook and prepared meals at home on festive days, contributed to his superiority toward his wife. This man had a demeaning profession, but at home he could have the standing he lacked at work.[8]

One man, a university lecturer in his fifties, described to me women's ignorance in terms of the way they speak. He explained that the loud penetrating voice that some women have is a sign of ignorance. It did not seem to matter to him that the woman would not otherwise be heard in surroundings where her thoughts are not counted. I once asked him why he thought my neighbor, a housewife recently married to an army member of staff, listened to music from her radio so loud that the voice quality broke. To my ear, it was no longer music. He explained that this habit indicated my neighbor's mentality: "It is simple ignorance. Such women do not understand anything."

This explanation links gender deficiency to social structure. Women of lower social classes, not women in general, are ignorant. According to the university man, education contributes to making the distinction between the social categories: it is in part a question of inherited mental inferiority, the "bad customs" *('adat sayyi'at)* of her kind of people, and in part a question of being a woman, which makes one more vulnerable than a man to having such deficiency. A woman's ignorance is a result of her belonging to the inferior sex, which does not have access to the resources the strong sex has. According to this man, the *akhdam* are ignorant and dirty and do not know good manners. Their ignorance is the result of being brought up in an atmosphere where bad customs and manners are bred.

Proverbs and sayings *(amthal)* are perhaps the most illuminating examples of misogyny. There are naturally many positive ones, too, though, such as "The wise woman builds her own home" (*"Al-mar'ah al-hakimah tibni baytha"*) (Khan 1933, 63). That means a woman should not let anyone else be in charge in her

8. In reference to Sana'a, Gabriele vom Bruck (1996) has argued that low-category men are believed to bear feminine qualities, which in part explains their low status socially. In Aden, I have not encountered such qualities among men in this category.

household. The negative sayings can be divided into two categories: first, those that degrade woman mentally and, second, those that depict her as a satanic being or a source of evil. "The minds of women are in their knees" belongs to the first group. It carries a similar message as "Women are deficient in mind and in faith." These two are rather straightforward and require no further explanation. The saying "The man who listens to women is one of them" carries the message that men are better off not consulting their wives when making decisions. If that saying is directed to men, another is addressed to women: "The chaste woman does not frequently leave her husband's home." A similar message lies in the following proverb, repeated by older women in particular and not always in a negative sense: "The woman has two places, the home and the grave."

Sayings that imply women's evil nature compare women either with Satan or with such vicious animals as snakes and scorpions: "A woman is like a scorpion. When she shows her teeth, she is not smiling."[9] The use of these negative proverbs about women was discouraged during the early years of the PDRY, and the government made an effort to eradicate them. In his speech to the Women's Union congress in 1976 , President Salim Rubaya 'Ali expressed the concern as follows:

> The Yemeni Woman was and is still deprived of her rights of equality with man. Not only that, but she was also despised and considered a worthless thing. This social intercourse was not the end of the matter but what is most striking is that the Yemeni Woman is treated by grievous beating and painful words in the case of any occurrence of the simplest family differences. It is no wonder if we say that the father, the brother and the husband are the legitimate floggers and perhaps two of the three agree to execute together the punishment of flogging.
>
> As for exploiting and oppressing the woman in the house, this has become an indisputable matter which cannot be argued and when you attempt to dis-

9. Some of these negative proverbs are reproduced in Women's Union documents in order to illustrate the inferior position of women in a culture patterned by "negative customs" and the "feudal" and colonial rule that prevailed in Aden and the countryside prior to independence, a state of affairs that the Women's Union fought with the slogan "Against Ignorance and for the Love of Work" (see General Union of Yemeni Women 1977, 12–13). In contrast, Yacub Khan's collection of Adeni proverbs from 1933 does not contain a single negative proverb on women (see Khan 1933).

> cuss it, you simply discuss the possibility of sunrise from the direction of sunset. (General Union of Yemeni Women 1977, 3–4, translation given in source)

The official attempt to eradicate degrading notions of women proved fruitful, in particular when combined with other measures to change women's role in society. In the course of women's increased participation in education and the labor market, where they could show that they can perform the same tasks as men and often even better, and when capable women became nationwide public figures, the ideas of women's innate inferiority met with other kinds of representations whenever gender roles were debated. When men talked about women, the practice of uttering "May Allah honor you" after the word *woman* was slowly replaced by such expressions as "Women are half the society," "Honor any woman like your sister," and "the new Yemeni woman," which was also repeated in radio broadcasts and in the official rhetoric of "women's emancipation" *(tahrir al-mar'a).*

By the time of Yemeni unification, talk about women's inborn deficiency was no longer the custom in Aden, but it was soon replaced by another type of negative thinking about women: an educated woman as a marriage partner came to be resented. The question of whether an uneducated bride is preferred to an educated one was hotly debated in the early 1990s. In the debate, many men irrespective of age, education, and occupation expressed their preference for an uneducated wife because, as they put it, an educated woman makes too many demands and does not easily comply with the role reserved for her in his house. A workingwoman has her work concerns first in her mind and thus neglects her husband's needs and is bad at running the household and bringing up the children. The concern was more about workingwomen's alleged disregard of the household duties than about their chastity. As Salim put it, "The Yemeni man likes everything to be ready for him when he comes home."

Educated women were shocked by such attitudes among men, even though in many families such ideas were nothing new. As a middle-aged woman in a public office put it, "Our leaders talk about democracy, but in their homes there is no democracy at all." Unmarried university students felt particularly uneasy with the wave of "traditional thinking." In the Medical College, I was told, female students made a deliberate choice in favor of a professional career over marriage when they chose to study medicine in the first place. Such a choice has become a real option, but only if the young woman's parents support her.

Men of Custom and Women of Religion

Although young women seem to accept with fatalism the idea that education is a problem in the marriage market, senior workingwomen often find it difficult to accept such thinking. One female reader responded to male readers who in issues of *al-Thawra* newspaper in 1991 supported the idea that an uneducated wife is better than an educated one:

> I find it depressing to know that such opinions are held by our Yemeni youth. It seems many of those men who responded to the debate have condemned educated women without justification.
>
> Many Yemeni men seem to think the oriental man is governed by customs, traditions and religion. But what about the oriental woman? By what is she governed? The oriental woman and the Yemeni woman in particular is governed by religion before she is governed by tradition.
>
> Marriage should be considered an arrangement in which two people become one and not a system of master and a slave, as I have observed in many families.
>
> Do you think that when a woman leaves her home to shop or to go to work or visit a friend her virtue is at stake? I believe it is impossible for a husband or brother to leave his job or school in order to escort his female relatives through the streets.
>
> We Yemenis know good manners. . . . The chaste woman who goes out takes her chastity wherever she goes.
>
> Yemeni men, are you going to leave your jobs to act as an escort service? If men are unwilling to disrupt their lives to adhere to this custom and our society persists in demanding that it continue, then no woman will be able to go outside of her home for any reason whatsoever.
>
> I would like to add that we should not forget that we live in a society which is still conservative.
>
> Marrying an educated female is not the problem many men believe it is. The difference educated women can make to our society is that the learned wife will raise a new generation of literate youth.[10]

The female author of this op-ed piece argues from the point of view of the modern, educated workingwoman. She establishes the dignity and moral integ-

10. Op-ed piece by Arwa Muhammad in *al-Thawra* (winter 1991), as translated and reprinted in *Middle East Times,* Yemen edition (Feb. 1991), 2.

rity of the educated woman in the qualities that she draws from "religion" and contrasts those characteristics to men's alleged sloppiness in complying first and foremost with these superior principles. She argues that for men the high values of religion come second, after the morally secondary qualities that "customs and traditions" can provide. Further, she argues that the educated woman carries her moral integrity and chastity in her mind and is therefore capable of guarding her own morality without male guidance. To her mind, a marriage that unites two people unmatched intellectually results in nothing but slavery, where the husband is the master and the wife has to comply to his every whim. Thus, she hints at the prevalence of servile relations in some homes. In Aden, as in other parts of Yemen, acting as a servant is generally considered degrading. A marriage based on master-slave relations is thus morally questionable and incompatible with the high values of religion.

By applying the moral repertoire assigned to religion, the female author of the op-ed piece invokes positive forces to justify her claim that the educated woman is the best wife. By linking illiteracy to a lack of knowledge in how to act properly, she launches strong moral arguments connected to religion to justify women's rights to an education. She points to the conflict between men's insistence on guarding their womenfolk and women's need to move freely in performing duties outside the home. For her, there is no need for guardianship because women aspire to their religion's high moral values. This line of argumentation follows the revolutionary discourse on "women's emancipation"—that is, that the woman's chastity lies in her mind. But the author deviates from that discourse by drawing on a morality she calls "religion."

At that period, a year after Yemeni unification in 1990, many women felt that men had suddenly turned their backs on the ideals of the revolution and returned to values typical of the preindependence era when illiteracy was still common. A middle-aged woman working in an executive position in a foreign company and who had participated in the liberation struggle told me bitterly: "I thought we had passed this already. As if men have not learned anything. Now they demand that we workingwomen should again have a male chaperone to accompany us performing our work duties. I cannot anymore make trips round the country, which is part of my work, without asking my grown-up son or my husband to accompany me. It does not matter that I have a company car and a driver. I thought we had passed this stage of thinking already." This woman considered the new atmosphere to be so bad that after the devastating civil war in 1994, she left the country. But not only workingwomen remained critical of the new wave of "traditional thinking." Men, too, used hard words to describe the situation. An unmarried government accountant in his early thirties put it this way: "We have turned the historical clock a hundred years backward."

In the summer of 1992, this change was accompanied by the replacement of the 1974 Family Law with the Personal Status Law, which allowed men to take a cowife. Even though the number of polygamous marriages did not rise extensively in Aden, many people felt that the mere possibility gave men a powerful weapon to put wives in their place. As one man, a government employee in his early forties and married with children, described his situation, "I have told my wife that I might take another wife. She did not seem to like it, but said nothing. I am not yet sure about this, but it is good that we now have the chance. Maybe in the future." When I asked him if he was happy in his present marriage and if he would like to keep his present wife, he replied, "Yes." But most people I asked, men and women, considered polygamy a negative custom that only rich people and those in power practice. The bad economic situation that emerged in Aden after unification made people consider polygamy not a viable option, but simply a curiosity.

The Perfect Woman

How do men see women in positive and idealistic terms? Many men I talked to valued women's company, whether they were family members, neighbors, or work colleagues. Men tended to view with apprehension the lack of a woman to talk to. In many offices, I observed nonkin men visiting female employees just to have a chat. Despite the wave of sexual segregation that swept over Aden in the early 1990s, workplaces remained unsegregated. A workingwoman who received male guests in her office did not get a bad reputation. Instead, people tended to think that she was very popular, or at least this is what they said. When the streets were "veiled" and women adopted a reserved and hostile attitude to nonkin men as part of avoidance, workplaces continued to be havens for men who wanted to see a female face and engage in friendly communication. But women, too, preferred the easygoing atmosphere characteristic of Adeni working life, which lacked tension and the fear of losing one's reputation and included socially egalitarian rather than selective interaction.

Nevertheless, when asked whether a woman can engage in conversation with a man in her own house, most people replied: "Only if the man is her close relative or someone she cannot marry" (*"Min al-aqarib aw al-harim"*). This normative answer is the rule many a man would like his wife or sister to follow, but without restricting him from meeting nonkin women. Even though both men and women gave this answer, it does not mean that the rule was actually followed. Like normative notions in general, this rule was referred to in order to invoke the positive implications that the mentioning of the rule brings about. In guiding actual practice, however, a rule is an insufficient lead to scrutinize moral principles, as Pierre Bourdieu has pointed out about rules in general (1977, 17).

Those men who thought they did not have emotionally much in common with their wives felt bad about it. But men also prefer a wife who is a good housekeeper. As Salim put it, the ideal *sayyidat al-manzil* is the one who keeps the home in order. A wife who is lazy, careless, and indifferent to household duties risks getting the reputation of a bad wife among relatives and in the neighborhood. She might be called a *brinsiyyah*, "princess," the "one who sleeps late and fails to get up earlier than the rest of the family to prepare breakfast." Greediness and extravagant demands for jewelry and clothes are other bad qualities a wife can have, from a male point of view. They seem to be a constant source of complaint. Such complaints are often about the alleged greediness in negotiating the marriage payments. Some men feel that women's desire for jewelry is endless and that this insatiability destroys the man and the marriage.

However, if men are economically able to provide and are happy with the marriage, they like to buy new rings and bracelets for their wives, thus evincing their satisfaction with the marriage. As we saw earlier, the ability to pay extravagant amounts in marriage payments is also a source of boasting. One young man who was married in 2001 told me enthusiastically that he was able to pay fifty thousand Yemeni rials[11] in jewelry and cash to his bride. He succeeded in raising this amount not on his own efforts—he was too young to have managed to save enough—but thanks to help from his kin: every earning member had

11. This marriage was contracted in the early 2001, when the highest amounts paid as *mahr* in Aden reached around one hundred thousand Yemen rials. Since Yemeni unification, amounts paid in Aden tend to follow with some delay what is paid in the capital, Sana'a, where amounts climbed up to half a million rials at that period.

contributed. It was a matter of family pride to be able to marry off the young man in a respectable and prosperous way even though the family was not particularly wealthy. Some members, including the head of the family, worked in the Persian Gulf countries and could command much higher salaries than if working in Yemen. The issue of high marriage payments is not simple among men, as this example shows. Meeting a high *mahr* can be both a distress to an eligible bachelor and a merit from which the family benefits as a whole (see more on this topic in Dahlgren 2005).

Even though men often spend most of the day and evenings outside home and seem uninterested in the family, a happy marriage and home seem to be a top priority to every man. Getting married in the first place is preferred by men, even though remaining a bachelor does not mark a man the same way as a woman. But men prefer to marry an "easy" woman—that is, a woman who is sympathetic to his needs and aspirations, who listens to him and obeys when needed, and who does not make his life miserable by making him slave away in trying to meet her never-ending demands. Men are usually not very suspicious about their wives' possible misbehavior and indecency and allow them to move freely outside the home. But a man might take measures to control his wife if there is talk about her *(kalam nas)*. In divorce cases in the Aden Divisional Court, men's accusations of *zina* (illegitimate sexual encounter) appear occasionally, but it is seldom the only cause for divorce. The fact that it is rarely the only cause does not mean, however, that women do not cheat on their husbands. Their cheating is simply a matter difficult to prove.

Some men do like to exercise control over their wives in their everyday comings and goings. This practice seems to be more usual among recently married young people than among older people. Because most men spend the day and evening outside the home, they cannot be 100 percent sure what their womenfolk are engaged in while out of sight. If family or neighborhood rumors indicate that something is wrong, senior female family members might be engaged to solve the problem. A woman who goes out too often might provoke marriage disputes. One workingwoman in her midthirties complained to me that her husband had become increasingly irritated after two years of marriage because her working hours were unusually long by Adeni standards. She worked from seven in the morning until three o'clock in the afternoon, and when arriving home, she often felt so tired that she only wanted to take a nap. Her husband, who arrived from

14. A woman smoking a *mada'a,* a water pipe for tobacco, in her house in Ma'alla. Photograph by the author, 1991.

work around noon, had meanwhile become hungry and was waiting to be served his lunch. The dispute was about his not allowing her to make visits to her family members and friends in the evenings when she otherwise would have time. When planning a marriage, some men demand that they be consulted when the wife wishes to leave the house, even when she wants to visit her mother. Even though this custom seems to be dead, some young women, a few approving and others disapproving, referred to it as a fact in present-day marriage.

The Strong Woman

The accounts of the woman's weakness in comparison to the man's strength are, however, only one side of the story. According to the opposite view, the woman is the strong party, and the man the weak one. Such images use physical features as proof. Men usually feel anxious about a woman who is taller than the average man or plump. Such a woman is called "strong" *(qawiya).* But more than physical supremacy men fear mental or spiritual powers in a woman. Men fear women who practice *zar,* a type of healing that invokes spirits, or who engage with supernatural forces in other ways. In September 1932, a number of men from well-known families filed a petition to the authorities demanding the end of *zar* in the colony. The men were concerned by the influence that the *'alaqa,* the woman healer and leader of the *zar* ring, had on their wives.[12]

During the colonial times, when large areas of Ma'alla and Shaykh 'Uthman were occupied by "Public Women's Lanes" and "Prostitutes' Lines,"[13] the brothels were often run by female procuresses. These women tended to be notorious in their reputation as "very bad women." Often of senior age, the procuress controlled the running of the business and the relations with the customers. In order to be admitted, men needed to get the procuress's approval. Thus, these women exercised power over men's access to extramarital sexual services. In complaints filed to the authorities throughout the twentieth century on disturbances that widely spread prostitution caused to the neighborhood, the procuress was the one usually pointed out as the source of evil.

In 1939, a citizen called "Ali Nagi" and other residents in his street in Ma'alla issued a complaint to the civil secretary regarding two procuresses: "[W]e are respectable people and there is a very bad lady called Mariam and Aisha Bedwiyas ladies in houses no. [numbers omitted]. . . . They are bringing prostitutes and men in their houses and drinks Bhang etc. The smoke of the Bhang Hashisha comes to my room up and the men drink wine in her house and they spoiled the lane of a respectable families. They made the houses and the streets worse than a prostitutes lanes."[14] This application was not directed against prostitution as such, but against the activities of the two named procuresses.

Women's Lib

In the official women's emancipation *(tahrir al-mar'a)* discourse, we can read the idea that men (as a gender category) subordinate women. In this rhetoric,

12. India Office Records (IOR) R/20/A/2906, Zar, petition filed on Sept. 14, 1932, by Syed Abdulla Aidaros and others.

13. These names come from colonial files (IOR R/20/B/991, Prostitutes, and R/20/A/1285, Venereal Disease). The legitimate areas that the British authorities had established for prostitution were also called *chukla* or *chakla.*

14. IOR R/20/B/990, Prostitutes; an English-language letter, probably written by a professional scribe. The word *bhang* comes from Sindhi language and refers to an intoxicating drink made from leaves available on the Indian subcontinent.

women's subordination is described as inherent in the "feudal ideology" and "colonial system," which "viewed women as inferior beings" (General Union of Yemeni Women 1977, 12). Men, as carriers of the feudal ideology, consolidate the domination of men over women (General Union of Yemeni Women 1977, 13). Even though the revolution brought forth a more positive outlook on women as "half the society" and as "sisters of every man," the "feudal ideology" continued to survive, in particular in the family. In ordinary people's accounts, the idiom of feudal ideology is not used, but the same phenomena are called "our customs and traditions" *('adat wa taqalid haqqana)* or ideas that are "backward" *(takhalluf).* As in the female reader's op-ed piece given earlier, many women think that it is men in particular who are subject to this "backward thinking." Even though the *tahrir al-mar'a* politics clearly came from above as a government policy, it gained wide support among the population, men and women alike, as I witnessed when talking to many people.

Women typically describe women's plight before independence as life "inside four walls." A woman who does not work outside home is called *galisa fi-lbeit,* "the one who sits at home." Women accordingly might say that they gained freedom and rights only with independence. As a twenty-six-year-old unmarried woman who worked as a typist in a factory explained the situation after independence, "The woman became liberated from oppression, and she started to work outside home alongside her brother the man" *("Tathrir al-mar'a min al-zulm wa kharugaha lil-'amal li-muasa'idat akhiha al-ragul").* Even though this woman was only a child when independence came, she had acquired the thinking that women's position in society had changed with the revolution. Her father worked as a health assistant, a nursing profession typical to men, and her mother was a housewife until she died. The woman was born in Aden, like her father, and had assumed the rhetoric typical to many people that emphasizes the difference between the colonial period "when there was no freedom" and the period after independence when "everybody gained their liberty." In her view, the idea that every man is the brother of the woman is equivalent to the idea inculcated in men—that every woman is the sister of the man.

The benefits that women consider the revolution to have brought to all women include access to education, the possibility of getting work outside the home, and the chance to choose one's husband. Highly educated women value most the opportunity for a professional career. In men's accounts, the expression "new Yemeni woman" is the metaphor for the changes that came in women's situation during the PDRY. But some women think that although the woman gained more opportunities to "improve herself," as it is expressed, the man has not "learned new ideas."

I investigated this question in particular among workingwomen. Although most were happy with the state of gender equilibrium in the workplace, one group of professional women complained about men's behavior. The women in this group were civil and electrical engineers working on large construction sites. "I hope that in the future the man and the society will respect [*yihtarimu*] the woman more than what happens today," expressed a thirty-one-year-old civil engineer after telling me of her problems with both working and managing a family. She was married to a car mechanic, and their first child had been born a year earlier. Her father was an emigrant from North Yemen and had his own small business. Her mother was a housewife and took care of the engineer's baby while she was at work. At home, the engineer's husband assisted her with the housework, a fact that raised positive reactions among the other female engineers present when I talked to this woman. Nevertheless, at work she had experienced negative attitudes among male coworkers.

In the beginning, her father did not accept her choice to become an engineer. "It is not work suitable for a woman," both parents had repeated. But she had made up her mind, and after she finished her studies in the Technical Faculty with good grades and started in her first job, they finally approved her choice. People in general do not know what engineers do, so the profession is not appreciated, the fourteen female engineers I met in a big construction site explained to me. Only five out of the fourteen were married even though these women were in their late twenties and early thirties. It seemed to me that women in this profession are in a situation similar to what I was told about female medical students, where the possibility of remaining unmarried is a risk that women students have to consider when choosing such a profession in the first place. The female civil engineer experiences humiliation in front of male workers when she hesitates to climb up to high places. The work sometimes requires physical strength that young women do not have. Heat on the site also creates trouble. "Men should learn new ideas," one of the engineers stated.

The engineers complained also about men's attitudes toward female chiefs. I did not hear this complaint in any other workplace. Men usually have accepted the fact that a woman can act as a superior, provided that she is capable and has the right education. Her personal capacities and behavior are also considered. I often heard a male colleague praise a woman in a superior position with the expression "She is a very capable woman." One of the engineers, however, explained to me: "It is not difficult to find a job after graduating, but it is hard to gain acceptance from coworkers. They do not want to have women in leading positions. Men have difficulties in accepting a woman above him. Only once she has gained their trust and confidence do they accept her." All the others shared her view.

Not all the young engineers had it easy at home. A thirty-year-old civil engineer told me that her husband, who works in a similar position on the same site, did not participate at all in household chores. He left it up to his wife to take care of the couple's one-and-half-year-old child and all the household chores. Her normal morning routine entailed getting up at 5:30 to prepare breakfast for the family. The three-member family had their own apartment, which was an otherwise comfortable arrangement, but she did not have any female relatives nearby to share the household chores. She had to travel extra hours each day by a route taxi to take her son to her mother's place for daycare, and after finishing work in the afternoon, she again had to travel to pick him up. When she arrived home, she would find her husband having his nap. She would heat up the lunch she had prepared the previous night and kept in the refrigerator. After lunch, she was busy fulfilling the young child's needs. Each evening between six and eight, she would spend with her husband and son. After eight o'clock, she would again start preparing for the next day's meals. If not too tired after dinner, she would read the newspapers and magazines or just watch television. She told me that she retired to bed after the late-night daily Arabic series finished, as so many other Adenis did.

One of the engineers, Ibtisam, was a member of the Yemeni Socialist Party, the ruling party at the time I met the engineers.[15] Politically active and a member of the party committee on the building site, she had been thinking in a wider perspective about the problems the female engineers have. When I asked unmarried women if they intended to give up working when or if they marry, all seemed to be of the opinion that working is preferable to staying at home. In particular, if the family has economic problems, it is better that the woman works, they said.

15. This conversation took place in autumn 1989.

But if there are children and nobody to take care of them, then the woman should stay at home. Ibtisam, unmarried like most of the others, commented during the discussion: "It is not right to quit working after so many years in education. It is better to interrupt for a while and then return to work."

I then asked the engineers what was their motivation in taking a job in the first place. All present explained that the main motivation to work is a career, not earning a living. Ibtisam wanted to put the answer in a different way: "Another reason for me to work is to become economically independent. Because in the East, you know, the woman is the Other and considered dependent on the man. When you are economically independent, you are no more dependent on a man." Unlike the others, she wanted to contextualize her ideas on women and working life to more universal ideas of women's subordination in the "East." Quite untypical of Adeni people in general, she used the expression "the Other," familiar from Western feminist vocabulary. The idea of liberating the woman from economic dependence is common in Socialist Party propaganda. But her idea of the "Eastern" woman being "the Other" is not familiar from party rhetoric and manifests rather exceptional thinking in Aden, where women's subordination and emancipation are usually argued in terms of more concrete injustices, such as the sealing of women inside four walls, the use of degrading names for women, and the prohibition of a woman's ability to make her own decisions. Also, in the Women's Union agenda, empowering the woman and making her independent of the man are the priorities. The union's activities involve teaching women skills such as literacy, typing, machine sewing, health education, legal rights, and sports. In these activities, however, it is not a question of mere economic freedom from the man, but also liberation from being intellectually unfit to manage one's own affairs (General Union of Yemeni Women 1977, 45–52, and 1986, 7–22). But I had never before encountered the reference to the woman as "the Other" when talking with the Women's Union activists or reading their pamphlets.

But Ibtisam's political activities were not limited to the workplace party committee only. She was also the ideological secretary of the local branch of the Women's Union and in charge of educational activities that the branch held in residential areas. On Saturdays, she participated in meetings between local women and women from the Soviet Union who resided in the area. The latter were mostly Russian housewives who had accompanied their husbands who worked on the same large construction site as the engineers. These Soviet women taught local women stitching and needlework: no politics were involved in the meetings. The only joint sports activity was chess. They celebrated International Women's Day together and held other parties. It seemed doubtful to me that Ibtisam acquired her feminist ideas from encounters with the Soviet women, and I asked her if this was the case. She said that she liked to read and to learn about other countries' women in magazines and books. Her taste for sports was also different; she played tennis and badminton with a female friend in the local sports club once a week.

Ibtisam, age twenty-nine at the time, was the eldest daughter in a family of seven children. The family had moved to Little Aden from Lahig, the governorate north of Aden, after her father had got a job in a big factory as a machine operator. Her mother, who came from the same village as the father, had been a housewife *(rabat al-bayt)* all her life. At home, it was Ibtisam's duty to prepare lunch each day, but the rest of the day she was free. On Fridays, the only holiday of the week at that time, she washed the laundry with her mother and sisters. She did not complain about her brothers' skipping all these household duties. Instead, she was happy in her family's division of work, which left her enough time to carry on with her political and sports activities.

While discussing problems that the female engineers faced at work and women's problems in Yemen in general, the engineers wanted to ask me questions also. One of them asked about women's problems in my country. I said that in Finland women do not have equal pay with men. All were surprised and asked how that was possible. I told them that there are historical reasons and that men have led the trade union. The same engineer then asked why women in Finland do not fight, and I said that they do, but their demands are disregarded. Everybody looked pleased, and one said that at least on one point Adeni women have it better than women in Europe.

Working for a Living or for One's Own Benefit

When interviewing women in different working positions, I asked all 253 interviewed about their motivations for working. Only a few had taken the job in order to become independent from their husbands. Quite unsurprisingly, the tendency seemed to be that women from modest social backgrounds had taken a job in order to support the family, and those from affluent families and with higher education asserted career aspirations, the need to develop skills at work, and the wish to gain more knowledge *(ma'rifa)*. Very few women acknowledged having taken a job just to get away from home.

In order to get comparative material in my survey of workingwomen, I asked 59 women who do not work outside the home about their ideas on women and work. I met these women either in their homes or in the Women's Union clubs. Most seemed to approve of the option given to women to participate in the labor market, but many thought that the woman should first acquire an education. When I met Nadhira in her home in Crater, she told me she was forty-eight years old, the daughter of a soldier *(askari)*, and born in Aden around 1943. She did not attend school but was not married until she had reached the age of eighteen, which was considered rather "old" in that period of time. She had married later because her husband, a cousin, was some years younger than she. He worked as an accountant, a white-collar employee in the British administration, a highly valued position at a time when few Adenis had the chance to join government ranks occupied by Indians and the British. The husband was exceptional in another respect, too, in that he looked after the children when Nadhira went out to make visits. When the husband died, her nine children were already old enough that she did not have to take a job to support the family. Taking a job was not to her liking in the first place, she asserted, and she also did not want to work because she was *ummiyya*, illiterate. "Working outside home is only for those women who have education; otherwise, the woman should stay at home as a housewife. That is how it should be, I think," she told me. Even though some of her eldest children worked, she complained about economic problems because her eldest daughter was getting married, and Nadhira had to supply furnishings for the daughter's new home, as is the custom.

A slightly younger woman, Intisar, thirty-four and a housewife like Nadhira, had similar thoughts about women working outside the home: "A woman should have education if she wants to work. Otherwise, there is no point, and she should stay at home." This woman, the daughter of a taxi driver who moved to Aden from Shabwa[16] in the early 1960s when she was a child, was "liberated" from illiteracy

16. The Shabwa governorate northeast of Aden comprises areas that are considered the most "traditional" in terms of family relations and women's lives. During the PDRY era, Shabwa was

(mutaharrir min al-ummiyya), as the expression goes. When I asked her if she would like to get more education and learn some new skills, she replied that, yes, she would like to learn dressmaking and stitching and knitting. Indeed, that is why she had come to the neighborhood Women's Union club and joined the sewing class. Otherwise, her days were busy, and she did not want to have a job. "I don't have to work," she said. Her husband worked as a manual laborer in a nearby factory, and other members of the extended family helped support the family. Each morning she would get up around five o'clock to perform her morning prayers. Then she would sleep again until six o'clock and then prepare breakfast for her husband and four children. After they all went to school or work, she would go to the Women's Union club to meet other women and attend the sewing classes. At lunchtime, she would go back home and prepare lunch for the whole family.

Thirteen people lived in her household, and she received help from her maternal uncle's wife, who lived with them along with some members of her husband's parental family. In the afternoon, the adults in the house would take a nap. Before resting, Intisar would perform her *dhuhr* prayer. By four o'clock in the afternoon, she would be up again, take a shower, perform her afternoon prayers, and have a cup of tea. In the late afternoon, the children would go back to school. In the evening, she would watch television with her children and other family members. At nine o'clock in the evening, she would start preparing dinner and after eating continue watching television until the daily Arabic series ended. This was her routine every day, and she complained that she did not have enough time for visiting relatives and friends. On Fridays, she washed laundry, made visits, and, if there was time, did some knitting. The house where the family lived was small, and Intisar would have liked her nuclear family to live by themselves, without the extended family. She had high hopes for her children, the girls as well as the boys, and wanted them to enter the university and become physicians or engineers so that they could contribute to the household economy and the family would not have to rely on relatives' income.

Su'ad, age eighteen at the time, was one of those who did not manage to get a husband who would support her aspirations. She was born in al-Beidha, a

---

the area where the Women's Union had least success in its work and where the overall changes the government made were actively resisted.

province across the former border. Her father, who originally came from Yafi' on the southern side of the former border, was the proprietor of a kiosk, and her mother was a housewife. Su'ad was born while the family lived in the North. She had been married for only four months before I met her and had moved to her father-in-law's house.

With ten people in the same household, she received help from her mother-in-law, in whose kitchen she sat.[17] She got along well with his family and was allowed a degree of time of her own, which she liked to spend in the Women's Union club. There she was able to meet other young women and take advantage of the various courses available, she asserted. She had left school at the sixth primary class and was trying now to catch up with the help of the classes the club organized. She attended courses on machine sewing, pattern making for dresses, and typing. She had high aspirations for learning some vocational skill and wanted to take a job of her own. But her husband prevented her. He wanted Su'ad to stay at home and forget thoughts of going out to work. The husband himself was an emigrant in Saudi Arabia, working at a petrol pump. Su'ad thought he was jealous because he was not able to keep an eye on her, so she hoped that in the future things would change and that she would be able to work, but for the moment she just wanted to be a good wife.

Not every young woman I talked to was prepared to wait for her husband to acquire a more tolerant attitude, though. I met Farida, age eighteen, in a literacy class run by another Women's Union club. Despite her young age, she was already divorced and had returned to her father's home. She was born in the North Yemeni town of Ibb, where her parents had originally come from, and had moved to Aden in childhood. When she was only thirteen, her father contracted her marriage to an older man, an emigrant living in Saudi Arabia. The marriage did not work out, and she finally told her father that she did not want her husband anymore. Just as he had organized the wedding, he now arranged the divorce. Farida did not attend the court sessions herself, and her father acted as her representative *(wakil)* in front of the judge. The husband spent a long time living abroad, but when he finally visited home, she told him that he was too old and

17. "Where one sits" is the local expression for where one lives. See my article on space and sociability, Dahlgren 2008.

that she did not want him. Farida did not even know his age and stated simply that he was "very old."

When she was a child, her parents, a policeman and a housewife, did not put her in school, and she had remained illiterate until now. Her aim was to learn to read and write and later to join vocational training to become a nurse or a typist. When I asked her what would be a suitable job for a woman, she replied, "A physician or anything, there is no limit." Nonetheless, she was not yet ready to say she was content. She said she would be happy when she finally graduated from a nursing or commercial school. If her choice to leave the unhappy marriage in order to obtain an education meant also a choice between marriage and work, it remained to be seen what would become of her pursuit of a career. This choice did not seem to trouble her because she was just excited about learning. I asked her if there were moments of happiness in her life, and she replied, "Yes, when I study."

For some women, not working is neither their own nor their husband's choice, but a matter of circumstances. Huda was fifty-two and unemployed when I talked to her. Her husband, who had retired some years ago, used to be a carpenter *(naggar)* with his own workshop. When she had worked earlier, she had been a messenger in a government office. She had liked her work but had been forced to leave it once unification came and the office moved to Sana'a. There was no question of her moving to the new capital to continue her job. She said she would take any job that suited her qualifications. She was illiterate at the time but had a long work history. I asked what she thought were suitable jobs for women, and she replied: "It depends on her education; any job is good for a woman if she is qualified." Her native Adeni father, who had died a long time before Huda and I talked, had worked as a guard *(haris)* in a government office. Her mother was born in Aden, too, and had been a housewife all her life. Huda's husband's income was not high, but together they could earn enough to keep up a decent standard of living for their family of seven children. After her eldest son came of age, he started to help support the family alongside his parents. The son's wife participated in household chores and helped Huda in providing everything for the twelve-member household.

Earlier, when Huda still worked and the children were small, she and her husband had an arrangement by which he would look after the children when she was at work. When Huda told me that her husband looked after the children while she was working, the other women present in her neighbor's flat in Ma'alla where we were sitting burst into laughter. These women were her own age and even younger, but the mere thought of a man looking after children made everybody, irrespective of age, laugh. "This we have not seen elsewhere!" cried one of the younger women. To heat up the discussion, I declared that my husband was a good cook and often prepared food at home. I also added that I shared all household chores with him. While he vacuumed, I mopped the floors. One of the young women present, a twenty-five-year-old university student, who earlier had worked as a secretary in a mixed-sector company, replied to me abruptly: "You are a bad housewife!" I asked her why she thought that way, but she gave no specific reasons: "That is simply how it is," she replied. There was no way I could convince her that a husband should take care of the housework if his wife works, something that many career women I met demanded from their husbands and any rejection of which they found difficult to accept.

The Unworthy Husband

The examples given in the previous section show that when women complain about men, rather than criticizing men in general they focus on a bad-behaving husband. They often point out the particular shortcomings the husband has and the concrete problems that are present in the marriage. Interestingly, although women I talked to criticized a husband for failing to give a helping hand at home, I heard no one point to that problem in their brothers despite the fact that boys are never instructed in doing household chores at home. When I asked working-women if they faced any problems with a job outside the home, a typical complaint was the double burden at home. This discrepancy gets multiplied by the fact that women tend to have longer working days than men do. In factories, where most of the factory floor workers are women, the working day starts at 7:00 in the morning and ends by 2:00 or 2:30 in the afternoon. In offices, I observed that female employees as a rule arrived earlier than their male counterparts. The early-arriving employees sometimes had to spend the morning hours waiting around, without being able to resume work, because the keys to the office cabinet where everybody kept their papers were held by a male superior.

Women also tended to leave work later than men. After *qat* became available in the market every day following unification,[18] some men started to leave the office after midday prayer, hurrying to purchase a bunch of *qat*. Many women, however, had to rely on transportation provided by the employer and for that reason kept longer working hours. But as one highly educated middle-aged woman who worked in the judiciary explained to me, "The Yemeni man is not bad." What she meant was that in Aden there is no "macho" *(raggaliyya)* culture as in some other areas of the Middle East. She was speaking from experience, having been involved as a barrister in hundreds of marriage litigation cases.

In Aden, marriage is in general not considered simply one option among others; it is a "must" for every person, women in particular. In talking about this duty, people referred either to what they called "our customs and traditions" or to "our religion." Just as in other places, people considered marriage a religious duty. When talking about customs, it was explained to me that a woman has to marry because it is in marriage and raising children that she finds her proper place. In the official rhetoric of the "new Yemeni woman," a woman is constructed in the dual role of "mother" and "builder of society" alongside the man. This formulation was also inscribed in the Constitution adopted in the PDRY in 1970.[19] During the course of the changes in the PDRY, however, more and more women started to consider the option of remaining unmarried and having a professional career. For some, this "option" was a reality they had to swallow after failing to find a proper husband. For others, it was truly a deliberate choice. One such woman was Samira.

When we met, Samira had passed her thirties and worked as a planning officer in a foreign company. She had a university degree and had carried out further studies abroad, too. Despite being already highly qualified, she still looked for further opportunities to improve her skills and to make her work more interesting. She could have stayed abroad, but she preferred to come back to Aden and pursue her career there. She lived in her parent's home, unmarried and without

18. Before unification, *qat* was available for sale only on Thursdays and Fridays.

19. The 1970 PDRY Constitution reads: "to develop political awareness amongst women to enable them to play a productive role in society for the realisation of educational and cultural tasks within the family, and to assist women to benefit from their rights as laid down in the Constitution on the basis of equality with men" (chap. 2, art. 58).

a family of her own. Some years before we met, she had come to the conclusion that she would never marry. This was not a deliberate decision, but a conclusion she drew after reviewing her options. "I will never find a man who will support my aspirations," she told me as we sat in her room. "Why not?" I asked. "Because of the kind of person I am and the kind of things I want in life, a Yemeni man would never allow me to be as I am," she replied. We talked about women who never marry, and I said that it's no longer such a shame for women not to marry. I mentioned what I was told about medical students. "It is not that I would not want to marry and have children of my own; I just will never be able to find such a man. I could not enter a marriage that is against my wishes," Samira uttered.

In her home, a typical extended family household of three generations, she lived with her mother; her older brother, his wife, and their two children; and a younger sister and her four-year-old son (the sister's husband worked abroad and visited only occasionally). Samira's two older sisters lived in the same area, within walking distance, and had adult children. Samira was happy with her family; she had a room of her own and a life where nobody asked about her comings and goings. She and her brother brought money into the household. Because she contributed to the household economy, she could make decisions that affected everybody in the household. Working long days, she did not have to bear the responsibility of taking care of the household chores.

Her mother was rather old and spent most of the day resting or taking short naps. It was the younger sister who prepared food for the entire family, cleaned the house, and washed everybody's laundry. Samira was sometimes tough on her sister if things were not the way she liked them to be. She also made her sister serve her. In most homes, it is usually the husband who likes to be served and dictates how food is cooked, but here it was Samira. She even criticized her sister if the food was not to her liking. The younger sister obeyed her and did not argue; after all, there was nobody else permanently in the house whom she had to obey because her husband spent long periods abroad.

In exchange for being able to boss her sister, Samira entertained the sister's young son while his mother was busy in the kitchen or doing other household chores. Samira liked to spend time with all the children in the house and participated in disciplining them if need be. She felt that the children were almost her own, and on most nights she slept in the same room with her mother, sister, and the young boy. The children were apparently happy in her company and did not seem to care whose lap they sat in. All the women tended the children of the household, and in their roles there was little difference as to who was the actual mother. The children did make the distinction in what they called the adults in the household, but in the actual terms of such a situation a female relative of the mother might be much closer to a child, in particular if the mother works and spends long hours away from home.

In Samira's life, her sibling's children filled her desire for children of her own. A strong woman such as Samira, with a family who accepts her decision not to marry, does not have any problem with the situation. Samira's economic independence contributed to her position as an independent woman. Her friends also supported her; she was an active woman much liked by everybody. When she was young and still in school, she had had a sports career. She had played volleyball and soon became so good that she was accepted into the women's national team. The team once had a female coach, but for the national cup competition the coach was male. After unification, women's sports were deprived of official support, and sportswomen such as Samira had to give them up.

Samira's decision not to accept just any man in order to get married is not exceptional in Aden. Still to this day, some women have to use indirect ways to accomplish an independent life. The usual way is to marry someone who pleases the family, but if the marriage does not turn out to be satisfactory to obtain a divorce and continue living as a divorced woman. With a respectful divorce—that is, one accepted by the woman's family and the people around her—a woman can enjoy much more freedom than if she remains entirely unmarried, a *bikr* (virgin). In her confident looks and determined personality, Samira lacked the insecurity that some young unmarried women who have reached their late twenties often have. Being unmarried did not put her moral integrity at risk. In her self-confident attitude, Samira embodied the "women's lib" politics.

How Is Marriage Contracted?

Let us then proceed to look at marriage and family, the locus where all kinds of gender conceptions meet and collide. At the beginning of this chapter, I described Salim's marriage arrangement, which exhibits some of the typical features of negotiating and contracting a marriage prevalent even today. Traditional marriage is a contract between two families. This kind of marriage is referred to locally as "customary" and is distinguished from "modern" and "Islamic" marriages. Young people especially call the customary marriage a marriage with "love after the wedding," distinguishing it from a free match—that is, marriage initiated by the couple, which is called "love before the wedding" and was described to me as the characteristic modern marriage.

When planning a marriage in the traditional way, the bride's family inspects the groom and his family's background. The particular factors investigated and evaluated include the prospective groom's work position and salary; the residence he can provide for his bride; the roots and origin *(asl)* of his family and its social position; his family's reputation *(sum'at al-usra);* and what particular merits and virtues *(mazaya)* his family can take pride in. The requirements focus on both the prospective groom's personal qualities and the qualities that determine his family's social standing.

The latter qualifications link to the old *kafa'a* principle, the "equality" of marriage partners, customary in Yemen since the times preceding Islam, which later adopted it. *Kafa'a* has a variety of manifestations. One interpretation of it is that the groom and the bride must be matched socially, so that the bride preferably comes from the same social category as the groom or from a lower group. The opposite is not possible because the children inherit their social standing from the father. The only two exceptions to this rule are the elite *sada,* the alleged descendants of the Prophet, whose daughters should marry only among the *sada,* and the *akhdam,* who traditionally stand outside the scope of other groups' possible marital choices.[20]

There are several variations in how the *kafa'a* principle is adopted around Yemen. Abdalla Bujra explains that in the town of Hureidah in Hadhramaut, the rule is interpreted with religious arguments and is restricted to equality in descent *(nasab)* only. Descent classifications refer in practical terms to social status groups.[21] Another somehow broader interpretation includes also such factors as religion (both parties must be Muslims), status (a slave man may not marry a free-born woman), character (spouses must be mentally compatible), wealth (the man is able to support his wife and maintain the kind of life she was used to in

20. On the *kafa'a* rule, see Serjeant 1967, 285. For a comparative note on the practice, see Mundy 1995, 173–75, and vom Bruck 1992–93.

21. On the ideology of descent, see Bujra 1971, 93–94, and Dostal 1989.

her paternal house), and permission of the woman's guardian *(wakil)* (Bujra 1971, 93–94; see also Dostal 1989). Gabriele vom Bruck (1992–93) explains that among the Zaidi *sada* of North Yemen, the *kafa'a* rule has had many interpretations throughout history.

In today's Aden, compatibility between the spouses in a marriage that does not follow the customary way means similar education, small age difference (the man is a few years older), a height difference (the man is slightly taller than the woman), and compatible character. In a traditional marriage, however, other factors dominate. As in other areas of Yemen, of central importance is the family's descent status. In Aden, members of religious minorities, in particular Bohoras and Khojas, tend to marry in their own group, but marrying out of the group is not an obstacle for a Shafi'i man. Territorial considerations are perhaps more important than these other requirements in choosing the spouse. A man whose roots are outside Aden must marry from his own tribe or native area. Territorial preferences can manifest themselves in other ways, too. A woman might want to stipulate a condition in the marriage contract about place of residence after the wedding. I was told that especially after the Yemeni unification some women demanded that the family shall not move out of Aden, in particular to Sana'a.

From the perspective of propriety *(adab)* in marriage arrangements, interesting qualifications are the ones that have to do with the family's reputation—its virtues and merits. A good reputation involves such positive qualities as respect, honor, generosity, piety, modesty, and the performance of good deeds, such as establishing religious endowments or engaging in welfare activities. Performing one's work admirably and cultivating knowledge *('ilm)* are also noticed. Negative qualities include, among other things, immodesty, bad habits, improper behavior, excessive use of *qat* or alcohol, untidiness, greediness, laziness, vulnerability to corruption, and ignorance of Islamic values. The latter values encompass all the virtues but refer also to observing the prayers and fasting during Ramadhan.

The family is considered to be a unit that functions as one. Any family member can harm the good reputation and respect of the entire family. Expectations for behavior vary according to age and gender. Children are usually considered *guhhal* (pl. of *gahil,* ignorant) lacking in *'aql* (reason, common sense), and in need of parental supervision. People have different opinions about at what age a child reaches maturity. A forty-eight-year-old uneducated woman I talked to who lived on her deceased husband's pension considered that children reach *'aql* as early as the age of twelve. Children's upbringing is, according to her, the mother's responsibility alone, but both parents decide on their education. According to her, boys and girls are received differently because they are different. When a boy is born, it is a big joy, and a lamb is slaughtered. Women express their happiness, give three ululates *(zaghadir),* and rattle metal pots *(taza),* but in the case of a girl, they give only two ululates, and no slaughtering takes place.

Some people discriminate when receiving a newborn only when it is the first child. Some women explained to me that it is a bad omen if the first baby is a girl because it might mean that the woman will give birth to girls only. Others thought that the sex of the first baby is an issue because of the great disappointment the arrival of a girl causes to the husband. This was the opinion of a twenty-eight-year-old woman who, after graduating from university, stayed at home to take care of her children. In her view, children do not reach *'aql* until eighteen, and therefore the mother is needed at home to instruct them. In her family, the husband alone made the decisions, but the children's upbringing was both parents' concern.

Some people think that boys and girls reach physical maturity *(nadj)* at different ages. A fifty-two-year-old male physician explained that children gain sense *('aql)* after reaching maturity *(ba'd sanat al-bulugh).* Because boys and girls reach sense, physical maturity *(nadj),* and social maturity *(bulugh)* at different ages, it is necessary that they also marry at different ages. According to him, boys should wait until they are thirty years old before marrying, but girls can marry much younger. He had married his own daughter after she had finished secondary school at eighteen to a man who was not a relative. The husband had then died suddenly. The daughter, now twenty-two, had returned to her father's house as a widow without children and supported herself with her own salary. The father stated that the age difference in maturation between boys and girls is owing to the fact that girls are expected at puberty to spend time after school at home participating in household chores, whereas boys are allowed more freedom without obligations and parental supervision. Girls are expected to control their behavior and act responsibly at an earlier age than boys are. Because of the differing expectations for girls concerning sexual modesty, too, it is vital that they learn to restrict themselves at an early age, which boys do not have to do, he concluded.

A twenty-two-year-old unmarried university graduate who was in his first job explained the idea of maturity: "According to the law,[22] marital age for girls is fifteen. My personal opinion is that this is not a proper age. Marital age should be eighteen or twenty, when she has reached her intellectual maturity [*al-nadj al-fikri*]. This is so because marriage is not meant for fulfillment of physical needs or for any other single purpose only. It is sharing, something that binds and that is experienced together, and for establishing a family and taking responsibility. A person who is only fifteen might not understand these responsibilities while she is still in school. A young person's rationality [*'aql*] can be seen from her behavior toward her surroundings and toward other people."

This young man emphasized the woman's responsibility in building a happy family. However, in a customary marriage the bride is expected to be very young, and because it is the husband who is supposed to make the decisions, her rationality is not required. Different expectations of boys and girls have to do with the division of labor in marriage, which is based on the idea that men and women are inherently different in character and capacities. The ideal family combines the good qualities of both sexes. When looking for a suitable match for a son or a daughter, parents and relatives have this notion in mind. It was explained to me that because young people do not have any experience in taking on the responsibilities in family life, it is natural that the parents negotiate the match.

How much the offspring are consulted regarding the planned marriage depends on the family. Out of twenty-six people to whom I posed the question, "Who in the family should decide on the son's and daughter's marriage?"[23] none would allow the daughter to decide on her own. One woman was willing to let her son decide himself, but regarding her daughter she required that the parents make the decision together with the girl. This woman was in her fifties, born in Shaykh 'Uthman, and retired from working as a seamstress. She had not attended school but had learned to read and write in a course organized as part of the national literacy campaign.

22. This man refers to the Personal Status Law, Law no. 20 of 1992; this interview was done in 1998.

23. In autumn 1998, I interviewed twenty-six people about family and marriage: seventeen women and nine men, all married with children.

Most of the people I asked, both men and women, thought that parents should make the decisions in conjunction with the young woman or man concerned. Five women thought that parents alone should choose the son's spouse, whereas six parents (two men and four women) considered that a groom should be selected by parents alone without the daughter's approval. Among the latter group was a forty-five-year-old man who kept two wives, each with children in two separate apartments where he alternately slept in a fixed routine. However, when I put the question the other way round and asked whether a daughter should be able to decline a match chosen by her parents, he replied, "Yes." Only one parent said no, a man age forty-one, born in Ta'izz, North Yemen, a section chief in a government office. While working in the administration in Aden, he had maintained his contacts in his home area, where he had property and income from the land.

Marriage Ideals

The parent's views about marriage decisions can be contrasted to young people's views on ideal marriages, which I also investigated. The young people I talked to were male and female university students, mostly still unmarried. I asked one class to write an essay at home on Yemeni marriage and another one on ideal marriage.[24] Most of the essays dealt with the division of work in the family. One female student wrote:

> When a girl becomes a wife her life changes. She knows her duties from before as they are taught to her. She should be the foundation of the family. The girl in Arab society is created to found a happy family and successful life. This is her gift to her country. Yemeni husbands prefer their wives not to be employed, even if that would improve their life. I think this is not ignorance but an instinct

24. In autumn 1991, I asked two classes of first-year students at Aden University, altogether thirty-four male and female students, to write an essay at home on either Yemeni marriage or ideal marriage. Both topics brought forth similar accounts, which indicate that the students viewed Yemeni marriage in terms of a normative, ideal marriage even though they raised several actual problems. These students were English-language students, so they wrote their essays in English.

> in Arab men. . . . Yemeni men want a wife to obey all their orders, even if she cannot, without any discussion. But naturally there are some exceptions. Generally the Yemeni husband wants his wife to do everything in the house, cleaning, washing, taking care of children etc. This is our customs and traditions.

In this account, the young woman alludes to the differences in men's and women's roles in marriage in a slightly critical tone that was typical of other young women. In between the lines, we can read her disapproval, based probably on her own experience, of the fact that the woman bears all the responsibility for running the household. She seems also critical of the fact that after graduation the woman can seldom expect to have a career but rather has to settle for running the household, in which she has been instructed at home before the marriage. She also points out that the wife's salary might be needed to make ends meet, a typical complaint of the postunification period when high inflation caused problems even among "middle-class" families. However, instead of being openly critical, she explains all this in terms of the inevitability created by the prevalence of "our customs and traditions." She concludes her essay by stating: "The wife is the engine of the house. The woman generally in Arab society seems oppressed, but this is a wrong theory. As the woman has many important duties, the man also has other duties which might be more difficult. The Yemeni family lives a simple life. The most important thing is to raise strong youth to serve his country."

In the student's essay, the family roles are based on compatibility. She addresses the problems a young highly educated woman faces in an era patterned by "modern" expectations of women—that is, an era in which a woman should acquire a higher education and obtain the same qualifications as a man, but also one in which the family life is saturated by "customs and traditions" that impose quite contrary role expectations. Whereas women have had to face these role conflicts, though, men have not experienced similar challenges to their role. The kind of problems that a marriage imposes on men is not the issue of her essay. In order to solve the problems in marriage and to "raise the happy family," it is the woman who has to compromise; otherwise, the family will suffer. As she explains, "Divorce in Yemen is rare, like in most Arab countries, and family relations are strong. This is because of the clear and serious instructions of our Islamic religion." In her essay, reference to Islam is only another way of making the point that family life is governed by some inevitable structures that a woman like her has little power to change.

"Customs and traditions" seem here to be something unavoidable, something that her generation of young women, torn between conflicting social expectations, just cannot sidestep. Her essay nicely describes the way "customs and traditions" touch men and women differently.

Here is how a male student describes the same discrepancy in roles in marriage:

> Before we used to have a traditional marriage, but now changes take place that affect both men and women. In the countryside, the man always prefers his wife to be younger and often he prefers that she be from his own family or other close relative. There is also another important thing, the wife must adhere to the work in his house, and he must not allow her to leave the house except to visit her relatives or near neighbors. These days some youth try to get free of these customs and traditions by the pretext of the recent development in our society, but most of them still adhere to this traditional way because it is the best one. A dangerous thing appearing in our society is that the youth delay their marriage, and the reason is the dearness of payments for marriage.

It becomes evident from this piece that this male student is a proponent of the marriage he calls "traditional," even though he uses indirect language to show his approval. In the traditional marriage, women's and men's roles clearly differ. The wife takes care of running the household and refrains from leaving the house unless with good reason, and the husband takes care of earning money and guides the family with his decisions. This young man does not approve of the "recent developments" in society or of their effects on the family, which instead should be run according to custom. In a typical male complaint, he raises the question of high marriage payments. The essay was written in 1991, when the economy had slowed down and inflation made even well-to-do people's earnings insufficient. The 1974 Family Law was still in force in Aden and other southern governorates, although the limitation on the *mahr* was largely no longer observed, especially in the countryside.[25]

25. Another male student describes how in his hometown of Mudia in Abyan, some hundred kilometers northeast of Aden, *mahr* had reached 3,000 dinars (78,000 rials), even though the law limited it to 100 dinars. In the Shabwa governorate, farther east of Aden, the highest amounts went up to 4,000 dinars (104,000 rials).

Another male student describes gender roles in the traditional marriage in Islamic terms: "Islamic religion limited the rights and duties of husband and wife. The man always goes out while the woman takes care of the house and everyone does this willingly, so the man is always the head of the family." Instead of talking about customs and traditions, this young man explains that it was Islam that created the division of labor in the domestic field. By his reference to Islam, he invokes the authority that it can cast on his argument concerning women's willingness to submit to men's rule in the family. This young man was obviously aware of the sacrifices some women have to make when contracting a marriage like this.

As noted earlier, however, not only men adhere to the traditional marriage ideal. Many young women I met in Aden who were at the age of finishing their education tended to discuss gender relations in marriage in similar terms. A young woman who after graduating from university took up her first job as supervisor of a factory line explained to me that when she marries, she will have to leave her work. I asked why, and she told me that men usually do not want their wife to work. To my second "Why?" she replied: "Because he is a man." For

15. Men spending an afternoon chewing *qat* in a fishermen's hut in the Sira Island. Photograph by the author, 1992.

her, the male role behavior was a fact that the woman simply has to cope with the best she can.

Marriage as a Battlefield

Not every female student tended to view the division of work in the family negatively. One female student phrased the division in a rather romantic way: "In the afternoon when he returns home he finds that everything is prepared and ready for him. After they have their lunch, they take their rest. After six o'clock, they can have a nice time together."

This account describes marital life in terms of affection between the spouses. Not very many students, however, viewed marital relations in terms of "love after marriage," as the traditional marriage is called, or in terms of happiness and mutual understanding. Even though many students considered marital harmony as an ideal, not everybody tended to expect it in his or her own case. The possibility of romantic feelings growing in the course of marriage between the spouses was presented only as a remote possibility. Instead of harmony and understanding, some students expected only disagreement and discord. In the following female student's essay, the idea of marriage as a battlefield comes up:

> But after the honeymoon problems start between them, and you cannot find a finite reason for these problems but always you find that there is no strong base for this marriage. All of us know that some families marry their daughters and sons when they are only 16 or 17, so they are still boys and girls, not men and women. They have not enough experience of life or responsibility. Or if there is big difference in their educational level, maybe the husband's level is higher. Or maybe one of them is from a higher social class. So always you will find them quarrelling even about simple things, their life is full of problems mornings and evenings and always the wife takes her children and leaves her home and goes to her father's house.
>
> Also you know that most men in our society chew qat and spend all their salaries in buying it, they do not think about their household needs, wives or children. Also most women are greedy, they want everything: more clothes, jewelry etc. and the husband cannot give his wife what she wants. So she quarrels with the husband and leaves her home. Sometimes these cases reach the court and then they divorce.

In this young woman's account, marriage is certainly not a bed of roses. She accuses men of neglecting their marital duties and responsibility in providing for the family. But interestingly she finds fault not only in men, but in women, too. She states that most women are greedy and express ever-increasing demands to the husband for clothes and jewelry. It is men who usually present such a claim.

If men resent "greedy" women, women consider the ideal partner one who is not addicted to the vices many Adeni men are accustomed to: *qat,* alcohol, and tobacco. Before unification, women tended to speak about *qat* chewing in very negative terms. At that time, *qat* consumption was limited to weekends only, and few women took it at all. It was widely believed that *qat* represented a major social problem in Yemen and negatively affected family life. After unification, *qat* was "freed" and restrictions on it lifted, and many felt that the situation ran out of control. Men started to consume it on a daily basis, and a large number of women started chewing. People just had to acknowledge that there was nothing they could do to save the family from this malady. Another female student points out in her essay that it would be difficult to find a man for a marriage partner who would not spend his time and money in smoking and chewing and drinking alcohol. A third female student puts the problem as follows: "The ideal couple are ideal parents. So they must divide the responsibilities of looking after their children. Unfortunately some parents are careless in bringing up their children, especially those who are alcoholics, heavy smokers and qat chewers."

Marriage "Is Like Gold"

In male students' essays, complaints regarding high marriage payments appeared often, a burden to every man who wants to get married. A male student explains in his essay: "Today men cannot marry because dowers are very high and we cannot pay it. For this reason the poor youth cannot marry. But rich youth can get any girl they want. To conclude I want to say that Yemeni marriage is very expensive, it is like gold." This young man is concerned about his chance of getting married while still young. He expresses his anger toward wealthy people, who can "just take any girl they want." In between the lines, we can also read his disappointment with the opposite sex, who not only make excessive demands, but also accept a suitor just on the basis of his affluence. This young man thinks like many men in Aden do, that life would be much easier if young women just controlled their greediness.

Some students described the ideal physical features that are commonly held as desirable in a marital partner. A female student wrote about the looks the woman should have to be appealing in the marriage market: "The desired woman is about medium height and rather plump. She has curly hair and dark eyes with narrow eyebrows. Her nose is small and short, and her lips are thick. She has a friendly smile exposing her white teeth. She looks friendly and is wearing a T-shirt and a leather jacket." To give a visual aid, the student had attached a photo cut from an Arab women's magazine where the woman of the description was exposed. The detailed illustration of physical features considered attractive in a woman in this essay makes the point that a woman's potential as a bridal candidate is measured on the basis of her physical appearance as well as her personality. The attractive woman's clothes in the photo are not the usual attire of young women in the street, but something women might wear inside the house in all-female gatherings when they dress up for each other.

The three main criteria that parents follow in choosing a bride for a son are her level of education, her beauty, and her family's social standing. In choosing a groom for a daughter, parents usually have no physical criteria, but they do emphasize his economic potential.

Even though in many female students' essays the idea of the inevitability of certain customs and traditions patterns their views of marital life, not everybody discusses these traditions neutrally. The student who starts her essay by describing the desired woman directs open criticism toward some prevalent features in marriage:

> Our religion Islam is very strict in treating the husband and refuses to give the wife any kind of freedom. For example, the wife cannot go out or receive any guest (even her mother) in her house unless she informs her husband. It instructed the wife to be a slave and servant for her husband. Although we are proud of our religion Islam's instructions, I think the woman must be treated as a human being. The husband must exchange opinions with her because most women are more clever and wiser than men.
>
> In Yemen, marriage used to be based on woman's obedience and she could not discuss with her husband about anything. She could not say "no" at all, but recently there has been some change and nowadays a woman can discuss

> everything with her husband and give her opinion and suggest solutions to any problems he has. These days many wives have convinced their husbands to stop chewing qat and to save their family finances. Also some women have managed to make their husbands stop drinking alcohol and help them in taking care of the children together.

Here the young woman points out her discontent regarding the way that women are treated in a traditional marriage. She uses hard language in describing how men treat women in such a relationship, as if women are slaves or servants. In her mind, such a union lacks mutual respect and the qualities of a humane life. But her pessimism is not overwhelming; she sees changes taking place and bringing about elements of sharing, respect, and mutual understanding in marital relations, the kind of ideals found in a modern marriage based on partnership.

A female student who supported a "love before the wedding" type of marriage wrote that the most important feature of any marriage is mutual understanding. Her father was a piloting engineer, and her mother worked as a librarian. On the ideal spouse, she wrote, "I would like to have a husband who respects marriage. His physical appearance is not important. He should be compassionate and respectful. We should respect each other's families, thoughts, working situation and most of all, we should trust on each other. He should also be highly educated like me, so that we can understand each other." About the positive example her family has given her, she continues: "My understanding and caring family has taught to me that woman have same rights as the man. This is why I expect that my husband assist me in household chores. I do not mean that he would have to know how to cook or to clean but that whenever I need he is there to help me. I do not have any intention to stay at home and become a housewife except during the time when I have a baby."

For this woman, her father represented the norm for her future husband. She also wrote that a long engagement time is necessary so that the future spouses can properly get to know each other. This time, she explained, "is [needed] as we live in an Islamic society, which does not allow boys and girls freely mix and meet each other." She ends her essay in a pessimistic tone by stating that, considering the times, she does not believe that her dreams will come true. She refers here to the tightened atmosphere as gender segregation returned and women's movement outside the home became an issue. Nonetheless, her thoughts on the ideal marriage reflect the ideas that the revolution was said to have brought to Aden. In her essay, we can hear the "new Yemeni woman" talk.

Both male and female students' essays express the confusing thoughts that marriage raised in their minds. On the one hand, they describe marital relations in terms of a battlefield, and on the other hand they present mutual harmony—even at the cost of one party's compromising—as the highest goal in conjugal relations. Female students discuss how to avoid disagreements that are destined to appear owing to the discrepancy in men's and women's marital behavior. Because the customs and traditions—sometimes explained to be caused by Islam—are immovable and difficult for an individual to change, personal qualities assist in coping in this rough field. Marital harmony often presupposes that women must make compromises, something most of the female students were prepared to do.

The essays also reveal prejudices against the opposite sex: women want only money, and men are careless and vulnerable to intoxicants. Expectations of quarrels regulate the joint decisions. Many students saw the clear and strict division of labor they describe as the way to overcome disagreements and to prevent the dissolution of the marital bound. After all, the purpose of marriage is to "educate strong youth to serve his homeland," as many students put it. In the students' essays, personal aspirations are subject to the family unit's well-being; in marriage, both sexes acquire new roles that leave little room for personal initiative in a traditional bond.

In their essays, the students describe aspirations they have in contrast to the inevitable constructs in the institution of marriage. Although their descriptions are evidently idealistic because few of them had personal experience of marital life at that time, they also reflect the ideas the young people have gained in observing conjugal life at home and among other people close to them.

In the students' essays, we can also read how these young people viewed the ideal comportment each sex is supposed to manifest in marriage. The ideal wife takes care of the household, and the husband concentrates on providing for the family. But the hard economic burdens the family faces in trying to make ends meet can force the wife to take a job outside the home; otherwise, her place is at home taking care of the family's well-being. Children's upbringing is the wife's duty, and the more educated she is, the better equipped she is in guiding and educating her children. Therefore, there is no contradiction if she first gains higher education and then stays at home. The female students often left to the husband the decision regarding whether they should take a job or not. This solution is based on the thinking that it is the husband who has the duty to guide the family and to make the decisions regarding each family member's future. In these students' ideal accounts, the familial ideology is argued in terms of "customs and traditions," on the one hand, and as part of "our religion Islam," on the other. Some female students tended to view these ideologies negatively, however, contrasting them to ideas of equality between the sexes, the core gender ideology linked to the revolution.

Gender Ideologies Emerge

On the basis of what I have discussed in this chapter, I can outline three different ideals for gender relations. In particular, these ideals are telling with regard to female gender roles. Because these ideals clearly stand for separate ideologies, I outline each respective ideology in the left column of table 3. The middle column gives normative ideals for proper comportment, and the right-hand column briefly describes what kind of practices each ideology allows and where it sets the limits for agency.

As table 3 indicates, for women, "customs and traditions" and "religion" stand for different ideals and therefore should not be mixed. One of the most striking differences between the two has to do with rationalizations used in explaining the segregation of the sexes. Based on the idea that women are irresponsible beings, lacking *'aql* (reason, understanding, common sense), customary ideology maintains that they should be isolated from the opposite sex so that they cannot cause harm to their male guardians. Religious discourse, in contrast, does not present women as a being without understanding or sense of personal responsibility, but it does maintain that the sexes should be separated from each other so that the divinely established order is not shaken. What is common to both custom and religion is that women and men are thought to have separate, complementing roles, but the two differ regarding what these roles are. Whereas religious ideology allows the woman an active role, customary discourse objectifies her and presents her from the male's point of view. In contrast to both of them, revolutionary ideology presents the woman in a dual role as mother of the new generation and agent in her own right alongside the man in building the society.

According to customs and traditions, women obtain their public recognition through membership in the male lineage. As Paul Dresch puts it, "[T]he idiom of

Table 3. Three ideals regarding women

Ideology	Adab *Discourses (Representations of Propriety)*	*Activities and Practices (Limitations and Resources)*
"Customs and traditions" (*'adat wa taqalid*). "Women have no *'aql* [reason]."	Women need to be protected. "The chaste woman does not frequently leave her house." Women should not be in professions that require rational judgment.	veiling and seclusion calling women bad names prestige system male guardianship giving birth to sons
"Religion" *(din).* "A woman can gain *'aql* through learning, but her basic task is to serve her family."	There are clearly marked areas where women are supposed to limit their activities. A woman should study to become a good Muslim and mother.	religious and general education work in certain fields martyrdom through motherhood segregation the "Islamic dress"
"Revolution" *(thawra).* "Everyone can improve himself or herself through learning."	Women should participate alongside men in building up the society while also acting as good mothers. Women and men are equal in marriage. Everybody's duty is to study. State politics work toward women's emancipation *(tahrir al-mar'a).*	education and work outside the home occupational and political career Family Law (1974) and marriage counseling

shared honour through shared male descent is the starting point for most social accountancy; the map, if you like, on which bearings of all sorts are laid. By itself it says nothing about females" (1989, 44). In this representation, women are identified as daughters, sisters, wives, and mothers to a man whose honor depends on them. A woman's proper behavior is her entire family's concern. Dresch's definition describes well the patriarchal logic in the intersex relations.[26]

26. Following Joseph (1999, 12), we can define patriarchy as the privileging of males and seniors and the mobilization of kinship structures, morality, and idioms to legitimate and institutionalize gender and age domination. See also Dahlgren 2007a.

In the religious discourse, women are represented as different from men because of their basic role as mothers in caring for and nurturing their families. Women are directed specifically to this role as the means by which they can climb the hierarchical ladder of religious striving for a share of paradise. In an ideal society, a woman's role is limited to areas that enhance her role as a good mother. Her *'ilm* (learning) is needed to give the best possible education to her children, whereas a man's *'ilm* is there to guide and to take responsibility for the family, as the students' essays so clearly manifest.

The revolutionary discourse represents a wholly different view of women. As women become economically independent from men, they no longer stand under the custody and control of the patriarchal kin, whether contextualized as God-created roles for genders or as an emblem to "our customs and traditions." In the last column of table 3, "activities and practices" can be analyzed as both resources and limitations. What is a resource in one situation can be a limiting factor in another, as I attempt to show in the next chapter. By presenting the ideologies in relation to practice, I want to emphasize their role in guiding positive morality in human communication. Thus, they form part of moral frameworks. But the idea that a moral framework is based on action cannot be limited to looking at the framework only as an ideology. In chapter 7, I come back to the question of how society functions with conflicting ideas of what is proper and morally upright and elaborate further the notion of a moral framework. Before that, though, I invite the reader to join me on the streets and in the houses of Aden.

6 Five Social Maps and a Mystery

If you look at Aden in time instead of space it is the most varied sort of island.

—FREYA STARK, *East Is West*

IN THIS CHAPTER, I focus on moments that I myself experienced while spending time with people in cars, offices, homes, and places of worship and ritual. In trying to give words to these experiences, I tried to keep in mind that one should not presume any direct, unmediated link between normativity and practice. Not only have gaps between norms and acts to do with what Pierre Bourdieu has held, that normative rules seldom dictate the outcome (1977, 17), but it is also a particular problem in studies that consider the discursive tradition and practice of Islam (see Asad 1996).[1] Scriptural Islam (i.e., Qur'anic deliberations) is discussed as if it were a hidden hand guiding practice without any human mediation in interpreting words considered divinely ordained.

Here I not only discuss normative notions as interpretations that become manifested in events and action, but also in particular focus on normative notions as tools for a particular purpose—that of acting in a morally proper way. I thus approach action as an embodied manifestation of virtue and good conduct, locally understood as *ahlaq* and which I analyze as expressions of *adab* (proper comportment). As I contended earlier, morally argued gender notions constitute essential elements in the different moral frameworks that I outline in this book.

The focus here is on what kind of normative notions arise in everyday interaction and on what kind of embodied manifestations they have acquired. I also observe how social limitations and impediments, such as sex segregation and social hierarchy, influence gender interaction. By approaching these structural elements from the point of view of action, I want to emphasize the role that agents themselves have in "making gender" (Ortner 1996, 1). I do not disregard

1. I elaborate on this point in chapter 7.

the fact that structures have a long-term and durable influence on action, on the one hand setting limitations and on the other providing scopes of variations that action can have in any given place.

Action is not based on voluntarism; it takes place in a dialectic relationship to prevailing structural prerequisites. As Sherry Ortner (1996) has suggested, the term *making* has a double meaning when operating in social sciences. On the one hand, it points to the way cultural categories, such as gender, are constructed or "made." This is the passive, "constructivist" sense of the word *making*. On the other hand, it has a more active aspect from the actor's point of view. It is how actors "enact," "resist," "negotiate," "contest" the world as given and in doing so "make" the world. The result of this latter "making" may be the reproduction of old social and cultural structures, or it might produce something new and not always something the actors anticipated (Ortner 1996, 1). In order to test how the moral frameworks talked about in the previous chapter work in practice—that is, in informing agency—I describe moments in which I myself participated and attempted to apply what I had learned about propriety.[2]

I start by following the social maps of three men and two women. They all are people whose talents and abilities to master their surroundings I admire. Yet they come from very different social backgrounds. The first case study tells about a professionally well-positioned man and how he invokes different normative orders in his daily communication. By following him, the reader will see how prevailing social hierarchies become manifested in daily encounters. This exploration provides us a round trip in Aden, a city marked by social and gender divisions of all kinds. Then I follow the patterns of movement of a lower-middle-strata young woman who is "chauffeured" from one place to another. This story is followed by a description of a professionally active woman with a low social background whose exceptional moral comportment has gained her the reputation of a *mu'addaba*, a person with excellent manners. Then I explore the social maps of two highly educated men whose relationships to kinship networks become crucial to what kind of choices each has to make. At the end of the chapter, I look at a supernatural incident I experienced while staying in a friend's home

2. Even more important than my observing other people in order to learn about the "local ways" were people's comments about me and my agency. The latter moments provided invaluable information about how agency and talk about it are interconnected.

and explore how each of us involved—the young woman, her old mother, and I—drew different conclusions from the event.

The Well-Connected Man

At the time I knew him, Muhammad was a man in his late forties (again, all names are pseudonyms). Owing to his earlier central position in the town's administration, he had many acquaintances and knew basically everybody in the town. However, this was not the only reason for his excellent "local knowledge"; this knowledge also stemmed from his personal capacity to orient himself in different social spheres and to address people of varying backgrounds. We started our first day together on a January morning in 2001 when Muhammad picked me up in his brother's car, which he had borrowed for the day. He had promised to act as my *wusta,* mediator and sponsor, to help me get the necessary permissions to carry out my studies in what involves the town's judiciary. We headed to his previous office in Crater because he wanted to have some breakfast first. Muhammad was not inhibited in his movements. Instead of parking his car in the street outside the governmental compound, he drove through the gate and left the car in a place reserved for the senior employees. We walked along a long corridor into his former secretary's office. The secretary, a woman in her thirties and modestly dressed, greeted us by uttering, "Sabah al-kher" (Good morning). Without getting involved in any deeper ceremony of greeting with his former closest coemployee, Muhammad stepped into his former office as if he were still the *mudir* (director).

The office was empty; it was, after all, before nine o'clock and not the time yet for people in executive positions to arrive at work. He ordered his former employee in a straightforward way to pick up some breakfast from the nearby teahouse and to prepare the tea for us. While we waited for the breakfast, Muhammad made use of the office telephone. We were left waiting for some time, and Muhammad lost his temper. He called the secretary and in a loud and rude manner asked her where the tea was. He also ordered the secretary to take care of some business of his. The woman did not object; he was, after all, her former boss. According to my observations in Adeni working life, boss-secretary relationships are more often based on friendliness and trust than on arrogant bossing around. Instead of addressing his former employee in a friendly way and recognizing the former working alliance, however, Muhammad invoked the straightforward and rude manner of addressing persons in a socially lower position.

After having breakfast, he called the secretary to clean up after us, and we exited the office and returned to the car. Once we drove out of the gate, Muhammad suddenly halted the car in the middle of the street and stepped out. From the car window, I could see that he was hurrying to greet in the most respectful and polite way some men in uniform. They exchanged kisses on both cheeks, shook hands, and applied the long formula of greeting, invoking such expressions as "Kef halak?" "Al-hamd'ulillah, bi kher," "Wa ant kef halak?" "Tayib, insh'allah," "Kef sahatak?" "Wa kef al-sughl? Kathiran, eh?" and so on. Everybody looked happy in a polite way; this is the way a person's social respect is formally expressed in greeting. Muhammad exchanged news with the two northern high military officials in a relaxed and natural way without expressing any signs of hurry. I became troubled; the car stood in the middle of the road and blocked the traffic. After several minutes of chatting with the men, Muhammad finally came back to the car and drove away. He turned to me and explained: "These are very important people; they know the president personally. Very important." I understood; as the ruling elite left the town after unification to take positions in the new capital, and really important people were now far away, there were fewer chances to bump into such people.

In the greeting formula we just observed, "Islamic" expressions such as "Thank God, I am fine" and "God willing, everything is alright" were used. Such expressions emerged in the Adeni everyday vocabulary after unification. Before that, these expressions were not common and represented the kind of talk typical only to people with a strong religious sense. Since unification, the use of such phrases no longer indicates whether a person is very religious-minded or not, but most people simply started to use them. In this same way, the *basmala*—the formula *bismillah al-rahman al-rahim,* "in the name of God, compassionate and merciful"—started to decorate all printed matter, even small handwritten notes. In the encounter on the street, Muhammad explained to me in the car, it was important to use such language, invoking "Islamic" notions because the two men were from the North and had important positions. Some other people told me that this is the way high people in the North greet each other. People did not tend to think that northerners were more religious, but because northerners often consider Adenis as lesser Muslims, lacking religion, it was important to express to them one's adherence to religious decency.

We continued on our way to the Aden Divisional Court. Being a man who knew everybody in the town, Muhammad slowed down as he spotted some municipal workers, called "sweepers," collecting garbage in the street, a menial job practiced usually by the *akhdam*. These men were dressed in worn-out and dirty blue coats and overalls, the typical uniform and color of a manual worker at that time. "Kef halak?" Muhammad greeted from the car window one of the garbage collectors. The man addressed looked glad to see Muhammad and replied, "Ahlan!" (Hi!). Then he engaged in a short discussion with Muhammad on his work. No formalities were exchanged or hierarchies invoked. The sweeper had the easygoing way of addressing people and disregarding formalities or positions that is typical to the *akhdam*. Because these people do not expect any respect from other people, they likewise do not bother to express deference to other people. For Muhammad, this was not an encounter where he wanted to invoke recognition of social position; instead, he engaged in an easygoing and friendly conversation.

Finally, we arrived at the courthouse. This time Muhammad settled for leaving his car outside the gate, and we walked in. In the long corridor of the court, Muhammad spotted some close friends walking in front of us. The friends, three men of Muhammad's age, did not see us right away, which sparked him to make a practical joke. He shouted in the men's direction: "Who are those criminals?" The men, startled, turned with angry faces. But once they saw their old friend Muhammad, smiles of happiness spread on their faces, and everybody exchanged slaps on each other's palms, a gesture invoked after a good joke. They all exchanged kisses on both cheeks and engaged in a rapid chat. "These are my very old and good friends," Muhammad explained to me once we left them. This was an encounter of close friends where no formalities were expressed, because it is equals who share so many things, including a sense of humor. In such company, even insulting comments can be uttered, which otherwise might be hazardous and risk fatal consequences.

Following Muhammad's social maps, we have so far met mostly men from different social backgrounds. During this round trip, we have met people from the lowest social category (the garbage collectors), a woman from the lower middle class (his former secretary), men from the upper middle class (his friends), and representatives of the new elite (the men in uniform). As we can see, Muhammad applied different greeting formulas to each one of them. His choices, however, did not follow any particular pattern such as social hierarchy.

A chance to further observe Muhammad's encounter with women came on another morning when Muhammad picked me up from my residence in Khormaksar. When I entered the car, a brand new Jeep belonging to another brother, I noticed that his two brothers sat in the back seat. His elder brother was a physician and worked in Sana'a, and the youngest brother had an engineering job in a gulf country. The latter was the owner of the fancy Jeep. Both were visiting their father's home, where Muhammad, divorced, lived at the time. Muhammad wanted his two brothers to meet some young women who worked in his office. When we arrived at the office, the youngest brother told me that these two women were his classmates from secondary school and that he had not seen them since then. He was a handsome young man in his late twenties and still unmarried.

We entered a small office room and met two very beautiful young women who were surprised and seemingly happy about the visit. However, hands were not shaken and kisses not exchanged, and in the beginning the atmosphere was a little tense. The only physical sign of recognition and anticipation was the eye contact and smiles between the people present. It seemed to me that the deference was linked to the atmosphere that emerged in Aden after unification. By that time, many young people in particular started to express restraint in front of the opposite sex. This restraint was in line with the unwritten rules of avoiding nonkin opposite sex and respecting sexual segregation. The youngest brother was the only man in the paternal household who observed the daily prayers, and the others said that he was more religious than the rest of them.

Despite the initial restraint in the encounter, it did not take long for the youngest brother and the two women to become engaged in a lively discussion, exchanging news on what each had done since leaving school. It turned out that neither of the two women was married. Even though no outsiders were present, everyone in the room was aware of the "risks" that some people think lie in such a meeting. To express awareness of the risks is to act with deference and restraint. For women, particular pieces of cloth such as head scarves and face veils can operate as an instrument in acting with restraint. But this kind of "risky" encounter is possible in the relaxed atmosphere of Adeni working life, where male and female coworkers *(zumala',* sing. *zamil)* meet routinely and where visitors can engage in lengthy discussions with a representative of the opposite sex. This atmosphere was not affected by the tightened sexual segregation that emerged in Aden in the early 1990s.

In the encounter between these young unmarried people of the opposite sex, I observed some restraint that was more than an expression of considering the risks of the encounter. Acting with deference also indicates adherence to particular rules of social interaction, often explained as "Islamic." Following such rules in comportment rewards a person morally. In particular among young people, launching such an "action code" means also engaging in a particular type of flirting. In such flirting, the woman first acts in a hostile way toward the object-man. She slowly eases the encounter by sending small signals to the man, encouraging him. Spheres patterned by sexual segregation and the women's modest dress play important roles in flirting.[3] In the present encounter, Muhammad respected the rules of the game and did not shake hands or exchange kisses. But avoiding these gestures was not the only way of addressing women in Muhammad's repertoire. In the courthouse on our previous outing, we had met a female lawyer, an acquaintance of both Muhammad and mine, and he had shaken hands with her.

So far we have seen that in addressing people of different social standing and of both the same and opposite sex, Muhammad did not apply a fixed behavior. Instead, he seemed to have a variety of repertoires in his greeting activity. Let us consider one more example. One day I was concerned about the tightened security situation outside Aden because I was due to travel to Ta'izz, a northern town a couple of hundred kilometers away. I asked Muhammad for his opinion, and he suggested that we go and meet some people in the Interior Ministry to find out if I needed a permit to travel outside Aden. It was early 2001, and I had heard rumors of sporadic clashes along the highway to the north. I was hesitant about his proposal to go to the ministry because it was my understanding that as a foreigner I should not enter the Interior Ministry premises unless "invited" there. No problem, Muhammad asserted, he would take care of it. For him, someone who knew everybody in the town, nothing was impossible.

We drove in his brother's car to the gate of Aden Security. Instead of halting and explaining our business to the guards, Muhammad announced his

3. I discuss such "*hijab*-flirting" in Dahlgren 2006a.

professional position and in the face of surprised armed guardsmen continued driving on inside the gate. We headed to the director's office, and Muhammad explained to the secretary that we wanted to meet the *mudir* (person in charge). An audience was immediately granted to us. We shook hands formally with the high-ranking officer, a small man of mature age dressed in uniform and with a friendly smile and a curious face. We all sat down, and I began to follow with amazement the scene Muhammad had arranged. With politeness and respect in his voice, he presented me to the police officer. This time he chose to invoke "Islamic" rhetoric in addressing the awkward situation. He started by introducing me and explained to the officer that I was a scholar of Islamic studies from abroad. The officer certainly understood, Muhammad elaborated, that it was of the utmost importance that he engage in supporting my concern and in this way provide a service for studies on Islam in Yemen.

The officer was immediately drawn into the rhetoric Muhammad launched. He took a relaxed position in his executive chair and put a pious look on his face. He explained to me how he had personally always valued Islam highly and understood the importance of my research. Once the introduction was made, and I became connected to an acceptable rhetoric, my problems were no more problems. They were his shared concern, the officer explained. He was ready to assist me in all possible ways. "Ayy khidma!" (Any service!), he affirmed to me. At the end of the discussion, we all uttered, "Khalas!" (Finished, that's it!), the magic word that finalizes all deliberations. Now everybody could take his or her rest, and the secretary brought tea for all of us to drink.

In another time and period, in particular during the PDRY era, Muhammad would perhaps have used another rhetoric, that of the revolution. He would possibly have introduced me as a scholar of the Yemeni revolution or the "new Yemeni woman," a friend of the Palestinians, and, all in all, a *sadiq* (friend). During the colonial period, it was customary to add affirmations of loyalty to the British king (or queen) and the country in whatever petitions people had to file to the colonial authorities.[4] Even though Islamic studies would not have

4. When I was reading the colonial archives in the India Office in London, it became evident to me that this manner of writing official documents was typical of the scribes who wrote the petitions on behalf of ordinary people. Such affirmations could have been simply a formula that people knew "belong" in a particular situation and place.

been the biggest concern of the high official in whose office we were sitting, he was immediately drawn into the game of words, where positive meanings were invoked and linked to a person lacking credentials. There was no artificiality in anyone's deliberations (especially in my astonished face in the beginning), and the encounter took place in an amicable atmosphere.

But it was not only a question of pulling the right strings; Muhammad had obviously calculated that the simple police officer would find it difficult not to cooperate when Islamic rhetoric was launched. Muhammad obviously also wanted to present me as a morally upright person. More than that, however, in this situation, like on many other similar occasions in Aden, I could benefit from the social capital of a person already acknowledged and recognized in the society. A "mediator" such as Muhammad introduced me to new people by linking my business to recognizable and acceptable speech formulas. He did so in a skillful way peculiar to a person who masters his social surroundings. This way I could "borrow" Muhammad's social respect *(karama)* to promote my investigations. Encounters such as this one provided me with invaluable knowledge of how social relations in Aden are maintained, upgraded, and launched by agents in practice.

This is not the whole issue, though. By following Muhammad's social maps, we can know how relations between people of varying social standings and between the sexes are not "made" in a fixed set of social reproduction. In his encounters with different people during my outings with him, Muhammad applied a variety of rhetoric that links to different normative frameworks. In meeting the garbage workers, the female lawyer, and his old friends in the courthouse, he put aside social hierarchies and the practice of avoiding the opposite sex. Nor did he apply Islamic rhetoric in addressing these people. This kind of easygoing communication between people is typical to the revolutionary repertoire that promotes equality between people irrespective of social and gender divisions. As I explained earlier, the "new ideas" that the revolution introduced include the message that each person should be judged according to his or her merit rather than according to social divisions or hereditary principles. In everyday communication, this approach means invoking neither social status nor gender avoidance in encounters between people.

In contrast to these three encounters, Muhammad addressed his former secretary, the men of the new elite, and the young women who worked in his office with more restraint and social distance. His meeting with the men in uniform was very formal; social standing was manifested in the way he addressed these people and in his acting with submission in front of them. He was utterly polite and expressed no signs of hurry, even though his car was standing in the middle of the road. In contrast, in the way he greeted his former secretary, no formalities were present from his side; instead, he was straightforward and even rude. He applied the social resource of his higher social standing toward her. He showed impatience and a sense of haste, qualities that are considered to express very bad manners. In Aden, impatience is considered one of the worst human traits, and an impatient person risks losing respect in front of others. Muhammad did not ask how the woman was, nor did he show any interest in her news. His behavior was simply impolite and lacking manners.

But as a socially superior person he could act that way. When social standing is invoked, the inferior individual should show deference and respect to the socially higher person. As I explained earlier, in Adeni working life I observed in various places that the boss-secretary relationship is usually not based on such hierarchies. Because gender interaction in working life is free and easygoing, so is communication between people of different social standings. This kind of everyday communication manifests the revolutionary discourse that maintains the implication that all social and gender divisions should be done away with. In work life after unification, the easygoing manner remained, even when segregation of the sexes reemerged in other fields of life.

In meeting with the two young women, Muhammad acted again in a different way. As a measure of partial avoidance, he did not shake hands or exchange kisses with them, even though he knew the women well and asked their news. He thus showed respect to the women, whom he knew as people who do not want to shake hands. By acting with restraint in front of the two unmarried women, Muhammad invoked gender avoidance in a milder form; full avoidance would have required him not to visit the women in the first place. What happens in gender avoidance in practice is that men are expected to show restraint in front of a woman and to wait for her to take the initiative. In such acts of communication, the exchange of words and eye contact take place on the woman's terms. Men are supposed to observe the micro gestures in her face and other signs she gives and then to act accordingly. The length and depth of contact also depends on the woman; the man should not cross the line drawn by the woman. By *not* doing certain things, Muhammad showed respect to the women.

Encounters where restraint is expressed, based either on social standing or on gender avoidance, manifest a society divided in social and gender terms. As I have maintained, the revolution tried to do away with all social divisions, whether based on social status or ethnic origin or gender. These divisions, however, persisted throughout the PDRY years. After unification and in particular after the 1991 Gulf War, when families of the old elite returned from exile, social standing again became an issue to be observed in addressing people. This tendency was accompanied by heightened gender segregation, which gained enthusiasm particularly among members of the youngest generation. As I discussed in chapter 5, university students explained in their home essays that such segregation is established according to "our customs and traditions" or because "our religion says so." For them, avoidance and deference are part of the culture that their parents' generation attempted to do away with.

For Muhammad, who clearly belongs in this "parent generation," invoking such avoidance or deference was simply a means to operate in situations where he anticipated that this was the right way to act. I came to learn about his views during our discussions. On one occasion, we were together in the court and observed a difficult divorce case in which an elderly woman had applied for divorce after twenty-five years of ill treatment by her husband. After the court proceedings finished, Muhammad commented to me: "We have stepped a hundred years backward." He noted that when the 1974 Family Law was in effect, the woman could have expected more justice than what was now the case. He was puzzled about why the woman had not thrown the good-for-nothing husband out of her house earlier.

Muhammad is a typical highly educated member of his generation. He received his university degree abroad, in a "friendly" eastern European country where, while studying, he mixed with local women, married one of them, had a child, then divorced. He also learned to drink vodka and approved of the manners of his temporary home country. He was not religious and did not observe daily prayers. His afternoons were reserved for *qat* chewing, a habit that had replaced his earlier preference for alcohol. He maintained a critical attitude toward postunification changes, and, being a typical Adeni, he was suspicious of anything that comes from the North or from Saudi Arabia. In his view, northerners are backward people who want to destroy the tolerant culture of Aden. As he preferred it, everybody should mind their own business. Nevertheless, in addressing the members of the Sana'ani elite, he expressed quite contrary qualities: respect and recognition of social status as well as the tendency to apply Islamic expressions in greeting formulas.

When meeting with the high-ranking police authority, he exhibited yet another pattern of behavior. In this meeting, Muhammad launched "Islamic" rhetoric in addressing the situation but did not resort to invoking social hierarchies. After greeting the high official as if equal with him, he applied Islamic utterances such as "al-hamd'ulillah" and "mash'allah" and started linking my problem and personality to this rhetoric. In Muhammad's deliberations, my matter became "Islamic" in character. The way he presented my work invoked positive connotations that have to do with the blessings and common good that the practice of Islam brings about. For the police officer, this linking provided him with an acceptable framework to become engaged in the matter. By choosing the Islamic rhetoric, Muhammad opted for the gambit where the officer would not have had a chance to decline assistance; it was after all for a "good cause" that this authority figure would be cooperating. For the officer, accepting the rhetoric and becoming involved in it provided a chance to present himself as a pious man who readily volunteered to help a person whose primary concern was presented as Islam. But I am sure that the official would not have refused his cooperation, anyway, because he was a nice man and visibly interested in learning about me and my business in Aden.

By accompanying Muhammad as he moved around the town in different contexts and social settings, we have come to know how he invoked different patterns of greeting and addressing people. The choice of rhetoric did not depend on the scene; it did not matter whether he met the person in the street or behind a director's desk. His activity was guided by some other logic: earlier I called his choice of framework in each situation an "action code." But before getting into the final conclusions on Muhammad's mastering of his surroundings, let us follow some other people's social maps and see whether similar codes arise. Because invoking social connections is not merely a matter of greeting and addressing people, in the following case studies I focus on other aspects of social communication. The next case looks at invoking connections for direct purposes. The case concerns an active young woman whose daily activities took her to several places round the town. Unlike most people, however, this young woman did not move from one place to another on her own. She was chauffeured by car.

Please Pick Me Up at 5:00 p.m.

Sa'ida was a woman in her late twenties when I met her. She had recently graduated from Aden University and was now working in her first job as a secretary for the administration at the university. She lived in her parental home, a tall traditional Craterian building with four floors, erected as one family's abode. Retired for many years, Sa'ida's father, the patron of the house, used to work as a foreman in a British company in the port area. Sa'ida's mother, a mother of five daughters, had always stayed at home and looked after the household. The father's elderly unmarried brother also lived in the house. Two of Sa'ida's married sisters, along with their husbands and their small babies, had been given a bedroom each on the first and second floors. Sa'ida was the youngest child, and she shared a bedroom upstairs with another unmarried sister. Her eldest sister, married with children, lived on the other side of the same street a block away. This sister often visited the family and spent evenings with them because her children were already grown up. When the family celebrated religious feasts, they all gathered in the small living room on the ground floor, and the eldest daughter recited the Qur'an.

Sa'ida was a beautiful young woman at the time and was conscious of her advantages in the marriage market, but she was not yet ready to tie the knot. She first wanted to get experience in working life, she explained to me. Her parents were liberal-minded when it came to their children's marriage arrangements. They trusted Sa'ida and let her come and go as she pleased.

Sa'ida and her family belonged to a small Shi'a minority of the Indian-origin Ithn'ashari community, the Khojas, which has its religious center in Iraq. Unlike Bohora women, Khoja women are not distinguishable from other people through any characteristic costume.[5] The family's ancestors came from India long ago. This small religious community, which is also called Ja'fariyya and Imamiyya, had in January 2001 only some eight hundred members in Aden who customarily intermarried inside the community. Unlike among the majority of Shafi'is, among the Khojas not only the groom and his family stand for the wedding

5. Bohora women wear a two-part outdoor outfit made of colorful thick cotton cloth with a special headgear.

expenses, but also the bride's family contribute to purchases for the new home, such as the furniture. Because of the close relations inside the community, wedding payments remain low,[6] and all the members contribute to collecting funds for them. Sa'ida was not convinced that the groom candidates among the community were the best for her, which is probably another reason why she was not in a hurry to marry. She knew that she would bring happiness to her parents by choosing a man among her own community, though.

However, her possible marriage arrangements did not stop her from going out and meeting people. In her daily communication, she did not observe gender avoidance. She had several male friends and colleagues with whom she socialized. This principle extended to her networks of movement, and it was these male friends and colleagues she used to chauffeur her because they had access to a car. Managing this system was essential to her because she never took public transportation, and nobody in her family had a car.

Why she did not use public transportation puzzled me when I first came to know her. If anything in Aden is well organized and runs smoothly, it is public transportation. After gender segregation reemerged in the early 1990s, and women were told to be more "careful" when going places, buses and route taxis (sing. *bass*) remained public spaces where women's sovereignty tended to be respected whether they were escorted by a man or not. Sa'ida's refusal to rely on public transport seemed to serve some other purpose. It was neither a class issue—that she would mind traveling in the same bus or *bass* with socially lower people, a practice that can be called "class avoidance"—nor a matter of her parents' objecting to her using shared taxis. Nor was it that Sa'ida minded walking or appearing in public spaces. On the contrary, when going to pray[7] or to participate in religious celebrations in the community's mosque, she always walked. She also walked whenever she wanted to do some shopping in the *suq tawila* and other market streets in Crater. I finally came to the conclusion that her preference for being chauffeured seemed to be a matter of social networking.

6. In early 2001, I was told in the Ja'fariyya mosque that *mahr* amounts paid upon marriage ranged from ten thousand to twenty thousand rials, which at that time was about one-tenth of the highest amounts paid in Aden.

7. The Ja'fariyya mosque has a separate area for women to pray upstairs, above the men's praying area.

One evening I got a chance to test my presumption. I was visiting Saʿida's home, and after I spent some time with her parents and others who happened to be at home, Saʿida asked me if I would like to go shopping with her. She fetched her overcoat and scarf, and after she tied the scarf in her own personal style, we walked to the nearby shopping streets. Saʿida had lived all her life in Crater and knew the *suq* (bazaar) much better than I did. She introduced me to new routes through some narrow alleys and took me to small music stores that I had not visited earlier to buy cassettes of Yemeni music. She even took me to a local restaurant to have dinner, something women seldom do because they prefer to dine at home even though many restaurants have a "family section."[8] When moving around in the *suq* and visiting shops with Saʿida, I observed how easygoing she was in her communications with shop attendants, mostly young men who were unfamiliar to her. In her manners, there was no sign of restraint typical to gender avoidance. She was actually very good in making small talk with male shop attendants, and with that skill she could invite better service and lower prices than what I usually could manage myself.

When the time for us to go home approached, I suggested to Saʿida that I walk her home and take a *bass* because I was living in another part of the town. Saʿida refused; first, she said she did not need me to accompany her home, and, second, she insisted that she wanted to organize a car to take me home. It was no problem for me to go on my own, so I objected. Besides, I wondered where she could get a car because it was already late. She insisted, though, and grabbed my hand to lead me to another street where she pulled me into a shop. She wanted to make a phone call and took the opportunity to ask a familiar shopkeeper for his private telephone. She had to make several calls before she finally reached an available young man with a car. It was interesting to observe her conversations; with a friendly but determined voice, she explained her need to the person on the other end. The friend she caught this time was a former fellow university student, a young man of Saʿida's age with a well-paid job. The car, a typical upper-middle-class sedan, belonged to his father and was equipped with "*hijab* tape"—that is, the car's back seat windows were covered with dark film tape to block the view

8. A family section is a separate area reserved for women and couples that is often cut off from the main hall by a curtain.

from outside. However, Sa'ida preferred to sit in the front seat next to the driver so that she could keep up a conversation with the fellow whose reward was the chance to have a chat with her.

On other occasions, when I accompanied Sa'ida as she went around the town, I observed the same phenomenon. The young men whose services she was able to use were not reluctant to come and help her. The former student colleague who came to pick us up in the *suq* explained to me when we were waiting in the car for Sa'ida to do some shopping that he was always willing to help her. He did not question the relevance of the help: on the contrary, he thought it was natural to help a young woman who did not have a family member to drive her. He also enjoyed talking to her; after gender segregation reemerged in the town, the chances to meet young women were few and far between, and he seemingly liked her, even though there was no flirting between them. The arrangement looked quite innocent from both sides: the woman needed the car and the man was willing to rescue her from any inconvenience. Besides that, his reward was a chance to have a chat with a pleasant member of the opposite sex, an opportunity highly valued among men after the changed atmosphere. In a sense, this arrangement was an "exchange" in the classical anthropological meaning.

On another afternoon, Sa'ida came to pick me up in a car driven by another colleague of hers from the university. This man had a more senior position, was married, and had children. I learned that Ahmad met Sa'ida quite often, and it was he who Sa'ida always preferred to chauffeur her around. But there was no romance or sexual affair between them; they were simply good friends. I again sat in the back seat, and Sa'ida next to the driver. Along the way, Ahmad took from his pocket a small box and showed it to Sa'ida. The box contained jewelry he had just bought for his wife. He wanted to hear Sa'ida's opinion of his purchase. In the box were a beautiful golden necklace and a ring, the kind of valuables a husband buys for his wife that is not actually a part of the *mahr* as signed in the marriage contract, but a token of appreciation in the marriage. Sa'ida studied the valuables carefully, the way people investigate the value of *badla dahab* (wedding gold), and gave informed comments about them.

This was not the only time this man chauffeured Sa'ida and me. He and Sa'ida appeared to have a trustworthy relationship. And because there was no flirting between them, they seemed to have the kind of friendship relationship that emerged in Adeni working life after women joined the labor market in large numbers. Now we were on the way to al-Mansura, the district that lies north of the isthmus, to meet Sa'ida's best friend, Nuria. Sa'ida had agreed to help me carry out some interviews, and the first person we visited was her friend's mother-in-law. Ahmad left us by the gate of Nuria's marital home and agreed with Sa'ida on the time he would come back to pick us up. Nuria came to the gate of the house, a small veranda that separates the entrance to the living room and the gate to the narrow street. The two friends greeted each other affectionately, and we went in. The two were seemingly happy to see each other, and there was no end to the kisses and embraces exchanged. It was the kind of meeting between two young people of the same sex who share affectionate feelings for each other, something quite common in Aden. Parents get worried about same-sex relationships only if they learn that their son or daughter is sexually involved with the friend. From Sa'ida's face, I could see that she was fully devoted to her friend and extremely happy to meet her again.

When Sa'ida took off her overcoat, I could see that she had specially dressed for the occasion, wearing a smart miniskirt and a tight blouse, the kind of "best clothes" young women wear when they want to dress up stunningly and look fashionable and attractive. There was no question that she had dressed particularly for her friend. Even her hair was different: she now had a special hairdo. Nuria teased her about her looks, and Sa'ida appeared pleased that Nuria noticed. Later that evening when we visited Nuria's parental home, Sa'ida kept her overcoat and head scarf on without revealing her dress or nice hairdo.

Nuria's mother-in-law was already an old woman and very reluctant to be tape-recorded. However, in a patronizing tone Nuria told her that she would just have to accept that the interview would be recorded. I did not want to push the old woman and soon realized that taping was a big mistake. When replying to my questions, the old woman covered her mouth with her *shaidor*[9] and uttered minimal answers. Some of my questions had to do with the evil eye *(al-'ain).* Nuria and Sa'ida were amused by the old woman's reactions to the tape recorder and my questions about spirits and evil forces. When I asked her what she did in

9. The *shaidor* is the old-fashioned women's outdoor cloak, a black piece of cloth that is sewed together on the lower part and thus serves as a dress and is wrapped over the head with the upper part. Old and less wealthy women still wear this outfit and often hold it tight around their face by their teeth.

order to drive away Satan, she shouted, "Mafish haga!" (There is no such thing here!). The old lady could now barely keep still on her cushion. I felt extremely troubled for upsetting her and wanted to finish as soon as possible.

Suddenly something startled us all. A table clock unexpectedly went off. It was not an ordinary ringing alarm clock, but one designed as a miniature of the Grand Mosque in Mecca. The alarm voice was a *mu'adhdhin*'s call to prayer: "Allahu akbar. . . ." Everybody burst into laughter—everybody, that is, except the old lady, who was very upset. Coming at a wrong time, the prayer call was completely out of place. The wrong timing made the call ridiculous, for nobody would otherwise laugh at a prayer call. Nuria got up and silenced the clock, and we continued the interview. After we finally finished, the old mother hurriedly stood up and disappeared to the room behind us. I could hear her immediately start to pray. When we left the house sometime afterward, she was still praying and did not come to say good-bye to us. Nuria looked apologetic and explained to me that I should not worry about her. "She is already old and believes in all kinds of superstitious things [*khurafat*]. Don't worry!" Ahmad was already waiting for us in the street, and we stepped into his car. This time Sa'ida preferred to sit in the back seat next to her friend, holding her hand.

In these encounters with Sa'ida, I learned how she operated her social connections. In a way, they showed an active agency of a determined woman who comes and goes as she pleases. Even though she was young and unmarried, nobody else could tell her what to do, where to go, and whom to meet. Her parents were moderate people and trusted her in her comings and goings. The fact that she did not have a brother probably added to her freedom. Brothers often monitor and control their sisters. Unlike many other young women in her position—that is, approaching her thirtieth birthday and still unmarried—Sa'ida was not worried about her chances of getting married. She was a confident young person who knew what she wanted and did not hesitate to go for it. Although determined, she was not pushy and seemed to be liked by the people around her.

In getting to know Sa'ida, I came to know a young woman whose sovereignty was quite remarkable. Her parents were already old, and she had a loving and caring relationship with them. Like her parents, her sisters did not intervene in her decisions. She shared her secrets with her closest friend, Nuria. Even though Sa'ida's agency distinguished her from those people who allow other family members to intervene and influence them in personal decisions, it did not mean that she did not honor her family's and community's traditions. In her friend Nuria's home, I noticed how amused she was by the old mother's fear of the tape recorder and how she agreed with her friend that it was a matter of superstition. For her, such fears were irrelevant and indicated the old woman's lack of knowledge *(ma'rifa)* and ignorance of modern life. But she did not consider supernatural phenomena nonsense. When we were sitting in Nuria's parents' home, Nuria's sister came to return a book she had borrowed from Sa'ida. It was a book of horoscopes translated from English into Arabic and published in Lebanon. When the sister returned the book, Sa'ida and Nuria became excited and started to read it aloud. Sa'ida asked my birth date, and they both engaged busily in reading my horoscope. I said that I considered horoscopes to be superstition, but the two women did not agree. It was something interesting that fascinated them, not superstition.

But I still did not know very much about Sa'ida's religiosity until late one evening when she came to pick me up from my residence. With plenty of enthusiasm in her voice, she explained that she wanted to show me "how customs and traditions are performed in Aden today." She took me through the dark and quiet streets of the main market into a quarter on the edge of the old town. Outside a typical Craterian two-storied house was stretched a *makhdara,* a tentlike shelter of plastic cloth that entirely hid the opening of the house, typical for wedding parties held in a home. Joyful conversation could be heard from inside, and outside, in the street and under the *makhdara,* men and boys leaned against the wall or squatted, waiting for the party inside to finish. Entering the front door, we came into a small *maglis,* living room, full of women of different ages sitting and squatting on the floor. A big cloth was spread on the floor, covering most of the space in the small room and acting as a "table" *(ma'ida)* for eating.

The hostess of the party, a woman in her forties with three children, was busy. She supervised everything in the kitchen and saw that her little helpers took out new food each time a bowl became empty. The mistress of the house took care that all visitors ate as much as they wanted of the special food prepared for the occasion. The food served was not typical Adeni food. A closer look showed me that it was more Indian than Adeni, even though Indian cooking, too, has influenced the Adeni cuisine. There was cooked meat with bones, cooked vegetables in sauce, rice, small *puri* bread, *sambusa* (pie), *halwa* (sweets), and *khir* (sweet almond milk, in Arabic called *halib bil-luz al-san'ani*). When I commented to Sa'ida that some of the food items had "Indian" names, she nodded approvingly. "These people came from India a long time ago and kept their traditions," she explained.

An empty cup was placed in the middle of the table into which each guest, without any fuss, put a small sum of money. As we entered, a middle-aged woman picked up the cup and held it in her hand, then closed her eyes and remained quiet for a while before putting her money into it. It seemed as if she had made a wish of great consequence while placing the money in the cup. Perhaps she made a vow, Sa'ida explained to me.[10] If her wish were someday to come true, she would be obliged to take gifts such as clothes *(kiswa),* money, and various kinds of food and incenses to the mosque or a similar gathering. The money collected in the cup was used to cover the expenses for the food, and I was told that anything left over would later be taken to the mosque and distributed among the neighborhood poor.

The setting for this gathering was like that at any women's dinner party. Nothing mystical was in the air. People looked relaxed and happy, engaging in lively conversation when not busy eating. Children came and went, and the men looked as bored as they always do in the presence of their wives. The air was not full of *bakhur* or other incense, and no drums or music was played. But this was not just any women's visiting occasion *(ziara),* but a ritual where divine forces were invoked and the blessings of a holy man called upon. The ceremony is called *nadhr* (vow). It is carried out as a *mawlid* ceremony dedicated to Imam Ja'far al-Sadik, the patron saint *(wali)* of these Shi'ite Muslims with origins in India. The possibility of engaging the blessings *(baraka)* of a patron saint and gratefulness for a miracle are at the core of this ritual.

Sa'ida told me the hostess's story. The woman's young son had become seriously ill some years earlier. Nothing seemed to make him feel better. She then went to the mosque of Ja'far al-Sadik to pray for her son's recovery and made a vow. When the boy finally improved, the woman understood that the *wali* had replied to her call, so she felt the obligation to fulfill her vow. From then on, every year in her house she organized a ceremony of gift giving and gratitude on the

10. The content of the vow is not a secret but shared in the community. Everybody is naturally concerned to follow the "success" of the wish for which the vow is made.

day of the imam's death (Rajab 22). Earlier that same day, a *ziara* (pilgrimage) had been performed in Aden, and the *fatiha*[11] was read in the mosque. Because the woman's vow was a private one, the tradition of organizing the *nadhr* will die when she who started it passes away.

Preparing and serving traditional food forms the core of the ceremony. The *nadhr* is organized not only as an occasion to enhance the blessings of a sacrosanct *wali,* but also as a chance to unite the female part of the community by preparing and consuming food that is held as traditional and specific to the group. The celebration I attended was an all-female gathering and of its kind not unique. When visiting the Khoja mosque on another occasion, I was told that many people come to the mosque to invoke a vow or they might do it elsewhere. A person can make a vow in the name of any of the twelve imams the Ithn'asharis consider important. Some of the imams "specialize" in fulfilling particular needs: traveling, insurance, health, or other matters. Each imam has a particular holiday. The Khojas are not the only ones to invoke a vow in this mosque. People who belong to other religious communities sometimes come and try it. In the mosque, I was told of a Shafi'i man who had come here with a fatally ill child: doctors had told him that the child would not recover. There was nothing medicine could do for the child. Somebody had suggested that the man make a vow, so he did, and as if by a miracle, the child recovered. Since then, on the day of his *nadhr,* the man comes to the mosque and brings food, presents, and money, whatever he sees fit.

In these stories, *nadhr* is not presented as a superstition, but as an actual means of accomplishing something urgent and important. It is an act of individual initiative that the community supports. Observing Sa'ida during the ceremony, I could see that she had a similar serious attitude about it. Like all the other participants, she put money in the pot on the *ma'ida,* and her decision to tell me the hostess's story indicated that she truly believed in the custom. In her respectful and proper manners during the ceremony, she manifested to those around her that she belonged to the community.

Making a vow has nothing to do with acts of traditional healing *(shifa'),* such as the use of amulets (sing. *hirz*). Many people consider these two things mere superstitions *(khurafat).* One version of such a practice includes inserting money

11. The opening sura of the Qur'an.

and a written charm in a leather wallet dedicated to a *wali,* to whom it is presented if the vow is fulfilled.[12] This practice involves no local Islamic institutions, such as the mosque and its imams. The master of the ceremony is a healer called *sahib al-kitab,* and he is perceived as a man with unique healing propensities and the capability to invoke supernatural forces, yet not possessing religious charisma or blessing. Such healing is not understood to belong to Islam, but it is not forbidden by it, either, and is used as a precaution taken in times of distress. Men tend to be more critical of such things, and some told me that only women are vulnerable to such "backward" *(mutakhallif)* practices. According to this view, not only do such healers spread superstitions, but they are also against Islam.

In these encounters with Sa'ida, I came to learn how she negotiated her religiosity in relation to traditions, modern phenomena, and demands for a purified Islam. For Sa'ida, horoscopes were an interesting new thing, but they had nothing to do with what she considered the superstitions of her friend's mother-in-law's acts and behavior. Nuria, her friend, was a modern, highly educated working woman who did not allow her old mother-in-law to patronize her. Instead, she had taken charge at home, even though it was her marital home, and she was normatively supposed to be the underdog here. For her, the mother-in-law was an illiterate old woman with backward habits. Nuria had a sympathetic yet distant relationship to the old woman, her husband's mother, whose ideas she could laugh at without any restraint.

Sa'ida, like her friend, was a modern, highly educated working woman. For her, going around as she pleased was part of her identity as a modern woman. She knew that operating such a wide network of male acquaintances and friends could be a risky business if those who advocate the home as a women's proper place or those who follow a purified Islam were to learn of it. She had heard stories of an Adeni woman in Sana'a who had landed in trouble with the police simply by sitting with her own brother in a car. Even though nobody expected anything similar to happen in Aden, people were wary in the new situation. That was why Sa'ida, too, was careful in choosing the place where she made her phone calls and where her male friends would pick her up.

12. In describing similar practice in Little Aden, Oliver Myers explains that it is applied to girls only (1947, 185).

As I learned in my encounters with Saʿida, everything has its right place; invoking something in a wrong place will render it meaningless. But places are also tied to the demands of time. Just as the call to prayer in Nuria's home came at the wrong time, resulting in laughter, so would not respecting the sequences of the *nadhr* be out of the question. What is proper in one context might be improper in another. People such as Saʿida know what is right in each situation; that is why she was respected among those who knew her as a person with proper manners. In engaging in the practices that formed the course of her life and by always invoking the right repertoire of knowledge, she constituted herself as a moral person.

For her, it was not a problem to combine modern phenomena (horoscopes) with traditional practices (*nadhr* ceremony) and simultaneously to show respect toward the demands of purified Islam (by operating discretely in her driving networks). Everything has its time and place; the secret lies in knowing what is proper in each context. I leave Saʿida here and continue my journey into learning how normative expressions come up in everyday practice. The next case involves a professional woman, senior to Saʿida and different from her in many ways.

16. Adenis have various physical features, reflecting the town's cosmopolitan past. "Ethnic" origin became an issue in Aden only after unity. Here the diversity of a neighborhood in Crater is pictured. Photograph by the author, 1991.

The Woman with Outstanding Manners

Nur was a woman in her forties at the time I knew her. Despite her modest background, she had pushed her way through school and had a successful working career. She was married and had a child to care for, but she did not live with her husband, who had moved to Sana'a in the early 1990s after the Adeni administrative elite was invited to take new positions in the postunification administration. Nur did not want to move; she had her work and activities in Aden and, aside from these factors, did not appreciate the intolerant atmosphere of Sana'a. Or this was how she put it to me, anyway. Nur was one of those Adenis who considered there to be a big difference between the new capital and Aden, one weighted in Aden's favor. Typical of the new Adeni-Sana'ani elite, her husband returned to Aden only on public holidays.

Her husband had a high position in Sana'a, but the family had kept their small house in the crowded part of Shaykh 'Uthman, where only modest housing can be found. Nur lived with her ten-year-old son, unmarried sister, and mother in a typical old one-family abode with a living room/bedroom, kitchen, and open-air middle-of-the-house veranda. While Nur worked and participated in political activities, her sister looked after Nur's son. Her mother was old and sick, and the responsibility for her well-being also lay on the sister's shoulders.

When I visited Nur's home, I could see that the sister was the real mistress of the house. It was lunchtime, and Nur and I had come only to have lunch. That afternoon Nur had to hurry to a meeting. I sat in an armchair in the living room with direct entry from the outer veranda, a narrow space that blocked the street's view of the room. Meanwhile, Nur changed into more comfortable clothes—the Adeni *dar'a,* a semitransparent voile dress. Her son came home from school and greeted us politely. He did not make any fuss about his mother's being at home. He was used to her comings and goings. At home, his aunt was the one to take care of his needs. Nur went to the kitchen and helped her sister carry the already prepared food to the plastic tablecloth spread on the floor. Nur worked rather long days compared to what is the custom in Aden, and it had taken us an hour to travel in two different *bass*es from her workplace in the peninsula to her home in mainland Shaykh 'Uthman.

Nur and her sister had quite different personalities. Whereas Nur was concerned about her work and other obligations outside the home, her sister was fully devoted to running the household and seldom went out. She usually met people only when they came to visit Nur or her, she told me. There was no question who made the decisions in the house; Nur occasionally commanded her sister in the same way I had seen husbands instruct their wives in other homes. Nur was the breadwinner of the house, and because her husband spent long periods away from home, she had taken on the role of head of household. This situation was not rare in Aden. When I did my small survey of households round the town, I noticed that workingwomen who used their salary for supporting the family—even if they were unmarried or young—had a significant say in decisions that involved the whole household.

Nur was very concerned about her image in the eyes of others. She was highly respected among her colleagues and widely known as a public debater. With her hard work, she herself had "made" her reputation; she had earned respect by becoming known as a woman of knowledge and of good manners. She did not have noteworthy family roots or high descent; in fact, it was the opposite. She could thus be characterized as one of those noteworthy Adeni women who benefited from the PDRY-era policy of giving opportunities to people irrespective of gender, ethnic background, or descent status.

Unlike most workingwomen of her generation with a high education, Nur was in the habit of covering her hair with a head scarf (*mandil,* not *hijab*)[13] even before it became socially mandatory. She dressed modestly and did not wear any gold or makeup. Her skin color was rather dark, and she had more "African-type" features than "Indian type"—two labels Adenis tend to use if they have to describe a person's physical features.[14] She was very much concerned about her public appearance and reputation. Following her during her daily activities

13. Women tend to make a distinction between the *hijab* and the *mandil:* the *hijab* is religious headgear, whereas the *mandil* is just a scarf. The difference is in the ideological motivations behind the woman's decision to cover her hair.

14. People talk of "African type of hair" and "Indian type of hair": the former is curly hair, the latter straight. Because Aden has historically accommodated people from both the west (the African coast and the Horn of Africa) and the east (the Indian subcontinent and Indonesia), the physical features of the people who live in the town differ considerably. Adenis usually do not make an issue of a person's basic appearance, except for that of the *akhdam*—that is, people whose dark skin color and "African-type" features link them to the mythical stories of origin.

provided me with insight on how a person who is considered a *tayyiba* (good person) with *mukarim al-akhlaq*, noble traits of character, gains that reputation and cultivates it in her daily practice.

One day I visited her in her office. It was morning, before ten o'clock, and not all of her colleagues had arrived. Once I opened the office door, I could see her smiling face behind her desk. She always smiled cordially when she saw anyone she knew. She received me with happiness in her voice and greeted me amicably by kissing both my cheeks and asking about my well-being. I reciprocated with the same questions to her, and she replied, "Al-hamd'ulillah, kull bikher" (Thank God, everything is fine). When her colleagues started to arrive, she greeted everyone with similar concern for the person's well-being. Typical for any Adeni office, the room was small and crowded and accommodated several people's work desks. In fact, more people worked in the room than there were desks. This was not a problem if not everybody was present; the things on top of the desks were placed in a locked cupboard or desk drawer at the end of each working day, and nobody left his or her things lying around. When the colleague arrived in whose chair I was sitting, Nur hurried to offer her own chair to me. I declined and said that she should be sitting because she was working, and I was only visiting. After this exchange of rationalizations for what was a common good in the situation, my point of view won, and Nur settled for occupying her desk.

One of her colleagues had problems at home. Nur was aware of the problems and asked her about the situation. The nature of these problems did not become clear to me, but I could see that everybody in the room was aware of the colleague's situation. Nur comforted her. Just as I have seen in other workplaces, colleagues shared their "news" each day, and everybody knew in detail other people's problems and worries. There was an atmosphere of trust among these people united by the bond of being *zumala'* (work colleagues, "comrades"). The fact that an outsider, me, was present did not worry Nur's colleagues. They knew that I was Nur's friend and thus adopted an easygoing attitude toward me. In this way, I "borrowed" Nur's *karama* (respect) and became immediately accepted by them. The respect they felt for Nur extended to me; even though I did not possess Nur's qualities, I could benefit from the position of being "under her reputation." This is social reckoning based on linking people to those with whom they have a bond, not unlike the qualities of ancestral reputation, family status, or claim to honor *(sharaf)* in tribal society.

In addition to being a very cordial person who showed concern and care for the people around her, Nur exhibited a larger societal caring for people in need. This human trait is in Aden linked to "Islamic" conceptions of virtues and meritorious deeds and differs from the idea of social welfare. One day Nur and I were traveling in a *bass* on our way from Ma'alla to Crater. When the car started to climb the hill to the "Gate of Aden," as the narrow pass up the mountain to the entry of the old town of Crater is called, I pointed to the luxurious villas that rich northern businessmen had erected. I said to Nur that I did not think that such villas were something that the town exactly needed right now. At this time, in 1998, the economic situation was so bad that even middle-income people had difficulties in making ends meet. Many people, often women with children, were forced to go onto the streets to beg. Among the begging people were many children on their own. It was not an easy time for anyone, and the situation made people either depressed or angry. I often had discussions with people about the economic catastrophe. In this particular situation, I took up the issue because I wanted to hear what Nur had to say in a public place with strange people around.

Nur immediately took the point and cried out loud: "*'Ayb!* [Shame!] It is shameful that those people build such houses when people are starving. Such disregard is *haram* [wrong according to Islam]." In the passenger taxi, other travelers seemed to share our views, judging from the faces around us that expressed approval of her statement. I noticed that Nur addressed her words not only to me, but also to the entire "audience" of the *bass*. In her statement, she raised a strong condemnation of the disregard and lack of concern. She did not identify the target of her disapproval, but all of us sitting in the car understood that it was addressed to the new elite. This elite comprises business families who benefited from the town's property market after the government in the early 1990s issued a decree that made land and housing private property again. Few of these business families actually lived in Aden; some were from the North, and some had roots in Hadhramaut and businesses in other peninsular countries. Because few Adenis actually have the wealth and means to engage in profitable business, severe resentment has arisen against these new investors, and people tend to view them as lacking concern for communal needs.

A disregard of the common good, arrogance, and selfishness are traits that dishonor a person, and in her statement Nur addressed those elements of ill manners. First, she invoked that such behavior is shameful in the sense of *'ayb.*

However, she did not settle for this "milder" notion of impropriety. She declared that it is *haram,* thus invoking the religious categories of what is commended, acceptable, avoidable, and prohibited. The difference between these two concepts of socially condemned behavior is clear. If seen from the point of view of either mild or severe impropriety, the notion of *'ayb* is used when, for instance, instructing a child not to do something, whereas *haram* shows the limits a person cannot cross without violating a religiously sanctioned common good.

In her statement, Nur constructed herself as a socially respectable person, a *tayyiba,* and as someone with *mukarim al-ahlaq*. By indicating concern for socially deprived people, even though everybody in the car could see from the way she was dressed that she herself was not poor, she presented the image of a person with social concern. That she also addressed her concern in religious terms enhanced the idea that she is a good Muslim. By invoking the term *haram,* she reminded people of the presence of God and of the limits God has set on people. Disregard for other people's needs and promoting selfish interests are dishonorable acts not only in front of people, but also in front of God.

This was not the only time that I became involved in a conversation about morality and propriety in a *bass.* These taxis are scenes where people earlier unknown to each other often engage in discussions about topical matters. Once as I was traveling from Khormaksar to Ma'alla, the car passed by the big foreign hotel located at the junction of the road to the isthmus. Outside the hotel was a young foreign-looking woman dressed in a very short miniskirt, tight blouse, and startling makeup. When spotting her, I thought to myself, "My goodness, I hope nothing will happen to her."

Before I turned to check the reactions of the other passengers in the car, a man sitting behind me shouted laughingly at the woman and called her a whore. I turned toward the man and with my facial expression signaled that his comment was to my mind improper. The man looked first a bit confused by my reaction but then continued laughing and pointing at the woman. This man, probably in his forties, dressed in a dirty and worn-out T-shirt and slacks, was accompanied by a woman of similar age, probably his wife, whose *shaidor* was likewise old and worn. She joined the man in laughing and pointing at the woman. At this point, two men sitting at the back of the car started criticizing the man's comment. These men were slightly junior to him and dressed in clean white shirts and straight slacks, the usual government employee outfit. One of them said in a critical tone: "You should not call any woman such indecent words!" A heated discussion followed between the three men.

At this point, the poor-looking woman expressed her opinion. She defended her companion and said that she did not think that there was anything bad in his comment. The two men disregarded her and continued to criticize the man. The issue was how men should react to women who are "free" *(hurra),* as women who move around as unrestricted as men are called. By raising their objection to the man's behavior, the two men in the back seat also addressed me, a "free" woman.

This incident came to my mind as I was sitting with Nur in the car. Some eight years had passed between the two occurrences, and I wondered how different the atmosphere was now. The kind of ideational framework upon which Nur placed the discussion of morality was clearly different from the agenda of the conversation eight years earlier. If Nur had participated in the earlier incident, she would have raised similar concerns as the two government employees. She was an advocate of women's rights and active in different women's initiatives. Based on our conversations, I got the idea that she shared the ideals of women's emancipation promoted by the PDRY regime. Nevertheless, in her everyday interaction with people, whether they were familiar to her or not, she preferred to invoke images that were linked to piety and Islam.

Nur wanted to present herself to the people around her as someone who embodies modesty, restraint, and generosity. That is the image of a proper Muslim who measures her words and deeds from a religiously informed moral point of view, even though in our discussions I never got the impression that she was very religious. For her, religious comportment represented the highest form of social propriety. By applying the qualities that are commonly understood as belonging to religious morality, she cultivated in her mind the most ideal forms of proper comportment *(adab).*

But Nur's religiosity was of a particular character. Unlike other people for whom observing religious obligations forms a vital part of daily life, she was not in the habit of performing the five daily prayers. Characteristic of people of her generation, she did not pray that way, nor did she share the gender ideology typical of many young people linked to "religion," as indicated in the students' essays quoted in the previous chapter. Nur considered that such views on gender roles belonged to the past. Religiosity in her was embodied in religious awareness and a conscious introduction of religious virtues. Her approach was different from the usual manifestations of religiosity, such as praying and fasting. Although she did not observe the daily prayers, it did not mean that she was less of a Muslim. To her, religiousness was a matter of consciousness and consideration, and her religion provided her with a resource pool on which to draw in making the best of her everyday interactions with other people.

Being generous and having a concern for the needy sectors of society have particular conventions in Adeni society. Conscious of this relationship, Nur exhibited her generosity within socially sanctioned limits. Such generosity builds a person's *karama* (reputation). On another day when we were traveling in a *bass* from Crater to Ma'alla, the car stopped at a traffic light at the beginning of the Madram Road. This was a place where a large number of beggars of all ages patrolled the passing cars to ask for alms. Accompanying them were young boys who provide services to the drivers, such as cleaning the windscreen or selling newspapers and paper tissues, in exchange for a little money.

The "traffic light beggars," a common feature in Sana'a, came to Aden after unification. People viewed this phenomenon as one of the negative things that accompanied unity. When these people first came to Aden, they were called "messengers of Ali Abdullah Salih," in a ridiculing jest referring to the alleged backwardness of northern society. The newcomers were also called "Tihama people" as if they all came from the hot and humid coastal area in the North.[15] While we were waiting for the light to turn green, a group of beggars approached our car. Nur took out her purse, and hands reached out toward her. "No!" she cried with an angry face to the first woman who approached. She leaned forward and slipped the coin into the hand of a woman with a baby standing behind the first woman. The light changed, and the car jerked forward. Nobody else made an effort to give a coin to the begging hands. Nur had manifestly given her alms to a local poor woman and dramatically rejected a "Tihama person."

However, Nur wanted to explain her behavior to me. She said that it is unacceptable that these people "whose profession is begging" have come to Aden. "They do not deserve our generosity. They should have stayed where they came

15. Adeni people consider these people as *'abid* (former slaves, a group of people believed to be descendants of African slaves that were brought to the Arabian Peninsula until early twentieth century) or *akhdam* (the "pariah" category believed to be descendants of Ethiopian invaders of A.D. 500). See Walters 1995 and 1996.

from. It is their profession anyhow. These people do not engage in anything respectful. They will always be as they are."

By handing a coin to the woman in need, Nur committed a merited deed. From a religious perspective, she engaged in an act of *sadaqa,* or almsgiving, which in both scriptural and local practices of Islam is considered a pious deed. Helping the poor by almsgiving is an activity that redounds on the person socially as well. However, as we can see from this incident, almsgiving or any other act becomes meaningful only if it makes sense socially. In this particular situation, almsgiving has to respect the local social organization. Not everybody should be given alms; almsgiving is merited only if directed to the right people. The negative attitude toward the "Tihama people" tells about social exclusion and manifests the idea that only the town's native poor people "belong" to the system of almsgiving and thus to social hierarchy with the accompanying duties and obligations.

By handing the coin to the "right" poor person, Nur exhibited a consciousness of these social imperatives and thus respected the underlying social predicament. By giving alms to a person who is included in the social hierarchy, Nur participated in social exchange. Had she given alms to the wrong people, she would have gained the reputation of someone who holds in contempt not only the morality of almsgiving, but also the prevailing social order.

However, to me Nur wanted to stress the immorality of the "Tihama people." What positive thing can be gained from an act that is linked to immorality? Almsgiving as a form of social security in a society with collapsing state services not only is part of the religious concepts of moral personhood, but also manifests a concern for the common good. Engaging in such moral activities requires a consciousness of the shared meaning of giving; otherwise, it does not merit a person to act as such. In this way, morality is tightly linked to social knowledge.

Even though Nur was highly educated and her knowledge was widely admired, she behaved very modestly in front of people. It always struck me how humbly she presented herself in front of people she talked to. This humbleness was not a result of her devaluing herself. On the contrary, by expressing deference and modesty, she invoked positive reactions from people with whom she communicated. This became apparent to me when we met with different people in the street or in any public place we went to. When meeting someone new or somebody from whom she maintained a social distance, she expressed shyness *(istihya')* and restraint. This restraint was manifested in her bodily movements. When greeting such a person, she lowered her gaze and made an obeisance. This way her body posture expressed submissiveness. By her act of shyness toward a person, she gave that person the chance to respond to her submissiveness. In the encounters I observed, people tended to react to her restraint with positive approval. Because Nur was a well-known person in the community, few people took her shyness as a mark of nonexisting or weak public standing. Her age did not require her to act with shyness in front of other people. Her act of shyness was perceived as a token of respect and commitment to the person, which was the way she seemed to like it. Because people were aware of the extent of her learning *(ma'rifa)*, her submissiveness in front of people who perhaps could not claim a similar reputation *(karama)* was taken as a sign of excellent manners.

Nur's bodily postures reminded me of the way elderly women greet a person socially higher than they. I came to wonder whether in fact Nur was acknowledging her humble social background this way. However, this was not a question I could ask her because to suggest that someone has a low social origin is not considered proper. Besides, Nur was a proponent of the ideas of equality connected to the revolution where status concerns are not raised. She probably was aware of how people expected her appearance to indicate her low social origin. She knew that she could not gain respect by disregarding that fact; instead, she consciously manifested in her actions piety, learning, and generosity. By acting with deference and shyness in front of people, she repeatedly constructed the image of a socially lower person, which then gave her the chance to make others reconsider their first impressions on the basis of the qualities of high morality she put forward. For me, it was fascinating to learn how in her everyday encounters Nur mastered structural inevitabilities and resources.

Kinship Networks and How to Make Things Happen

In the earlier case studies, we observed how social divisions and hierarchies are acted upon in daily life and how social reputations are "made." The cases also brought up details on how propriety and morality are acted upon in everyday practice. With the case study in this section, I examine, on the one hand, how kinship networks are used to create social resources and, on the other, how kinship ties can put up obstacles to personal endeavors to such an extent that the ties have to be renegotiated. The actors in this study are ʿAli and Ahmad, two men in their late thirties who were connected by friendship and work.

Ahmad was the son of a local shaykh in what was the preindependence Upper ʿAwlaqi Sultanate (in the present-day Shabwa governorate), some 150 kilometers northeast of Aden. Because of a popular uprising in the area after independence, the family had to leave the area and settled in Sana'a. When Ahmad reached the age of maturity, his father arranged his marriage with his cousin, a *sharifa*[16] woman with education and personal aspirations outside the home. The marriage did not work out; as a final reason for divorce, the dissatisfied wife claimed that Ahmad had not been able to arrange for her a house that would meet her social standing *(bayt shariʿa)*. Ahmad was not sorry that this marriage organized according to the family conventions had ended in divorce. He thereafter concentrated on acquiring an education and promoting a career that was independent of his position as the hereditary tribal chief. His studies brought him to Europe, where he met ʿAli, and they became close friends. While studying in Europe, Ahmad attained the "new thinking," as ideas on social and gender equality are called in Aden. In due course, he returned to Yemen. When unification came, tribal systems were reintroduced in areas outside Aden. However, Ahmad did not want to have anything to do with his family's regained position in the native territory. Instead, he settled in Aden in his uncle's house, where he could continue to lead a lifestyle he had become used to while living in Europe, including, among other things, visiting bars and meeting women who did not observe gender avoidance.

ʿAli was also born in the countryside, but he was the son of an ordinary tribal man with vast areas of land in the present-day Abyan governorate. His father moved when still at a young age to Aden and became involved in the struggle for independence. The family preferred that ʿAli first finish his studies, get a good position, earn some money, and obtain a flat before marrying. So he and his fiancée, a cousin some ten years his junior, had to wait for many years. The marriage had been agreed upon before ʿAli went abroad. When ʿAli finally managed to get a house of his own, the wedding was organized in the native village. After the

16. *Sharif* (fem. *sharifa*) is an honorable title accorded a member of a holy house—that is, a family that can claim descent from Prophet Muhammad.

wedding, his wife moved to Aden. The marriage was a happy one, and the couple had been blessed with a daughter and son, the preferred combination and number of children.

'Ali's house was different from most homes I visited. The fact that it was a nuclear family unit was not unusual, but more peculiar was that during the afternoons and evenings, men occupied the only *maglis* (living room): 'Ali usually chewed his *qat* at home, so his friends and neighbors visited him on a regular basis. While 'Ali entertained his guests, his wife had to stay in the kitchen or visit her father-in-law's home in another part of the town, where women occupied the entire flat. When visiting 'Ali's house, I seldom met his wife. If she was at home, I went to meet her in the kitchen, but she rarely came and sat with us in the *maglis,* even if no men were around. 'Ali was in the habit of reading books and newspapers while chewing and did not want to invite people to a more conventional *qat makhdara,* where the men might smoke *mad'aa*[17] or *shisha*[18] and talk lively while chewing. 'Ali's *maglis* was the kind of typical "traditional" room with cushions on the floor near the walls and with no other furniture except a TV set.

One afternoon I was visiting 'Ali, and Ahmad soon joined us with his *qat.* As often happened, 'Ali was concentrating on reading a book and making notes. Ahmad and I engaged in conversation. Ahmad started to tell me what his sister, a student in her early twenties, had said to him the other day. Ahmad had told her about me and asked if she would like to meet me. The sister's reaction had infuriated him. She had said that she would never meet a Christian. She had also asked her brother to discontinue meeting me, warning him that I might influence him negatively.

Ahmad had earlier told me about his family when I visited his home. The family had a two-floor apartment in a colonial-era block of flats, in which Ahmad had a room of his own on the roof while the rest of the family lived downstairs. I had met some of his brothers and male cousins while sitting in his room, where he has a habit of receiving visitors while chewing. These relatives had a respectful attitude toward me, and I had good conversations with them. The patron of the house was Ahmad's paternal uncle, who was seldom at home during the

17. A tall water pipe in which the leaves of locally cultivated tobacco are smoked.

18. A small water pipe for imported scented tobacco.

afternoons, so I never met him. His uncle was tolerant of Ahmad's way of life and allowed him to come and go as he pleased, a grown man with his own income and social networks.

Ahmad had told me earlier that one of his younger sisters was very religious and a *muhaggaba*,[19] as he called her. But I was nevertheless quite astonished by the sister's reaction. During my time in Aden, I had often met people who were very religious, but it did not stop them from talking to me. I had encountered hostile attitudes toward me as a "Christian" in some areas east of Aden and in the North, but in Aden I had never experienced such reactions. Ahmad started to criticize his sister's attitude. He said that it was a token of ignorance and that his sister did not have any understanding that even according to Islam, Christians are considered to belong to the same religious tradition. "I am going to ignore her comments. She should not tell me whom to meet," he said finally.

'Ali now became engaged in the discussion. He said that young people are often so naive because they do not have the knowledge of how things are. Such intolerance does not belong to Aden. "Aden is for all," he said. He told us that after his younger brother joined one of the intolerant Islamist groups, he had kept some distance from the brother. "You cannot influence them; once they are drawn to such a movement, they do not listen to you anymore." 'Ali chose to avoid meeting his younger brother, and the latter only rarely visited his house. When he came, he did not sit down and talk with anyone present, and he was not in the habit of chewing.

'Ali's reaction was typical of what I had seen earlier. Since the beginning of the 1990s, militant Islamist groups had become vocal in Aden, among them the Salafis and the jihadists.[20] The presence of these two groups of Islamic "purifiers" affected the atmosphere negatively. Before unification, the Muslim Brotherhood

19. A woman who wears the *hijab*, the "religious costume" as it is viewed in Aden.

20. The Salafiya represent an Islamic reform movement that was inspired by the Egyptian intellectual Muhammad Abdu (d. 1905). It derives its name from the call to follow the path of the forefathers, as presented by Ibn Taymiyya (d. 1328) (Lapidus 2007, 518; Weismann 2001, 263). The jihad movement in Yemen has been linked to both al-Qa'ida and the murder of the secretary-general of the Yemeni Socialist Party, Jarallah Omar, in 2002 (see Carapico, Wedeen, and Wuerth 2002). On the origin and connections of Salafi and jihad groups in Yemen, see Burgat 1999; Monet 1995, 29–30; and Weir 1997.

was functioning in Aden, but its activities were suppressed, and it never drew such a reasonable following as the new groups. Those who resented these groups' aims simply avoided having any contact with them. With their coming, a new form of social avoidance emerged, marking a line of tolerance between people who are pious "real Muslims" and those who are in one way or another deficient from the ideal. This avoidance is guided by knowledge of where these groups are active in the city so that visits to such areas can be limited. When in 2001 I lived near a Salafi mosque in Khormaksar, some people advised me not to go out when the praying moment approached because the street would be full of Salafi supporters from other parts of the town.

Both Ahmad and 'Ali, as senior members of their family, were in the position to disregard junior siblings' disapproval of their acquaintances and way of living. But neither of the two tried to discipline these siblings or to use their superior position in the patriarchal kinship hierarchy. When thinking about this, I remembered what Suad Joseph has suggested, that the sibling relationship is two sided (1999, 12–13). Even though the younger sister and brother could hardly expect their elder brothers to do as they say, they could do something: they could resort to a discourse about a "blasphemous" *(kafiri)* way of life that purifiers believed to prevail in Aden and in this way launch an authoritative disapproval of their elder brothers' way of living.

During the 1990s, a wave of public disapproval arose against the earlier tolerant alcohol customs. Those who promoted such tight interpretations of Islam—including some mosque imams, activists in militant movements, and ordinary people—were in the forefront in disapproving and condemning these customs. Before unification, it was no problem for men to sit on the pavement outside a bar and consume beer. After the early 1990s, though, that was no longer possible. During that same period, the Seera Beer Factory in al-Mansura, which produced the popular local beer, as well as nightclubs, restaurants, and alcohol stores were violently targeted. Drunken people in the streets and prostitutes hanging in bars experienced harassment, too.

Junior family members' intolerant position and the no longer tolerant public attitude did have an effect on Ahmad and 'Ali's lives. These two friends earlier simply had to hide their drinking from the family and kin. Now that bigoted people could be anywhere, they had to be careful in the street, too. The biggest problem seemed in both families to come from the younger siblings, whose religious awakening had made even other members of the two families consider their deeds from a more puritanical perspective.

Ahmad and 'Ali tried to ignore and avoid the intolerance that had arisen in the family. Neither of them "corrected" his own behavior, but they did not engage in trying to influence the younger relatives, either. There simply was no longer any positive connectivity between them. From the senior brothers' point of view, the family relationship had been distorted by the junior members' connection to small-minded religiosity. As 'Ali explained his relationship to his brother, "You cannot influence them anymore." For the junior siblings, adherence to a powerful religious ideology had changed their relations to their closest relatives. It was no longer up to the elder brother to supervise and provide an example of what was right and what was wrong.

In this new atmosphere, Ahmad had changed his consumption habits. He now chewed *qat* every day, taking the intoxicant that is permissible according to local interpretations of Islam and that the fanatics for some reason do not attack, even if they do not favor it, either. Ahmad explained to me that he had developed the habit of arriving home from a bar so late that everybody was already asleep. He even had taken measures in anticipation of possible trouble with the law if confronted on the streets at a late hour, when the militia patrolled the streets and occasionally stopped people. Ahmad had become a member of the ruling party and kept his membership card with him to avoid trouble. On a couple of occasions, merely flashing the president's party membership card had saved him from harassment.

'Ali had taken another way to solve the same problem: he rarely drank anymore. Instead, he chewed *qat* every day. Buying *qat* for daily consumption was naturally expensive, but because almost every man in the town now did the same thing, there was no way a concerned family member could limit the consumption. *Qat* chewing had become a dominant custom, and those who opposed it were unable to stop it. Even though Ahmad had a reasonable salary, his *qat* and alcohol expenses were so high that he was constantly short of money. To solve the problem of serving his daily needs, he had to borrow money on a regular basis. When payday came, he always paid his debts, but that meant very little was left for the rest of the month.

He was in a vicious cycle of borrowing and keeping up contacts with those who were able to help him. His basic network of borrowing included male kinship members. However, Ahmad did not use any particular planning in his finances and borrowing. Thus, his need for money hit when he was in need of either *qat* or alcohol—that is, around lunchtime for *qat* and in the early evening for beer. This was the time of the day when everybody who had the habit of chewing was either at home having his lunch or already in the place where he enjoyed his *grass.*[21] For Ahmad, this meant that he had to know where each person he borrowed from usually was; otherwise, he would have to make futile trips to his relatives' homes around the town.

As I explained earlier, Ahmad had made his own way and refused the hereditary position that he was entitled to. He also insisted on staying unmarried and resented offers to arrange a new union according to family conventions. After settling in Aden, his relationship to his kin had taken new forms. His actual, practiced relationships to his kin focused now on the family residing in Aden and in particular on those male kin members who on a regular basis helped him keep up his consumption habits. Ahmad was aware that if these relatives found out that he spent money on alcohol, they would no longer help him. Many of his kin were rather conservative and resented such aspects in Adeni cosmopolitan life. He put on a different face in front of his relatives from the one he wore with his friends and work colleagues. Kinship for Ahmad was now a network of social security, a safety net that helped him meet his consumption needs.

Kinship is a different issue in Aden than it is in Shabwa, where Ahmad's family comes from. But Aden is not detached from the tribal structures of the countryside because ties and obligations do not disappear when people move to the city. Affinities might be put on hold and taken up when the time is right. As noted earlier, this happened when 'Ali got his business in order and informed his family in the village that the marriage, planned years earlier, could now be organized. However, in Ahmad's case the situation was different because he refused his patrilineal duties. But he had not left his kin, as happens when a member of a tribe becomes alienated from his group, leaves the unit, and joins another one. Instead, Ahmad renegotiated the nature of his kinship relations. For him, kinship was as important as it had been previously—it was serving his needs. Although the young family members in both 'Ali's and Ahmad's families placed other concerns before family ties, for Ahmad and 'Ali such total negation was not at issue.

21. *Grass* is an old word for *qat* that dates back to the colonial period.

17. A woman preparing *iftar,* the food that is taken to break the day's fast during the fasting month of Ramadhan. Photograph by the author, 1992.

A Mysterious Occurrence and Three Attempts at Interpretation

Let us then go to the final case study. The following story has to do with a strange incident that happened one weekend while I was visiting a family whose daughter is a friend of mine. The case study concerns how significant events are interpreted, contextualized, and linked to larger systems of meaning when people try to understand something that cannot be comprehended by reason.

One early afternoon on a quiet weekend I was sitting with my friend Fawzia in her home in Ma'alla, interviewing her old mother on the topic of *zar.* This spirit possession activity was in the old days common in Aden, despite the colonial authorities' occasional attempts to ban or limit it, often at the request of concerned men whose wives were involved with it or of puritanical religious leaders.[22] The street, which was located in the outer edge of Ma'alla facing the slopes of Mount Shamsan and leading to the district of al-Qallu'a, used to be famous in the old times for accommodating several reputed *'alaqas*,[23] practitioners of *zar,* in whose home *zar dairas* (*zar* circles)[24] were regularly held. In this neighborhood, two *zar* rings were still held on a regular basis. Someone would bring a sick woman to be healed with *zar.* The *'alaqa* who lived next door to Fawzia's house had passed away some time earlier, but the most famous *'alaqa* still lived at the start of the street. Even though a well-known *'alaqa,* this woman, Mariam, was now a *hagga*—that is, a woman who has made the hajj to Mecca and expected the respect that a *hagga* can claim.

During the course of the 1990s, intolerant people made the practicing of *zar* difficult. At the time I visited Fawzia in 2001, Mariam performed healing by reading the Qur'an. Operating with spirits and mystic forces had changed in other respects, too. A fortune-teller had taken the place of the *'alaqa* as the one to whom people would turn when they had problems with the supernatural. In the

22. See India Office Records (IOR) R/20/A/2906, Zar, the colonial official file on petitions against *zar* in the 1920s and 1930s.

23. The term *'alaqa* (sing.), the colloquial name for practitioners of *zar,* comes from the Amharic language and means "chief" or "dignitary" (Kapteijns and Spaulding 1994, 9). In the old times, many of the *'alaqas* in Aden were of Abyssinian or other African origin, but the ones I met or heard of were Aden-born Arabs. The British administrators thought that the origin of *zar* was in Abyssinia, where a man called Ababadar, shaykh of Harar, established it (IOR R/20/A/2906, Zar, office notes dated Jan. 7, 1924). People with whom I have spoken say that *zar* in Aden originates from 'Imran, a village behind Little Aden, where the *'alaqas* had a *wali,* a holy man. The *'alaqas* would take to this *wali* whatever presents were brought to a *zar* ring. In his study on Little Aden folklore, Myers explains that *zar* is locally believed to have been introduced from ancient Egypt (1947, 197nB).

24. In a *zar* session, people sit on the floor in a ring or circle.

clairvoyant's house, people came to learn the fortune that she could see in a glass of water into which she tossed coins.

Fawzia's mother told me about how *zar* had been conducted a long time ago, during her childhood and until Fawzia's youth in the early 1970s. We were sitting on sofas in the first living room of the flat, which one entered after crossing the small veranda with stairs to the gate that led to the street. From this room, one could go into the second living room, furnished with traditional furniture—cushions circling the walls and a television set. This second room led to a small lobby with an entrance to the kitchen, the *hammam* (bathroom), and the stairs to two upper floors, with three bedrooms. It is a typical Ma'allan house of an extended family. Fawzia's father had died, and the breadwinners of the family were now Fawzia's elder brother and Fawzia herself, unmarried and without a family of her own. She had her own bedroom, but she preferred to sleep in the room her mother shared with Fawzia's younger sister and the sister's young son. Her sister's husband worked in the Emirates and seldom visited home. Fawzia's elder brother and his wife had built a bedroom on the second floor, on top of his mother's and sisters' bedrooms.

That afternoon Fawzia, her mother, and I were sitting in the outer living room next to the veranda toward the street. I had taken a seat in the sofa next to Fawzia. I was making notes while Fawzia's mother told me details of the *zar* sessions in which she had participated. Her account was so detailed that I suspected that she herself had acted as an aid to the *'alaqa,* even though she strictly denied it. This thought came to my mind because I knew that the custom was that an *'alaqa* had a staff of young girls, often Somalis, to help her in organizing the sessions.

Suddenly something strange happened. I heard an abrupt noise behind my back, like the sound of rats running fast down a wall.[25] I turned violently and pulled back my head because I expected something to run over me. Others in the room were also shocked; we looked up the wall behind my back and saw drops of water bursting violently from the wall and the ceiling. After seeing the drops of water I was relieved; after all, I had expected a huge creature to

25. At that time, I lived with a family in Khormaksar in a colonial-era wooden house, where every night rats ran in between the thin wooden walls and ceilings, causing similar noises.

run down the wall onto me. After recovering from this initial shock, I realized that there was something strange about water bursting from the wall. Fawzia's first reaction was to rush to the kitchen to fetch a rag to wipe away the strangely emitted water while it was still running down the wall. Her mother just sat paralyzed in her armchair.

Meanwhile, Fawzia's sister rushed from the kitchen, alarmed by the noise that came from the violently bursting water and from our screams. Relieved, I suggested that the water must have been caused by a leak from upstairs. However, the others did not share my relief. Fawzia said that there was no water pipe upstairs, just a bedroom with a big wardrobe. To be sure, we climbed upstairs to see if for some reason there was water. But there was nothing—just the heavy wardrobe and no sign of water at all. Fawzia and I even climbed up to the second floor, but to our disappointment we saw nothing there either. We went back downstairs to the living room, where Fawzia's mother, still very upset, was sitting in her armchair.

Fawzia, her sister, and I started to speculate about where the water could have possibly come from, but the old mother did not participate in our discussion. I suggested that the water must have come from the neighbor. Fawzia rushed to explain that the neighbor's house was a mirror image of this house and that the water pipes were on the other side of that house, not along this wall. Nevertheless, she went and knocked on the neighbor's door. Nagib, the neighbor and a friend of everybody in the family, was not at home, and we couldn't consult with him until the next day. We kept on inspecting the place where the water came from, but there was no sign of water anymore. We could find no explanation whatsoever, and we all remained quite upset about the strange incidence.

The situation was puzzling; I was still quite jerky about the unpleasant experience and saw that Fawzia's mother, who kept on sitting absolutely silent next to me, looked very troubled. Fawzia continued to ponder where the water could have possibly come from. It was not a large amount of water, but the strange mystery of water bursting out so roughly as if it came from inside the wall troubled her, too. It had never happened earlier, she said. Fawzia was no longer in shock and continued talking to me about her childhood experiences with *zar*. Yet her mother remained quiet; while Fawzia and I talked, she looked gloomy and with her small narrow eyes viewed me with suspicion. I could not escape the feeling that the old woman thought that I had caused the water, the supernatural event, to happen because I had insisted on talking about evil spirits. Or perhaps she thought that I represented some sort of evil force that had made the mysterious water appear.

I felt quite annoyed about the situation, and after I calmed down, I suggested half-jokingly that the water must have appeared because we were talking about *zar.* I expected the mother to react to my suggestion and to air her concern. She forced a smile, and Fawzia replied blatantly that she did not believe in such things. I could see that the incident troubled the mother, but she was not willing to talk about it. Instead, she tried to make fun of it, but I could see that her jokes did not amuse her either. The mystery of the water remained unresolved, and it seemed to me that there was no reason for it. More than the supernatural incident itself—even though thoughts of something evil awaiting my family came to my mind—I was worried that Fawzia's mother was seemingly disturbed by the strange incident.

I had been invited to stay in this house for some days, and that evening I heard the mother, who sat upstairs, listening loudly to the Qur'an recitation on her radio. It was late in the evening, and I sat downstairs with Fawzia. The whole house was filled with the vociferous voice echoing from the radio. I told Fawzia that her mother must be upset because of what happened and that maybe she thought it had happened because of me; after all, the water had come down right from above the place where I was sitting, and it had never occurred earlier. Fawzia continued to express her rejection that something supernatural had happened: "We will ask Nagib tomorrow; I am sure the mystery will be then resolved," she said. "You should not think that my mother has any bad thoughts about you," she continued. "She really likes you, just as everybody else in the family does." I suggested to her that her mother must be listening to the holy word because she was so upset. "No, that is how she is; she is in the habit of listening to the radio," Fawzia tried to reassure me.

When thinking of the day's ordeal and the discussions we had had, I came to the conclusion that out of the three of us, Fawzia was the only one who refused to interpret the events in any way related to the supernatural. At least, this unconcern was the image she wanted to maintain: "My mother is an old woman; we should respect her as she is," she concluded. I was still not really convinced about what she had said about her mother and went to bed with confusing thoughts in my mind.

The next morning Fawzia and I had breakfast in the kitchen, and I asked her if her mother had slept well after the stressful day. She convinced me that everything was all right. After breakfast, Fawzia went to see if the neighbor was at home. Nagib, the government employee, came and greeted us all. Fawzia explained the situation, and Nagib looked as puzzled as we did. He affirmed that there was absolutely no water source on this side of his flat. Even though the whole incident remained an unresolved mystery, the next day the mother had regained her calm, and she smiled warmly at me. I concluded that listening to the Holy Book had acted as a purifying ritual for her and brought back her peace of mind.

This was not the first time that my presence had caused an elderly woman to suspect that the forces of evil were present. As I mentioned earlier in this chapter, when interviewing Nuria's mother-in-law, my tape recorder had caused the old woman to become upset. In order to purify herself after being exposed to suspicious forces, she resorted to an immediate connection to God. Just as had happened in Fawzia's house, the younger generation of women in Nuria's marital home, too, saw the old woman's behavior as a token of superstition *(khurafa).* As they explained to me, they did not believe in such nonsense.

Regarding what happened in Fawzia's house, there was some space to believe that a supernatural event had taken place. Fawzia, however, refused to believe that any such thing had taken place. At first, I suspected that she was only denying it in order to please me, but I later became convinced that she meant what she said. We had many discussions on our worldviews and on matters of religion and belief. Fawzia was, like Adenis at large, a devout Muslim. However, unlike many other career women of her generation—she was born in the late 1950s—she was in the habit of observing the five daily prayers on a regular basis. Her mother had studied in a *mu'alama kuttab,* a Qur'an school, in a village outside Aden, and she had taught Fawzia matters of faith.

Fawzia was, like her mother, very religious, but her religiosity was quite different from the old woman's. She once told me that she had learned to submit to Islam in her childhood, when her grandmother and mother had taught her how to pray. Since then she regularly observed the daily prayers. Unlike her mother, she did not listen to religious preachers because she thought that their way of interpreting Islam was not in accordance with what she thought her religion was about. For her, religion was a personal matter, and she objected to the way some mosque leaders had of incorporating social and political messages in their sermons. For instance, she could not accept what those men said about women's decency and veiling: "A woman's morality is in her mind, not in her donning the veil. Look, even prostitutes here carry the veil," she once told me.

Her religiosity did not guide her view of society around her; instead, she had the typically Adeni leftist view on social problems and solutions to them. She talked about her personal aspirations, her relations to her family, her work, and her future plans against the background of being a highly educated working woman and an activist in both a small leftist political party and in the women's movement. She considered her mother's involvement in *zar* and the mother's listening to the imams' conservative messages as behaviors that belonged to the past.

In her childhood, Fawzia often accompanied her mother in the neighborhood *zar* rings and learned the knowledge of *zar* healing. At that time, people used to visit all kinds of healers and participate in big *ziara*s (pilgrimages) organized in the Hashimi mosque in Shaykh 'Uthman and in the 'Aydarus mosque in Crater. The *ziara*s used to gather folk healers of different kinds. Her mother once took her to the Hashimi mosque to have a headache healed by a folk healer. The healer put a thin iron rod through the skin of her forehead and let blood run out. Still today, Fawzia has a small mark, like a tattoo, on her upper forehead. Fawzia recalled that she once saw a woman playing with fire and pushing an iron stick into her throat. It was also customary to make vows on the occasion of the Hashimi *ziara,* after the "big *'id*"—that is, the *'id al-adha* following the hajj period. Those who succeeded in their vows brought money and small gifts of food to the mosque's *wali.*

Even though Fawzia had been exposed in her childhood to what she later considered two different forms of faith, upon adulthood she developed the idea that one was mere superstition. The other one reckoned with her "modern" worldview, marked by higher education, leftist political activism, and devotion to the cause of women's liberation. By declining to admit that her mother was upset because of me, Fawzia did not want me to feel uncomfortable for her mother's sake and tried to protect me. I was, after all, a guest in the house and thus must be treated in the best possible way. During my stay in the house, everybody did their best to meet all my needs and to make me feel comfortable. On my part, I expressed concern for the well-being of the old mother, whose generosity I had been allowed to enjoy. For me, it was a matter of attempting to behave in a virtuous way, the way I had learned that such reciprocity was culturally sanctioned.

For the three of us directly involved in the mysterious incident, different approaches to the supernatural made us take different positions in the aftermath of the event. But this was not all; what each of us considered proper action in the confusing situation contributed to the way each of us acted in relation to the others. In the aftermath of the mysterious occurrence that launched the reactions, the primary concern for all of us was to restore a balance. As I thought about everything that had happened, I also thought that the event as such was not the only level where we considered our action. More important was the level where personal and intersocial relations were reaffirmed. In this case, it was particularly Fawzia's agency in seeking a balance in my and the old mother's reactions of confusion that was important to the way things turned out. Because none of us finally understood what really had happened, the way each of us coped in the situation contributed to the restoration of amicable and cordial relations between us. Finally, even though the event still remained obscure, we could anyhow utter "*Khalas!*" (That's it, finished!), the magic word that ends all deliberations and permits everybody to relax (*Ittakhid rahatak!* Take your rest!).

Conclusions

In this chapter, I have discussed how propriety and morality come up in addressing and greeting people, operating with social networks, advocating virtue and high morals, renegotiating kinship ties, and, finally, dealing with different forms of spirituality. The same moral principles that people used in their talk, as presented in the previous chapter, came visible in action, too. In putting myself as a scholar in the middle of these events, I wanted to emphasize my understanding that talk about agency corresponds with my observations on agency in concrete events, such as those described in this chapter. More than that, by taking an active role in the events, I tested whether I could manage in these different situations by applying the moral frameworks I had learned from people's talk.

7 Morality, Causality, and Social Praxis

> [P]eople are not merely playing out a structure, they are each a locus of reason and construction, using complex embodied imagery that they are trying to fit to what they perceive and experience.
>
> —FREDRIK BARTH, "Boundaries and Connections"

IN THIS CHAPTER, I draw together the material I have presented so far and attempt to outline a theoretical argument. My starting point here is that my ethnographic material speaks of heterogeneity in norms, ideal models, and moral representations. As I concluded in chapter 5, three distinct and separate discourses on propriety emerge in people's talk. In chapter 6, we observed how a person can shift from one moral framework to another smoothly, often without visible conflict. What I want to draw from this observation is that moral frameworks are not tied to persons; that is, these ideologies influence the way people act and talk in particular situations whether the person adheres to a particular ideology and its morality concepts or not. From this perspective, I argue that people are users of resources of the moral frameworks and have become accustomed to changing from one *adab* (propriety) discourse to another in their agency and talk. That people in Aden change their reference framework when moving from one social context to another is in itself nothing peculiar; this happens everywhere. The point here is to focus on how the contextual nature of social interaction is "made" in practice and how people relate to social dynamics. These moral frameworks "are there" because their coexistence organizes social communication, not because adherents of particular ideologies bring different viewpoints to particular everyday situations.

When observing this heterogeneity in notions of propriety in Aden, I never had the impression that anomaly or confusion would prevail either in everyday practice or in moral commentary. What fascinated me in my ethnographic encounters was how people in everyday communication easily moved from one moral framework to another. Does this suggest that these people lack moral integrity or that they do not have a shared moral order characteristic of a culture that can be considered "authentic" or "solid"? Does my finding of contested moralities suggest that the Adeni society consists of several moral orders that live alongside each other in one community? To answer these questions we need first to look at what unites these people and how they mark the boundary between themselves and groups counted as "others." Again, I find the concept of *adab* useful in examining what unites and what divides these people in terms of identity and belonging. Anita Fábos's study of ethnic identity among Sudanese expatriates and exiles in Cairo provides an interesting comparison. Egyptians and northern Sudanese share the "same pool of cultural knowledge," as Fábos puts it, owing to their common Islamic and Arab heritage, so *adab* provides an ethnic vocabulary that marks the uniqueness of the northern Sudanese from other groups with the same cultural background (1999, 127). According to Fábos, the ambiguity that comes from both emphasizing the values shared with the majority community and highlighting a difference from them, as manifest in superior comportment, characterizes the northern Sudanese people's identity construction in Cairo (214).

An outline of general characteristics that people apply in describing what it is to be "Adeni" involves in a similar way notions of nation, religion, and communal specificity. As I noted in chapter 2, unlike many other parts of present-day Yemen, Aden, throughout its history as an international port, has been part of regional, intercontinental, and global movements of people and commodities. This position was further strengthened during the late 1950s, at the height of colonial times, when Aden became the third-busiest port in the world and when many of those families that today form the settled population of the town came here.[1]

1. In the 1955 population census, reflecting the British policy of distinguishing people according to descent, the population was divided into categories based on race, religion, and country of birth. These three indicators produced the following population groups: Arab (Aden), Arab (protectorate), Yemeni, Indian, Somali, British, European (Other), Jews, Other (including Palestinians, Syrians, Lebanese, other Arabs, and Americans) (Aden Colony 1955a, 10). If in the 1946 census the group "Aden Arabs" formed half of the population according to place of birth, in 1955 their share had dropped to 37.9 percent. As the population of Aden increased from 80,516 in 1946 to 138,155 in 1955, the number of people coming from the eastern and western protectorates and

From the idea of Aden's unique position as manifest in its history comes the idea that Adeni people have a particular identity different from that of the people of other parts of present-day Yemen. Furthermore, Aden's uniqueness comes from the understanding that the people of Aden today do not necessarily share the place of origin or the ancestors or traditions of their grandfathers that is considered typical to other areas of Yemen (although it is not necessarily true). On the one hand, the ambivalence in relation to other parts of Yemen is manifest in the shared idea of common "Yemeni" descent, an identity that culminates in the positive feelings in regard to Yemeni unity as a long wished-for dream. On the other hand, Adeni people make clear distinctions between themselves and what they call *dahbash*[2] and *badu,* abusive names for fellow Yemenis. *Dahbash* is the offensive name used for North Yemenis who visit the town. It is often uttered in the street and traffic because the northerners' driving style causes irritation to Adenis accustomed to more orderly traffic behavior. At the core of this abusive discourse is the idea that the *dahbash* are people who have no understanding *('aql)* or manners *(adab).*

In similar terms, although *badu* literally means "bedouin," a category to which only a minority of countryside people belong, it is the term of mockery for people from the surrounding countryside or anyone who behaves in an "uncivilized" way, as contrasted to being a *hadhari,* a civilized town settler. This concept holds that the *badu* are "backward" *(mutakhallif)* and that they engage in customs that disgrace a person *('adat sha'na ma'aba).* Such customs, according to this Adeni stereotype, involve certain wedding practices, the way men talk negatively about women, and some features of the imagined typical countryside marriage. This name is not, however, used of people who have settled in Aden permanently and have become accommodated to the ways of life of the town.[3] As I pointed out in chapter 2, Adeni people are open to newcomers, and it is easy for anyone of whatever background to become an Adeni.

---

from the Kingdom of Yemen in particular rose in proportion to that of locally born people (Aden Colony 1955a, 12).

2. One version of the meaning of the pejorative name *dahbash* indicates that *d* stands for *dawlah* (country), *h* for *hikmaha* (its leader), *b* for *balatia* (thieves, criminals), *a* for *awla-hum* (the first one of them), and *sh* for *shawish* (a soldier).

3. Bujra (1970) emphasizes this point, too.

A third marker of Adeni identity has to do with Islam. More than 90 percent of present-day Adenis are Sunni Muslims of the Shafi'i school. Not everybody expresses his or her faith manifestly—observing the five daily prayers, visiting the mosque on Friday prayers, fasting during the Ramadhan, or making the hajj to Mecca—but even those who do not do these things in a regular way still consider themselves to be proper Muslims. The rituals are as they are, but people tend to think that merely performing the rituals does not make one a proper Muslim. For such people, Islam is present as moral guidelines. At the core of these principles are the Islamic sanctions that divide the world into what is recommendable, permissible, avoidable, and prohibited. The idea that religion is a private matter has historical roots in Aden, and it was not brought here by the colonial rule or by the Socialists.

However, after unification with the North and with the influx of returnees from the conservative gulf countries, many people became more concerned about practicing their faith according to visible manners. These changes were accompanied by the "new veiling" phenomenon and the spread of the idea that a "proper" Muslim woman should cover her hair. Even though the majority of the young women I asked about the name of the headgear they wore called it a *mandil* (scarf), emphasizing that it is not a *hijab* (the Islamic headgear), they often explained the change of costume by reference to Islam. "This is what our religion Islam requires" was the typical answer. But not only women adjusted their appearance to meet "Islamic" criteria; politicians, former leaders of the PDRY, also now took to the habit of fiddling with a rosary while appearing on the television in order to demonstrate their piety.[4] Some people resorted to making the hajj to Mecca to manifest religiosity and to be called by the respected name *hagg* or *hagga*,[5] as in the case of the woman in chapter 6 who had earlier been known as an *'alaqa* (leader of a *zar* ring). Nevertheless, the idea that Adenis are not proper Muslims—an idea entertained by some people in the North and during the PDRY era as propagated by Saudi Arabia—is troubling to many Adenis.[6]

4. This new practice looked rather awkward in Aden, where men are not in the habit of carrying a rosary.

5. A person (male or female) who has carried out the pilgrimage to Mecca.

6. One such account is in Meneley 1996, 99–100. Elite Zabidi women were, according to Anne Meneley, shocked to see how Adeni women "had absolutely no concept of how to behave

It is simply understood that Adenis practice their faith in a different way and that they are more tolerant than other Yemenis to variations in forms of religious adherence and practice.

In this way, Adenis negotiate a community identity in both positive terms, by identifying with town life and its social networks, and negative terms by emphasizing their distinction from people who do not respect the town's openness and easygoing way of life. This latter element has gained weight in the course of the 1990s with the influx in 1991 of Yemenis from conservative gulf countries following the first Gulf War. These people brought along conservative ideas that many Adenis consider alien to Aden, and Adenis resent the Saudi interference in Yemeni politics. Alongside the returnees came proponents of militant Islam, some returning from the "Holy War" in Afghanistan.

As the backgrounds and roots of Adeni people differ, so do their ideas of traditions. One day I was sitting in a newspaper office browsing through old newspapers in the archives when the women who worked in the room started a heated discussion on how traditions should be observed. Present were four women of different ages and backgrounds. Ramadhan and *'id* were approaching. The four women were sitting quietly performing their tasks when suddenly the youngest of them initiated a discussion on *'id* preparations. She announced enthusiastically that it is a must to prepare *burr* (a kind of wheat porridge) in a traditional *naswa* (clay pot) for the *'id*. She was very excited by the thought that the holy month was approaching and by all the special things that would happen in her home while celebrating it.

Judging from the faces of the other women, I saw that they thought this young woman was unfamiliar with the local customs; after all, she had only recently moved from the North and was working in her first job. Her costume signaled that she was different from the other women. She was wearing a black *abaya* (overcoat), a *niqab* (face veil with eyeholes), and black gloves. Her outfit was unusual job attire at that time (autumn 1998) in an Adeni office—in particular in a section where only women worked—whereas in Sana'a it was the typical office woman's costume.

---

appropriately in public." Zabidi women view their propriety primarily in terms of *din haqqana*, "our religion" (1996, 96), from which Adenis were believed to deviate.

The other women did not share her enthusiasm. The two middle-aged women, who had the usual job attire of that period, a Western-type skirt with a long-sleeved blouse and no head covering, looked at her with pity in their eyes. One of them replied to her that there was no such obligation and that even if there was such a tradition someplace in the North, it was up to each person to decide whether to follow it or not. The young woman was left alone with her excitement, and the others continued their work without saying anything.

The contrasting ideas are not owing to differences in background only, though. As I held in chapter 2, socially stratified Aden hosts different social traditions that mark the social groups and categories. Until the late twentieth century, it was customary for a son to follow his father's occupation, a custom that contributed to the reproduction of the social hierarchy. However, during the time of the PDRY, this tendency was counteracted with the coming of universal education and job opportunities that made it possible for people of modest backgrounds to acquire positions that their fathers and mothers had never dreamed of. The new opportunities were also open to the *akhdam,* and some of them had even acquired high-ranking positions in the army. These policies resulted in a generation gap in terms of work career and educational qualifications, as I explained in chapter 2.

Traditions According to Taste

Aside from the influence of the different backgrounds of people, ideas of tradition vary at another level, too. It is the question of different moral frameworks and how the notion of "tradition" is interpreted as constitutive of morality. What might be called the "customary model of traditions" presumes a centuries-old way of living, often represented as "the Yemeni way of life." In gender terms, this notion of "tradition" is institutionalized in such social phenomena as the patriarchal family, with its gendered division of labor and women's seclusion from affairs outside their domestic sphere. Limitations to women's and men's propriety are regulated from the point of view of these social institutions. Words such as *'urf* and *'adah* refer both to customs and to the customary law[7] applied in varying

7. Other terms are also used in customary law; see Dostal 1989 and Weir 2006 for an introduction to tribal law.

forms outside Aden, from where many people in town originate. But in conversations about aspects of the customary way of life that people view negatively, the word *takhalluf* can appear. It refers to "bad customs" and "backwardness,"[8] matters that should be eradicated in order for the tradition to be acceptable. The earlier practice of displaying a woman's bloodstained *futa,* underskirt, after the wedding night is one such "bad" custom.

Second, the notion of tradition bears a meaning in an Islamic framework. As I explained in chapters 2 and 4, from the twentieth century on the idea of what Islam is and what stands outside it has become polarized into two positions represented by two prominent figures, Shaykh Muhammad bin Salim al-Bayhani and Shaykh ʿAli Muhammad Bahamish. It is not a question of ritual practice only. The two approaches stand for a different orientation to Islamic scholarly tradition, too. Whereas the Bahamish type of Islam in interpreting sharia has tended to rely on classical *fiqh* manuals, the new *qadi*s who function in mosques[9] develop their own interpretations directly from the Qur'an and the sunna, thus following Bayhani's example. The question of *ʿurf* as a source of Islamic law also divides these two camps.

A third idea about tradition can be outlined in the framework of the revolution. As I maintained earlier, the discourse of revolution constructed an idea of a nation deprived of its Arabic and Yemeni identity during the colonial past and in the countryside during the feudal *(iqtaʿi)* times. This deprivation was seen as caused in part by the Indian cultural penetration, as I explained in chapter 2. The postcolonial rulers subscribed to Arab unity and the idea of "one Yemeni homeland."[10] The mission was to rid tradition of feudal and backward elements[11] and thus to

8. As an example of the use of word *takhalluf,* see how ʿAida ʿAli Saʿid, a prominent figure in the Yemeni women's movement, discusses negative customs in family relations prevalent still in the countryside in her newspaper column in *Sawt al-ʿUmmal* on the draft of the Personal Status Law (*Sawt al-ʿUmmal,* Apr. 30, 1992).

9. See note 94 in chapter 2 regarding the increase in the number of *qadi*s in Aden.

10. On this national ethos, see Halliday 1990, 99–139, and 2000, 55–70.

11. As A'ida Yafaʿi, leader of the Women's Union during the late 1970s, put it, "We might think that men are the cause of women's situation; but men are not the cause because they are governed by the feudal and tribal social relations of the society itself. When we declare that we want to be equal to men, we want to be equal in rights but we don't want to be equal if men are trapped in underdeveloped thoughts. In an underdeveloped society men have underdeveloped ideas and

"give vitamins to old ideas," as it was explained in drafting the 1974 Family Law (see chapter 4). In this mission, both traditional and religious rationalizations were used to introduce change into society, a tactic that is similar to those used in other Middle Eastern countries (see Eickelman and Piscatori 1996, 25–26).

Traditions and Social Exclusion

Alongside the use of the two stereotypes *dahbash* and *badu,* Adeni identity is negotiated by making a distinction from the *akhdam,* too.[12] This distinction is argued in particular in terms of traditions. Traditions can uplift a person, but they can also degrade him or her. The discourse of distinction is evidently talk of propriety, even though it is expressed in negative terms. What the "*akhdam* are" is the opposite of what the people with claim to respect are.[13] As noted earlier, the *akhdam* are a social category of people with a despised origin. Commonly believed to be the descendants of Ethiopian occupiers who ruled the area with oppression and violence during the fourth to sixth century A.D., these people are said to carry the burden of their vicious ancestors, who lacked the local Arab people's manners and positive qualities.[14] In popular belief, the *akhdam* are also descendants of slaves; their grandfathers are believed to have acted as slave fighters in the Ethiopian army when it invaded the southern part of the Arabian Peninsula. Likewise, it is believed that people of Hamdan, the forefathers of the present-day two main tribal confederations of the northern highlands, the Hashid and the Bakil, terminated the foreign occupation. According to the story, the Hamdan enslaved the slave

we don't want equality in this. . . . They have inherited the way they are from thousands of years of backwardness" (quoted in Molyneux 1979, 12).

12. What follows here regarding the *akhdam* people represents common beliefs, prejudices, and assumptions that other social categories of people maintain about them. These accounts are in no way a fair characterization of the *akhdam* and do not represent my views on them.

13. To fight the prevailing misconceptions, the people called *akhdam* have recently formed associations to eradicate the bad image and inferior position they are subjected to in Yemeni society. To replace the stigma linked to the name *akhdam,* the activists have attempted to introduce a new meaning for it: "servants of Allah."

14. Scholars are not unanimous in their views of the origin of the *akhdam*. Serjeant accepts the idea that their origin is linked to the Abyssinians but suggests that part of the non-Arab population of this "class" might be aboriginal people that predate the Arabs (1967, 287).

fighters again but set them free after some time on the condition that these people be banned from everything that the free people enjoy.[15]

This "historical" disgrace marked these people and continues from generation to generation to stigmatize them. Each new generation is believed to carry not only its ancestors' appalling traditions *(taqalid)*, but also those ancestors' unmannered behavior and contemptible customs *('adat)*.[16] One old man recalled to me how during the British time the *akhdam* were banned from attending school and how he and other schoolchildren used to throw stones at the *akhdam* children if they tried to come near his school. A small portion of the public prostitutes come from this social stratum, too. Many people believe that prostitutes come only from among the *akhdam*,[17] thus linking prostitution to the "despicable" occupations these people are presumed to practice.

During the colonial era, the *akhdam* were segregated from other social "classes," and at one point the British even considered nominating a separate *qadi* for the *akhdam* to solve their particular problems. These problems were linked to poverty and to the specific marriage customs the *akhdam* had. Among these customs was the practice of paying very nominal payments upon marriage *(mahr)* and the tendency among both men and women to change marital partners and to divorce rather easily. Another custom had to do with a type of "temporal exchange" marriage the *akhdam* had.[18] In this system, two men agree to marry two women for a certain period and then to exchange wives after a certain time

15. Since the 1994 civil war, which was won by the northern troops, many people think that Aden is again under northern occupation. The Adenis claim that the *akhdam*, who enjoyed a relatively good time during the PDRY era, are repressed again because the northerners are Hashid and Bakil.

16. The *akhdam*, however, should not be confused with another social group that also carries the stigma of their grandfathers, the *'abid* (literally "slaves"), who are considered to be descendants of slaves brought from Africa as late as the early twentieth century.

17. Records on public prostitutes in Aden, which the British kept during the early part of the twentieth century and which are stored in the India Office Records in London, contain an entry on the "origin" of each public woman, indicating that only a small minority seems to have been of *akhdam* origin. Some present-day prostitutes I have met are from social categories other than the *akhdam*, even though there are also women from the latter social group, too.

18. This custom should not be mixed up either with *mut'a* (temporal) marriage of the Twelver Shi'a or with exchange marriage *(zawaj al-badal* or *zawaj shighar)*. The latter is practiced in Aden,

has lapsed. The official *qadi*s nominated by the British felt that they could not solve these specific problems because the problems stemmed from local customs, and there was no mention of them in the Islamic law manuals that were used to solve marital problems in the court.

These kinds of stories have contributed to the idea many people hold today that the *akhdam* are not proper Muslims. Some people also told me that the *akhdam* do not bury their dead in the way considered proper for Muslims. According to such prejudices, the *akhdam* might bury their deceased outside their huts and sometimes even under the mud floor of their dwellings. One man told me that he was intrigued by this question, and so he went and asked one *akhdam* man about the matter. The man convinced him that they bury their dead in the same way other people do—that is, by carrying them to a public cemetery. This example is exceptional; people usually do not query the *akhdam* regarding such prejudices. Few people who are not *akhdam* have anything to do with them, and in case someone knows any of them from the neighborhood or from work, that person prefers not to socialize with them because it is considered improper to mix with the *akhdam*.

Custom, the Everyday Manifestation of Tradition

In common language, "customs and traditions" *('adat wa taqalid)* form a phrase, but in actual fact these two words refer to two different conceptual entities. Where *'adat* tell about practical ways of doing things, *taqalid* inform one about the heritage of a group of people. "Bad customs" *('adat sayyi'at)* and "habits you are blamed for" *('adat sha'ina)* draw the line regarding the ideal way a person is expected to present himself or herself in front of others. *'Adat* can change within a generation, such as marriage customs, whereas *taqalid* persist and constitute more permanent parts of a group's identity.

According to what old people have told me about Adeni society during the colonial era, various social categories differed from each other on the basis of *taqalid*. But the dividing line between "respected" social groups and the *akhdam* is

---

but it is not in accordance with sharia or *qanun* (law) if *mahr* is not paid (as indicated in both the 1974 Family Law and the 1992 Personal Status Law).

not drawn only on the basis of what kind of traditions each is supposed to have, but also on the idea that the *akhdam* are considered to have no *taqalid* at all. One middle-aged professional woman from a *mashayikh* family that had moved to Aden from Hadhramaut explained to me the way the *akhdam* are: "One day they buy a TV set, and the next day they sell it. They do not have a plan." "Not having a plan" means to this woman not only that the *akhdam* do not have any order in their everyday deeds, but that they have not inherited a morality that guides those deeds. This is the stuff that people consider all persons inherit from their family. An intellectual man in his sixties explained this same matter to me as follows: "*Qat* is their biggest vice. A man and his wife chew *qat* together, and when it's all gone, he takes a radio set or anything they have, brings it to the market, sells it, and buys more *qat*. They don't feel shame in divorcing randomly and not planning for future." Some people tend to see the lack of *taqalid* in positive terms, too. As this same man explained to me, "The *akhdam* are really different from the rest of us. Everything is different in their life, they do not have *taqalid*, but only *'adat*. This is the best thing about them; they are free from the obligation of heritage." To this man, the *akhdam* "way of being" was a source of admiration; it was freedom that only those people could possess. He continued: "The three best qualities of the *akhdam* are that they are generous, courageous, and free in sexual matters."

He continued by telling me that in the North the *akhdam* have historically been more restricted than in Aden: for example, in the North the names of the early imams and members of the Prophet Muhammad's family such as "'Ali," "Zaid," "Ja'far," "Husayn," and "Hassan" used to be forbidden to the *akhdam*, but not in Aden. In contrast to the dominant attitude toward the *akhdam*, this man admired them for their freedom from the "ties that bind"—that is, the traditions of their forefathers, although it was for this reason in particular that the majority of the population despised them. Their freedom in sexual matters, this man explained to me, means that the *akhdam*'s marriages do not involve large sums of money and are not as formally organized as they are for the rest of the population. A woman can easily obtain a divorce from her husband and marry a man she likes more. She just pays back to him the *mahr* he paid her upon marriage. According to him, *akhdam* women do not feel ashamed to divorce and remarry this way.

In other aspects, too, women among the *akhdam* are freer than other women. They worked outside the home long before other women began to, and they acted as independent entrepreneurs, which few women can do, even today. "Besides, the *akhdam* women never veil, they move around freely among men and don't feel ashamed to have their meal in a *mat'am* [local restaurant].[19] Akhdam men and women can even chew *qat* together, something other people never do," he explained to me.[20] The positive image this man maintains of the *akhdam* is probably owing to the fact that in his childhood in Ma'alla he used to play with *akhdam* children from the neighboring shanty area, a matter that was not common during the colonial time. "I lived among them, and my best friends were among them," this man recalled.

In contrast to the previous views, some people maintain that the *akhdam* do have traditions. An upper-middle-class man in his fifties told me that the *akhdam*'s traditions are simply different from those of other people. "It is not that they don't have traditions, but that their traditions are different from ours," the man said. In the Adeni way of thinking, the forefathers' merits accumulate over time and contribute to the honor of the living descendants, providing cultural capital. Because the *akhdam* are considered to have an ill-reputed past, and because their origin is viewed as despicable, it is believed that they do not have any such cultural capital to build upon.

Talk about good and bad traditions is also a discourse on purity. Good traditions "purify" a person, link him or her to the glory of the ancestors, whereas bad traditions manifest how the person is limited to reproducing his or her ancestors' "impurity" and "bad manners." But purity is not the only marker that distinguishes groups with honor from those they should avoid having any contact with. The old saying "Take your meal with a Jew, but do not make him your friend; take a *khadim* [singular of *akhdam*] as your friend, but do not share a meal with him" is illustrative. It is based on two different kinds of distinctions. Ideas of impurity prevent an Arab with honor from eating with a *khadim*, whereas concepts of moral integrity stop him from relying on a Jew. According to the tribal ideology, both Jews and *akhdam* are considered to be "weak" *(da'if)* people and thus

19. Local restaurants that only men are supposed to frequent. Some *mat'ams* have a "family section," an area often separated by a curtain that is meant for women, even if in male company. Women seldom go to a restaurant without a male escort.

20. In fact, non*akhdam* men and women do chew *qat* together; members of the same family, neighbors, or close family friends can spend an afternoon together chatting and chewing.

in need of the protection of "strong" *(qawi)* groups as well as lacking the claim to honor *(sharaf)*.[21] As Abdalla Bujra points out, these groups have no ascribed religious status either because they have no ancestors who are religious leaders (1971, 14–15). These groups lack "religious capital," as manifest in the concepts of *baraka* (blessing) and piety that elevate a person.

As in India, in Aden people view the society in terms of "pure" and "impure" people. Robert Serjeant asserts that the fact that in Aden the *akhdam* specialize as sweepers (in contrast to *akhdam* in the countryside, who act as agricultural laborers), "n'est pas loin de faire d'eux une sorte de caste d'intouchables" (almost renders them as a sort of untouchable caste) (1967, 287). As the middle-aged *mashayikh* woman referred to earlier explained to me, "These people do not wash themselves, and they wear dirty clothes. Their houses are without running water, and the food they eat is not clean. You cannot have your meal with such people." Thus, respectable people cannot exchange visits with them. This uncleanliness, according to the woman, also prevents marriages between *akhdam* and other groups.

Even though the concept of impurity in relation to the *akhdam* is clearly symbolic, this woman preferred to explain their impurity to me in terms of hygiene. She worked in the health sector and was aware of the Western principles of cleanliness that came to Aden first with the colonial rule and after that with the national health system based on World Health Organization standards.[22] The concept of impurity does not come from the body itself, but from the way the body is symbolically constructed as impure.

Many non*akhdam* people explained to me that this group's difference to other social groups arose from their involvement in jobs that are not considered proper for "respectable" people. The *akhdam* can perform tasks where they come in contact with wet and dirty materials, such as in cleaning work, garbage

21. The "weak" people are weak in the sense that they are not armed, fighting men. The "strong" groups are the ones who have the right to bear arms (Serjeant 1967).

22. In the health system, Western concepts of purity have been in part combined with Islamic principles of cleanliness, in particular in regards to maintaining personal hygiene, exposing the body, nursing the sick, and treating the dead. See al-Bayhani on issues related to women's sexual organs and exposure of the female body in visits to a doctor (1950, 27–33); see also World Health Organization 1981.

18. The *akhdam* often live in makeshift huts erected with whatever building material they can find. Photograph by the author, Crater, 1991.

collection, masonry, butchering, bloodletting, circumcision, and barbering.[23] In the old social hierarchy, such "dirty" jobs were reserved for people whose claim to propriety did not prevent them from performing such work or for others who for subsistence reasons had no choice but to take such jobs. The former category consisted of many *akhdam* people, together with other low-category people such as the *'abid* (descendants of earlier slaves), and the latter group consisted of, among others, Somalis, other Africans, and North Yemenis (see chapter 2).

One middle-aged man in his late forties, a teacher by profession, divided the *akhdam* into three subcategories according to how "dirty" the business is that they are involved in. The upper category consists of those who perform clean but simple tasks under someone's service, such as messengers and guards. In the middle category are those who perform tasks that involve dirt and service, such as sweepers, cleaners, garbage collectors, and barbers. The lowest category

23. Serjeant says that people in Hadhramaut consider these jobs demeaning and defiling. He mentions two types of occupations that demean: body services of any sort and "unclean" work, in particular anything that involves handling human excrement or animal dung (1980, 130).

consists of "very dirty people who have no manners [*ahlaq*] at all and who behave like animals. They don't take care of their hygiene or wear clean clothes, and, besides, they are always involved in all kinds of illegal businesses. They perform despicable things such as prostitution."

Social Hierarchy and Propriety

The talk of *akhdam* is evidently talk of social hierarchy. These explanations are the kind people use in describing the inevitability of *akhdam* people's low position. But because the *akhdam* are considered not to be part of normal social exchange, which is manifested among other things in visiting patterns, in greeting and addressing people, in participating in mutual help networks, and in conducting marriage arrangements, they therefore stand outside society as imagined by non*akhdam* people. However, the "society of the people with respect" relies on services the *akhdam* perform. Sweeping the streets, serving the tea in the offices, and collecting garbage, among other things, are the kinds of essential tasks in which the *akhdam* specialize. Without their contribution, the society would not run. The *akhdam* thus constitute a community that belongs to society but whose exclusion from society forms the imagined society of the majority population.

"People with respect" are thus dependent on the *akhdam*, and there is some reciprocity between the two groups, too. Not everybody tries to avoid or can avoid contact with the *akhdam*. Some people provide housing for *akhdam* families in exchange for services they can provide. In Khormaksar, I visited a colonial-era villa where the owner of the house had allowed an *akhdam* family to stay in his yard even after unification, when families became owners of houses that were previously owned by the state and rented for a minimal rent. In contrast to this owner, in Khormaksar in the early 1990s some people started to build fences round their villas, and some tried to evict the residents of the huts erected in their compound.

In the house I visited, the owner had allowed the *akhdam* family to stay in the one-room former servant's house, but he had also sealed the view between the two houses with a high fence in the yard. The owner, an elderly man who lived on his own, used the services of the *akhdam* family in exchange for this arrangement. The children of the servant's house shopped for the man and came whenever the owner banged on the wall that separated his kitchen from the *akhdam* family's abode. These services included small repair jobs and other errands in the house. Communication between the two houses took place through the kitchen window of the owner's house, which was covered with fine iron mesh and gave a view into the small yard of the servant's house and allowed visual contact. The owner was on friendly terms with his tenants, whom he did not charge any formal rent. But on one occasion when a misunderstanding came up, he criticized them to me: "These people have no understanding; they are only *badu*." He thus offered the kind of friendliness that lacks all respect, indicative of the general nature of the relationship between non*akhdam* and *akhdam*. Because the *akhdam* are not expected to have any manners, other people do not have to utilize this category of social virtue in relations with them.

In Aden, having a housemaid or servant was rare at the end of the 1990s, unlike in colonial times, when it was a rule in every financially established family. In Ma'alla, I once participated in a women's *qat* party organized in the flat of a woman who had a job outside the home and for that reason did not have time for household chores. Her husband was an immigrant in a gulf state with a salary reasonable enough to have a servant in the house. The housemaid was a young *khadim* woman whose duties included preparing the *maglis* (living room) for the Thursday afternoon *qat* parties. She cleaned the room and organized the cushions and the low tables so that each one of the guests had a comfortable place to sit and take her rest. Before the guests arrived, she put sufficient drinking water in the refrigerator to cool, heated charcoal on the gas stove for incense burners and *shishas* (water pipes where scented tobacco is burned), and brought soft drinks from the shop downstairs. When the guests arrived, she took care of everybody's overcoats and brought drinks, ashtrays, and whatever anyone needed. After everybody had been served, and all were taking their rest, she sat in the corner of the room and started chewing *qat*. Even though her presence was allowed in this company of upper-class women, nobody talked to her, and she had to settle for listening while others exchanged news and views.

Akhdam women act as coffee makers in men's *qat* gatherings or the like. In Khormaksar, I once participated in a men's *qat* party where a *khadim* woman was invited to prepare and serve coffee. She was not a prostitute. She had a daytime job as a typist in an office in Ma'alla, and in the evenings she occasionally provided services for men she knew. She told me that the host of the party had called her at her workplace and asked if she could come in the evening to his place and help with the catering. During the party, when she was not busy with catering, she sat next to me, the only woman in the company, and chewed her *qat* while talking to me. The other guests ignored her presence, assuming that she was a prostitute whom the host had invited for his own pleasure. All the men present treated me in the same way they addressed other men—exchanging views, telling news, and making jokes. I felt embarrassed for the sake of the woman but understood that her presence in such a party was considered socially *haram*.

As noted earlier, though, not all accounts of *akhdam* and the services they provide are negative. People who know the *akhdam* understand that they have an important role in the society. An old man who works as a director in an educational establishment praised the role the *akhdam* played during the 1994 civil war, when the northern army bombarded Aden. In the confusion that prevailed among many Adenis at that moment regarding whose side to take in the war,[24] the *akhdam* stood against the invading forces and defended their town. "The *qaba'il* [tribesmen] under whose protection we townspeople were supposed to be left Aden unprotected. When rumors spread round the town that northern tribesmen would come and loot, the *akhdam* heroically defended Aden until the last moment," this man explained.

Gender and Distinction

The *akhdam* are an interesting social group from a gender perspective, too. Some *akhdam* men act as *muzayyin*s, drum players who are asked to attend traditional weddings to accompany the bridal couple to the stage in the *zafaf* party. One of the most popular *muzayyin zafaf* groups in Aden in the 1990s consisted of three young men who were transvestites. In the wedding parties where they performed, they dressed in long *galabaya*s (cotton robes) or just slacks and shirts with a scarf tied loosely round their heads. All three had long hair reaching the shoulders, untypical of the local young men's short hairstyle that is usually short

24. Even though people were disillusioned about the practical outcome of the unification, not everybody thought that leaving the union with the North—a decision promoted by the secessionist move launched by southern leaders in the midst of the war in May 1994—was the right choice.

and well cut.[25] Men in the countryside surrounding Aden typically wear a scarf, whereas Adeni men in general seldom wear a scarf or turban as head attire. But the way the group members tied the scarf was not typical even of men from the countryside, but instead resembled the way some women do it. Their physical appearance when they were not performing, too, distinguished them from the entire population.

Men like these *muzayyin* are considered "harmless" and "not dangerous" in female company. In this sense, they are not considered men, who are understood to jeopardize the reputation of women who are outside their *ahl* (family) or who are not *aqarib* (close kin). Such men are thought to cause no harm and can be allowed to spend time in female company without being seen as a problem, even if the women in their presence are *haram* to them.[26] Thus, they are allowed to enter the women's *harim* (harem), or "private sphere."

Not all transvestites are from the *akhdam* category, of course. Some transvestites are hairdressers and beauty salon *(koiffer)* owners (who, unlike barbers, are not *akhdam*). I met the owner of one such beauty shop located in Khormaksar. He had a full bridal service in his salon, including renting out wedding dresses, doing makeup and henna, styling hair, doing pedicures, and so on. On one busy Thursday afternoon, his salon was full of customers being attended to by his assistants, and the customers' friends and relatives were there as well: all of them were women. The owner, dressed in a white *galabaya,* supervising his assistants and seeing to it that every customer received the best treatment, occasionally engaged in lively discussions about how to apply makeup and what kind of dress best suited a particular customer. He was soft-spoken and kind, without the typical restraint that is expected from men. His body movements and the way he held his hands expressed exaggerated femaleness typical to Adeni transvestites. The way he enthusiastically engaged in planning a customer's treatment indicated how he had a passion for women's beauty. After leaving the *koiffer* with a friend of mine, I commented to her that the man certainly knew his job. My friend, a woman of my age, replied that such men are not considered "dangerous"; it was all right that he ran the salon, and he was very popular among the local women.

25. Pop idols George Michael and Michael Jackson, whose songs were extremely popular in Aden in the 1990s, probably influenced the look of typical Adeni young men at this time.

26. Possible marriage partners according to limits set in the Qur'an.

From a gender perspective, the *akhdam* are distinguished from the entire population in terms of restrictions to personal freedom and mobility, too. Although it was stated to me that *akhdam* women are free to do what they like, they resembled more the way the *akhdam* men are thought to be rather than how women in general are supposed to behave. "The *khadima* woman is *hurra* [free]," some people proclaimed to me.

Restrictions for women were argued in terms of "not feeling shame." Things normally allowed for a man only, such as marrying and divorcing as he pleases, are considered to make a woman vulnerable to losing her reputation. Other more everyday issues—such as going to a local restaurant to have a meal, buying *qat* as often as one wants to and consuming it in a mixed-gender company, and moving outside the home without considering whether it is proper or not—apply to *akhdam* men and women in the same way. In people's commentaries, gender division thus fades away when it comes to the *akhdam*, a division that is otherwise always emphasized.

Non*akhdam* people consider the *akhdam* to differ from other members of the society in sexual morality as well as in lacking a gender division that otherwise organizes ideas of morality and propriety. The *akhdam* are also thought to lack a strict division of labor inside the household based on the familial ideology in which men and women complement each other in the tasks and duties they perform. And finally, the practice of sexual segregation is not thought to apply to the *akhdam*. Segregation includes the idea of "protecting" women from nonkin men—that is, those who are not *ahl* or *aqarib*—secluding the sexes in their everyday chores, and practicing avoidance, which both sexes are expected to follow while outside the home or when guests arrive at one's home. Thus, the *akhdam* are thought not to have a gender division in responsibilities that would contribute to accomplishing moral personhood as constituted separate to men and women. As a consequence, the *akhdam* do not manifest the virtue that is familiar to other social groups' gender conduct, rationalized in terms of either "what our religion says" or "this is our customs and traditions." However, promoting women's mobility and autonomy, allowing women similar roles in society as men, and downplaying sexual segregation, as the gender ideology of the revolution had it, resembles interestingly the way the *akhdam* are considered to be.

On the basis of the previous accounts regarding the lack of propriety among the *akhdam* and the material presented in the previous chapters on good manners, an idea of *adab* within the local context can be outlined. To summarize the prejudices described earlier, the *akhdam* lack *adab,* first, because they are not proper Muslims; second, because their traditions *(taqalid)* are reprehensible (or they lack them outright); and, third, because they act without a plan, solving their problems outside the socially conventional means. These three explanations link first to religion, second to traditions, and third to rationality. That the *akhdam* also lack both ideas of men's and women's separate spheres and the institutions connected to these spheres puts them in clear contrast both to what is considered as "religion" and to "our customs and traditions," thus complementing the first two prejudices.

The point here is to describe how *adab* is argued in negative terms, as a discourse of distinction, and how propriety is discussed in terms of lack, deficiency, and the legacy of *asl* (roots). In chapters 5 and 6, I described how positive notions linked to *adab* arose in how people act virtuously and in how people talk about propriety. These characterizations include generosity, cordiality, moral integrity, concern for the socially vulnerable, piety, modesty, restraint, and "learning" *(ma'rifa).* If we contrast these virtues to those characterizations that mark

19. Transvestite men acting as traditional wedding musicians who accompany the couple to the stage in a wedding club. Photograph by the author at a wedding club in Crater, 1991.

the alleged moral deficiency of the *akhdam,* we can note that the *akhdam* were pointed out in particular for lacking modesty, piety, restraint, moral integrity, and learning. These people can be generous and cordial, but their generosity is not reciprocated. People with a claim to respect engage in social exchange only with those who advocate morality and in activities that manifest social propriety. As we saw in chapter 6 with the case of Nur, she carefully avoided handing alms to the "wrong beggars"; doing so would not have won her social merit.

Morality, Propriety, and Place

In chapters 5 and 6, I pointed out how ideas of propriety have different contextualized manifestations. What is proper in one situation might be improper in another. The notion of "customs and traditions" that appeared in many accounts was distinguished from what was understood as "religious," on the one hand, and what the revolution was presented to have brought along, on the other. When talking about the uneven attributes of strength and weakness in relation to gender, people contextualized it with the phrase "our customs and traditions." As a counterideology to that, the revolution was presented to have eradicated bad customs, including the idea of men's and women's uneven capacities.

If "customs and traditions" and "revolution" were the only frameworks people use in contextualizing notions of propriety, it might have been natural to apply a traditional/modern dichotomy in analyzing those rationalizations. The evident variation in applying this concept pair could have been explained simply by pointing out how notions of tradition and modernity should be seen in their diversity, not as systems of fixed experiences and meanings, as Dale Eickelman and James Piscatori have rightly suggested (1996, 24).

But this variety characterizes Adeni society, too. It is clear that there is neither a unified idea of traditions nor only one representation of modernity. As I have pointed out elsewhere (Dahlgren 2000, 158), one can identify at least four different notions of what is modern in Aden, just as one can show how tradition has several contextualizations. The modern includes the pragmatic approach that can be called "customary modern," which is about combining a centuries-old lifestyle with selected elements of the modern to make life a little more comfortable but without changing the structural constitution of that life. Men are clearly the agents of this selective type of modernity, whereas women devote themselves to playing the role of recipients of whatever men decide to acquire. Sheila Carapico and Cynthia Myntti have described this phenomenon for two northern Yemeni areas (1991, 27). According to them, the selective approach to modern technologies resulted in new consumption practices that became available to families with a son or husband working as a migrant in one of the prosperous oil economies elsewhere in the peninsula or further overseas.

The second idea of what is modern links to the British colonial legacy and its "Western" way of life. The British ways still prevail in the administrative system, in infrastructure technologies, and in the ideas of good life that the upper-income sectors of the society embrace, such as receiving education and health care abroad. In continuity with what the British started, the third notion of the modern emerged with the revolution, which in principle subscribed to the work that the colonialists had left unfinished—that is, unifying the area, building a nation-state, establishing central rule, and enlarging the scope of societal services. As I pointed out in chapter 2, some British-introduced phenomena were readopted simply by changing their color. In terms of economics, the revolutionary government's modernizing efforts included establishing a locally based national industry, creating a domestic market, and improving the capacities to consume. In contrast to the British, the revolutionary government's policies transformed gender relations by opening education, the job market, and politics to women and by issuing a new family code. It is noteworthy that men and women talk in similar terms about "revolution," and advocates and opponents of women's liberation can be found among both men and women.

The fourth notion of modernity can be outlined within the framework of Islam. Islam presents an alternative future for the nation and includes a message that involves women, too. According to this idea, which emphasizes the compatibility of Islam and the modern, the orthodox discursive tradition of Islam can be turned into a societal practice by using both traditional media (such as the mosques) and modern digital technologies. In particular, young people are involved in promoting this form of the modern, and it remains to be seen what it will bring forth in Aden.[27]

27. On the emergence of this discourse after the time period covered in the current study, see Dahlgren 2007b. For research on such issues as Islamic consumption, the media and the constitution of the discursive, and nondiscursive public participation in "Islamic" terms in other places

Just as there are different representations of the "modern," so do notions of "traditions" differ among people, as I explained earlier in this chapter. In contrast to the conventional understanding of social processes discussed in terms of the traditional/modern divide,[28] however, in Aden the movement is not exclusively from the traditional to the modern. As the setbacks in rights that Adeni women experienced during the 1990s indicate, the society is characterized by an intense struggle between various ideas of modern and traditional, with no definite winner between the two. Among the varying notions of modernity and tradition, though, some representations have gained over others and become hegemonic. As my ethnography suggests, the "revolutionary modern" seems to be the hegemonic discourse of modernity. Nevertheless, the notion of "revolution" does not stand only for the modern. As I argued earlier, "revolution" represents a particular interpretation of tradition, too. In addition, I have suggested that the term *revolution* refers also to a particular way of acting and arguing religiosity.

The way people use the notion of "our customs and traditions" indicates that it is closest to what I earlier outlined as the "customary model of traditions." But like the notion of "revolution" in respect to modernity, the notion of "customs and traditions" does not stand for only a particular representation of the past, "*the* traditional." Out of the various notions of the modern, the concept "customs and traditions" represents the selective and pragmatic approach to modern phenomena that I called the "customary modern." It also represents a particular form of religiosity, as I pointed out earlier.

The ethnography presented in earlier chapters reveals the limits of the traditional/modern dichotomy as an analytical tool in one more respect. As we saw in chapter 5, some people used the term *religion* as a notion of contextualization. This term, which does not indicate that "customs and traditions" and "revolution" are un-Islamic or lacking religion, was used alongside these other terms. As the woman who addressed male readers of *al-Thawra* newspaper, quoted in chapter 5, put it, "The Yemeni woman is governed by religion before she is governed by tradition." Ladislav Holy, in his study of the Berti of the Sudan, asserts in a similar vein that these people distinguish between custom and religion

---

in the Middle East, see Eickelman and Anderson 2003a; Salvatore 2001; Salvatore and Eickelman 2006b; and Salvatore and LeVine 2005b.

28. An illustrative example is Makhlouf 1979, a study of Sana'ani elite women.

(1991, 129–40). Even though the Berti view custom as embedded in religion, the two stand for separate categories. Holy calls them "a kind of discourse about the world" (138).

Religion in Different Contexts

If religion and religiosity have different manifestations, as I argued earlier, then it is necessary to elaborate what "religion" here *is* in the first place and how it relates to what in anthropology is understood by the notions of religion and Islam. These questions require a definition of Islam that is not limited to its discursive traditions and holy texts. The notion of diversity in conceptualizing Islam and the idea that it can be embedded in other discourses about the world echoes Holy's definition of a "nonnormative" Islam. According to him, the diversity that exists alongside the core beliefs and common Islamic symbols consists of numerous ideological and practical accretions (1991, 1). If, however, we refute the idea that this diversity implies an existence of multiple "Islams," the way Abdul Hamid El-Zein (1977) has suggested, we have to distinguish for analytical purposes between the discursive tradition and the practice of Islam.

Talal Asad (1996) suggests that this separation is brought about by respecting the principles that guide the constitution of what he calls "Islamic discursive tradition." According to him, not everything Muslims do can be counted as Islamic discursive tradition. To outline this discursive tradition, he takes as the analytical starting point an instituted practice into which Muslims are inducted as Muslims in a particular context and with a particular history. Instead of "orthodoxy," he calls this practice "orthopraxy" because what is essential here is the establishment of a right way.[29]

Asad (1996) criticizes El-Zein's model of a plurality of Islams by pointing out how this model denies the specific significance of orthodoxy. According to Asad,

29. "The discourses in which the teaching is done, in which the correct performance of the practice is defined and learned, are intrinsic to all Islamic practices. It is therefore somewhat misleading to suggest . . . that it is orthopraxy and not orthodoxy, ritual and not doctrine, that matters in Islam. . . . A practice is Islamic because it is authorized by the discursive traditions of Islam, and is so taught to Muslims—whether by an 'alim, a khatib, a Sufi shaykh, or an untutored parent" (Asad 1996, 14).

critical to Islamic discursive tradition is that it constitutes a doctrine—a teaching—that notes the correct process of teaching as well as the correct statement of what is to be learned.

Drawing on what Asad elaborates and on Holy's idea of diversity in religious practices, we can note that in this book Islam is present in three different discourses, one of which is specifically called "religious" *(dini)*. As the ethnography I presented earlier suggests, people have different approaches to faith, a fact that comes up both in talk about religion and in the practices in which people engage. There is nothing surprising here; as Reinhold Loeffler has suggested, religious practice in any Islamic community is patterned by diversity rather than by communality (1988, 246–50). According to him, diversity has been a secondary concern in anthropology concerned to find the general pattern, the norm, and the shared culture. Loeffler argues that Clifford Geertz has made ignoring diversity a methodological postulate in his suggestion "to put aside at once the tone of the village atheist and that of the village preacher" (Geertz 1993, 123). As a consequence, we have become used to thinking in terms of the worldviews of "the" Azande or "the" Balinese (Loeffler 1988, 247).

In his critique of Geertz's famous definition of religion (for this definition, see Geertz 1993, 87–125), Loeffler argues that more than faith, religion is knowledge: "One should probably say that belief takes on the quality of knowledge, or, even better, that belief and knowledge are not strictly and abstractly separated" (1988, 270).[30] According to him, seven factors are critically operative in the formation of individual worldviews: (1) the individual's personality, including mode of perception, psychoanalytic constitution, intelligence, memories, needs, and so on; (2) his social and political interests; (3) his socialization and education; (4) the social milieu where he is living; (5) his existential situation; (6) the perceived empirical evidence of certain beliefs; and (7) the preexisting worldview. It is in the field of forces constituted by these factors—constraints as well as opportunities—that the individual's worldview is forged.

30. Loeffler further suggests that the structure and inner logic of religious hypotheses contain challenges and obstacles to belief that he calls "the threat of disaster," "the test of success," and "the explanation of free association." People engage these techniques in testing religious hypotheses and in explaining away the uncertainty that the application of these hypotheses in practice sometimes creates.

From the perspective of the present book, Loeffler's list of what factors contribute to the way religion is conceptualized in human practice is relevant but not comprehensive. What is missing links to the questions my book raises. One discourse is particularly called "religious," but similar considerations are made in reference to two other discourses outlined in this book: Why is one thing particularly explained as being "according to our religion," whereas something else is considered to be in line with "our customs and traditions"? And is the reference to revolution a mere political statement? To solve this problem, the concept of propriety *(adab)* is again useful. As I have maintained throughout this book, the notion of propriety stands at the center of all action; deeds are evaluated from

20. North Yemeni men, called "*dahbash,*" on a visit to Aden. Photograph by the author, 2001.

the point of view of propriety, and in talk distinguished formulas of propriety inform statements on practice. On the basis of my ethnography, I suggest that we need to include in Loeffler's list both morality and propriety among the factors that contribute to the formation of worldviews.[31] What people of my ethnography consider "religion" is at its core a distinct code of propriety. They articulated this idea by stating "this is what our religion says" and in other similar comments. This kind of speech formula refers to the particular message that the concept "religion" is understood to convey.

Morality Codes

Concepts of morality and proper comportment separate religious discourse from other discourses outlined in this work. The dividing lines between customs and traditions, religion, and revolution is not belief, which takes various manifestations according to the principles outlined by Loeffler, but rather different morality codes and the knowledge that informs them. We can call these morality codes *moral frameworks,* borrowing the term from philosopher Charles Taylor (1989, 19–20, 26). In what follows, I attempt to examine how Taylor's moral philosophy helps me to organize my ethnographic findings.

This mission, however, is not unproblematic. Signe Howell asserts in her introduction to the collected volume *The Ethnography of Moralities* that anthropologists have by and large ignored the theoretical challenges of the empirical study of moralities, even though moral philosophy has had a long intellectual tradition. For anthropologists, it is a problem to apply theories that do not concern themselves with locating the moral subjects within actual social and cultural worlds (1997, 8). Questions of morality in earlier Middle Eastern anthropological studies tended to be tied to the concept of "honor," whether linked to its alleged opposite, "shame," or not. This canon had its culmination in the classical volume *Honor and Shame,* edited by J. G. Peristiany in 1965. In such studies, the concept of honor has been presented in a way that separates this geographic area from

31. In addition, I think that we need to consider that in the Middle East there are no strict limits between acts that involve religion and other acts. As Fadwa El Guindi has asserted, flexibility characterizes the movement from religious to profane, with time and space affecting this movement (1999, 77–96).

other areas of the world where concerns of honor have also been raised, such as Latin America. Even though the Middle East certainly is a case of its own among the cultures of the world, pursuance of ethnographic research strictly within the notion of "honor and shame cultures" has contributed to a parochialism of the Middle East. The anthropology of moralities has in particular contributed to this trend. Because recent studies have spoken in favor of comparative studies across regions (e.g., Bayat 2001; Gran 1998; Kandiyoti 1996; Keddie 2002) and have questioned, among other issues, the way honor has been pathologized in "Muslim moralities," the way to discuss moral questions as part of general anthropological discussions has been opened.

In the present book, I have attempted to outline a moral order that consists of three parallel and contesting moralities that are operative according to context yet are nevertheless not tied to place. In particular, I have focused on how these different moralities present matters of propriety in everyday practice. In order to emphasize the dynamic relationship between the three moral codes and social reality as well as to avoid a perspective that views morality and propriety as principles of mere social control and reinforcement of the status quo, I have focused on issues of diversity and flexibility. To describe this multiplicity of moralities, it is not enough to use such general concepts as "morality." In my attempt to go beyond such concepts, I find Taylor's "moral framework" concept useful (with certain reservations, to which I return later) because it focuses on the relationship between agent and morality. Taylor's moral philosophy is also attractive from the perspective that he attempts to restore the centrality of goodness in morality, which, according to him, modern moral theory often forgets (as described in Abbey 2000, 49). As my ethnography suggests, common good manifested as a "personal goodness" is a central value in propriety in Aden. People do not act out propriety merely for negative considerations—that is, to escape sanctions—but in an attempt to express goodness and respectability.

According to Taylor, moral frameworks give shape and meaning to individual's lives and provide answers, no matter how tacitly, to the existential questions about the purpose, conduct, and direction of human life. One's framework provides guidance about moral questions in the broad sense, in relation to others, and with regard to what is meaningful and rewarding for a person. A framework incorporates qualitative distinctions and provides the sense that some actions, modes of life, and modes of feeling are incomparably of higher value than others

(Taylor 1989, 19–20; see also Abbey 2000, 34). Taylor uses the term *moral framework* as a synonym for *strong evaluation,* a concept he distinguishes from *weak evaluation.* According to Taylor, strong evaluation involves motivation in judging desirable actions and thus their qualitative worth (1985, 15–44, in particular 16, 18, and 1989, 26). Ruth Abbey, who has studied Taylor's thinking, suggests that it is better to consider moral frameworks as *consisting* of a series of strong evaluations (2000, 35). Living within such strongly qualified frameworks is constitutive of human agency, Taylor suggests, and stepping outside these limits would be tantamount to stepping outside what we would recognize as integral, undamaged personhood (1989, 27).

But if we look at the ethnography in this book and at the way propriety is acted upon and talked about in Aden, we can see that Taylor's idea of moral personhood is not exactly relevant here. First, people in this study do not seem to acquire some particular moral framework but instead use different frameworks contextually in their agency, smoothly moving from one framework to another. Second, the idea that a lack of moral framework places a person outside "undamaged personhood" and the mere field of human agency is problematic in the case of the *akhdam.* These people are said to lack the moral integrity and customs ("human agency" in Taylor's terms) that other social groups claim to possess. But the representations of the *akhdam* do not place them outside what is considered to be the scope of human agency. The *akhdam* certainly engage in agency, but the kind of affairs they engage in and the way they do it is considered improper and lacking all positive moral qualities. The "otherness" of the *akhdam* is not an ontological fact, but rather a social fact. Thus, we need to combine these two ethnographic facts with Taylor's concept of moral frameworks to be able to benefit from his concept.

Equally interesting is Taylor's idea of how people position themselves with respect to other people by means of principles of morality. This positioning relates to Taylor's concept of the dialogical self (1989, 36),[32] where identity is dependent on dialogical relations with others. According to Taylor, a self can never be described without reference to those who surround it (1989, 35). More than that, the self in general is a psychological blurring of boundaries between self and other (Abbey 2000, 68).

32. Taylor draws his idea of the dialogical self from Bakhtin. See Abbey 2000, 67.

Taylor's idea of selfhood or identity in relation to surroundings sounds like a form of universalism. We therefore need something to connect his dialogical self to the present ethnography. For this purpose, Suad Joseph's ideas of *relationality* and *connectivity* as characteristic of images of the self in the Arab world are useful (1999, 11–12). Her idea of the constitution of selfhood focuses on power relations inside families. Patriarchal connectivity is, according to Joseph, the particular form of relationality in Middle Eastern families, patterned by patriarchy. In refuting both individuality and corporatist ideas in the shaping of self in Arab families, Joseph explains that relationality is a typical form of selfhood to societies that value linkage, bonding, and sociability (1999, 9).

In these systems, persons achieve meaning only in the context of a family, which is the locus of survival and, in particular for women, often the only possible existential option. Joseph explains that persons in Arab societies are embedded in relational matrixes that shape their sense of the self. Although connected primarily to kinship and other relations of proximity, these matrixes shift and are situational. On this basis, Joseph constructs her concept of "connective personhood." By "connectivity," she means that persons do not feel autonomous; rather, they are an extension of significant others, and others are an extension of the self in the kind of process Taylor calls the "blurring of boundaries" between the self and others.

In my descriptions in chapter 6 of Nur's agency in making everyday choices and in chapter 5 of Salim's account of how he was the agent of his life, we can see an evaluation of the qualitative worth of agency. These persons made the evaluations in the process of considering the outcomes of each of their choices in the eyes of others. But it is difficult to draw the line between a person's own internalized decision making, which presupposes the social consequences of the choice, and a person's openness to other people's interventions in the way Joseph theorizes the issue. The motivation to act in a particular way is clearly selfish here, though, which naturally raises the question: Does the etiquette of propriety spark agency that is motivated by manipulation of the available resources? What actually is at stake, or, to turn the question around, what has the most merit in each moral framework? Before going into these questions, we have to deal with the problem of the accessibility of the moral frameworks in question. What kinds of processes are involved in the internalization of the guidelines of the three moral frameworks outlined in this book—the revolutionary, the customary, and the religious? How are the frameworks institutionalized?

The Institutionalization of Moral Frameworks

As I mentioned earlier, the focus of this book has not been the institutionalized forms of the three moral frameworks outlined here. Nevertheless, in order to demonstrate that each framework is a distinct entity, I want to take a brief look at where the frameworks are located and how they are institutionalized as I understand them. Each framework has its own "*'aqils*" (wise men). To start with the question of where these repertoires are located, we first have to see how the community is understood in each one.

In the revolutionary framework, as it is ideally presented, the community is the society that is part of the nation-state. The society is understood to be divided into different fields—economic, political, social, and cultural. The family is the core unit of society, but each person is also directly a member of society, a citizen. In this framework, men and women are seen to work alongside each other in building up the society.[33] Even though within this framework notions of equality and equitable opportunity are often celebrated, state and party functionaries constitute the "wise men" of this framework. Among them, some prominent women have occasionally appeared.

In the customary framework, the paramount reference is kinship in the form of a patrilineal family line. The community consists of lineages, the bearers of the forefathers' traditions, because the ancestors' history is embodied in the present-day generations. As Andre Gingrich has asserted in reference to marriage arrangements in a northern Yemeni tribal context, genealogy is not merely an a posterior ideological legitimation of the present day by means of references to the past. It is also a statement about the foreseeable future. Genealogical statements play an elementary and self-understood part in these a priori considerations (1989, 81–82). The genealogical line is counted according to male members of the family, and senior men in particular have the role of "specialist" in this representation. Women are counted only according to their relationship to a significant male. This relationship can be described by Joseph's concept of patriarchal connectivity, as discussed earlier. At issue are both age and gender hierarchy. The paramount resource that

33. "Society" here refers to an ideological construct. Social scientists tend to distinguish between state and (civil) society. For such an approach in the Yemeni case, see Carapico 1999.

the framework offers consists of relations that the kinship arrangements provide. The community consists of families and lineages, organized socially in a hierarchical order, each with traditions of its own. Outside this system of respected social strata lie the "nonrespectable" groups, such as the *akhdam*.

During the late colonial period and the PDRY era, the community coexisted in a more or less oppositional relationship with the state, each of the two having its own judicial system. As explained in chapter 2, this system was part of the "custom" the British claimed not to touch. During the PDRY era, family regulation according to the state law was possible if the parties concerned brought their disputes to court in the first place. State power was not so mighty that its disciplinary machine could have forced people to face the law if they did not voluntarily bring the dispute forward.[34] After the state apparatus moved to Sana'a from Aden following Yemeni unification, the customary framework reemerged as a stronger institutional determinant than the revolutionary framework, the latter now not having any main institutional support.

In the religious framework, the organizing unit is the community of the believers, the *umma*. The state is not necessarily in contradiction with it, provided that the state does not limit its activities. The community strives to transform the state into an "Islamic" state where no other source except the sharia serves as the basis for legislation. As representative of the new coming of a solid institutional basis for this framework, after the civil war in 1994 the Constitution was amended to enact Islam as the only source of law in the republic. Men and women have their own special roles in the Islamic community, which are different but not necessarily hierarchical. However, because the "wise men" of the religious framework tend to be male, women's role in defining the institutional basis of this framework is not the same as men's. Central to the religious concept of community is the "Muslim family," the unit that Martha Mundy has described in ideological terms as the "timeless, divinely regulated nucleus . . . lying at the heart of Islam" (1995, 91).

34. There were some famous exceptions to the usual state noninterference in personal matters. One was the case of bigamy that the authorities raised in the early 1980s against 'Ali Salim al-Bidh, at that time deputy prime minister, a popular personality, and, after unity, a member of the presidential council (see Lackner 1985, 94). Many other cases of polygamy went unnoticed, including the one during the late 1980s of my neighbor with two wives.

The Art of Being a Person with Respect

Alongside the institutional dimensions, moral frameworks as I outline them here have embodied manifestations, too, in the way they inform and become informed by the body. In the anthropology of practice, bodily dispositions are most often discussed in terms of Bourdieu's *habitus.* To my purposes, however, I perceive *adab* to be a notion more suitable in trying to establish a link between knowledge and embodiment. As a concept of "proper comportment," *adab* is the term for the embodiment of the finest traits of moralities manifest in human existence and agency. As such, it can be compared to *habitus,* the capacity for structured improvisation.[35] Both are sets of transposable dispositions, which allow agents to act and react in certain ways. *Habitus* is intersubjective and the site of the constitution of a person in action; it describes a system of dispositions that are both subjective and objective (Bourdieu 1977, 78–87; Postone, LiPuma, and Calhoun 1993; Thompson 1991). Being an embodiment of all that is idealized in a particular framework, *adab* is, like *habitus,* a structured structure, a system of durable dispositions that generate and organize practices and representations in a way that they can be objectively adapted (Bourdieu 1977, 78–87).

Whereas *adab* entails no structuralist prerogatives, *habitus* tends to be linked to a structural nominator. Bourdieu talks of a class *habitus,* or dispositions that are generated in relation to the homogeneity of the conditions of existence and social dispositions available (1977, 80, 83). To escape from the inevitable social determinism of the concept of *habitus,* Bourdieu introduces the term *bodily hexis* to denote personal qualities in deportment, gesture, and physical presence (1977, 82, 86–87, 93–94). This move separates *habitus* from the individually acquired qualities in human agency, qualities that become possible through acquisition of knowledge. According to Bourdieu, the modus operandi that defines practical mastery is transmitted in practice, without attaining the level of discourse. A child imitates not models but other people's action. She learns by observing

35. Brinkley Messick, focusing on textual *habitus* in discursive practices, compares Bourdieu's *habitus* to Ibn Khaldun's *malaka,* translated as "*habitus*" in Latin. According to Messick, the two concepts share an emphasis on the bodily basis and implicit qualities of the dispositions involved, reference to language models, and emphasis on the importance of repetition/practice for inculcation and reproduction (1993, 19n7).

gestures and postures: ways of walking, tilts of the head, facial expressions, ways of sitting, tones of voice, styles of speech, and so on. But acquisition of *habitus* does not imply mechanical learning. In the application of principles coherent in practice, a child learns to make a *habitus* his or her own in the form of a principle generating conduct that is organized in accordance with a rationale (Bourdieu 1977, 87–88).

Even though *adab,* like *habitus,* is linked to a person's social background,[36] it should not be understood as a reproduction of social determinants.[37] What is essential in the concept of *adab* is that it is the embodiment of knowledge related to particular *intellectual* and social dispositions. Islamic *adab,* for instance, is related to religious sanctions, a matter that emphasizes the role of knowledge in internalizing norms, and involves the inner and spiritual life in its fulfillment. In *adab,* knowing, doing, and being become one (Metcalf 1984a, 5, 10). *Adab* can be cultivated beyond the mere social determinants. In Aden, a person who "does right" or "who acts like a good person" *('alehu ahlaq),* as proper comportment is often described, gains a good reputation *(karama)* in the eyes of members of the surrounding society. The essential aspect of Islamic *adab,* that knowledge is not separate from its internalization and that no knowledge can exist outside its realization,[38] is relevant in Adeni social practice, too, because moral commentary on issues of gender and family tends to involve the question of consistency in moral dispositions (knowledge) and individual action (internalization of the knowledge).

Brenda Farnell has argued that Bourdieu's concept of *habitus* lacks an adequate conception of the nature and location of human agency (2000, 397). To elaborate on her point, Farnell asks what exactly *habitus* is and how it connects with what people say and do (2000, 402). For her, the causal link between unconscious, habituated generation, which Bourdieu calls the dispositions of

36. As Barbara Metcalf argues, classical *adab* books were not written for Muslims in general but addressed to particular social groups (1984a, 4).

37. William Hanks reminds us that *habitus* allows a way out of mechanical reproduction while still accounting for continuities (1996, 239).

38. Ira Lapidus explains that "Islamic knowledge," *'ilm,* "is not just intellectual knowing, but knowing charged with feeling. *'Ilm* is insight—an experience of the reality of what is known" (1984, 39).

habitus, and actual agency remains unclear. According to her, Bourdieu has simply replaced "rules" with "dispositions" in a deterministic way that he cannot escape. Bourdieu's theory, in its attempt to remove rational choice as a determining factor in accounting for what people say and do, depends on the assumption of a hidden apparatus by means of which people draw on implicit knowledge that is acquired through social experience and socialization (Farnell 2000, 403). The basic problem in Bourdieu's theory, Farnell argues, lies in his Cartesian division of body and mind into two ontologically separate entities. In order to avoid the Cartesian divide, Farnell suggests a so-called causal powers theory (404).[39]

The causal powers theory is based on the idea that in the physical world, original sources of activity exist. Natural phenomena have powers and forces intrinsic to their structural design. The activity of such substances at work is causation, the power to produce real consequences (Farnell 2000, 408–9). With the notion of causal power, the recovery of the notion of person as a causally powered (not causally determined) dynamically embodied center of action who is engaged in multiple kinds of semiotic practices becomes possible (Farnell 1999, 348). In this way, the analysis of practice avoids the separation of language and thought from practical activities.

In a phenomenological critique of Bourdieu's concept of *habitus,* Michael Jackson argues that as in Foucault's notions of discursive formations and discursive practices, Bourdieu excludes autonomous subjects from the anonymous labyrinths of culture. In a vein similar to Farnell, who argues that dispositions linked to *habitus* simply replace rules as forces that determine action, Jackson points out that Bourdieu's attempt to avoid subjectivism in his theory leads him to speak of the *habitus* in objectivist terms as "objective" or "embodied history" by means of which individual practices are merely produced or generated. Jackson instead argues for a theory that includes an account of such moments of social life when the customary, given, habitual, and ordinary are disrupted, flouted, suspended, and negated. At such moments, Jackson argues, crisis transforms the world from an apparently fixed and complete set of rules into a *repertoire of possibilities* (1996, 20–22). Once human action is acknowledged to entail

39. The notion of causal powers, influenced by developments in quantum physics, comes from Harré and is central in a new realistic approach in the philosophy of science (Harré and Madden 1975).

intentionality, the deterministic character of any a priori prerequisites—be they marriage rules, notions of honor, or normative gender ideals—can be avoided.

Regarding both *habitus* and *bodily hexis,* Bourdieu is concerned to argue that these knowledge repertoires exist in forms not entirely rationalized and that they are not acted or learned as "norms"; that is, social life does not reflect normativity. In approaching the ethnographic material presented here and the image that it draws of Adeni social dynamics, my concern has been to explore the knowledge repertoires the way they are at least in part normative in form, but which people can act upon consciously and which they can describe as objective realities.

Adab, seen as an embodiment of a particular knowledge repertoire, combines the body- and mind-related forms of knowledge in constituting internalized knowledge, or knowledge that is present in both practice and discourse. *Adab* should not be understood as behavior guided by some particular rules, but as a domain of action that combines the discursive and practical ways of dynamic human movement. The notion of *adab,* then, does not entail the Cartesian division of mind and body and the other oppositional dimensions that

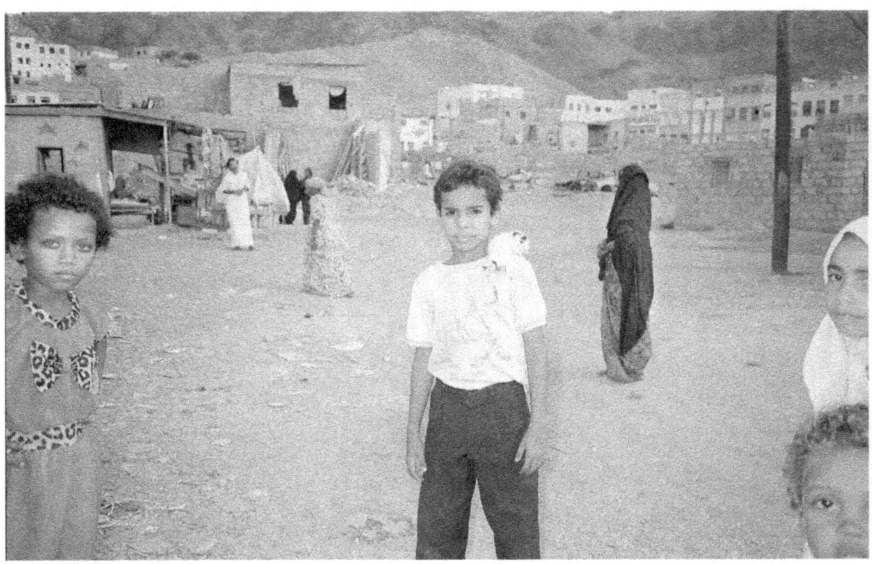

21. Helping a neighbor is considered one of the virtues in Aden. A poor neighborhood on the slopes of Crater. Photograph by the author, 1989.

often follow it in social theory, such as mental/behavioral, reason/emotion, and subjective/objective.[40]

Knowledge and Morality

To elaborate on the argument of three parallel moral frameworks that link to both practice and discourse, I find useful Taylor's suggestion that any theory of human behavior must take into account the way the people studied understand themselves (1989, 26).[41] Awareness of the principles of different morality frameworks presupposes knowledge. As Loeffler suggests, belief is to a large extent knowledge. Knowledge, as we know, is attainable by engaging in different forms of learning and education. As Marcel Mauss puts it, "In all . . . elements of the art of using the body, the facts of education [are] dominant" (1979, 101).

The principal responsibility for teaching children proper comportment lies with the parents. This process involves stages that a child is considered to go through in gaining bodily and intellectual maturity *(bulugh* and *rushd).* These stages are profoundly gendered. Boys and girls are considered to proceed along different routes in gaining maturity and to proceed at different speeds in that process. In chapter 5, I explained parents' views of the age children reach maturity, and all answers gave no indication of any gender difference. However, when inquiring about what is the best age for marriage, people immediately saw a difference. It was often considered that the girl reaches the maturity needed in marriage at an earlier age. It was explained to me that girls reach "reason" *('aql)* earlier than boys. At homes, instruction in adult duties and chores starts at an

40. As Farnell has pointed out, when treating the body as separate from the mind, Western social theory has understood physicality as natural rather than cultural and as a survival from our animal past. This bifurcation, according to her, has led to a valorization of spoken and written signs as "real" knowledge, internal to the reasoning mind of a solipsistic individual, to the exclusion of other meaning-making bodily practices. Such nonvocal bodily practices she calls "action signs" (1999, 343, 345–46). I discuss action signs and bodily postures in Dahlgren 2008.

41. Taylor makes a distinction between "external action descriptions" and the "language of thick description," borrowing the latter term from Geertz (Geertz 1993, 3–30). With this term, Taylor refers to language that is culturally bound as it articulates the significance and point that the actions have within a certain culture (1989, 80).

earlier age for girls, whereas boys of the same age are still allowed to run freely outside the home.

Even if the normative answer given to me in response to the question of who is responsible for children's upbringing tended to be "parents together," when visiting people's homes I noticed that because men as a custom are at home very little during the day and evening, children spend most of their time in female company. But the mother is not always the adult closest to the child. In Nur's case, discussed in chapter 6, we learned that her son was instructed, nurtured, and entertained by his maternal grandmother and his aunt, Nur's sister. The boy's father lived in another town, and his mother, a busy career woman and political activist, seldom spent long hours at home. In many other homes, I observed that both paternal and maternal grandmothers take care of children, even outside the time that parents actually spend in work. In general, the grandparental generation expressed attitudes about women's roles and possibilities in society that were different from their offspring's generation, which was the generation that had joined the labor market in masses in the 1970s and 1980s, as I explained in chapter 2. Women of the older generation were most often housewives who had spent their entire life inside four walls (Dahlgren 1998–99). Their daughters, who work outside the home, often rely on their help in childcare.

When reading the essays on marriage by young university students, whose views I described in chapter 5, I wondered where the young generation had gotten what appeared to me old-fashioned and conservative ideas about men's and women's duties and roles in marriage. I have not particularly investigated this question, so I can only preliminarily suggest that young people have adopted their ideas from their grandmothers, with whom they spent their days while their parents were working. A comparison of the elder- and middle-generation women's ideas about what women are allowed to do and what they should do as a vocation indicates that there tended to be much more choice and belief in the workingwomen's view of women's capacities; older women expressed limited ideas about a woman's capacities.

These attitudes reflect understandings of what is proper behavior for a woman and of men's and women's differing roles in society. When the present generation of older women was still young, discussion about women's roles and duties was flourishing in newspapers and civil societies. As I explained in chapter 4, during that period in particular three different camps emerged in the discussion. The very active Wahhabi religious scholar Shaykh al-Bayhani published his book *Ustadh al-mar'ah* (The Teacher of the Woman) in 1950 and appeared in many other public forums. This book can be described as an *adab* manual for women. However, when I inquired about the book's influence and its reception among women, I was told that it did not have so much influence. At the time of its publication, some women even questioned the blind preacher's right to educate women in how they should act, as Serjeant has reported (1962, 194n).

Puritanical attitudes regarding religiously sanctioned and recommended modes of action and being have never tended to gain a wide following in Aden. As I explained in chapters 2 and 4, in the spectrum of religious interpretation and preaching, al-Bayhani was countered by a longtime *qadi* of Aden, Shaykh Bahamish, whose interpretations reflected a more tolerant view of various types of religious practices historically typical to Aden. In contrast to al-Bayhani, Bahamish spoke in favor of variety in religious practices and gave religious approval of the cosmopolitan way of life that, among other elements, the British base and the commercial market that flourished around it brought to Aden.[42] In some marriage dispute cases, as I discussed in chapter 3, the learned shaykh tried to protect women, whose interests he felt were threatened. These two authorities were countered in the public sphere in newspapers, books, and discussions held in various clubs that I discussed in chapter 4, where demands for reforms in marriage and rights for women and their liberation from "backwardness" *(takhalluf)* were raised.

But the home is not the only place where socialization in moral values takes place. Public instruction also participates in bringing up "a new generation of good citizens to the state," as the role of the state educational system was often described to me in reference to the revolution's achievements. In primary schools, children of an early age are disciplined to observe absolute submission to the teacher's rule. Young boys and girls sit upright in their desks, raise their hands in a particular disciplined way when wanting to get the teacher's attention, and are expected to manifest in the tidiness of their school uniform the refinements of disciplined comportment. A skillful teacher captures the full attention of

42. There were limits to Bahamish's tolerance, of course. As I explained in chapters 2 and 4, the *qadi* participated in petitions against prostitution.

children who are noisy and wild outside of class by involving them in a dynamic interaction where the instructed topic acts like a ball tossed between the instructor and those instructed, as I observed in some primary schools. In this intensive teaching methodology, the teacher uses his or her body as a moving vehicle that draws and pulls the interacting forces into a dialectic game.

After unification, Qur'an schools were again allowed to operate openly, and at one stage young boys' not so enthusiastically performed monotonous repetition of holy verses was broadcast through loud speakers to the busy streets of the main market in Crater. This attempt to dominate the public square did not last long, however, and the market was soon again allowed to have its own noises. After that short period in the early 1990s, religious instruction found its place in the confines of mosques and other premises where children and adults are instructed in a variety of forms of Islam, Sufism included. Religious clubs, especially those for women, found their audience, too. During the 1990s, a variety of puritanical confederations found their way to Aden; new mosques devoted to the Salafi ideology, among others, were erected round the town, and old mosques were resurrected. As we saw in the case of Ahmad and 'Ali's religious younger siblings (chapter 6), young people in particular are drawn to these uncompromising communities. Yet in Aden the home and the public-school system, with its three hours a week of Islamic instruction, continue to provide the basic elements of religious education.

With regard to a plurality of moral frameworks, as in the case of the present book, it is not sufficient to note exactly how Islam and Islamic moralities are instructed. If we wish to trace the path of socially valuable knowledge, we need to follow chains from parents/grandparents to children and from public institutions to both members and outsiders of those institutions. Because the Aden society is not normatively monolithic—that is, guided by one hegemonic system of morality—chains of transmission of knowledge vary according to gendered social hierarchies, on the one hand, and to significant institutions that promote particular systems of norms, on the other. As I suggested earlier, in each moral framework outlined in this book the stakes are different. The primary motivation in adhering to a particular notion of normativity and in manifesting a specific kind of morality becomes transparent when we focus on basic "strong evaluations."

In chapter 6, I concluded that recognizing the existence of three parallel frameworks of morality allowed us to see how people understand moralities that guide their actions. In the beginning of that chapter, we followed Muhammad, who adopted various moral frameworks when addressing and greeting different people. As we saw, his choice of how to address the person he encountered did not depend only on the place of interaction or on the social status and gender of the person addressed. Instead, the choice seemed to correspond to his understanding on what was proper in each situation, evaluated on the basis of what he knew about the person he addressed and about the nature of the encounter, not to mention his knowledge of the requisites of each moral framework. However, in addressing people, he applied the conventions of social hierarchy selectively, which indicated that his conduct was not simply dictated by the obligations of respect and disrespect associated with different social hierarchies and their varying status positions, a point I discussed in chapter 1 with the examples from Michael Gilsenan's work.

The second case in chapter 6 concerned a young woman, Sa'ida, who built her social world, among other things, by operating a network of eligible men with cars. In this maneuvering, she carefully observed the conventions of what was proper in each place and situation and adjusted her agency accordingly. Her activity was guided by knowledge of propriety and the prevailing structural limitations. It manifested a mastery of her social prerogatives. Different approaches to supernatural phenomena were observed in her case, too. An old woman's fear of the tape recorder was contrasted to Sa'ida and her friend's seriousness about horoscopes. In participating in the *nadhr* ceremony, Sa'ida expressed sincerity in yet another type of belief: it was not a question of "modernity" being manifested in "secularity" or of a worldview based on "rationality" and "scientific thinking" replacing the "traditionality" in a belief in the supernatural in all different forms. Everything has its place, and as we saw in this chauffeured woman's case, observing the conventions of different situations brings merit to a person and creates trust and respect for her in her social environment. We can say that Sa'ida's freedom of movement was based on the trust she could generate based on her personality.

Then we followed Nur, the professionally and politically active woman whose sensitive concern for propriety was present in various scenes in her daily interaction with people. In her case, we could observe how Islamic piety is acted upon in everyday encounters. In Nur's agency, the finest traits of propriety and morality were consciously put in play. These traits were contrasted to her lack of inherited social standing, as embodied in her appearance, a fact she skillfully used in practicing *adab* virtues. She observed the prevalent social hierarchies but managed to manipulate her interpretation of those stratifications to her own benefit. Even though not a religiously learned person, Nur was well equipped with knowledge of Islamic *adab*. At the core of that *adab* were actions that could be valued as pious, modest, generous, and full of concern for the socially vulnerable. By operating on that knowledge, Nur could attract approval and respect.

At the end of chapter 6, we followed two friends, Ahmad and 'Ali, whose relationships to their own kin was constantly negotiated. As we saw, Ahmad refused the privileges that his belonging to a family high on the social scale prescribed for him—that is, a particular position among his people. Instead, he invested in education abroad to gain a good position in working life and society around it. In contrast to him, 'Ali followed the way of his grandfathers and engaged in a marriage negotiated for him by his father and the father of the prospective bride, a close relative. In this way, 'Ali combined resources that can be viewed to belong to two different moral frameworks. His marriage was according to "our customs and traditions," and his education and career were made possible by the resources the revolution brought about. Both 'Ali and Ahmad, however, experienced a clash with the intolerant expression of religiosity that alienated them from some of their closest family members. In their stories, we could follow how kinship relations are open also to conflict and renegotiation, never manifesting a stagnated "traditionality." In all these stories, we could see that the three moral frameworks do not represent a particular historical time or space, but rather are open for agency. The frameworks are neither tied to nor representative of some socially "autonomous" movement of the traditional or the modern. But what makes them relevant to an anthropology of morality is their deep-rooted meaning in making positive morality available.

Conclusions

By outlining three parallel moralities in this book, my purpose has not been to suggest an "Adeni worldview," an approach that is common in anthropological literature (e.g., see Boddy 1989 and Eickelman 1976). As Fredrik Barth puts it, there is not a finite and one-to-one relationship between cognitive models and social action, though the two are fundamentally connected (2000, 34). In the brief ethnographic sketches I presented in this book, my concern has been to outline general patterns in a person's agency as it can be observed and to talk about agency within the particular frameworks that people take into consideration in making sense of their experiences.

8 Conclusions

It cannot be born from a comparison but from a juxtaposition of two more or less distant realities.

—ANDRÉ BRETON, *Manifestoes of Surrealism*

BORROWING FROM the words of people introduced in this book, I have called the three moral frameworks outlined in this study *'adat wa taqalid* (customs and traditions), *thawra* (revolution), and *din* (religion). For analytical purposes, I have treated them as "moral frameworks," discussing them as repertoires of particular knowledge. As we saw in some of the ethnographic cases, at issue, first, are three different corpuses of knowledge; second, these sets of knowledge have to do with morality and normative action; and third, they are "repertoires" in that they contain resources and limitations that people can draw and talk about. I argued not only that both consciousness and habituation characterize people's relationships to this division and that they structure action, consciously or unconsciously, but also that they are also continually restructured in practice.

By approaching Adeni gendered practice and discussion about it from the point of view of three normative sets has not been an attempt simply to substitute the conventional dichotomy of traditional/modern with a new analytical "trichotomy." Instead, I have wanted to show how the three moral frameworks and their parallel coexistence allow particular social dynamics. Even though the third framework is called "religion," I have pointed out that it does not mean that it alone stands for Islam, but rather that Islam as a religion is present in all three frameworks, a fact that contributes to local Islamic variations. In the first and second framework, Islam is embedded with other sources of knowledge, even though it is not made the central reference. Religious practices such as performing a *dhikr*[1] in a mosque, reciting some "extra" prayers in praise of a

1. The "remembering" of God, a central Sufi ritual.

holy man according to need, and performing the *salat* prayer with what accompanies it (i.e., performing the *wudu'* or "little washing," covering the head and body, repeating the prayer formula, and prostrating) are all acts of prayer and expressions of Islamic faith, but only the third one belongs to the religious framework in the sense outlined here. From a historical point of view of Islamic tradition, all are local forms of practicing the faith and expressions of how Islam is culturally present in Aden.

As I explained earlier, by "knowledge" I mean that each framework contains material that can be acquired as knowledge and that each has its own specialists who embody the highest knowledge of that framework. These frameworks can be called "ideologies" in the sense that each has proponents and opponents and that each is institutionalized in a variety of forms ranging from popular movements and political parties to state institutions and religious establishments. However, my purpose here has not been to focus on supporters and adherents of each knowledge repertoire and the way it is institutionalized, but to focus on "ordinary people" (as distinguished from specialists and activists) and their agency. I have also wanted to show how every person active in Aden has to take into consideration the parallel coexistence of mutually contradicting and opposing moralities and normativities. Most of the people I have met while in Aden are not manifestly proponents of particular ideologies and do not belong to political parties or militant groupings; rather, they negotiate their lives by taking into consideration the contesting nature of reality. At an individual level, the repertoires are embodied in the refinements of a person's *adab,* ideal comportment and propriety as manifestations of embodied knowledge and virtue. Given that the society is patterned by contesting realities, state policies cannot have straightforward effects, as we saw in chapters 3 and 4 in the case of the two family law reforms.

Because the focus of this book has been the relations between men and women, I have been particularly interested in seeing what structural prerogatives organize the field of gender interaction and what cognitive means people have for interacting in the prevailing circumstances. Here I have relied on the anthropological use of the word *cognitive,* meaning a system received from previous generations rather than something that a child develops when growing up. In that sense, a cognitive system can also be called "collective representation," "culture," or "ideology" (Bloch 1989, 106). In an attempt to avoid a structuralist analysis and a determinist emphasis, I have focused on the ways and means people have at their disposal as agents in coping with the structural prerogatives. I have also emphasized the intersectional nature of all social hierarchies. By approaching the different moral frameworks as limitations and resources rather than as fixed entities, I have focused on everyday practice as the site where the competing frameworks become manifested. Moral frameworks contain idealized representations of things and matters, as I explained at the end of chapter 5, but their actual deployment in practice is where they get their full meaning.

The acquisition of knowledge in each framework can be viewed as a prestige system, following what Sherry Ortner has argued with reference to gender, as drawn from Louis Dumont's concepts of hierarchical society. In relation to gender, a prestige system "defines what men and women are as well as what they are (or should be) trying to accomplish or to become, and it defines how they can and cannot go about that project" (Ortner 1981, 360–61). But it is not sufficient to mention that such prestige systems exist. Instead, I have studied how prestige systems, as I described them in chapter 2, are acted upon and embodied in comportment and have shown a variety of available prestige systems and their normative nature. Even though in Aden acquisition of knowledge is also clearly linked to hierarchical prestige systems, acquiring knowledge as such is not limited to or reserved for particular (elitist) groupings. But knowledge does contribute to particular persons' prestigious position in a community—as in the *fuqaha'* (Islamic scholars), for example. The acquisition of knowledge passes along any lines, however blurred they might be, between public and private spheres. As I pointed out in chapter 5, even an old illiterate housewife living inside four walls can participate in discussions characteristic to the public sphere.

However, that is not the whole issue: also relevant here is how knowledge is used not only in defining social hierarchies, but also in redefining them or merely neglecting them. As Deniz Kandiyoti has put it, social institutions do not solely reflect unitary patriarchal logic (or some other logic for that matter, either, I must add) but are the site of power relations through which gender hierarchies are both created and contested (1996, 17). In Aden, knowledge repertoires as I outline them constitute corpuses of local knowledge that agents consciously and habitually draw from in their everyday action and discourse. In this sense, the repertoires can be considered to provide conceptions about the actions people engage in. These conceptions refer to socially established zones of space and mark different spaces with a particular repertoire, thus linking the space with embodied

22. "Welcome!" waved this repairman in one of the colonial-era blocks of flats in Ma'alla. Photograph by the author, 2001.

knowledge. It is not a question of "behaving" correctly in a given social space, but of dynamic agency, which gains specific merit by drawing on the resources and limitations of a particular space marked by socially meaningful knowledge.

In this book, I have discussed how Adeni people consider contesting ideas of propriety that concurrently give meaning to the social reality. Recent studies on emerging public spheres in the Middle East pay attention to "public subjects," activists of militant and less militant movements and public institutions such as *fatwas,* newspapers, or the Internet, leaving the sphere of "ordinary" life experiences unexplored. Although distancing themselves from the Habermasian notion of free subjects engaged in debates with modern methods of communication, such studies reproduce the understanding that only active agency counts in constituting the public sphere. Studies on Islamic initiatives have pointed out variation in the forms and methods that agents may engage in their agency (see Deeb 2005, 2006; Mahmood 2005), but the focus nevertheless remains political or "Islamic" activism. In this book, I have explained how "ordinary" people—that is, nonactivists and "nonpublic" people—participate in constituting, reforming, and creating the discussions and happenings of the public sphere. In analyzing agency in this participation, I contrasted agency to prevailing structures in order to emphasize the procedural nature of the constitution of a public sphere.[2]

I further explored how positive moral values and proper comportment are manifest in everyday life and how they are present in local definitions of gender and idealized relations between the sexes. In challenging the conventional understanding of the movement from traditional to "ever more" modern, I called attention to the complex relationship between modernity and the traditional. This complexity was highlighted also by the interconnection that I attempted to show between traditions and modern processes with a variety of Islamic and other ideological representations.[3]

In focusing on the constitution of the public sphere, I stressed the dialectical relationship between structures and agency. In emphasizing that moral frameworks are not tied to persons but are context bound and consist of capacities, resources, and limitations, I highlighted the role of learning and knowledge in the making of social practice. But the idea inherent in the moral framework called "religion"—namely, that the answers to all social problems can be found within Islam only—puts this framework in a position clearly different from the

2. By emphasizing the procedural nature of the public sphere, I do not mean to create a link to procedural concepts of the public space characteristic of Hannah Arendt's thinking. See Benhabib 1992, 80–81.

3. Ideological in the sense William Hanks (1996, 234) uses the word, as ideas rather than classical ideologies.

other frameworks discussed. It remains outside the scope of this book to show how in the future this morality discourse gained further institutional ground and how it challenged gender relations in Aden.

By looking at virtues and the public good, I wanted to call attention to the positive driving force or causality in people's agency as an alternative way of seeing the gendered social practice in a Middle Eastern cultural context, a context that was earlier framed by the honor/shame approach, which tends to explain social comportment only in terms of avoidance, limitation, and lack. *Adab*—the notion of delicacy, refinement, and embodiment of virtue—also allows us to focus on the very process of making. More than that, when people advocate the shared notions of virtue and decency in agency and talk about these things, they participate in constituting metadiscourses particular to the public sphere. By following Charles Taylor's idea that the public sphere is metatopical, the method here allows for the incorporation of people from various social positions into the analysis, thus avoiding exclusive attention to institutionalized social formations or to elites. I have also discussed how Islam is embedded in the society's overall social dynamics. The analysis concentrated on Islam as an everyday manifestation, not as an abstract doctrine beyond people's everyday life. In regard to studies that focus on emerging public spheres, this book thus offers one more perspective on viewing complexity in an urban Middle Eastern context.

By choosing gender as the topic of this book, I wanted, first, to argue in favor of an inclusive understanding of gender in social construction and, second, to contribute to the scholarly project of transforming gender into a fundamental, omnipotent concept in the study of any Middle Eastern community, not just a topic in studies that focus on women. I wanted to discuss gender as part of new anthropological studies influenced by postcolonial feminist approaches that consider gender as a primary organizing principle in complex relations between the sexes that are embedded in other social divisions. By going beyond sexual segregation, I wanted to challenge the idea that men's and women's social worlds are reducible to public and private spheres, respectively, with power limited to the men's or public sphere.

The idea of social dynamics as constituted in tension between a diversity of context-bound normative representations adds one more perspective to the recent debate about permanence or fluidity of social structures such as the patriarchal family in today's Middle East. The family tends to have various manifestations, and its internal hierarchies might not necessarily be that straightforward as models of patriarchy present. Other family types such as those led by women have always existed alongside the normative family. On that basis, however, one cannot suggest that patriarchal power structures have come to a state of fluidity. In the Adeni case, anyhow, variety in family forms is no new phenomenon.

Finally, to say something about the permanence or fluidity of social processes in the Middle East, each study has to be anchored to the concrete social surroundings with respect paid to local historical variations. The themes and topics of public discourses and struggles presented in this book are common to other Middle Eastern urban environments, but the ways they interact with particular historical structures, both conventional and action bound, are unique to Aden.

Appendixes | Glossary | References | Index

Appendix A

Field Survey Statistics

Table A.1. Profession of female survey subjects

	n	%	Labor Statistics (%)[1]
A. Administration and management			
Judges, directors, chairpersons, rectors	7	2.3	(3.6)
B. Highly educated professionals			
Lawyers, teachers, engineers, accountants, supervisors, editors, physicians	72	23.2	(32.6)
C. Institute-trained professionals			
Clerks, secretaries, TV announcers, nurses, midwives, archivists, laboratory technicians	78	25.1	(32.4)
D. Production and transport workers, artisans			
Machine operators, production recorders, and seamstresses	73	23.5	(16.8)
E. Agriculture, fishing, sea fare			
Agricultural workers	4	1.3	(0.1)
F. Service work			
Sweepers, messengers, cooks, child attendants	19	6.1	(13.5)
G. Sales work			
Shop assistants	—	—	(0.9)
H. Students			
In higher education	3	1.0	(—)[2]
In school	7	2.3	—
In literacy classes	8	2.6	—
I. Unemployed	5	1.6	(60.2)
J. Women at home			
Married, widowed, and divorced	27	8.7	(—)
Divorcées and widowers who returned home	5	1.6	(—)
Unmarried	3	1.0	(—)
K. Work not classifiable	—	—	(0.2)
L. Immigrants	—	—	—

Table A.1. Profession of female survey subjects (continued)

	n	%	*Labor Statistics (%)*[1]
M. No information	—	—	—
Total	*n* = 311	100.0%	100%

1. Percentage of the same occupational category in official labor statistics concerning employed women (PDRY 1990, 126). In this statistic, *n* is 4,693, which indicates that the data are far from complete. Here I compare my field data with the official statistics in order to indicate that my data, even though limited, matches well with the official statistics.

2. Students and women at home are not classified in the labor statistics.

Table A.2. Profession of female survey subjects' husbands

	n	%[1]	*Subject n*
A. Administration and management *Army officers, managers and directors, chairpersons, professors, businessmen, rectors, judges*	21	10.0	(7)
B. Highly educated professionals *Lawyers, teachers, engineers, accountants, supervisors, editors, physicians*	39	18.5	(72)
C. Institute-trained professionals *Clerks, accountants, nurses, midwives, inspectors, archivists, technicians, police inspectors*	51	24.2	(78)
D. Production and transport workers, artisans *Machine operators, drivers, mailmen, electricians, military privates, policemen, mechanics, carpenters, builders*	60	28.5	(73)
E. Agriculture, fishing, sea fare *Farmers* (muzari'un, fellahun)*, fishermen, sailors, shepherds*	2	1.0	(4)
F. Service work *Sweepers, messengers, cooks, guards, sanitation workers, plumbers, porters* (hammal)*, barbers* (hallaq)	6	2.8	(19)
G. Sales work *Shop and kiosk assistants,* qat *sellers, street hawks*	4	1.9	(—)
H. Students *In higher education*	2	1.0	(3)

Table A.2. Profession of female survey subjects' husbands (continued)

	n	%[1]	*Subject n*
In school	—	—	(7)
In literacy classes	—	—	(8)
I. Unemployed	6	2.8	(5)
J. Men at home	—	—	(35)
K. Work not classifiable	—	—	—
L. Immigrants	6	2.8	—
M. No information	14	6.6	—
Total	*n* = 211	100.0%	*n* = 311
		(Subject unmarried = 100)	

1. *n* = 211.

Table A.3. Profession of female survey subjects' fathers

	n	%	*Subject n*
A. Administration and management			
Army officers, managers and directors, chairpersons, professors, businessmen, rectors	24	7.7	(7)
B. Highly educated professionals			
Lawyers, teachers, engineers, chief accountants, supervisors, lecturers, physicians	14	4.5	(72)
C. Institute-trained professionals			
Clerks, accountants, nurses, midwives, inspectors, archivists, technicians, police inspectors	25	8.0	(78)
D. Production and transport workers, artisans			
Machine operators, drivers, mailmen, electricians, military privates, policemen, mechanics, carpenters, builders	60	19.3	(73)
E. Agriculture, fishing, sea fare			
Farmers (muzari'un, fellahun), *fishermen, sailors, shepherds*	34	11.0	(4)
F. Service work			
Sweepers, messengers, cooks, guards, sanitation workers, plumbers, porters (hammal), *barbers* (hallaq)	24	7.7	(19)
G. Sales work			
Shop and kiosk assistants, qat *sellers, street hawks*	14	4.5	(—)
H. Students			
In higher education	—	—	(3)

Table A.3. Profession of female survey subjects' fathers (continued)

	n	%	*Subject n*
In school	—	—	(7)
In literacy classes	—	—	(8)
I. Unemployed	15	4.8	(5)
J. Men at home	2	0.6	(35)
K. Work not classifiable			
Qadis, *Qur'an teachers*	4	1.3	(—)
L. Immigrants	3	1.0	(—)
M. No information	92	29.6	(—)
Retired and deceased			
Total	*n* = 311	100.0%	*n* = 311

Table A.4. Profession of female survey subjects' mothers

	n	%	*Subject n*
A. Administration and management			
A school headmaster and a children's day-care centre director	2	0.6	(7)
B. High educated professionals			
Teachers	2	0.6	(72)
C. Institute trained professionals			
A nurse and a community midwife	2	0.6	(78)
D. Production and transport workers, artisans			
Factory workers (machine operators) and a carpenter	5	1.6	(73)
E. Agriculture, fishing, sea fare			
Farmers (fellahat), a fisherman, a sailor, and a shepherd	7	2.3	(4)
F. Service work			
Messengers, a sweeper, and a cook	10	3.2	(19)
G. Sales work			
A shop assistant in a state retail shop for clothes	1	0.3	(—)
H. Students			
In higher education	—		(3)
In school	—		(7)
In literacy classes	—		(8)
I. Unemployed	3	1.0	(5)
J. Women at home	270	86.8	(35)
Housewives			

Table A.4. Profession of female survey subjects' mothers (continued)

	n	%	*Subject n*
K. Work not classifiable			
An artist	1	0.3	(—)
L. Immigrants	1	0.3	(—)
M. No information			
Retired and deceased	7	2.3	(—)
Total	*n* = 311	99.9%	*n* = 311

Appendix B

Commentary on the Family Law, Law no. 1 of 1974 in Connection to the Family (1976)

1. Marriage is a contract between a man and a woman who are equal in rights and duties (§2).

2. The family of the bride-to-be is forbidden to agree on her engagement on her behalf without her consent (§3, §5).

3. All marriages shall be registered with the marriage registrar (*ma'dhun*, §6a).

4. Legitimate marriage age for men is set at eighteen and for women at sixteen, and the age gap between the spouses is restricted to twenty years for women under the age of thirty-five (§7, §9).

5. Two witnesses, who are of sound mind and of legal age irrespective of sex are required to witness the signing of the marriage contract (*'aqd*, §8); the marriage contract may be concluded by proxy (§10).

6. Bigamy *(ta'addud al-zawjat)* shall not be allowed except with the written permission of a competent divisional court, which, however, shall not grant such permission unless either of the following two conditions are met:

- the wife is declared by a medical report to be barren, provided that the husband was unaware of her barrenness prior to marriage;
- the wife is proved by a medical report to be suffering from a chronic, contagious, or infectious disease that is incurable (§11).

7. Prohibited degrees are set from the point of view of the man, who is forbidden to marry his roots and branches or those of his parents or the first degrees of his ancestors; in addition, he is prohibited from marrying any woman with whom his roots and branches had sexual intercourse or the roots and branches of a woman with whom he had sexual intercourse (§12, §13); fosterage limits a man from marrying a woman who acted as his wet nurse immediately following his birth (§14). A marriage that flouts these

provisions is rendered void even if not consummated (§14.2). These prohibitions are not against levirate marriage (of a widow to her husband's brother) or sororate marriage (of a man to his deceased wife's sister), although levirate marriage is practiced in Aden. Judges and barristers with whom I spoke were ambiguous about it. Because the law now protects the woman's right to maintain her children even if she remarries, she might not want to stay in her agnatic home if she has a choice. The latter provision is clearly in favor of the woman, but it can also be seen to liberate the man from a duty to marry his deceased wife's sister or his expired brother's wife as customarily might be his duty.

8. Expenses of the conjugal home shall be borne by both husband and wife according to their means (§17); husband and wife share their joint life expenses, but where either of them is unable to provide, the other spouse shall be liable for maintenance of the family (§20). Both the father and the mother share the burden of maintenance of children, but in case either of them is incapable of doing so, the other shall bear the maintenance alone (§22).

9. The amount of *mahr* (bride wealth) is limited to one hundred Yemeni dinars (§18); no other amounts whatsoever shall be paid in regard of marriage (§19).

10. Maintenance of children continues until the girl marries or works and the boy completes his studies, starts to work, or attains the age at which his equals earn their living (§24).

11. Both son and daughter, if well off, shall maintain their poor or idle parents provided the parents do not obstinately choose to remain idle (§24).

12. Unilateral divorce *(talaq)* is prohibited (§25).

13. No divorce is effective without the leave of a competent divisional court, and the court shall not grant such leave unless the matter is first referred to the People's Committee, all attempts to reconcile have failed, and it is found that the divorce is justified by reasons that render it impossible for the married life and the happy union to continue (§25b).

14. The court shall not grant leave for more than one divorce at a time (§26); every divorce is reversible except the third one (§27); a reversible divorce shall not immediately terminate the marriage, and the husband has the right to return to his wife during her *'iddat* period after obtaining a return certificate from the *ma' dhun,* provided she agrees to such return (§28).

15. Both spouses have the right to make an application to the court for the termination of the marriage *(tafriq)* for any of the following reasons:

- the other spouse is suffering from an incurable disease that renders conjugal union impossible, proven by a medical report and provided the other spouse was not aware of the condition prior to the marriage;
- the spouse's absence for a period exceeding three consecutive years;
- if the well-off spouse refuses to maintain the other who is badly off, after a reasonable respite up to three months issued by the court;

- where there is proof of harm *(dharar)* done by one spouse to the other or of serious discord *(shiqaq)* between them to the extent that it has become impossible for the married life to continue and the court has failed to reconcile the spouses (§29)

The wife shall in addition to the application for termination have the right to apply for a judicial separation in case the husband has married another woman in accordance with §11 of this law (§29.2).

16. Concerning the harm *(dharar)* caused by the divorce to the divorced party and the required compensation to be provided, the law differs according to who caused the marriage to terminate. If the court finds that the husband was the cause of discord and that the wife would "suffer misery and distress," it may award the divorcée reasonable compensation that can exceed maintenance for one year (§30a). If the wife is the cause of discord, the court may award the husband a reasonable compensation that may exceed up to the amount of the *mahr* (§30b).

17. Part III of the law deals with *'iddat,* the waiting period the wife must observe after divorce or death of her husband before she can remarry. During this period, the spouses' legal rights and obligations are not entirely extinguished. The length of the period depends on several factors, including her being pregnant, the reason for the termination of the marital union, and reversibly divorced husband's death during her *'iddat:*

- The *'iddat* of a divorced woman who is not pregnant is ninety days (§31), but if she is pregnant, it continues until the delivery or miscarriage of the baby (§33).
- The *'iddat* of a woman whose husband dies is four months and ten days (§32).

If the husband dies during her *'iddat* following a reversible divorce, she shall observe the *'iddat* stipulated for death, and the previous period of *'iddat* is not counted (§36a); in similar circumstances following an irreversible divorce, she only has to continue her *'iddat* that follows a divorce—that is, ninety days (§36b); in case the marriage was not consummated, *'iddat* follows only if the husband has died (§35).

18. Part IV of the Family Law stipulates for legal paternity and is divided into two chapters: the first one dealing with requirements for paternity during a valid marriage and following such union, but the second one stipulating for paternity following an improper marriage. A maximum period and minimum period of pregnancy are also stipulated here:

- A legitimate pregnancy shall not last less than 180 days (about six months) and not more than "one calendar year" (it is not indicated which calendar is in question, §37).
- Paternity by husband (*nasab,* descent) is counted by lapse of the minimum period of pregnancy from the date of signing the marriage contract (§38a.1).

- If the spouses did not meet during the pregnancy, the husband's paternity cannot be proved. If either of the two conditions are not met, the husband has the right to acknowledge or claim his paternity (§38b).

19. Paternity of a child whose mother is divorced or widowed shall be counted to the former husband within a period of one year provided the woman does not admit the lapse of her *'iddat.* In case the child is delivered after the period of one year, the husband or his heirs have a right to claim the paternity (§39); in case the woman admits the lapse of her *'iddat,* the former husband's paternity is proved if the child is delivered within 180 days from the date of such admission and within one year from the date of the divorce or the husband's death (§40).

20. Paternity in an improper marriage shall be proved in the following cases:

- If the child was born 180 days or more after the consummation of the marriage
- If childbirth occurs after abandonment or separation and if the child is born within one year from the date of the abandonment or separation (§41)

Even without the existence of any marriage, when a woman and a man have had sexual intercourse outside wedlock, and the woman gives birth to a child, the minimum and maximum periods of pregnancy are counted, and the paternity of the man is proved (§42).

21. A man can claim paternity and filiation of a person of unknown parentage in case the difference of age between the two allows such filiation (§43). A further requirement is that the person acknowledged as filiated agrees (§44).

22. Requirements for custody are set from the point of view of the child's best interest. A custodian must be of full age, of sound mind, and able to take care of the child and look after his or her affairs (§45). The mother has the right to custody of her daughter up to the age of fifteen and her son up to the age of ten even if she has remarried. If the court finds the mother or her possible new husband completely unqualified to have custody, proved to the court by a report on the social circumstances prevalent in the family, the court can decide otherwise and cancel the mother's custody. The child's interest is the paramount concern (§46).

23. Final provisions of the law deal with punishments that follow from actions contradicting the provisions of the law. The strictest consequences follow for any person who "concludes, notarizes, or contributes toward concluding or notarizing any contract of marriage contrary to the provisions of this law" and include a fine not exceeding two hundred Yemeni dinars or imprisonment for a term not exceeding two years or both such punishments (§49a); a subsequently milder punishment (fine of one hundred Yemeni dinars or imprisonment for one year or both) awaits any person who contravenes any of the provisions of the law (§49b).

Glossary

Terms are given with diacritical marks here, although these marks—other than ayn and hamza—do not appear in the main text. Words are listed according to the English alphabet. This list does not include all Arabic or non-English words used in this text.

abaya: women's overcoat
'abīd: literally "slaves"; social category of people believed to be descendants of slaves
adab: proper comportment, manners
adabiyy, adabiyya: a person with manners
'ādah, pl. ***'ādāt:*** custom
'ādāt sayyi'āt: bad habits
'ādāt sha'ina: customs that degrade
'ādāt wa taqālīd: customs and traditions
ahl: family
akhdām, sing. ***khadim:*** literally "servants"; social category of people with despised origin
akhlāq: manners
'alaqa: mistress of *zār*
'alēhu/'alēhā akhlāq: person with good manners
amthāl: proverbs
aqārib: close kin
'aqil: wise man
'aql: sense, reason, rationality
'ardh: honor
asl: roots, origin
ayah: Somali domestic aid
'ayb: disgrace, shame
al-'ayn: evil eye
badla dahab: wedding gold
badu: pejorative name given to people from the countryside

bakhūr: incense

Bangala Shaytān: Free Masons' house in Maʿalla

baraka: blessing, spiritual power

basmala: invoking the formula *bismillah al-rahmān al-rahīm* (in the name of God, most gracious, most merciful)

bass: route taxi

bayt sharʿī: sharia quarters; legal term for marital abode that corresponds to wife's social standing

bikr: virgin

Bohoras: Shīʿa community, Mustaʿilī Ismāʿīlīs

bulūgh: social maturity

burr: wheat

dafʿa: payment for marriage preparations

dahbāsh: pejorative name given to northern Yemenis

dar'a: women's voile dress

dhakar: male

dharar: damage, cruelty

dhikr: literally "remembrance"; Sufi ritual of recollecting the names of God

dīn, dīnī: religion, religious

fānūs: kerosene lantern

fāsid: irregular marriage

faskh: court dissolution of the marriage

fātiha: opening sura of the Qur'ān

fiqh: Islamic jurisprudence

fuqahā', sing. ***faqih:*** individuals learned in Islam

futa: men's loincloth or women's underskirt

gāhil, pl. ***guhhāl:*** ignorant person

galabaya: cotton robe

gālisa fi-lbeit: house-bound woman

gandar: gender

hadharī: city-dweller, civilized

hāgg, hāgga: person who has performed the hajj to Mecca

hajj: pilgrimage to Mecca

hakam: arbitrator

halwā: sweets

hammam: bathroom, toilet

haram: Islamically prohibited

harim: women
hijāb: religious headgear
hirz: amulet
hurra: free
'īd: (Islamic) holiday
'īd al-adha: feast of sacrifice, holiday following the hajj
'iddat: the waiting period a woman has to observe after termination of marriage
ijtihād: legal reasoning through which the jurist derives law on the basis of the Quran and Sunna
'ilm: knowledge
inhitāt al-mar'a: women's inferiority
imam: religious leader
imāma: men's turban
iqtā', iqtā'ī: feudal
islah: reform
Islah Party: Yemen Congregation for Reform Party
Ithn'asharīs: Khoja community, Twelve Imam Shī'as
jabr: compulsion, compulsory marriage
jebelis: "people of the mountains"; temporary workers who came to work in Aden from Kingdom of Yemen during the colonial era
jins: gender, citizenship
kafā'a: equity principle
kāfirī: infidel
kalam nās: people's talk
karāma: honor, respect, reputation
khalas: finished, "that's it"
khātiba: bride searcher
khīr: (Sindhi) milk, sweet almond milk
khitān: women's genital cutting
Khojas: migrants from Sindh and Gujarat
khubz: flat bread
khul': women's no-fault divorce with compensation to the husband
khurāfa: superstition
khutba: engagement
kiswa: wedding trousseau; cloth that covers a *wali*'s grave
kizb: lying
koiffēr: beauty salon, hairdresser

kufīyya: men's scullcap
kufu': equal according to *kafā'a* principle
lailat al-dukhla: the night following a wedding; penetration
madā'a: tall water pipe to smoke locally cultivated tobacco
madhhab: Islamic law school
ma'dhūn: marriage and divorce registrar
maglis: living room
mahr: wedding payment; women's property that is due upon the signing of the marriage contract or deferred
mahr mu'ajjal: deferred marriage payment
mahr muqaddam or ***mahr mu'ajjal:*** prompt marriage payment
mā'ida: table, tablecloth
makhdara: tentlike shelter erected outside the house
mandīl: head scarf
al-mar'a al-gadīda: the new Yemeni woman
al-mar'a nusf al-mugtama': "women are half the society"
ma'rifa: knowledge
mashayikh: plural of ***shaykh,*** social category of people with noble descent
maskin, pl. ***masākin:*** dwelling
mat'am: restaurant
mawlīd: birthday, saint's day celebration
mu'addab, mu'addaba: person with fine manners
mu'adhdhin: mosque caller for prayer
mu'alama kuttāb: Qur'ān school
mudīr: director
mufisha: prostitute
muhaggaba: woman dressed in *hijāb*
muqaddam, pl. ***maqādima:*** headman who recruits labor
muqaddiyya: wedding assistant
Musta'ilī Ismā'īlīs: Daudi Bohoras (main branch of Bohoras) with *dai* (spiritual leader) in India
mut'a: temporary marriage
mutakhallif: backward
mut'amar: People's General Congress
muzayyin: traditional wedding players
nadhr: vow
nadj: physical maturity

nafaqa: maintenance
nasab: descent, affinity, kin
nāshiza: disobedient, rebellious woman
nikah: marriage
nikah al-badal or ***nikah al-shighār:*** exchange marriage
niqāb: face veil with eye holes
niswa, nisā', pl. ***niswān:*** woman, women
Nizārī Ismā'īlīs: Khoja community, followers of Aga Khan
nushuz: disobedience
purdah: seclusion (colonial-era expression)
pūri: bread cooked in oil
qabila, pl. ***qaba'il:*** tribe
qadi: judge
qa'ida: (Moroccan) the code of conduct
'qal: (Moroccan) reason, God's will
qānūn: law
qāt: mild narcotic shrub
qāt makhdara: *qāt* session
qāwī: strong
qishr: spicy hot drink made of coffee husks
rabat al-bayt: housewife
raggaliyya: "macho" culture
riggāl sālih: folk healer
rushd: maturity
ruti: bread baked with yeast
sada, sing. ***sayyid:*** social category of people who claim descent from the Prophet Muhammad
sadaqa: alms
sadīq: friend
sāhib al-kitāb: healer with supernatural forces
al-sahwa al-islamiyya: re-Islamization
sakan: dwelling
salat: prayer
sambūsa: triangle-shaped pie
sayyidat al-manzil: mistress of the house, housewife
shaidor: women's outdoor garment
sharaf: honor

sharia: God's way to humankind, understood as the Islamic law
sharīf, *sharīfa:* noble person
shaykh: honorific title; in Sufism, a spiritual guide
shifā': traditional healing
shiqāq: marital discord
shirk: adoration of forces other than God
shīshā: small water pipe for smoking foreign, scented tobacco
subhia: tea party following a wedding, given by the groom's mother
sunna: Prophetic example
sūq: market
surung: people who provide day labor
ta'addud al-zawjāt: polygamy
tafrīq: judicial separation
tahkīm: arbitration
tahrīr al-mar'a: women's emancipation
takhalluf: backwardness
talāq: men's right to divorce by repudiation
talfīq: eclectic choice
taqālīd: literally "imitation"; tradition
tayyib, tayyiba: good (person)
thawra: revolution
thayyiba: nonvirgin
theshshem: (Moroccan) propriety
'ulamā' (ulema), sing. ***'alīm:*** religious scholars
umma: Muslim community
ummiyya: illiterate
unthā: female
'urf: customary law
usra: family
wahda: Yemeni unification in 1990
Wahhabism: religious reform movement that began in eighteenth-century Arabia aimed to eradicate popular Islam; official form of Islam in Saudi Arabia
wakīl: legal guardian
walī, pl. ***awliy':*** saint
waqf, pl. ***awqāf:*** religious endowment
wathaniyya: idolatry
wudū': minor ablution related to *salat* prayer

wusta: mediator, sponsor

zafaf: party where wedding celebration culminates

***zaghādīr* (pl.):** ululates

Zaidis: Shiʿa community from the northern part of Yemen

zamīl, zamīla, pl. ***zumalā':*** colleague

zār: spirit possession

zār daira: *zār* ring, a gathering to practice *zār*

zawj: marriage

ziara: visiting, pilgrimage

zina: adultery

References

Unpublished Sources

Aden's Bloody Monday. 1986. Pamphlet issued by Ideological Division, Secretariat of the Central Committee, Yemeni Socialist Party, Aden, Apr. Unpublished xylocopy.

'Ali, Salim Rubaya. 1977. Address by the assistant secretary-general of the Central Committee of the Unified NFPO and chairman of the Presidential Council on the occasion of the tenth anniversary of national independence. Unpublished xylocopy.

India Office Records (IOR), British Library, London

R/20/A/1284, Lists of Prostitutes

R/20/A/1285, Venereal Disease

R/20/A/1375, Prostitutes

R/20/A/2210, Qadi

R/20/A/2212, Prostitutes

R/20/A/2213, Prostitutes

R/20/A/2906, Zar

R/20/A/3452, Reformatory Club

R/20/B/990, Prostitutes

R/20/B/991, Prostitutes

R/20/B/1000, Qadhi

R/20/B/2681, Jewish Community

R/20/B/2810, Arab Reform Club

R/20/B/2813, Arab Women's Club

R/20/B/2833, Religious (Sharia) Courts

R/20/B/2904, Sheikh Mohammed Salim El Beihani

R/20/D/327, Religious Courts

Newspapers

14 Uktubr
Aden Recorder
'Adn Weekly
al-Ayyam Biweekly
Fatat al-Jazira
The Middle East
Middle East Times (Yemen edition)
Sawt al-'Ummal
Yemen Times

Published Sources

Abbey, Ruth. 2000. *Charles Taylor.* Princeton, N.J.: Princeton Univ. Press.

Abu-Amr, Ziad Mahmoud. 1986. "The People's Democratic Republic of Yemen: The Transformation of Society." Ph.D. diss., Georgetown Univ.

Abu-Lughod, Lila. 1986. *Veiled Sentiments: Honor and Poetry in a Bedouin Society.* Berkeley and Los Angeles: Univ. of California Press.

———. 1989. "Zones of Theory in the Anthropology of the Arab World." *Annual Review of Anthropology* 18: 267–306.

———. 1998. "The Marriage of Feminism and Islamism in Egypt: Selective Repudiation as a Dynamic of Postcolonial Cultural Politics." In *Remaking Women: Feminism and Modernity in the Middle East,* edited by Lila Abu-Lughod, 243–69. Princeton, N.J.: Princeton Univ. Press.

Abu-Rabi', Ibrahim M. 2004. *Contemporary Arab Thought: Studies in Post-1967 Arab Intellectual History.* London: Pluto Press.

Aden. 1961. *Reports for the Years 1957 and 1958.* London: Her Majesty's Stationery Office.

Aden Colony. 1941. *Ordinances Enacted during the Year 1941.* Aden: Cowasjee Dinshaw & Bros.

———. 1954. *Annual Report of the Department of Labour and Welfare 1954.* Aden: Government Press.

———. 1955a. *Census Report 1955.* Aden: Government Printer.

———. 1955b. *Law Reports.* Vol. 1: *1937–1953* (1 Aden L.R.). Aden: Government Printer.

———. 1962. *Law Reports.* Vol. 3: *1956–1958* (3 Aden L.R.). Aden: Government Printer.

Aden Colony Police. 1948. *Annual Report 1948.* Aden: Cowasjee Dinshaw & Bros.

———. 1961. *Annual Report 1961.* Aden: Government Printer. (Also IOR R/20/G/174.)

———. n.d. *Annual Report 1954.* Aden: Government Press. (Also IOR R/20/G/170.)

Ahmed, Leila. 1983. "Feminism and Feminist Movements in the Middle East, a Preliminary Exploration: Turkey, Egypt, Algeria, People's Democratic Republic of Yemen." In *Arabian and Islamic Studies,* presented to R. B.Serjeant on the Occasion of His Retirement from the Sir Thomas Adams's Chair of Arabic in the University of Cambridge, edited by Robin Bidwell and G. Rex Smith, 155–71. London, U.K.: Longman.

Ahroni, Reuben. 1994. *The Jews of the Crown Colony of Aden: History, Culture, and Ethnic Relations.* Leiden: E. J. Brill.

El Alami, Dawoud Sudqi, and Doreen Hinchcliffe. 1996. *Islamic Marriage and Divorce Laws of the Arab World.* CIMEL book series no. 2. London: Kluwer Law International.

Al-Ali, Nadje. 2000. *Secularism, Gender, and the State in the Middle East: The Egyptian Women's Movement.* Cambridge, U.K.: Cambridge Univ. Press.

Ameer Ali, Syed. 1929. *Mahommedan Law: Personal Law of the Mahommedans.* 5th ed. Calcutta: Thacker, Spink.

Amin, S. H. 1987. *Law and Justice in Contemporary Yemen: People's Democratic Republic of Yemen and Yemen Arab Republic.* Glasgow: Royston.

Anderson, James Norman Dalrymple. 1954. *Islamic Law in Africa.* Colonial Research Publication no. 16. London: Her Majesty's Stationery Office.

———. 1959. *Islamic Law in the Modern World.* New York: New York Univ. Press.

———. 1964. "The Isma'ili Khojas of East Africa." *Middle Eastern Studies* 1, no. 1: 21–39.

Anderson, Jon W. 2003. "New Media, New Publics: Reconfiguring the Public Sphere in Islam." *Social Research* (fall): 887–906.

Anderson, Michael R. 1990. "Islamic Law and the Colonial Encounter in British India." In *Islamic Family Law,* edited by Chibli Mallat and Jane Connors, 205–24. Arab and Islamic Law Series. London: Graham & Trotman.

———. 1996. *Islamic Law and the Colonial Encounter in British India.* Women Living under Muslim Laws (WLUML) Occasional Paper No 7. Available at http://www.wluml.org/section/resource/results/taxonomy%3A122. Accessed Nov. 15, 2005.

Asad, Talal. 1996. *The Idea of an Anthropology of Islam.* Occasional Papers Series. Washington, D.C.: Center for Contemporary Arab Studies, Georgetown Univ.

Aspects of Economic & Social Development in Democratic Yemen. 1981. Aden, Yemen: 14 October Corporation.

Badran, Margot. 1993. "Independent Women: More Than a Century of Feminism in Egypt." In *Arab Women: Old Boundaries, New Frontiers,* edited by Judith Tucker, 129–48. Bloomington: Indiana Univ. Press.

———. 2000. "Gender: Meanings, Uses, and Discourses in Post-unification Yemen 1–3." *Yemen Times* June 25, July 2, and July 9.

Barth, Fredrik. 1983. *Sohar: Culture and Society in an Omani Town*. Baltimore: Johns Hopkins Univ. Press.

———. 2000. "Boundaries and Connections." In *Signifying Identities: Anthropological Perspectives on Boundaries and Contested Values,* edited by Anthony P. Cohen, 17–36. London: Routledge.

Bawazir, Amin Sa'id 'Udh. 1997. *Halqat al-Qur'an wa majalis al-'alim fi masagid 'Adn.* Ta'izz, Yemen: Matabi' al-Mutanawwi'at.

Bayat, Asef. 2001. "Studying Middle Eastern Societies: Imperatives and Modalities of Thinking Comparatively." *Middle East Studies Association Bulletin* 35, no. 2 (winter 2001): 151–58.

Al-Bayhani, al-Shaykh Muhammad bin Salim bin Husain al-Kadadi. 1950. *Ustadh al-mar'ah.* Aden: Matba'at al-kamal.

Benhabib, Seyla. 1992. "Models of Public Space: Hannah Arendt, the Liberal Tradition, and Jürgen Habermas." In *Habermas and the Public Sphere,* edited by Craig Calhoun, 73–98. Cambridge, Mass.: MIT Press.

Bloch, Maurice. 1989. *Ritual, History, and Power: Selected Papers in Anthropology.* London School of Economics Monographs on Social Anthropology. London: Athlone Press.

Boddy, Janice. 1989. *Wombs and Alien Spirits: Women, Men, and the Zar Cult in Northern Sudan.* Madison: Univ. of Wisconsin Press.

Bonebakker, S. A. 1990. "Adab and the Concept of Belles-Lettres." In *'Abbasid Belles-Lettres,* edited by Julia Ashtiany, 16–30. Cambridge History of Arabic Literature. Cambridge, U.K.: Cambridge Univ. Press.

Bourdieu, Pierre. 1977. *Outline of a Theory of Practice.* Cambridge, U.K.: Cambridge Univ. Press.

Breton, André. 1972. "Manifesto of Surrealism 1924." In *Manifestoes of Surrealism,* 1–47. Ann Arbor: Univ. of Michigan Press.

Bujra, Abdalla S. 1967. "Political Conflict and Stratification in Hadramawt 1–2." *Middle Eastern Studies* 3, no. 4 (July): 355–75 and 4, no. 1 (October): 1–28.

———. 1970. "Urban Elites and Colonialism: The Nationalist Elites of Aden and South Arabia." *Middle Eastern Studies* 6: 189–211.

———. 1971. *The Politics of Stratification: A Study of Political Change in a South Arabian Town.* Oxford, U.K.: Clarendon Press.

Burgat, François. 1999. "Islamisme en Yémen." In *Le Yémen contemporain,* edited by Rémy Leveau, Franck Mermier, and Udo Steinbach, 221–46. Paris: Éditions Karthala.

Burman, Richie. 1991. *The Jews of Aden.* London: London Museum of Jewish Life and Kadimah Youth Movement.

Calhoun, Craig, ed. 1992. *Habermas and the Public Sphere.* Cambridge, Mass.: MIT Press.

Carapico, Sheila. 1999. "Contested Spaces: State and Civil Society." In *CCAS Report Focus on Yemen,* 1–3. Washington, D.C.: Center for Contemporary Arab Studies, Georgetown Univ.

Carapico, Sheila, and Cynthia Myntti. 1991. "Change in North Yemen 1977–1989: A Tale of Two Families." *Middle East Report* 170: 24–27.

Carapico, Sheila, Lisa Wedeen, and Anna Wuerth. 2002. *The Death and Life of Jarallah Omar. Middle East Report* online (Dec. 31). Available at http://www.merip.org/mero/mero123102.html. Accessed Nov. 20, 2005.

Carapico, Sheila, and Anna Würth. 2000. "Passports and Passages: Tests of Yemeni Women's Citizenship Rights." In *Gender and Citizenship in the Middle East,* edited by Suad Joseph, 261–71. Syracuse, N.Y.: Syracuse Univ. Press.

Certeau, Michel de. 1984. *The Practice of Everyday Life.* Berkeley and Los Angeles: Univ. of California Press.

———. 1988. *The Writing of History.* New York: Columbia Univ. Press.

Chakrabarty, Dipesh. 1997. "The Difference-Deferral of a Colonial Modernity: Public Debates on Domesticity in British Bengal." In *Subaltern Studies VIII,* edited by David Arnold and David Hardiman, 50–88. Delhi: Oxford Univ. Press.

Chelhod, Joseph, Dominique Champault, Lucien Golvin, Liliane Kuczynski, and Michel Tuchscherer. 1985. *L'Arabie du Sud: Histoire et civilisation.* Vol. 3: *Culture et institutions du Yémen.* Paris: Editions G.-P. Maisonneuve et Larose.

Cohen, David William. 1991. "'A Case for the Basoga': Lloyd Fallers and the Construction of an African Legal System." In *Law in Colonial Africa,* edited by Kristin Mann and Richard Roberts, 238–54. Portsmouth, Me.: Heinemann.

Colonial Reports Aden 1953 & 1954. 1956. London: Her Majesty's Stationery Office.

Cornish, William R., and G. de N. Clark. 1989. *Law and Society in England 1750–1950.* London: Sweet & Maxwell.

Coulson, Noel James. 1963. *A History of Islamic Law.* Edinburgh: Edinburgh Univ. Press.

Dahlgren, Susanne. 1998–99. "'The Chaste Woman Takes Her Chastity Wherever She Goes': Discourses on Gender, Marriage, and Work in Pre- and Post-unification Aden." *Chroniques Yéménites* 1998–99: 77–86.

———. 2000. "Traditions and Modernities in Aden, Yemen: On Studying Urban Middle Eastern Societies." In *The Middle East in a Globalized World,* edited by Bjørn Olav

Utvik and Knut S. Vikør, 150–82. Nordic Research on the Middle East no. 6. Bergen and London: Nordic Society for Middle Eastern Studies and C. Hurst.

———. 2002. "Family Legislation and Court Practice in Aden: The Role of the Judge in Three Periods of Modern History." Paper given at the Third Mediterranean Social and Political Research Meeting, organized by the European University Institute Mediterranean Programme in Robert Schuman Centre for Advanced Studies, Mar. 20–24, Florence, Italy.

———. 2003. "The Disobedient Wife: Family Law, Family Roles, and Gender Ideologies in Colonial Aden." Paper presented at the seminar "Family Relationships and Intimacy in a Globalizing World," Sept. 4–6, Rauma, Finland.

———. 2004. "Can a Woman Decide upon Her Marriage? The Case of Compulsory Marriage in Anglo-Muhammadan Court System in Colonial Aden." In *Women and Religion in the Middle East and the Mediterranean,* edited by Ingvar B. Mæhle and Inger Marie Okkenhaug, 135–48. Oslo: Oslo Academic Press.

———. 2005. "Women's *Adah* vs. 'Women's Law': The Contesting Issue of *Mahr* in Aden, Yemen." In *Le shaykh et le procureur: Systèmes coutumiers et pratiques juridiques au Yémen et en Égypte. Égypte/Monde arabe,* no. 1, 3rd series, edited by Baudouin Dupret and Francois Burgat, 125–44. Paris: Le Centre d'études et de documentation économiques, juridiques et socials (Cedej).

———. 2006a. "Segregation, Illegitimate Encounters, and Contextual Moralities: Sexualities in the Changing Public Sphere in Aden." In *Rewriting the History of Sexuality in the Islamic World,* special issue of *Hawwa: Journal of Women in the Middle East and the Islamic World* 4, nos. 2–3: 214–36.

———. 2006b. "Women with Too Many Rights: Men, Women, and the State in Pre- and Post-unification Aden." Paper presented at the conference "Arab Women, Past and Present: Participation and Democratization" organized by Georgetown University, Mar. 3–5, Doha, Qatar.

———. 2007a. "Islam, Custom, and Revolution in Aden: Reconsidering the Background to the Changes of the Early 1990s." In *Yemen into the Twenty-First Century: Continuity and Change,* edited by Kamil A. Mahdi, Anna Würth, and Helen Lackner, 327–45. Reading, U.K.: Ithaca Press.

———. 2007b. "Welfare and Modernity: Three Concepts for an Advanced Woman." In *Interpreting Welfare and Relief in the Middle East,* edited by Nefissa Naguib and Inger Marie Okkenhaug, 129–47. Leiden: E. J. Brill.

———. 2008. "Morphologies of Social Flows: Segregation, Time, and the Public Sphere." In *Gendering Urban Space in the Middle East, South Asia, and Africa,* edited by Martina Rieker and Kamran Asdar Ali, 45–70. New York: Palgrave Macmillan.

Daruwala, Pervez. 2002. *The Flames of Faith: The True Story of the Aden Holy Fire.* Available at http://members.ozemail.com.au/~zarathus/aden33.html. Accessed Nov. 12, 2002.

Deeb, Lara. 2005. "'Doing Good, Like Sayyida Zainab': Lebanese Shi'a Women's Participation in the Public Sphere." In *Religion, Social Practice, and Contested Hegemonies: Reconstructing the Public Sphere in Muslim Majority Societies,* edited by Armando Salvatore and Mark LeVine, 85–108. New York: Palgrave Macmillan.

———. 2006. *An Enchanted Modern: Gender and Public Piety in Shi'i Lebanon.* Princeton, N.J.: Princeton Univ. Press.

Doe, Brian D. 1965. *Aden in History.* Aden: Government Printer.

Dorsky, Susan. 1986. *Women of 'Amran: A Middle Eastern Ethnographic Survey.* Salt Lake City: Univ. of Utah Press.

Dostal, Walter. 1989. "The Structure and Principles of Customary Law among the Tribes of Yemen: An Anthropological Interpretation." In *Festschrift at the Occasion of the 19th Anniversary of the Department of Archaeology and Museology at King Saud University.* Riyadh, Saudi Arabia: n.p.

Douglas, J. Leigh. 1987. *The Free Yemeni Movement, 1935–1962.* Beirut: American Univ. of Beirut Press.

Dresch, Paul. 1989. *Tribes, Government, and History in Yemen.* Oxford, U.K.: Clarendon Press.

Dumont, Louis. 1980. *Homo hierarchicus: The Caste System and Its Implications.* Chicago: Univ. of Chicago Press.

Dupret, Baudouin. 1999. "Legal Pluralism, Normative Plurality, and the Arab World." In *Legal Pluralism in the Arab World,* edited by Baudouin Dupret, Maurits Berger, and Laila al-Zwaini, 29–40. The Hague: Kluwer Law International.

———. 2005. "What Is Plural in the Law? A Praxiological Answer." In *Le shaykh et le procureur: Systèmes coutumiers et pratiques juridiques au Yémen et en Égypte, Égypte/Monde arabe,* no. 1, 3rd series, edited by Baudouin Dupret and Francois Burgat, 159–83. Paris: Centre d'études et de documentation économiques, juridiques et socials (Cedej).

Eickelman, Dale F. 1976. *Moroccan Islam: Tradition and Society in a Pilgrimage Center.* Austin: Univ. of Texas Press.

Eickelman, Dale F., and Jon W. Anderson, eds. 2003a. *New Media in the Muslim World: The Emerging Public Sphere.* Indiana Series in Middle East Studies. Bloomington: Indiana Univ. Press.

———. 2003b. "Redefining Muslim Publics." In *New Media in the Muslim World: The Emerging Public Sphere,* edited by Dale F. Eickelman and Jon W. Anderson, 1–17. Indiana Series in Middle East Studies. Bloomington: Indiana Univ. Press.

Eickelman, Dale F., and James Piscatori. 1996. *Muslim Politics.* Princeton, N.J.: Princeton Univ. Press.

Eickelman, Dale F., and Armando Salvatore. 2006. "Muslim Publics." In *Public Islam and the Common Good,* edited by Armando Salvatore and Dale F. Eickelman, 3–27. Leiden: E. J. Brill.

Evans-Pritchard, Edward Evan. 1937. *Witchcraft, Oracles, and Magic among the Azande.* Oxford, U.K.: Clarendon.

Fábos, Anita Häusermann. 1999. "Ambiguous Ethnicity: Propriety *(Adab)* as a Situational Boundary Marker for Northern Sudanese in Cairo." Ph.D. diss., Boston Univ., Graduate School of Arts and Sciences.

Family Law, Law no. 1 of 1974. 1976. Official English translation, issued by the Information Department of the Ministry of Information. Aden, Yemen: 14 October Corporation.

Farag, Iman. 2001. "Private Lives, Public Affairs: The Uses of *Adab.*" In *Yearbook of the Sociology of Islam,* edited by Armando Salvatore, vol. 3: *Muslim Traditions and Modern Technologies of Power,* 93–120. Hamburg and New Brunswick, N.J.: Lit and Transaction.

Farnell, Brenda. 1999. "Moving Bodies, Acting Selves." *Annual Review of Anthropology* 28: 341–73.

———. 2000. "Getting Out of the *Habitus:* An Alternative Model of Dynamically Embodied Social Action." *Journal of the Royal Anthropological Institute* 6, no. 3: 397–418.

Fayein, Claudie. 1957. *Hakima: Kvinnlig läkare i Jemen.* Stockholm: Albert Bonniers Förlag.

Footman, David. 1986. *Antonin Besse of Aden: The Founder of St. Antony's College Oxford.* London: Macmillan in association with St. Antony's College, Oxford.

Foster, Donald. 1969. *Landscape with Arabs: Travels in Aden and South Arabia.* Brighton, U.K.: Clifton Books.

Fraser, Nancy. 1992. "Rethinking the Public Sphere: A Contribution to the Critique of Actually Existing Democracy." In *Habermas and the Public Sphere,* edited by Craig Calhoun, 109–42. Cambridge, Mass.: MIT Press.

Gavin, R. J. 1975. *Aden under British Rule 1837–1967.* London: C. Hurst.

Geertz, Clifford. 1993. *The Interpretation of Cultures: Selected Essays.* London: Fontana Press.

General Union of Yemeni Women. 1977. *Documents of the General Union of Yemeni Women.* First General Congress of Yemeni Women in Saiun, July 15–16, 1974. Aden, Yemen: 14 October Corporation.

———. 1986. *A Decade of Achievements.* Aden, Yemen: General Union of Yemeni Women.

Ghanem, Isam. 1972. "Social Aspects of the Legal Systems in South-West Arabia with Special Reference to the Application of Islamic Family Law in the Aden Courts." Master's thesis, Univ. of London, School of Oriental and African Studies.

———. 1976. "A Note on Law no. 1. of 1974 Concerning the Family, People's Democratic Republic of Yemen." In *Arabian Studies III,* edited by Robert Bertram Serjeant and Robin Leonard Bidwell, 191–96. London: Hurst.

———. 1981. *Yemen: Political History, Social Structure, and Legal System.* London: Arthur Probsthain.

Gilsenan, Michael. 1982. *Recognizing Islam: Religion and Society in the Modern Arab World.* New York: Pantheon Books.

———. 1993. "Lying, Honor, and Contradiction." In *Everyday Life in the Muslim Middle East,* edited by Donna Lee Bowen and Evelyn A. Early, 157–69. Bloomington: Indiana Univ. Press.

Gingrich, Andre. 1989. *How the Chief's Daughters Marry: Tribes, Marriage Patterns, and Hierarchies in North-Western Yemen.* Vienna Contributions to Ethnology and Anthropology no. 5. Vienna: University of Vienna.

———. 1997. "Inside an 'Exhausted Community': An Essay on Case-Reconstructive Research about Peripheral and Other Moralities." In *The Ethnography of Moralities,* edited by Signe Howell, 153–77. London: Routledge.

Goitein, Shlomo Dov. 1964. *Jews and Arabs: Their Contacts Through the Ages.* New York: Schocken Books.

Göle, Nilüfer. 1997. "The Gendered Nature of the Public Sphere." *Public Culture* 10, no. 1: 61–81.

Government of Aden. 1939. *The Aden Blue Book 1937.* London: Waterlow & Sons.

Gran, Peter. 1998. "Contending with Middle East Exceptionalism: A Foreword." *Arab Studies Journal* (spring): 6–9.

Granqvist, Hilma. 1931. *Marriage Conditions in a Palestinian Village.* Commentationes Humanarum Litterarum 3, no. 8. Helsinki: Finska Vetenskapssocieteten.

El Guindi, Fadwa. 1999. *Veil: Modesty, Privacy, and Resistance.* Oxford, U.K.: Berg.

El Habashi, Muhammad 'Umar. 1966. *Aden: L'Evolution politique, économique et sociale de l'Arabie du Sud.* Algiers: Societé Nationale d'Edition et de Diffusion SNED.

Habermas, Jürgen. [1989] 2003. *The Structural Transformation of the Public Sphere: An Inquiry into a Category of Bourgeois Society.* Oxford, U.K.: Blackwell.

Hale, Sondra. 1993. "Transforming Culture or Fostering Second-Hand Consciousness? Women's Front Organisations and Revolutionary Parties—the Sudan Case." In *Arab Women: Old Boundaries, New Frontiers,* edited by Judith Tucker, 149–74. Bloomington: Indiana Univ. Press.

———. 2005. "Activating the Gender Local: Transnational Ideologies and 'Women's Culture' in Northern Sudan." *Journal of Middle East Women's Studies* 1, no. 1: 29–52.

Halliday, Fred. 1975. *Arabia Without Sultans.* Harmondsworth, U.K.: Penguin Books.

———. 1979. "Yemen's Unfinished Revolution: Socialism in the South." *MERIP Reports* 9, no. 8 (October): 3–20.

———. 1990. *Revolution and Foreign Policy: The Case of South Yemen 1967–1987.* Cambridge, U.K.: Cambridge Univ. Press.

———. 2000. *Nation and Religion in the Middle East.* London: Saqi Books.

Al-Hamdani, Ahmad 'Ali, ed. 2005. *Al-mujahid Muhammad 'Ali Luqman: Za'id nahdhat al-fikriyyat wal-adabiyyat al-hadithat fil-yaman.* Beirut: n.p.

Hanks, William F. 1996. *Language and Communicative Practices.* Boulder, Colo.: Westview Press.

The Hans Wehr Dictionary of Modern Written Arabic. 1976. 3rd ed. Edited by J. Milton Cowan. Ithaca, N.Y.: Spoken Language Services.

Harré, Rom, and Edward H. Madden, eds. 1975. *Causal Powers: A Theory of Natural Necessity.* Oxford, U.K.: Blackwell.

Hickinbotham, Tom. 1958. *Aden.* London: Constable.

Hirsch, Susan F. 1998. *Pronouncing and Persevering: Gender and Discourses of Disputing in an African Islamic Court.* Chicago: Univ. of Chicago Press.

Holy, Ladislav. 1991. *Religion and Custom in a Muslim Society: The Berti of Sudan.* Cambridge, U.K.: Cambridge Univ. Press.

Hoodfar, Homa. 1997. *Between Marriage and the Market: Intimate Politics and Survival in Cairo.* Berkeley and Los Angeles: Univ. of California Press.

Howell, Signe. 1997. "Introduction." In *The Ethnography of Moralities,* edited by Signe Howell, 1–21. London: Routledge.

Al-Hubaishi, H. A. 1988. *Legal System and Basic Law in Yemen.* Worcester, U.K.: Billing and Sons.

Hunter, Captain Frederick Mercer. [1877] 1968. *An Account of the British Settlement of Aden in Arabia.* London: Frank Cass.

Ibn al-Mujawir, Yusuf b. Ya'qub. 1986. *Sifat bilad al-yaman wa makka wa ba'dh al-hijaz: Al-musammat tarikh al-mustabsir.* Beirut: Sharkat Dar al-Tanwir lil-Taba'at wa al-Nashr.

Ingrams, Doreen. 1949. *A Survey of Social and Economic Conditions in the Aden Protectorate.* Asmara, Eritrea: n.p.

———. 1970. *A Time in Arabia.* London: John Murray.

Ingrams, William Harold. 1937. *A Report on the Social, Economic, and Political Condition of the Hadhramaut.* Colonial Office, Aden Protectorate, Colonial no. 123. London: His Majesty's Stationery Office.

Ismael, Tareq Y., and Jacqueline S. Ismael. 1986. *PDR Yemen: Politics, Economics, and Society: The Politics of Socialist Transformation.* London: Frances Pinter.

Ismail, Salwa. 2007. "Islamism, Re-Islamization, and the Fashioning of Muslim Selves: Refiguring the Public Sphere." *Muslim World Journal of Human Rights* 4, no. 1: article 3.

Jackson, Michael. 1996. "Introduction: Phenomenology, Radical Empirism, and Anthropological Critique." In *Things as They Are: New Directions in Phenomenological Anthropology,* edited by Michael Jackson, 1–50. Bloomington: Indiana Univ. Press.

Al-Jamhuriyya al-Yamaniyya, Wazara al-Saun al-Qanuniyya. 1992. *Al-qirar al-jamhuriyy bil-qanun raqim 20 lisana m1992 bishan al-ahwal al-shakhsiyya 1992.* Aden, Yemen: 14 Uktubr.

Joseph, Suad. 1999. "Introduction." In *Intimate Selving in Arab Families: Gender, Self, and Identity,* edited by Suad Joseph, 1–17. Syracuse, N.Y.: Syracuse Univ. Press.

———, ed. 2000. *Gender and Citizenship in the Middle East.* Syracuse, N.Y.: Syracuse Univ. Press.

———. 2003. "Among Brothers: Patriarchal Connectivity and Brotherly Deference in Lebanon." In *The New Arab Family,* edited by Nicholas S. Hopkins, 165–79. Cairo Papers in Social Science, vol. 24, nos. 1–2. Cairo: American University in Cairo Press.

Joseph, Suad, and Susan Slyomovics, eds. 2001. *Women and Power in the Middle East.* Philadelphia: Univ. of Pennsylvania Press.

Kadivar, Mohsen. 2003. "An Introduction to the Public and Private Debate in Islam." *Social Research* (fall): 659–80.

Al-Kanadi, Manal. 2000. "Schemes for Elimination of Discrimination Against Women." *Yemen Times,* Aug. 13.

Kandiyoti, Deniz. 1996. "Contemporary Feminist Scholarship and Middle East Studies." In *Gendering the Middle East: Emerging Perspectives,* edited by Deniz Kandiyoti, 1–27. Syracuse, N.Y.: Syracuse Univ. Press.

Kapteijns, Lidwien, and Jay Spaulding. 1994. "Women of the Zar and Middle-Class Sensibilities in Colonial Aden." *Sudanic Africa* 5: 7–38.

Kapur, Ratha, and Brenda Cossman. 1996. *Subversive Sites: Feminist Engagements with Law in India.* New Delhi: Thousand Oaks.

Keddie, Nikki. 1988. "Ideology, Society, and the State in the Post-colonial Muslim Societies." In *State and Ideology in the Middle East,* edited by Fred Halliday and Hamza Alavi, 9–30. New York: Monthly Review Press.

———. 2002. "Women in the Limelight: Some Recent Books on Middle Eastern Women's History." *International Journal of Middle East Studies* 34, no. 3 (Aug.): 553–73.

Khalifa, Mohsin H. 1951. *Report on Social Conditions and Welfare Services in Aden*. N.p.: n.p.

Khalil, Fatima Abdul Qawi. 1972. "Indigenous Midwifery in Selected Villages in the Second Governorate of People's Democratic Republic of Yemen." Master's thesis, American Univ. of Beirut.

Khan, 'Abd Allah Yaqub. 1933. *Al-amthal al-'adaniyat*. Aden: Matb'a Ibrahim Rasim.

Khan, Abdulla Yaqub. 1938–39. "A Narrative and Critical History of Aden 1." *New Indian Antiquary* 1: 616–27.

Kidder, Robert L. 1978. "Western Law in India: External Law and Local Response." In *Social System and Legal Process*, edited by Harry M. Johnson, 159–62. San Francisco: Jossey-Bass.

Knox-Mawer, June. 1961. *The Sultans Came to Tea*. London: John Murray.

Knox-Mawer, Ronald. 1956. "Islamic Domestic Law in Aden." *International and Comparative Law Quarterly* 5 (Oct.): 511–18.

Knysh, Alexander. 1993. "The Cult of Saints in Hadramawt: An Overview." In *New Arabian Studies 1*, edited by Robert Bertram Serjeant, Robin Leonard Bidwell, and G. Rex Smith, 137–52. Exeter, U.K.: Univ. of Exeter Press.

Kour, Zaki Hanna. 1981. *The History of Aden 1839–72*. London: Frank Cass.

Lackner, Helen. 1985. *PDR Yemen: Outpost of Socialist Development in Arabia*. London: Ithaca Press.

Lambek, Michael. 1993. *Knowledge and Practice in Mayotte: Local Discourses of Islam, Sorcery, and Spirit Possession*. Toronto: Univ. of Toronto Press.

Lapidus, Ira M. 1984. "Knowledge, Virtue, and Action: The Classical Muslim Conception of *Adab* and the Nature of Religious Fulfilment in Islam." In *Moral Conduct and Authority: The Place of* Adab *in South Asian Islam*, edited by Barbara F. Metcalf, 38–61. Berkeley and Los Angeles: Univ. of California Press.

———. 2007. *A History of Islamic Societies*. 2d ed. Cambridge, U.K.: Cambridge Univ. Press.

Lateef, Shahida. 1990. *Muslim Women in India: Political and Private Realities*. London: Zed Books.

Laws of Aden. 1955. Containing the ordinances of the Colony of Aden in force on May 1, 1955, and subsidiary legislation made thereunder. Vols. 1–5, edited by J. V. M. Shields and D. L. Davies. London: Vacher & Sons.

LeVine, Mark, and Armando Salvatore. 2005. "Socio-religious Movements and the Transformation of 'Common Sense' into a Politics of 'Common Good.'" In *Religion, Social*

Practice, and Contested Hegemonies: Reconstructing the Public Sphere in Muslim Majority Societies, edited by Armando Salvatore and Mark LeVine, 29–56. New York: Palgrave Macmillan.

Lévi-Strauss, Claude. 1977. *Structural Anthropology 1.* Suffolk, U.K.: Peregrine Books.

Little, Tom. 1968. *South Arabia: Arena of Conflict.* London: Pall Mall Press.

Loeffler, Reinhold. 1988. *Islam in Practice: Religious Beliefs in a Persian Village.* Albany: State Univ. of New York Press.

Lunt, James. 1966. *The Barren Rocks of Aden.* London: Jenkins.

Luqman, Farouk. 1960. *The Aden Guide.* N.p.: n.p.

Luqman, Hamza 'Ali. n.d. *Asatir min tarikh al-Yaman.* Markaz al-Dirasat wal-Bahuth al-Yamaniyy, San'a'a. Sana'a, Yemen: Dar al-Masirah.

Lutfi, Huda. 1991. "Manners and Customs of Fourteenth-Century Cairene Women: Female Anarchy versus Male Shari'a Order in Muslim Prescriptive Treatises." In *Women in Middle Eastern History: Shifting Boundaries in Sex and Gender,* edited by Nikki R. Keddie and Beth Baron, 103–15. New Haven, Conn.: Yale Univ. Press.

MacLeod, Arlene Elowe. 1991. *Accommodating Protest: Working Women, the New Veiling, and Change in Cairo.* New York: Columbia Univ. Press.

Mahmassani, Abd al-Hafiz. 1962. *Ittihad 'adn ma'a imarat al-janub al-'arabiyy.* Beirut: n.p.

Mahmood, Saba. 2001. "Feminist Theory, Embodiment, and the Docile Agent: Some Reflections on the Egyptian Islamic Revival." *Cultural Anthropology* 16: 202–36.

———. 2005. *Politics of Piety: The Islamic Revival and the Feminist Subject.* Princeton, N.J.: Princeton Univ. Press.

Makhlouf, Carla. 1979. *Changing Veils: Women and Modernisation in North Yemen.* Austin: Univ. of Texas Press.

Maktari, Abdulla M. A. 1971. *Water Rights and Irrigation Practices in Lahj: A Study of the Application of Customary and Shari'ah Law in South-West Arabia.* Cambridge, U.K.: Cambridge Univ. Press.

Mann, Kristin, and Richard Roberts. 1991. *Law in Colonial Africa.* Portsmouth, Me.: Heinemann.

Mauss, Marcel. 1979. *Sociology and Psychology: Essays.* London and Boston: Routledge and Kegan Paul.

Meeker, Michael E. 1976. "Meaning and Society in the Near East: Examples from the Black Sea Turks and the Levantine Arabs. I–II." *International Journal of Middle East Studies* 7, no. 2: 243–70 and no. 3: 383–422.

Al-Mekkawi, Shaikh Abdul Kadir bin Muhammed. [1886] 1959. *A Treatise on the Muhammedan Law, Entitled "The Overflowing River of the Science of Inheritance and*

Patrimony" Together with an Exposition of "The Rights of Women, and the Law of Matrimony." Cairo: Moustapha El Baby El Halaby & Sons.

Meneley, Anne. 1996. *Tournaments of Value: Sociability and Hierarchy in a Yemeni Town.* Toronto: Univ. of Toronto Press.

Meriwether, Margaret L., and Judith E. Tucker. 1999. "Introduction." In *A Social History of Women and Gender in the Modern Middle East,* edited by Margaret L. Meriwether and Judith E. Tucker, 1–24. Boulder, Colo.: Westview Press.

Messick, Brinkley. 1993. *The Calligraphic State, Textual Domination, and History in a Muslim Society.* Berkeley and Los Angeles: Univ. of California Press.

Metcalf, Barbara Daly. 1984a. "Introduction." In *Moral Conduct and Authority: The Place of* Adab *in South Asian Islam,* edited by Barbara Daly Metcalf, 1–20. Berkeley and Los Angeles: Univ. of California Press.

———, ed. 1984b. *Moral Conduct and Authority: The Place of* Adab *in South Asian Islam.* Berkeley and Los Angeles: Univ. of California Press.

Miller, W. Flagg. 2002. "Metaphors of Commerce: Trans-valuing Tribalism in Yemeni Audiocassette Poetry." *International Journal of Middle East Studies* 34, no. 1: 29–57.

Mir-Hosseini, Ziba. 2000. *Marriage on Trial: A Study of Islamic Family Law.* London: I. B. Tauris.

———. 2003. "The Construction of Gender in Islamic Legal Thought and Strategies for Reform." *Hawwa* 1, no. 1: 1–28.

Moghadam, Val. 2002. Book review of *The Veil Unveiled: The Hijab in Modern Culture* (Gainesville: University of Florida Press) by Faegheh Shirazi. *International Journal of Middle East Studies* 34, no. 3: 597–99.

Mohanty, Chandra Talpade. 1991a. "Cartographies of Struggle: Third World Women and the Politics of Feminism." In *Third World Women and the Politics of Feminism,* edited by Chandra Talpade Mohanty, Ann Russo, and Lourdes Torres, 1–47. Bloomington: Indiana Univ. Press.

———. 1991b. "Under Western Eyes: Feminist Scholarship and Colonial Discourses." In *Third World Women and the Politics of Feminism,* edited by Chandra Talpade Mohanty, Ann Russo, and Lourdes Torres, 51–80. Bloomington: Indiana Univ. Press.

Mohsen, Safia K. 1990. "Women and Criminal Justice in Egypt." In *Law and Islam in the Middle East,* edited by Daisy Hill Dwyer, 15–34. New York: Bergin & Garvey.

Molyneux, Maxine. 1979. "Women and Revolution in the People's Democratic Republic of Yemen." *Feminist Review* 1, no. 1: 5–20.

———. 1982. *State Politics and the Position of Women Workers in the People's Democratic Republic of Yemen 1967–77.* Women, Work, and Development no. 3. Geneva: International Labour Office.

———. 1985. "Legal Reform and Socialist Revolution in Democratic Yemen: Women and the Family." *International Journal of the Sociology of Law* 13: 147–72.

———. 1989. "Legal Reform and Socialist Revolution in South Yemen: Women and the Family." In *Promissory Notes: Women in the Transition to Socialism,* edited by Sonia Kruks, Rayna Rapp, and Marilyn B. Young, 127–47. New York: Monthly Review Press.

———. 1991. "The Law, the State, and Socialist Policies with Regard to Women: The Case of the People's Democratic Republic of Yemen 1967–1990." In *Women, Islam, and the State,* edited by Deniz Kandiyoti, 237–54. London: Macmillan.

———. 1995. "Women's Rights and Political Contingency: The Case of Yemen, 1990–1994." *Middle East Journal* 49, no. 3: 418–31.

Monet, Paul. 1995. "Réislamisation et conflit réligieux à Aden: La structuration locale du champ islamique après l'échec de la secession de 1994." Paper presentation for the DEA d'Etudes Politiques, Institut d'Etudes Politiques de Paris.

Moore, Henrietta. 1994. *A Passion for Difference.* Bloomington: Indiana Univ. Press.

———. 1999. "Whatever Happened to Women and Men? Gender and Other Crises in Anthropology." In *Anthropological Theory Today,* edited by Henrietta L. Moore, 151–71. Cambridge, U.K.: Polity Press.

Moore, Sally Falk. 1977. "Individual Interests and Organisational Structures: Dispute Settlements as 'Events of Articulation.'" In *Social Anthropology and Law,* edited by Ian Hamnett, 159–88. London: Academic Press.

———. 1986. *Social Facts and Fabrications: "Customary" Law in Kilimanjaro, 1880–1980.* Cambridge, U.K.: Cambridge Univ. Press.

Moors, Annelies. 1995. *Women, Property, and Islam: Palestinian Experiences 1920–1990.* Cambridge, U.K.: Cambridge Univ. Press.

———. 1999. "Debating Islamic Family Law: Legal Texts and Social Practices." In *A Social History of Women and Gender in the Middle East,* edited by Margaret L. Meriwether and Judith E. Tucker, 141–76. Boulder, Colo.: Westview Press.

Mueller, Eric. 1985. "Revitalizing Old Ideas: Developments in Middle Eastern Family Law." In *Women and the Family in the Middle East: New Voices of Change,* edited by Elizabeth Warnock Fernea, 224–28. Austin: Univ. of Texas Press.

Muheirez, Abdullah Ahmed. 1985. "Cultural Development in the People's Democratic Republic of Yemen." In *Economy, Society, and Culture in Contemporary Yemen,* edited by Brian R. Pridham, 200–14. London: Croom Helm and Centre for Arab Gulf Studies, Univ. of Exeter.

Mundy, Martha. 1995. *Domestic Government: Kinship, Community, and Polity in North Yemen.* London: I. B. Tauris.

Myers, Oliver H. 1947. "Little Aden Folklore (with 4 plates)." *Bulletin de l'Institut Français d'Archéologie Orientale* 44: 183–234.

Nagi, Sultan A. 1976. "Historical Glimpse of Yemen." In *Democratic Yemen Today,* edited by Faruq M. Luqman, n.p. Bombay: n.p.

———. 1984. "The Genesis of the Call for Yemeni Unity." In *Contemporary Yemen: Politics and Historical Background,* edited by Brian R. Pridham, 240–60. London: Croom Helm and Centre for Arab Gulf Studies, Univ. of Exeter.

Najmabadi, Afsaneh. 1998. "Crafting the Educated Housewife." In *Remaking Women: Feminism and Modernity in the Middle East,* edited by Lila Abu-Lughod, 91–125. Princeton, N.J.: Princeton Univ. Press.

Nashat, Guity, and Judith E. Tucker. 1999. *Women in the Middle East and North Africa: Restoring Women to History.* Bloomington: Indiana Univ. Press.

Naumkin, Vitaly. 1993. *Island of the Phoenix: An Ethnographic Study of the People of Socotra.* Reading, U.K.: Ithaca Press.

Naval Intelligence Division, United Kingdom. 1946. *Western Arabia and the Red Sea.* Geographical handbook series. Produced and printed for official purposes during World War II, 1939–45. Oxford, U.K: n.p.

Nizan, Paul. 1987. *Aden, Arabie.* New York: Columbia Univ. Press.

Al-Noban, Saeed Abdul Khair. 1984. "Education for Nation-Building: The Experience of the People's Democratic Republic of Yemen." In *Contemporary Yemen: Politics and Historical Background,* edited by Brian R. Pridham, 102–24. London: Croom Helm and Centre for Arab Gulf Studies, Univ. of Exeter.

Omar, Sultan Ahmed. 1970. *Nadhrah fi tatwir al-mujtama' al-Yamani.* Beirut: Dar al-Tali'ah.

Ortner, Sherry B. 1981. "Gender and Sexuality in Hierarchical Societies: The Case of Polynesia and Some Comparative Implication." In *Sexual Meanings: The Cultural Construction of Gender and Sexuality,* edited by Sherry B. Ortner and Harriet Whitehead, 359–409. Cambridge, U.K.: Cambridge Univ. Press.

———. 1989. *High Religion: A Cultural and Political History of Sherpa Buddhism.* Princeton, N.J.: Princeton Univ. Press.

———. 1996. *Making Gender: The Politics and Erotics of Culture.* Boston: Beacon Press.

Paget, Julian. 1970. *Last Post: Aden 1964–1967.* London: Faber.

Parashar, Archana. 1992. *Women and Family Law Reform in India: Uniform Civil Code and Gender Equality.* New Delhi: Sage.

Parfitt, Tudor. 1996. *The Road to Redemption: The Jews of the Yemen 1900–1950.* Leiden: E. J. Brill.

People's Democratic Republic of Yemen (PDRY). 1974. *A Summary of the Experience of the Revolution in the Democratic Yemen from the Armed Struggle until the Quinquinnial Plan.* Aden, Yemen: 14 October Corporation.

———. 1977. *The Political Report of the Unified Political Organisation the National Front.* London: Russell Press.

———. 1979. *National Health Programme 1979–1983.* Aden, Yemen: Ministry of Public Health.

———. 1988. *A Summary of the Experiences of the Government.* Aden, Yemen: Government Printer.

———. 1990. *Statistical Yearbook 1988.* 6th ed. Aden, Yemen: Dar al-Hamdaniyy.

Peristiany, J. G., ed. 1965. *Honor and Shame: The Values of Mediterranean Society.* Chicago: Univ. of Chicago Press.

Postone, Moishe, Edward LiPuma, and Craig Calhoun. 1993. "Introduction." In *Bourdieu: Critical Perspectives,* edited by Craig Calhoun, Edward LiPuma, and Moishe Postone, 1–13. Cambridge, U.K.: Polity Press.

Al-Qadri, Husnia. 1998. "Gender and Health." *Yemen Times,* Nov. 2.

Rateb, Mohamed Farouk. 1988. *Civil Rights in the Light of Islamic Legislation (Five Studies).* Cairo: Aalam al-Kotob.

Reclus, Elisée. 1892. *The Earth and Its Inhabitants IX.* 17 vols. A. H. Keane. New York: D. Appleton.

Reilly, Bernard R. 1960. *Aden and the Yemen.* Colonial Office, no. 343. London: Her Majesty's Stationary Office.

Rewriting the History of Sexuality in the Islamic World. 2006. Special issue of *Hawwa: Journal of Women in the Middle East and the Islamic World* 4, nos. 2–3.

Roberts, Richard, and Kristin Mann. 1991. "Law in Colonial Africa." In *Law in Colonial Africa,* edited by Kristin Mann and Richard Roberts, 1–48. Portsmouth, Me.: Heinemann.

Rooke, Tetz. 2000. "The Influence of *Adab* on the Muslim Intellectuals of the Nahda as Reflected in the Memoirs of Muhammad Kurd 'Ali (1876–1953)." In *The Middle East in a Globalised World,* edited by Bjørn Olav Utvik and Knut S. Vikør, 193–219. Nordic Research on the Middle East no. 6. Bergen and London: Nordic Society for Middle Eastern Studies and C. Hurst.

Rubin, Gayle. 1975. "The Traffic in Women: Notes on the 'Political Economy of Sex.'" In *Towards an Anthropology of Women,* edited by Rayna R. Reiter, 157–210. New York: Monthly Review Press.

Sahlins, Marshall. 1985. *Islands of History.* Chicago: Univ. of Chicago Press.

Salvatore, Armando, ed. 2001. *Yearbook of the Sociology of Islam*. Vol. 3: *Muslim Traditions and Modern Technologies of Power.* Hamburg and New Brunswick, N.J.: Lit Verlag and Transaction.

Salvatore, Armando, and Dale F. Eickelman. 2006a. "Preface: Public Islam and the Common Good." In *Public Islam and the Common Good,* edited by Armando Salvatore and Dale F. Eickelman, xi–xxiv. Leiden: E. J. Brill.

Salvatore, Armando, and Dale F. Eickelman, eds. 2006b. *Public Islam and the Common Good.* Leiden: E. J. Brill.

Salvatore, Armando, and Mark LeVine. 2005a. "Introduction: Reconstructing the Public Sphere in Muslim Majority Societies." In *Religion, Social Practice, and Contested Hegemonies: Reconstructing the Public Sphere in Muslim Majority Societies,* edited by Armando Salvatore and Mark LeVine, 1–25. New York: Palgrave Macmillan.

Salvatore, Armando, and Mark LeVine, eds. 2005b. *Religion, Social Practice, and Contested Hegemonies: Reconstructing the Public Sphere in Muslim Majority Societies.* New York: Palgrave Macmillan.

Al-Saqqaf, Abou Bakr. 1999. "The Yemeni Unity: Crisis in Integration." In *Le Yémen Contemporain,* edited by Rémy Leveau, Franck Mermier, and Udo Steinbach, 141–60. Paris: Éditions Karthala.

Schacht, Joseph. 1964. *An Introduction to Islamic Law.* Oxford, U.K.: Clarendon Press.

Serjeant, Robert Bertram. 1962. "Sex, Birth, and Circumcision: Some Notes from South-West Arabia." In *Hermann von Wissmann—Festschrift,* edited by Adolf Leidlmair, 193–208. Tübingen, Germany: Selbstverlag des Geographischen Instituts der Universität Tübingen.

———. 1967. "Société et gouvernement en Arabie du Sud." *Arabica* 14: 284–97.

———. 1980. "Social Stratification in Arabia." In *The Islamic City,* edited by Robert Bertram Serjeant, 126–47. Paris: UNESCO.

———. [1957] 1981. "South Arabia." Reprinted in *Studies in Arabian History and Civilisation,* 226–47. Aldershot, U.K.: Variorum.

Shakry, Omnia. 1998. "Schooled Mothers and Structured Play: Child Rearing in Turn-of-the-Century Egypt." In *Remaking Women: Feminism and Modernity in the Middle East,* edited by Lila Abu-Lughod, 126–70. Princeton, N.J.: Princeton Univ. Press.

Al-Shamiriyy, Nagib. 1984. *Haquq al-mar'a fi tashriyy'at al-yaman al-dimuqratiyya.* Aden, Yemen: Dar al-Hamdaniyy lil-Taba'a wal-Nashr.

Sharma, Vijay. 1994. *Protection to Women in Matrimonial Home.* New Delhi: Deep & Deep.

Al-Sharqi, Ra'ufah Hassan. 1998. "Khalfiyyat hawl markaz al-abhath al-tatbiqiyyat wa al-dirasat al-niswiyyat bi-jami'at san'a'a." *Majallat al-Dirasat al-Niswiyyat* (Oct.): 7–22.

Shirazi, Faegheh. 2001. *The Veil Unveiled: The Hijab in Modern Culture.* Gainesville: Univ. Press of Florida.

Shukry, Hazem Ali. 1986. "Morphology of Greater Aden and Related Problems." Ph.D. diss., Aligarh Muslim Univ.

Smart, Carol. 1989. *Feminism and the Power of Law.* London: Routledge.

Stark, Freya. [1945] 1986. *East Is West.* London: Century.

State of Aden. 1964. *Law Reports* Vol.4: *1959–1960* (4 Aden L.R.). Aden, Yemen: Government Press.

Stevenson, Thomas. 1985. *Social Change in a Yemeni Highlands Town.* Salt Lake City: Univ. of Utah Press.

Stookey, Robert W. 1982. *South Yemen: A Marxist Republic in Arabia.* Boulder, Colo., and London: Westview Press and Croom Helm.

Tahir, Ahmad. 2001. *Al-islam wal-mu'amarat al-masuniyyat: Ma' watha'iq 'an al-hifl al-masuniyy fil-yaman.* Sana'a, Yemen: Markaz 'Abadi lil-Dirasat wal-Nashr.

Tahir, 'Alawi 'Abdullah. 1981. *Lutfi Iman: Darasah wa tarikh.* Aden, Yemen: 14 October Corporation.

Taminian, Lucine. 1998. "Rimbaud's House in Aden, Yemen: Giving Voice(s) to the Silent Poet." *Cultural Anthropology* 13, no. 4 (Nov.): 464–90.

Taylor, Charles. 1985. *Human Agency and Language: Philosophical Papers I.* Cambridge, U.K.: Cambridge Univ. Press.

———. 1989. *Sources of the Self: The Making of the Modern Identity.* Cambridge, U.K.: Cambridge Univ. Press.

———. 1993. "To Follow a Rule. . . ." In *Bourdieu: Critical Perspectives,* edited by Craig Calhoun, Edward LiPuma, and Moishe Postone, 45–60. Cambridge, U.K.: Polity Press.

———. 1995. *Philosophical Arguments.* Cambridge, Mass.: Harvard Univ. Press.

Thompson, John B. 1991. "Editor's Introduction." In Pierre Bourdieu, *Language and Symbolic Power,* edited by John B. Thompson, 1–31. Cambridge, U.K.: Polity Press.

Three Hours in Aden: A Short Descriptive Account of the Settlement, for the Use of Passengers, with a Map and Five Views. 1891. Bombay: Education Society's Steam Press.

Tobi, Jacob. 1994a. "Inheritance Rights of Jewish Women and Moslem Women in Yemen." *Proceedings of the Seminar for Arabian Studies* 24: 201–8.

———. 1994b. *West of Aden: A Survey of the Aden Jewish Community.* Netanya and Jerusalem: Association for Society and Culture and "Graphit" (Graph-Chen) Press.

Trevaskis, Kennedy. 1968. *Shades of Amber.* London: Hutchinson.

Tucker, Judith E. 1993. "The Arab Family in History: 'Otherness' and the Study of the Family." In *Arab Women: Old Boundaries, New Frontiers,* edited by Judith E. Tucker, 195–207. Bloomington: Indiana Univ. Press.

UNICEF and Ministry of Local Governments in the People's Democratic Republic of Yemen, Central Statistical Organisation. 1973. *Good Planning, Book 2.* Aden, Yemen: UNICEF and Government Printer.

Vom Bruck, Gabriele. 1992–93. "Enacting Tradition: The Legitimation of Marriage Practices Amongst Yemeni *Sadah.*" *Cambridge Anthropology* 16, no. 2: 54–68.

———. 1996. "Being Worthy of Protection: The Dialectics of Gender Attributes in Yemen." *Social Anthropology* 4, no. 2: 145–62.

Vuorela, Ulla. 1999. "Postkoloniaali ja kolmannen maailman feminismit." In *Rotunaisia ja feminismejä, Nais-ja kehitystutkimuksen risteyskohtia,* edited by Jaana Airaksinen and Tuula Ripatti, 13–37. Tampere, Finland: Vastapaino.

Walters, Delores. 1995. "Transforming Cultural, Racial, and Gender Categories: An Ethnographic Update on Social Relations in Two Northern Yemeni Communities." *Yemen Update* 37: 6–9.

———. 1996. "Invisible Survivors: Women, Diversity, and Transition in Yemen." Paper presented at the Middle East Studies Association Thirtieth Annual Meeting, Nov. 21–24, Providence, R.I.

Watha'iq al-mu'tamar al-'am al-rabi' lil-ittihad al-'am li-nisa' al-yaman. 1986. N.p.: n.p.

Watha'iq al-mu'tamar al-istithna'iyy lil-ittihad al-'am li-nisa' al-yaman 1981. 1983. N.p.: Mu'assasat al-Jundiyy lil-Taba'at wal-Nashr.

Webber, Sabra J. 1997. "Middle East Studies & Subaltern Studies." *Middle East Studies Association Bulletin* 31, no. 1 (July): 11–16.

Weir, Shelagh. 1985a. "Economic Aspects of the Qat Industry in North-West Yemen." In *Economy, Society, and Culture in Contemporary Yemen,* edited by Brian R. Pridham, 64–82. London: Croom Helm and Centre for Arab Gulf Studies, Univ. of Exeter.

———. 1985b. *Qat in Yemen: Consumption and Social Change.* London: British Museum.

———. 1997. "A Clash of Fundamentalisms: Wahhabism in Yemen." *MERIP Reports* 204: 22–26.

———. 2006. *A Tribal Order.* Austin: Univ. of Texas Press.

Weismann, Itzchak. 2001. *Taste of Modernity: Sufism, Salafiyya, and Arabism in Late Ottoman Damascus.* Leiden: E. J. Brill.

Welchman, Lynn. 1999. *Islamic Family Law: Text and Practice in Palestine.* Jerusalem: Women's Centre for Legal Aid and Counseling.

Welcome to Aden: A Comprehensive Guidebook. 2d ed. 1963. Guides and Handbooks of Africa. Nairobi: East African Printers Kenya.

Wenner, Manfred. 1984. "South Yemen since Independence: An Arab Political Maverick." In *Contemporary Yemen: Politics and Historical Background,* edited by Brian

R. Pridham, 125–46. London: Croom Helm and Centre for Arab Gulf Studies, Univ. of Exeter.

Wikan, Unni. 1982. *Behind the Veil in Arabia: Women in Oman.* Baltimore: Johns Hopkins Univ. Press.

Willis, John. 1997. "Colonial Policing in Aden, 1937–1967." *Arab Studies Journal* 5, no. 1 (spring): 57–91.

Women's National Committee, Republic of Yemen. *Status of Woman in Yemen.* 1996. N.p.: Women's National Committee.

World Bank. 1979. *People's Democratic Republic of Yemen: A Review of Economic and Social Developments.* Washington, D.C.: World Bank.

World Health Organization (WHO), Regional Office for the Eastern Mediterranean (EMRO). 1981. *Traditional Practices Affecting the Health of Women and Children: Female Circumcision, Childhood Marriage, Nutritional Taboos Etc.* 2d ed. Report of a seminar in Khartoum, Feb. 10–15, 1979. WHO/EMRO Technical Publication no. 2. Geneva: WHO.

Yemeni Socialist Party. 1979. *Proceedings of the First Congress of the Yemeni Socialist Party, Aden, 11–13 October 1978.* Moscow: Progress.

Al-Zafari, Ja'far. 1997. "Safinat al-amthal (al-'arabiyyat wa al-ingliziyyat)." *Majallat al-Yaman* 7–8: 95–191.

El-Zein, Abdul Hamid. 1977. "Beyond Ideology and Theology: The Search for the Anthropology of Islam." *Annual Review of Anthropology* 6: 227–54.

Index

www.ingramcontent.com/pod-product-compliance
Lightning Source LLC
Chambersburg PA
CBHW030254100426
42812CB00002B/432